SCOTTISH SPORT CLI

SCOTTISH MOUNTAINEERING CLUB
CLIMBERS' GUIDE

Published in Great Britain by The Scottish Mountaineering Trust, 2013
© The Scottish Mountaineering Club

ISBN 978-1-907233-15-9

Front Cover: Ian Taylor on The Prow (7c), Goat Crag, Gruinard (photo Richie Betts)

Frontispiece: Friendly Fire (7a), The Anvil, Loch Goil, Argyll. Climber Alan Cassidy (Photo Stone Country)

Back Cover: Jules Pearson on The Silk Purse (7c+), Upper Cave Crag, Perthshire (photo Fraser Harle)

Inside Back Cover Left: Vast Mango in Tardis (6c+), Arbroath Sea-cliffs. Climber Sadie Renwick (photo Cubby Images)

Inside Back Cover Right: Andy Simpson on Climb and Punishment (7b), Rob's Reed, Angus (photo Gary Latter)

Route descriptions of climbs in this guide, together with their grades and any references to protection are made in good faith, based on past or first ascent descriptions, checked and substantiated where possible by the authors. However, climbs lose holds and are altered by rockfall, rock becomes dirty and loose and in situ protection deteriorates. Even minor alterations can have a dramatic effect on a climb's grade or seriousness. Therefore, it is essential that climbers judge the condition of any route for themselves, before they start climbing. The authors, editors, friends and assistants involved in the publication of this guide, the Scottish Mountaineering Club, the Scottish Mountaineering Trust and Scottish Mountaineering Trust (Publications) Ltd, can therefore accept no liability whatever for damage to property, nor for personal injury or death, arising directly or indirectly from the use of this publication.

Production: Scottish Mountaineering Trust (Publications) Ltd
Typesetting: Ken Crocket, Tom Prentice
Diagram and map graphics: Susan Jensen, Matt Munro, Tom Prentice, Noel Williams

Some maps are derived from Ordnance Survey OpenData™
© Crown copyright and database right 2010

Printed & bound in India by Replika Press Pvt Ltd,

Distributed by Cordee, (t) 01455 61185 (e) sales@cordee.co.uk

SCOTTISH SPORT CLIMBS

A comprehensive guide by leading Scottish Sport Climbers

Coordinating Author Andy Nisbet
Edited by Rab Anderson & Brian Davison
Designed by Tom Prentice
Produced by Susan Jensen & Tom Prentice

SCOTTISH MOUNTAINEERING CLUB
CLIMBERS' GUIDE

Contents

Introduction & Acknowledgement	6
Environment	8
Safety	8
Guidelines for Sport v Trad	10
Technical	11
Climbing Walls	12
Weather Forecasts	12

Central Lowlands — 14
- Central Lowlands West — 18
  - **Dumbarton Rock** – by Dave MacLeod — 18
  - **Dumbuck** – by Dave MacLeod — 23
  - **Dunglas** – by John Watson — 26
- Central Lowlands East — 30
  - **Ratho Quarry** – by Rab Anderson — 30
  - **North Berwick Law Quarry** – by Rab Anderson — 32
  - **Dunbar Crag** – by Rab Anderson — 35

Argyll & Lochaber — 36
- Argyll – Cowal Peninsula — 40
  - **Tighnabruaich** – by Dave MacLeod — 40
  - **Miracle Wall** – by Dave MacLeod — 45
  - **Innellan Quarry** – by Dave MacLeod — 46
  - **The Anvil** – by Dave MacLeod — 47
  - **The Bastion** – by Dave MacLeod — 52
- Argyll – Loch Lomond — 53
  - **Ardvorlich** – by John Watson — 53
- Lochaber — 56
  - **Tunnel Wall** – by Joanna George — 56
  - **Steall Hut Crag** – by Dave MacLeod — 60
  - **Cat's Eye Crag** – by Tom Ballard — 65
  - **Ranochan Walls** – by Tom Ballard — 66
  - **Black Rock** – by Tom Ballard — 68

Es Tressider stepping out on Hamish Teddy's Excellent Adventure (7b+), Upper Cave Crag, Perthshire (photo Cubby Images)

Stirlingshire to Perthshire — 74
- Stirlingshire — 79
  - **Stronachlachar Crags** – by Dave MacLeod — 79
  - **Inversnaid Crag** – by Dave MacLeod — 81
  - **Strathyre Crag** – by Joanna George — 85
  - **Craigruie** – by Dave MacLeod — 88
- Glen Ogle — 89
  - **Glen Ogle Dark Side** – by Dave MacLeod — 90
  - **Glen Ogle Sunny Side** – by Dave MacLeod — 100

Perthshire	113
Bennybeg – *by Andy Nisbet*	113
Dunira – *by Andy Nisbet*	117
Lower Lednock – *by Andy Nisbet*	120
Newtyle Quarry – *by Dave MacLeod*	121
Upper Cave Crag – *by Joanna George & Rab Anderson*	128
Myopics Buttress – *by Joanna George & Rab Anderson*	132
Weem Crags – *by Joanna George*	133
Rockdust Crag – *by Joanna George*	144

Angus – *by Neil Shepherd* — 148
Kirrie Hill	152
Ley Quarry	161
Balmashanner Quarry	166
Rob's Reed	171
Legaston Quarry	180
Arbroath Sea-Cliffs	188
Red Head	218
Elephant Rock	219

Aberdeenshire – *by Neil Morrison & Tim Rankin* — 226
Boltsheugh	230
Newtonhill Cave	234
The Keel	236
Clashfarquhar Bay	238
Sportlethen	240
Findon Ness	242
Orchestra Cave	243
Red Wall Quarry	247
Cambus o' May Quarry	251

Highlands East — 256
South of Inverness	260
Dunlichity – *by Andrew Wilby*	260
Brin Rock – *by Andrew Wilby*	262
Creag Dhearg – *by Andy Nisbet*	264
The Camel – *by Neil Shepherd*	265
North of Inverness	268
Moy Rock – *by Andy Nisbet*	268
Princess Cairn – *by Andy Nisbet*	276
Little Torboll – *by Rab Anderson*	277
Creag Bheag – *by Rab Anderson*	279
Silver Rock – *by Simon Nadin*	283
The Powe – *by Joanna George*	286
Creag Dhubh, Loch Loyal – *by Simon Nadin*	287

Highlands West — 288
Duncraig – *by Neil Smith*	292
Leacanashie Woods Crag – *by Martin Moran*	293
Creag nan Cadhag – *by Paul Tattersall*	296
Grass Crag – *by Paul Tattersall*	300
Creag nan Luch – *by Paul Tattersall*	302
Creag an Oisean – *by Paul Tattersall*	309
Kuhjo Crag – *by Paul Tattersall*	309
Goat Crag – *by Paul Tattersall*	312
Am Fasgadh – *by Paul Tattersall*	317
Creag nan Òrd – *by Colin Meek*	320

The Islands — 322
Mull – *by Colin Moody*	324
Stac Liath	324
Balmeanach	325
Creag Ghillean	326
The Staple	326
Orkney	327
Castle of Yesnaby Quarry – *by Orkney Climbing Club*	327
Shetland	330
Raasmi – *by Al Whitworth*	330

Minor & Historical Venues — 332
Index — 333

Introduction & Acknowledgements

Costa del Sol it may not be, but Scottish sport climbing has a charm of its very own. There are varied rock types and some stunning venues, located in all areas from urban environments to the stunning glens of Coe and Nevis and the open country of the Northern Highlands. Cliffs such as Upper Cave and Tunnel Wall contain world class routes while Bennybeg offers the ideal beginners' venue. There are now over 50 crags, some with many sectors (Arbroath Sea-Cliffs has 25 and Glen Ogle 20), giving some 1300 routes and sport is now a major part of Scottish climbing.

Sport climbing in Scotland has certainly come of age and is no longer just about early season training or a poor weather option, but has its own attractions. Neither is it the sole preserve of the elite athlete for it has been truly opened up to all. You climb more routes in a day and can push your technical and physical limit without the worry of placing gear. Those advantages combine with accessibility and convenience for those with busy lives. And now that most climbers start on climbing walls, their first outdoor experience is likely to be one of the crags in this book.

It should be said that this has not been at the expense of traditional climbing, for many climbers alternate between the two, with the result that the continued activity and increased fitness allowed by the sport climbs is being put to good use in the traditional arena. Many of the sport cliffs lie in locations that are readily accessible for those on trips to and from the major traditional areas, so a combination is common. This also means that they can be used as fall backs when Scottish weather stops play elsewhere.

Happy hooking – Tim Rankin, left, on Dead Pull (7b+) and Wilson Moir on The Reinforcer (7c), Dirty Harry's Cave, Rob's Reed, Angus (photo Neil Morrison)

Sport climbing in Scotland started in the early '80s on the Angus sea-cliffs and Legaston Quarry. There was certainly some disapproval but Angus sandstone was given little importance in those days. Sport climbing gained publicity in the mid-'80s when a few bolts were used to reduce the danger enough to breach the impressive Tunnel Wall and Upper Cave Crag. Further development here was slow but continued steadily in Angus, although the climbing was generally by locals.

By the early '90s most keen climbers had sport climbing holidays abroad and opposition in Scotland had waned enough for pure sport venues like Glen Ogle to be accepted. But the developers were small in number and climbed hard. By the later '90s the number of crags was increasing and places like Weem, Inversnaid and Rockdust were established. Rockdust was the first where the majority of routes were lower grade and would have become popular more quickly had route descriptions been more easily available. By 2000 indoor climbing walls had become well established and with growing enthusiasm for sport climbing, combined with the bolting of more lower grade routes, soon everyone was able to enjoy some sport climbing. There has been some conflict with trad climbing, but now that guidelines for bolting have been established, both aspects of the sport are flourishing.

Although conglomerate crags had previously been considered for sport climbing, the first route was on The Camel in 1997. Recently the more solid versions of this rock have been accepted as ideal for sport climbing and a number of major conglomerate crags have been developed, like Moy Rock and Creag Bheag. In 2004/2005

Creag nan Luch became the first gneiss crag to be bolted. Bolting this traditional rock type worried many but the quality of the routes answered most of the critics. The gneiss crags of the North-West remain the closest to the boundary of what is acceptable for sport and seem likely to remain so, as the tradition of no bolting in the mountains remains unchallenged and is what makes British climbing unique.

Creating sport routes is expensive but in 2008 at Silver Rock came the first sponsorship of costs. In 2007 however, Orkney Council had paid for bolts at Yesnaby and it will be interesting to see whether outdoor sport climbing becomes sufficiently mainstream for this to be a regular source of funding as it is in France.

Dry Tooling has been intermittently used over the years as training for Scottish winter climbing. But abroad, increasingly hard dry tool climbing, often across roofs, has been used to reach ice formations. This aspect of the sport started in Canada but soon spread to Europe and elsewhere. Scotland doesn't have the same ice, but in 2003 Newtyle Quarry became Scotland's answer to roof tooling and quickly saw itself established on the world map, as exponents of this sport turned up to sample the hard core climbing on offer. In 2008/2009 Leacanashie Woods Crag was equipped for lower (but still impressive) grades, and the Aberdeen climbers bolted two routes near Newtonhill. These are at present Scotland's only three bolted dry tooling crags.

The four star system has been used for indicating quality. Don't take the stars too seriously, as sport climbs in particular are most satisfying when the biggest effort ends in a climax of success. That does seem to give an advantage to the harder climbs which tend to get more stars, and many of the authors climb hard, but remember that the star ratings are much more personal than trad climbs. Stars aren't given at Kirrie Hill, so see if you miss them. The route lines on the diagrams (topos) have generally been drawn following the line of bolts. This is not necessarily the climbing line, though of course each bolt will be clipped.

Acknowledgements

An impossible task to list them all, since everyone who has cleaned, drilled, glued, or just carried heavy rucksacks, has contributed to this guide.

To Scotland's trad climbers for realising that sport climbing is a companion, not a rival. The most thanks go to Jo George, who was the inspiration for this guide and who had it well established before she passed it on to me. To Rab Anderson, one of the pioneers of Scottish sport, who could have written the guide but instead has added his great knowledge to it. To the many authors who have helped with other sections than their own.

To Ian Taylor for teaching me how to drill and to Andy Wilby for cleaning up my mistakes, and to both for the loan of tools. To Dave Cuthbertson, another pioneer, for early help and supplying so many excellent photos. To Billy McKee for checking some sections and giving an independent opinion. To Dave Redpath for help with many crags. To Ian Taylor for help with several Highlands crags. To Stuart Burns for help with Dunglas, Tony Shepherd with the Arisaig crags, Raymond Wallace with The Powe, Tim Deakin & Don Husband with Orkney, Alex Thomson for updating the approach to Dunira and Greg Boswell for updating The Tube. To many others who have supplied photos and added their comments; Gary Latter was particularly helpful. To Brian Davison for editing some consistency into the text, Tom Prentice for the exciting new design of the book and overseeing its production and to Susan Jensen and Matt Munro for the hard graft of production.

As a personal comment, I had no idea when I took on the coordinating role for the guide just how much effort and expense was required by the bolters to create routes, and perhaps they are similarly unaware of the effort in producing a guidebook. I have enjoyed immensely learning about sport climbing in Scotland, including how to wield a drill, and hope that all the readers get similar pleasure from this guidebook!

Andy Nisbet, 2013

Environment

Access

The Land Reform (Scotland) Act 2003 established a statutory right of responsible access over all land and inland water in Scotland for the purpose of recreation and passage, subject to certain exclusions. The Scottish Outdoor Access Code provides detailed guidance on the responsible use of these rights.

- Take responsibility for your actions;
- Respect people's privacy and peace of mind;
- Help land managers and others work safely and effectively;
- Look after your environment;
- Keep your dog under proper control;
- Take care if you are organising an event or running a business.

Footpath Erosion

The number of walkers and climbers on the hills is leading to increased footpath erosion. Part of the revenue from the sale of this and other Scottish Mountaineering Club books is granted by the Scottish Mountaineering Trust as financial assistance towards the repair and maintenance of hill paths in Scotland.

Bird Life

When climbing, don't cause direct disturbance to nesting birds, particularly the rarer species, which are often found on crags (e.g. golden eagle, peregrine falcon, razorbill, guillemot, puffin, fulmar, kittiwake, cormorant, shag, buzzard, kestrel, raven). Usually this is between 1st February and the end of July, but on coasts it may be later. Intentional or reckless disturbance of nesting birds is a criminal offence with potentially large penalties and confiscation of climbing equipment.

Climbers are advised to try to find out the nesting situation at the location they intend visiting, such as from MCofS, but this information is advisory and not exhaustive. The MCofS relies on climbers to feed information back to them so they can pass it on, so you are encouraged to let them know if there is a nesting situation at a crag. For the latest information, try <www.mcofs.org.uk/advice-and-policies.asp>, then click on "nesting birds and climbing".

Vegetation

When cleaning routes in summer take care what you remove; some of the flora may be rare. Many crags are designated Sites of Special Scientific Interest (SSSI). This doesn't mean climbing is not allowed, but it may mean there are restrictions on activity. A Crag Code is available from the MCofS (see below).

Litter and Pollution

Do not leave litter of any sort and bury human waste carefully out of sight, far away from any habitation or water supply. Avoid burying rubbish as this may also pollute the environment. Be careful with toilet breaks, both from the point of litter and also offending observers, as some of the sport crags are quite public. If you take dogs to a sport crag, please pick up any waste.

Car Use

Do not drive along private roads without permission, and when parking, avoid blocking access to private roads and land or causing any hazard to other road users. Please adhere to particular parking requirements which are mentioned in the text, as many sport crags are close to civilisation.

Mountaineering Council of Scotland

The MCofS is the representative body for climbers and walkers in Scotland. One of its primary concerns is the continued free access to the hills and crags. Information about bird nesting issues, stalking and general access issues can be obtained from the MCofS.

Should you encounter problems regarding access you should contact the MCofS, whose current address is: The Old Granary, West Mill Street, Perth PH1 5QP, 01738 493 942, fax 01738 442 095, email <info@mcofs.org.uk>, website <www.mcofs.org.uk>. Detailed information on many of the topics below is found at <www.mcofs.org.uk/advice-and-policies.asp>.

Safety

MCofS/UIAA Participation Statement

"Climbing and mountaineering are activities with a danger of personal injury or death. Participants in these activities should be aware of and accept these risks and be responsible for their own actions and involvement."

Thr above is an extract and the full version is available at <www.mcofs.org.uk/ climbing-statement.asp>.

Personal Responsibility

Sport climbing is not without risk and one should familiarise oneself with the required equipment and the current means of best using this. Climbers should make their own assessment of the quality of any protection they use, both personal protection (climbing 'gear') and in-situ protection such as bolts, pegs, slings and lower-offs. It is up to the individual to assess whether such protection is suitable to take a fall or be used in any way. This is part of the risk assessment required by individuals to participate as safely as they wish to.

Liability

Climbers should understand the risk and their responsibility, and therefore cannot hold any other person liable for damages (including other climbers, first ascentionists/climb developers, guidebook authors and publishers, landowners and land managers etc.).

Lowering-Off

Most serious accidents occur during lowering-off. A climber being dropped (or not held at all) during lower-off is a common accident. Careful threading is also important; this video of good technique is worth watching <www.thebmc.co.uk/Feature.aspx?id=2766>. Of particular concern in sport climbing is the state of lower-off gear including in-situ krabs which deteriorate rapidly and should not be considered trustworthy. There are some climbs where it is worth taking a spare krab or maillon just in case.

Clip Sticks

Some climbs in this book have a first bolt high enough that a failure to clip could result in minor injury. Those wishing to increase safety should pre-clip the first bolt using a clip stick, something which many regular sport climbers own. They can also be used for working a route, or just pre-placing the quick-draws. Clipping the second bolt is often even more dangerous than the first (because you are higher), so be careful not to take in loads of slack for clipping if you are running out of strength; if in doubt you can stick clip it also.

Self Regulation

The placement of bolts to produce sport climbs is unregulated, so the quality of bolts is variable. Climbers developing sport climbs may have a personal connection to the crag which allows for informal checking of bolt quality. This can be backed up by feedback from visiting climbers. A small number of local bolt funds have been set up to help pay for replacement of old bolts and the MCofS supports this informal system and encourages climbers to support any local bolt fund.

Some of the crags in this guidebook were bolted a long time ago and particularly on wet crags and sea-cliffs, the bolts are showing corrosion. Others have been rebolted with the latest best practise. Climbers are recommended to take all precautions in case of bolt and particularly lower-off failure.

Children

Some sport crags are in child friendly locations, but take care, particularly not allowing the child to wander under climbers where a falling rock or dropped gear could cause an injury.

Sea-Cliff & Mountain Rescue

Contact the police, usually by phone (999 or 112). There are a few situations where ambulance instead of police is sufficient, but only if the venue is close to the road and particularly if there are others to help carry a stretcher (Bennybeg for example). Give concise information about the location and injuries of the victim and any assistance available at the accident site. It is often better to stay with the victim, but in a party of two, one may have to leave to summon help. Leave the casualty warm and comfortable in a sheltered, well marked place.

Ticks

Whether due to climate change or better reporting, being bitten by deer and sheep ticks is becoming more common. The altitude of many of the crags in this guide produces a high concentration of ticks. Tick bites are normally very itchy perhaps for several days but the serious problem is the chance of catching Lyme Disease. Prevention from being bitten is important, such as not sitting on the ground and checking for ticks on your clothing (they don't bite quickly like midges). Nowadays a tick hunt is always worthwhile on returning from a climbing venue. Ticks will bite and remain in place sucking blood and it is this direct link to your bloodstream that makes them dangerous. The risk of catching Lyme Disease is small, as most ticks are not infected and is reduced even further the faster the tick is removed (hours rather than minutes is fine). It is worth looking at the website for the charity Lyme Disease Action <http://www.lymediseaseaction.org.uk> for further information.

Alternatively, the website for Borreliosis and Associated Diseases Awareness UK <http://www.bada-uk.org> is very informative. Removal is best done with fine tweezers or a tick remover instrument which can be bought through that website. The plan is to remove them without squeezing or distressing the tick and causing injection of its contents into the bloodstream. So techniques like spreading Vaseline or any other chemical, or heat, are not recommended. Whether removing them with finger nails is safer than waiting for a number of hours for correct removal is unproven, but most climbers prefer to remove them as fast as possible. It is well worth learning the symptoms of Lyme Disease and going to your GP if necessary. Although country GPs are usually well aware of Lyme Disease city ones may not, and symptoms are hard to diagnose.

Guidelines for Sport v Trad

Sport climbing (fixed protection) and trad (traditional) climbing – using protection placed and removed during the ascent – coexist in Scotland and must compete, since no climb can be both. The decision on whether a climb or crag should be sport or trad is based on consensus, so anyone bolting and failing to consult takes the risk of their bolts being removed. An existing climb will not normally be changed, so 100 years of trad before sport appeared means that many crags are already established as trad.

Scotland is proud to be one of the few countries in Europe where bolts are not placed in the mountains, and this is the current consensus. In addition there is agreement (and not just amongst climbers) that wild places should not be modified by man, so placing of bolts in remote venues is not acceptable.

This means that the ideal sport venue has not previously been trad climbed, is not protectable by nuts and cams, and is close to the road. Perfect venues rarely exist so a consensus should be sought as to what level of suitability should be accepted. There must also be a consideration not to bolt up all good quality roadside rock, so that future bold trad climbers have places to put up new lines. The following refers to cliffs which meet the overall ethic of not being in the mountains or in a remote wild place.

1. Previous trad climbing – some crags have limited or poor quality trad climbs (proved by their lack of popularity) and these are generally acceptable for bolting providing there is the usual consensus, particularly with any first ascentionists who still might climb on the cliff. If the crag has not been climbed on, then the guidelines are less strict.

2. Not protectable – it is acceptable on a sport cliff to bolt poorly protected climbs or very steep ones with fiddley gear but not well protected crack-lines.

3. Remote – although this is perhaps harder to define, for obvious reasons most sport crags are readily accessible and found within 30mins from the road. If in doubt, consensus is again the key.

These guidelines are the same for summer and winter (drytooling), and for inland and sea-cliffs.

Equally, removal of bolts is unacceptable without consensus unless they have been recently placed and clearly break the current guidelines. Simply because a route could be trad climbed by someone good enough is not an excuse for de-bolting.

Bolting should be done with the best available equipment (stainless steel & resin) since bolts that rot away after a few years do no one any good. Remember no bolt or piece of rock is guaranteed and users should take responsibility for assessing the quality and safety for themselves.

Equipping of new sport climbs

It is urged that new climbs and crags should be opened in a responsible manner in accordance with the guidelines. Stainless steel bolts should always be used rather than cheaper options as these deteriorate rapidly and become dangerous. For lower-offs, use either a stainless steel lower-off unit or a double ring lower-off, which has the advantage of minimum visual impact and avoids the need to leave behind in-situ krabs. If possible, place bolt runners and lower-offs near good holds to allow safe clipping. For guidance on assessing the quality of bolts and their placement, the following downloads are recommended:

<https://www.thebmc.co.uk/bmcNews/media/u_content/File/equipment_advice/bolt_funds/Users_guideHR.pdf>

<https://www.thebmc.co.uk/bmcNews/media/u_content/File/equipment_advice/bolt_funds/Installers_guideHR.pdf>

For technical information on safe equipping of sport routes visit <www.petzl.com>.

There is a lot of useful information on <www.bolt-products.com/Glue-inBoltDesign.htm>.

Ethics

- Don't steal newer lower-off carabiners, replacing them with older personal gear.
- Don't top rope from fixed lower-offs, wearing them out.
- Having your clips in a route doesn't give you ownership of the route/crag for the day; share with other parties that may come to try.
- Occasionally quickdraws may be left on a route if a party intends to return. Don't see this as an opportunity to add to your own rack.

Technical

Distances

Distances in Directions are normally in miles to match with road signs and car mileometers. Where the measurement is precise (decimal point), it has been measured on a mileometer and doing so in your own car is recommended.

Distances in Approaches and at crags are in metres to match with OS maps and generally have been paced. For those wishing to be precise, most folk take between 60 and 70 double paces to 100m.

Maps

The relevant Ordnance Survey maps are listed under the heading for each crag (or group of crags). These are the 1:50000 map where the Landranger series is abbreviated as L followed by the sheet number, and the 1:25000 map where the Explorer series is abbreviated as E followed by the sheet number. It is not always necessary to have an OS map although it always helps for a first visit. Detailed maps are provided in the text for some crags, particularly if they are difficult to find and have several routes. For many crags, the small area shown on <www.getamap.ordnancesurvey.co.uk/getamap/frames.htm> is sufficient – you must type in the 2 letter and 6 figure grid reference of the crag or parking place (no spaces).

A larger area is shown on <www.bing.com/maps>. Locate and select the Ordnance Survey Maps, then zoom in and move to your desired location. Eventually the OS 1:50000 map turns into the 1:25000 version.

Another website has the OS map on the left and a Google Earth image of the same area on the right <http://wtp2recorder.appspot.com/wheresthepath.htm>. Using the map reference for the parking allows you to visualise your approach.

Map References

Eight figure GPS readings are given for the parking places and the crags, unless they are too large for this to be meaningful, and a few crags have not been visited with a GPS. A GPS should not be necessary to find the crags despite some being in trees and hard to find, but the readings can be useful if you have one. Note that GPS readings in trees and at the base of crags are less accurate than on open ground and 8 figures is the most that could be useful. Where the crag is approached from above, the GPS reading will be for the top of the crag. Also note that GPS readings are more accurate than the drawing of maps, so in some instances the position of parking places may not appear exactly on the road if positioned precisely on the map, although this won't hinder finding the parking place.

Grades

The sport rock climbs in this guide have been graded using the French scale which is commonly used for sport climbs worldwide and by most indoor climbing walls. The grade conversion table on the Inside Front Cover fold is a rough indication based on grades on Scottish routes. Fr refers to the French route scale used for sport routes, Trad refers to traditionally protected routes, Font refers to the Fontainebleau bouldering scale and V refers to the American V boulder scale. Grades are highly subjective and frequently argued about so please accept that this scale may not always tally with your experiences. A sport route may have an isolated move near a bolt which is technically harder then the expected trad technical grade. For wider comparison to world grading scales, visit <www.8a.nu>.

For those who have not climbed outdoors before, bear in mind that a given grade is likely to feel more difficult than equivalent routes indoors due to the requirement for rock reading skills and extra exposure, different weather conditions etc. The highest grade in Scotland is currently 9a. If you climb new routes, these should be graded for an on-sight ascent in good but normal conditions and attempt to gain a consensus with other climbers for the route grade. A few of the harder routes in this guide have been graded for redpoint because not everyone agrees about grading for on-sight, and some routes have never been on-sighted (yet!).

Routes which are particularly height dependent are often indicated in the text, but as this is hard to assess, some shocks may still occur. Grading information is in some cases scanty or even

Climbing Walls

lacking, particularly in some of the older or more obscure routes. On some of the harder routes in this guide, the grade is given for finishing the route by grabbing the belay. However, this is not the accepted norm and is increasingly viewed as being a tainted ascent. To avoid feelings of guilt and raised eyebrows from your climbing partners, clip it first. It is considered acceptable to have the quickdraws in place before an on-sight (if placed by a climbing partner) or redpoint ascent. It is also acceptable to leave the rope clipped in the highest bolt you have clipped during an attempt as long as you climb back to the ground without weighting the rope. This can be an important strategy on harder routes. For most, the down-climb must be done on the day of the ascent.

Definitions of Style

The accepted styles of ascents in sport climbing are divided into three different categories, in order of difficulty:

On-Sight – Leading the route cleanly without weighting the rope on the first attempt without any prior knowledge. This includes watching others on the route or receiving move information (beta) from other climbers. It is acceptable for the holds to be chalked.

Flash – Leading the route cleanly at the first attempt but with additional information gained by watching others or receiving beta from other climbers. Often called a betaflash.

Redpoint – Leading the route cleanly after a failed previous attempt or after working one or more of the moves. Redpoints may take between two attempts and a climbing career's worth of attempts to successfully complete.

Diagrams

Numbered routes will be found on diagrams close to the relevant text. The numbers of the climbs in the text correspond to the numbers on the diagrams.

Recommended Routes

* Good climbing, but lacking line, character, situation or balance.

** A very good route but lacking one or more of the features that would make it a climb of real quality.

*** An outstanding route of the highest quality, combining superb climbing with line, character, situation and balance.

**** One of the best climbs of its class.

Some of the climbs in this guide have been given fewer stars since their first ascent due to re-growth of lichen and/or vegetation. Careful cleaning will restore these climbs to their former quality.

First Ascentionists

The first ascentionist and year of the first ascent is given in the text. Sometimes in the Highlands areas, it is the person who bolted the route who is given credit even if they didn't climb the route first. This especially applies with bolting of easier lines, where cleaning and bolting takes much more effort than climbing the route. Lines which have been bolted but not yet climbed are marked as either open or closed projects. A taped first bolt is a sign that the route is a closed project. Please do not steal closed projects, as someone has put considerable effort and expense into cleaning and equipping these lines. Projects that have been abandoned, or where the bolter doesn't mind, are marked in the text as open and are fair game for an ascent.

Climbing Walls

There are around 25 climbing walls in Scotland, including walls in all the cities. Information and links are at <www.thebmc.co.uk> - click on climbing walls and download a Scottish climbing wall directory. The most popular are:

Glasgow Climbing Centre, 0141 4279550, <www.glasgowclimbingcentre.co.uk>

The Climbing Academy (Glasgow), 0141 4296331, < http://www.tca-glasgow.com>

Edinburgh International Climbing Arena, 0131 3336333, <www.eica-ratho.com>

Alien Rock and Alien Rock 2 (Edinburgh), 0131 5527211, <www.alienrock.co.uk>

The Ice Factor (Kinlochleven), 01855 831100, <www.ice-factor.co.uk>

McLaren Leisure (Callander), 01877 330000, <www.mclarenleisure.co.uk>

Avertical World (Dundee), 01382 201901, www.averticalworld.co.uk

Transition Extreme (Aberdeen), 01224 626279, <www.transition-extreme.com>

Inverness Wall, 01463 667500, www.invernessleisure.com/climbing-wall.asp

Gairloch Leisure Centre, 01445 712345

Weather Forecasts

The weather forecast is an important factor in

choice of venue. Even though most sport crags are at low level (away from the mountains) there is still a big difference between west and east in rainfall, temperature and wind. Many crags are in areas of low rainfall so are useful as a safe option. As well as predicting dry rock, wind and shelter from the wind are important to assess the midge risk, the further west the more the midge potential. The four choices are radio, TV, newspaper or internet.

Radio:
Radio 4 gives the most concise forecasts, although often lacking detail for Scotland. Radio Scotland forecasts are also good. The best combination is the Shipping Forecast on Radio 4 (5.54 pm) giving sea winds which are relevant to mountain winds, followed by the weather forecast (5.57 pm) with other details, particularly rain, snow and timing of fronts. On the Shipping Forecast, Mallin (west; Fort William and south), Hebrides (north-west) and Cromarty (east) are relevant. A Radio Scotland forecast then follows at 5.58pm, but usually doesn't overlap. The Shipping Forecast can also be found on <www.bbc.co.uk/weather/coast/shipping>. An Outdoor Conditions forecast is on at 5.13pm on Radio Scotland and another weather forecast at 8.58pm.

Newspapers:
Newspaper forecasts are poor compared to the information on tv, radio and the internet.

Television:
The BBC offers a better and more detailed chart than ITV. The Reporting Scotland forecast at approximately 6.55pm Monday to Friday is the best daily one.

Internet:
Use of the Internet has led to the withdrawal of good telephone forecasts. There are a wide variety of forecasts on the Internet, including: <www.mwis.org.uk> is the best mountain forecast. A mountain forecast is also available on <www.metoffice.gov.uk/loutdoor/mountain-safety>, with East and West Highland options. <www.bbc.co.uk/weather> and <www.metoffice.co.uk> give reliable forecasts. <www.wetterzentrale.de> gives 10 day synoptic pressure and temperature charts (speculative), and is the best access to a huge amount of technical information. <www.weatheronline.co.uk> gives a huge range of information including long range forecasts.

Midge & Bracken Forecasts
Sadly you have to make your own forecasts, unless you believe <http://2010.midgeforecast.co.uk>. Only the female midge bites (she needs blood for sexual reproduction) and she detects you by carbon dioxide from your breath. So if there is a breeze, you are hidden. As the larvae survive the winter in bogs, they are much worse in the west than the east. Midges also don't like hot sun, as it dehydrates them and frost is fatal. So despite their reputation, you can still climb in the summer, although windless cloudy humid days in the west are definitely not recommended. Crags in the trees are often windless unless there's good breeze, so worry about them too and beware the evening, particularly when camping. Midge repellent is close to essential on days like that, as well as a midge hood for belaying.

Climbing further east is probably more sensible; you will rarely be troubled on the Angus and Aberdeen coasts. Central places like Weem, Kirriemuir, Dunkeld and the Inverness crags will normally be fine during the day but not so good on a still evening. Up till the end of May and from mid September onwards (depending on the first frosts) should be fine in all places.

Many of the approaches to crags in the west are through bracken which can grow up to head height in mid-summer. While access is always possible, the longer approaches are not recommended. In the spring you wouldn't know the problem existed as you cross bluebell covered slopes. It is little more than an irritation at most of the current crags in the centre and east, but a few can become difficult to approach (mentioned in the text).

Books
The SMC publishes a wide range of traditional climbing guidebooks, and a comprehensive range of hillwalking and general interest guides to Scotland's mountains. There is usually a nearby trad crag for those who like to mix styles. Several of the sport crags listed in this guidebook also contain traditional climbs which are in the relevant guidebook. For more information see the booklist at the end of this guide or visit the SMC website <www.smc.org.uk>.

Central Lowlands

The sport climbs in this section all lie within easy reach of Scotland's largest two cities and, like Scottish sport climbs generally, offer a great variety in character. The most important crags are undoubtedly Dumbarton Rock and Dumbuck. These unusual volcanic plugs share the same rock, smooth and compact basalt, yet give very different climbing experiences.

Dumbarton features long technical and fingery lines such as Dum Dum Boys (7c+) or Unforgiven (7b) whereas all of Dumbuck's routes are short and sharp. Those who enjoy complex sequences which must be carefully deciphered and remembered will love basalt. Strength, even lots of it, will not be enough to avoid frustration! Its other main selling point is its smoothness; it will wear your arms out before your skin (probably the secret behind the strength of its devotees).

Dumbuck routes are particularly characterised by blocky pinches, toe hooking moves and the odd clever Egyptian (eg on If Six Was Nine 7c) on the 45 degree overhanging face. The eastern crags, North Berwick Law and Dunbar Crag aren't up there with some of the other crags in this guide for sure, but they do provide a fantastic resource for easy cragging near Edinburgh. Both provide great evening venues and a good selection of lower grade climbs at some friendly angles!

History by Dave MacLeod

The earliest developments in the Central Lowlands came fittingly from Rab Anderson in 1989 on North Berwick Law Quarry. His series of mid-grade routes, although short were an important step in the development of Scottish sport climbing, not to mention a welcome digression from the progressively more death defying trad routes which characterised Scottish climbing in the '80s. Since then, the presence of a keen local activist has been noticeably lacking on the eastern crags in general until Calum Mayland's string of worthwhile recent additions such as Aching Arms and Dragging Heels (6c+).

The Hiltis first came out at Dumbarton Rock in 1990. This was a controversial move at the time, not just within the climbing scene but with the Rock's owners, Historic Scotland. The bolts were removed and a climbing ban threatened, but after things calmed down development tentatively re-started in 1993 with the classic arete of Omerta (7c) by Andy Gallagher. Andy and climbing partner Cameron Phair went on to dominate the sport climbing scene during most of the '90s, producing a series of classics such as Awaken (7c+), Unforgiven (7b) and Persistence of Vision (7a+). The popularity of their mid-grade routes at Dumbarton such as Natural Born Drillers (7a) and Persistence underlines the significance of their efforts. Andy was particularly committed and saw off some frustratingly hard projects such as Voodoo Magic (8a+) and the aptly named Sufferance (8a). His futuristic attitude also left a legacy of inspiring, if occasionally optimistic projects.

Just as in the new routing scene, the early repeats of these routes have been dominated by a few loyal activists, with some exceptions. Early on, Mark 'The Face' McGowan accounted for a repeat of Dum Dum Boys (7c+ but given 8b at the time before Mark found a much easier sequence). Behind Andy and Cameron, who often repeated each other's routes quickly, Darren Stevenson and Paul Savage made early ascents of Awaken (7c+) and Stevenson contributed the excellent lower grade wall climbs on Dumbuck's headwall. A super fit and cool headed Craig Parnaby made

History

occasional appearances and quietly cruised his way through ticks such as Sufferance and Omerta without so much as a grunt. In 1997 Dum Dum Boys got a 3rd ascent from 17 year old Dave MacLeod, marking the start of a continuing interest in the area's top level routes.

Andy Gallagher and Cameron Phair were also responsible for developments at Dunglas in the 1990s. This small but superb gently overhanging basalt face provided mid-grade routes very reminiscent of Dumbuck but without the vicious angle. However, these routes fell into neglect until rediscovered in 2008 by John Watson and Colin Lambton, who added more bolts and routes, all of which provide punchy climbing between 6a and 7b. Bolting was previously 'sporting' but is now complete and generous.

Another youngster emerging at that time was Dave Redpath from Edinburgh who, like Andy Gallagher, wasn't scared of equipping and getting stuck into some blank looking lines. Redpath succeeded on short and beefy Second Sights (7c+) at Dumbuck. Dave MacLeod, after serving a thorough apprenticeship on the easier lines bagged a third ascent of Voodoo Magic (8a+). Voodoo got its first repeat from a strong French climber (Olivier Froideval) but lost all its best holds before MacLeod's ascent re-instated it as one of the country's hard classics. MacLeod also succeeded on the easiest of Andy Gallagher's abandoned futuristic lines at Dumbuck to give So Be It (8a+). Apart from a second ascent of this route Dave Redpath shied away from the repeats he was capable of in favour of going 'long term' on the scoop and seam project at Dumbuck. This superb line was indeed worthy of a large investment of time and effort, and would have been become Scotland's hardest sport route at the time.

Dave MacLeod spent a large chunk of 2004 sieging up at Dumbuck attempting the scoop and seam project, dubbed Devastation Generation by Redpath. By the end of the spring MacLeod became frustrated with it and concentrated on another line, coming away with Happiness in Slavery (8b+). Attempts resumed in the autumn and a successful redpoint came just before winter

Central Lowlands
1. Dumbarton Rock p18
2. Dumbuck p23
3. Dunglas p26
4. Ratho Quarry p30
5. North Berwick Law....p32
6. Dunbar......................p35

Minor Crags
7. Cambusbarron p332

Stirlingshire to Perthshire
8. Stronachlachar..........p79
9. Inversnaid p81
10. Strathyre.................p85

Stuart Burns in the Bahama Breeze (6c+) of Dunglas (photo Fraser Harle)

History

(left) Dave Redpath on Voodoo Magic (8b), Dumbuck (photo Stone Country)

(right) Neil Shepherd on Benny's Route Right-Hand (7c), Dumbarton Rock (photo Fraser Harle)

(opposite) Jules Pearson on Benny's Route Left-Hand (7b), Dumbarton Rock (photo Fraser Harle)

closed in. Devastation was Scotland's first 8c.

On-sights of the harder sport routes seem to be rare. Visiting John Dunne set the standard back in 1993 with an on-sight first ascent of Benny McLaughlin's project (Benny's Route 7c). Craig Parnaby made several impressive ascents, but modestly didn't shout about it. Newcastle star Andrew Earl 'flashed Dumbuck' on a flying visit, climbing several of the 7c/7c+s in a day. In 2003, the newly re-bolted Sufferance wall at Dumbarton saw a surge of activity with beta flashes of Dum Dum Boys (7c+) by Niall 'The Nipper' McNair and Tarrier (7c+) by Dave MacLeod. In 2004 Dave MacLeod re-bolted the remaining routes, making Dumbarton much safer and more user-friendly and improving the quality of the sport routes. Latterly, Alan Cassidy has worked his way through many of the routes awaiting repeats, his best effort so far being the second ascent of Slavery. Malcolm Smith made a fast repeat of Devastation, followed eventually by the original equipper Dave Redpath, 14 years after bolting it.

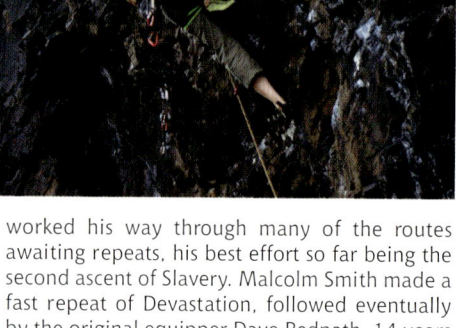

The future projects to inspire new generations of climbers are limited but spectacularly good! The complex looking wall right of Gentle Mass at Dumbuck is definitely possible. However, the immense bolted face routes on either side of Requiem at Dumbarton provide a world class challenge both in terms of quality and difficulty. These have been played on by McGowan, McKenzie, Parnaby, Gallagher, MacLeod and Smith, but even the individual moves haven't been done. Anyone for F9b?

History | 17

Central Lowlands

Dumbarton Rock

CENTRAL LOWLANDS WEST
There are three crags in the vicinity of Glasgow.

Dumbarton Rock - Dumbarton

(NS 400 745) L64 E347   Alt 5 - 20m   West facing
Maps p15, p18   Diagrams p19, p20, p21

Sitting by the river Clyde at the town of Dumbarton, this 70m high volcanic basalt plug is one of Scotland's finest low lying outcrops, featuring a wealth of bouldering (see http://dumby.info and Lowland Outcrops), sport routes and traditional lines. The crag is often buzzing with climbers on summer evenings, when it is a sun-trap, but is also frequented even in the depths of winter due to its quick drying and accessible nature. Virtually all the rusting bolts and in-situ gear were replaced in 2004 with stainless steel bolts and lower-offs. A few non-stainless steel bolts remain and these may eventually need replacement.

March and April are excellent months for friction, but conditions are frequently good all year. Midges are rarely experienced, except during very still summer evenings. Almost all the routes feature spectacular exposure disproportionate to their length, with a very pleasant outlook to the Clyde estuary. The climbing tends to be extremely varied from route to route, but always very demanding on finger strength and technical ability and the routes often have intricate moves which are difficult to flash.

AMENITIES
If visiting from further afield, it is perhaps best to stay in Glasgow (20mins drive). For a day visit, Dumbarton has a retail park with supermarkets, petrol stations and McDonalds. Buddha on Dumbarton High Street is one of a few good pubs. The Stonefield pub/restaurant (from the Brewer's Fayre chain) lies on the A82 about 1km in the Glasgow direction and serves good meals at very reasonable prices. The adjacent Milton Hotel also does good food.

RECOMMENDED TASTY BITES
There is a small corner shop halfway down Victoria road just 300m before the parking for the rock. It sells excellent hot rolls and homemade soup to takeaway. Best enjoyed with some Irn Bru for the full Dumby experience.

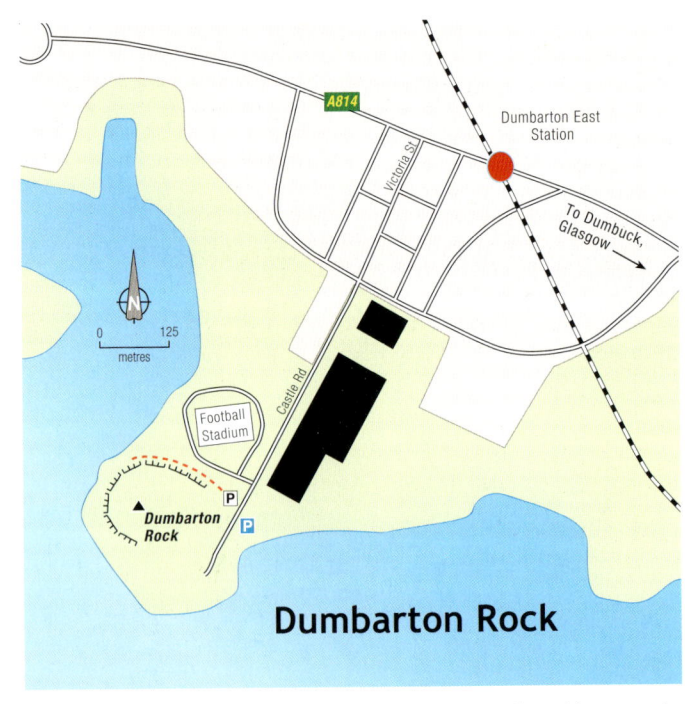

TOP TIPS
To get anywhere at Dumbarton Rock you need beta! Get as much as you can from the locals as it can make a huge difference on technical routes. Dum Dum Boys was originally given (8b) until a new sequence was found, knocking three grades off.

Dumbarton Rock

Central Lowlands

DIRECTIONS
From Glasgow, follow the A82 north-west out of the city past the Erskine Bridge then just beyond a Little Chef and service station at Milton, turn off for Dumbarton on the A814. After passing under the railway at Dumbarton East train station, take the second left into Victoria Street and follow this to a small car park on the right (there is also a car park opposite which has an adjacent manned security box; better for security).

From Edinburgh and the south, it is better to stay on the motorway network and follow the M8 through the centre of Glasgow to cross the River Clyde via the Kingston Bridge and continue past Glasgow Airport. Cross over the Clyde via the Erskine Bridge to join the A82 and the above route beyond the outskirts of Glasgow.

From Loch Lomond and the north, at the end of the A82 dual carriageway on the outskirts of Dumbarton turn off right, following the Town Centre signs around the Barloan Roundabout to take the first exit off left. Continue to the next roundabout, then turn left and take the second exit; both turns signed to Dumbarton Castle and Glasgow. Continue straight over the next roundabout and take the third right into Victoria Street to gain the car park at the end.

From Stirling (M9 Junction 10), take the A811 to Balloch to join the A82 and come in from the north as above.

There are frequent trains from Glasgow Queen Street, taking 25mins to Dumbarton East station.

APPROACH
Time: 2mins
From the car park, an alleyway leads round the rock to the boulders and the impressive main face above.

1 Payback Time! 15m 7b+
Andy Gallagher 1996
This is the bolt-line on the short wall left of a striking large corner near the left end of the face. The bolts do not start at the base of the crag (owing to nearby trad lines). Either abseil down the corner and belay, or climb a short, excellent and well protected finger crack on the overhanging wall below the ledge **Woops** (E4 6a) to reach the start.

2 Omerta 30m 7c *
Andy Gallagher 1993
The stunning and exposed left arete of the main smooth wall. Climb to a small hold below the obvious steep hand-crack leading to the arete. Make a desperate move into the crack then continue up the superb technical arete. The climbing is 7b after the ledge above the crack.

3 Persistence of Vision 15m 7a+ ****
Andy Gallagher 1997
This recent addition is now the most popular sport route in the area. Follow the line of bolts on the black slab directly below the central thin crack of Requiem to a lower-off. Moving out left then back right at the 4th bolt is the crux.

Dumbarton Rock

4 Abstract Art   12m   6c+   *
Dave MacLeod 2004
Balancy climbing on the slabby grey wall right of Persistence. Technical and intricate but ultimately amenable climbing; a good warm-up for harder things or a good challenge in itself.

There are bolted projects on either side of the thin crack of Requiem on the headwall. These have been bolted since the early 1990s but remain projects. Both are thought to be in the mid F9s! The following three lines lie on the intimidating right wall and are modern classics.

5 Dum Dum Boys   23m   7c+   ***
Andy Gallagher 1995
An excellent sport climb running the height of the smooth right wall. Move up the corner and onto the right wall. A hard move gains the base of the long ramp which is followed (sustained) to the ledge. Continue up the easier upper wall past another shake-out to the top.

6 Sufferance   21m   8a   ***
Andy Gallagher 1993
A first class sport route up the very smooth wall just to the right. The route is sustained and technical on small edges, with a traverse at half-height being the crux. Low in the grade.

7 Tarrier   23m   7c+   **
Mark McGowan 1993
Another superb climb, more cruxy than the previous two. From the top of the initial undercut flake, span to the right arete and make a hard move to gain the slopey shelf. An easier section leads to an excellent fingery finish.

8 Suffix   23m   8a   *
Ross Henighen 2006
The only link on the wall at 8a, starting up Sufferance, but moving into Tarrier from the jug after the crux to create a more sustained overall route.

Sufferance Wall

Doing the reverse (Tarrier start into Sufferance) is also 8a and often named **Endurance**.

9 Tolerance   30m   8a+ ★★
Dave MacLeod 2003
The obvious linkup to give a superb sustained pitch with some new climbing. Follow Tarrier to the end of the initial undercut flake. Break out left on sidepulls and make a hard lunge to a handrail (crux). Traverse left along the handrail past Sufferance to join Dum Dum Boys just before its crux (no reversing down this to jugs). Finish up Dum Dum Boys.

10 Negative Creep   10m   8b ★
Dave MacLeod 2004
Start up Appliance but break out left after the crux to gain a good sidepull. A long reach gains another big sidepull leading to a desperate crimping sequence to the finishing holds on the ledge. 7c to the last three moves, and the grade is definitely for clipping the belay rather than grabbing!

11 Appliance of Violence   10m   7b+ ★
Benny McLaughlin 1993
Right of the smooth main walls is another face with two prominent corner-lines. This route takes the short bolted overhanging arete between the corners and has a technical crux which needs some imagination and leads to easier laybacking

12 Bad Attitude   18m   7b
Andy Gallagher 1993
On the wall to the right of the right-hand corner, the left-hand of a trio of bolted lines gives technical balancy climbing.

13 Half Breed   18m   7b ★★★
Cameron Phair 1993
The central line of the trio takes the shallow groove, pulling leftwards from a flat hold at its top to join Bad Attitude above the roof.

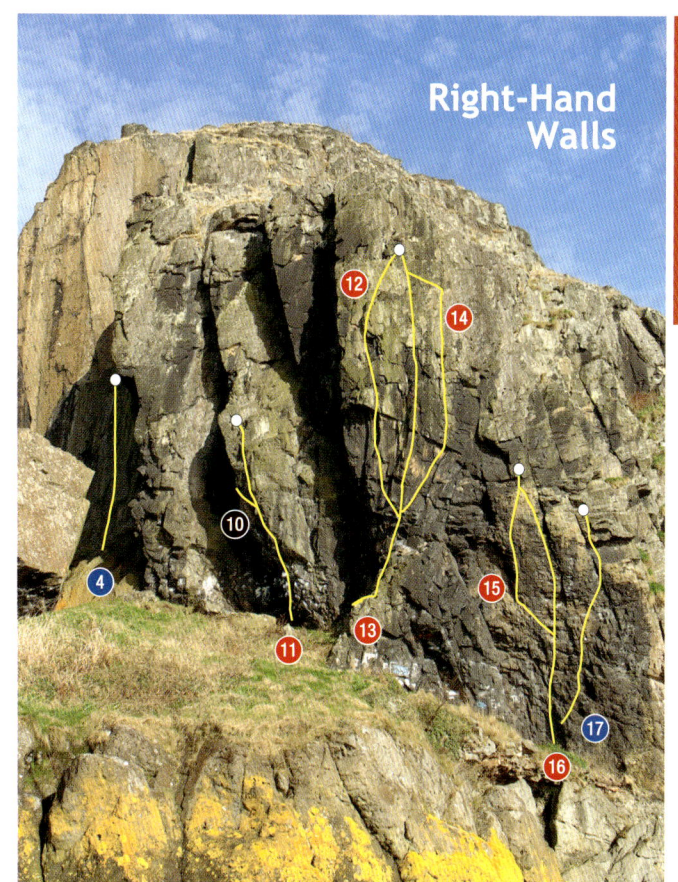

Dumbarton Rock

Right-Hand Walls

Central Lowlands

Dumbarton Rock

Kev Gibson using the Appliance of Violence (7b+), Dumbarton Rock (photo Fraser Harle)

14 Unforgiven   18m   7b ★★★
Andy Gallagher 1993
The right-hand line is the best of the three, with blind technical climbing on sidepulls.

15 Benny's Route Left-Hand   12m   7b ★
Glen Sutcliffe 1994
The overhanging wall at the end of the grass shelf has three bolt-lines. Move left at the 3rd bolt on the left-hand line and climb the steep arete on good holds to a hard section moving rightwards to the lower-off.

16 Benny's Route Right-Hand   12m   7c ★
John Dunne 1993
From the 3rd bolt, make hard moves rightwards, then follow the faint fault to the lower-off.

17 Natural Born Drillers   13m   7a ★
Cameron Phair 1996
From the edge of the shelf, follow the diagonal line of bolts across the wall to a crack. Climb this and use a fingerlock over the bulge to pull over (crux) and climb easier ground to the lower-off. Regularly failed on.

18 Casanostra   10m   6c+ ★★
Andy Gallagher 1997
This good little route can be found hiding on the right wall of a deep gully on the broken area of rock dropping into the Clyde. Drop down from the grassy base of the main crag onto the beach, or traverse above the sea if the tide is in. Climb into the gully just left of a large metal mooring. It was very popular for a while but people seem to have forgotten it's there! Interesting laybacking leads to a hard move followed by an easier finish on good holds. Starting from further left up the gully reduces the grade.

19 Consolidated   16m   8a (Font 7b+) ★★★
Andy Gallagher 1990s
This boulder problem has been included as an honorary sport route

Dumbuck

owing to its length and popularity. It lies just downhill from Appliance of Violence on the lower of two propped boulders. Sustained and technical, but with no hard moves. An eliminate problem which is somewhat difficult to describe, but a good rule of thumb is if you think it might be too high, it probably is!

Start at a head-height arete near the left end of the boulder on a sidepull and flat undercut. Traverse right on small holds on the lip and then drop down to better holds. Follow the line of parallel holds/ramps to a halfway stopping place. Pause here for a moment on an upside down rest on a toe hook, then layback past a tiny niche and continue right past a complex sequence on holds below the lip to reach triangular hold below the right arete. Finish up the arete or keep going at a low level to up the grade to 8a+.

Dumbuck - Dumbarton
(NS 4196 7453) L64 E347 Alt 50m North-West facing
Maps p15, p23 Diagrams p24, p25

This good sport climbing venue lies close to Dumbarton Rock on an obvious volcanic plug overlooking the main A82 Glasgow to Loch Lomond road. A visit is definitely worthwhile, especially if combined with Dumbarton Rock. The routes climb the large and obvious overhang on the craggy face to the right of a huge quarry on the north side of the plug.

The climbs are generally short, powerful and very sustained, being about 45-50 degrees overhanging. Although the easier, less steep routes are well worth doing the routes on this crag are mainly in the harder grades and they offer excellent climbing, which stays dry, even in heavy rain. The rock is a clean, fine grained basalt which gives powerful climbing, often featuring undercutting and interesting footwork.

Most of the routes are climbable during dry periods in winter, but the crag does suffer from some seepage. The crag sees the sun from about 2pm onwards and can be hot in summer evenings. Midges are rarely a problem as the crag is exposed to any breezes. There is a fantastic view down the Clyde estuary and across to the Southern Highlands. In general, March and April give the best conditions.

AMENITIES
See Dumbarton Rock p18

RECOMMENDED TASTY BITES
The Stonefield Brewers Fayre pub restaurant lies on the A82 about 1km in the Glasgow direction and serves good meals at very reasonable prices. The nearby Milton Hotel also does good food.

TOP TIPS
Finding the correct sequence can be frustrating; clever toe-hooks seem to be the secret to success on most of the harder routes.

DIRECTIONS
From Glasgow, take the A82 north-west out of the city past the Erskine Bridge to fork left onto the A814 for Dumbarton town centre at traffic lights just after a Little Chef and service station at Milton. Follow the A814

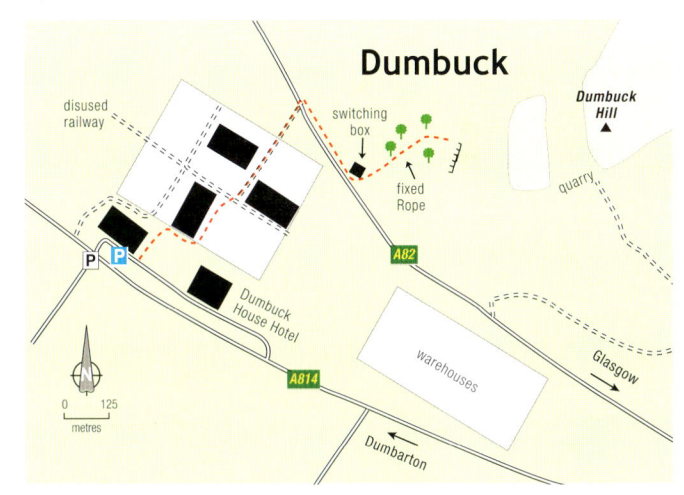

Dumbuck

for a short distance and pass a first entrance on the right to the Dumbuck House Hotel. Some 250m further on is a second entrance to the hotel and a wide industrial gateway on the left. In the evening, park at the side of the gateway (NS 4142 7453). During the day this can be very busy so park just inside the west entrance to the hotel (NS 4145 7452). If both are busy, park in Dumbuck Crescent on the right 100m further on. Dumbuck can be seen on the hillside above the hotel.

From the south and east, it is better to stay on the motorway network and follow either the M8 (over the Kingston Bridge) or the M74 through the centre of Glasgow and continue past Glasgow Airport. Cross over the Clyde via the Erskine Bridge to join the A82 and the above route beyond the outskirts of Glasgow. From the north, see the approach for Dumbarton Rock and instead of turning into Victoria Street, continue under the railway to reach the Dumbuck House Hotel. From Stirling (M9 Junction 10) take the A811 to Balloch to join the A82 and come in from the north as above. There are frequent trains from Glasgow Queen Street, taking 25mins to Dumbarton East station. From here walk east out of town along the A814 to the Dumbuck House Hotel.

APPROACH
Time: 15mins
Go in the west entrance to the hotel, unless you are already parked there, and 50m from the main road find a path through the trees, which leads away from the road – in 2010 there was a Public Right of Way sign strapped to a tree here. Follow the path to the A82 dual carriageway. Cross over and follow the road right (east) for 150m to a grey switching box just before a bend. Behind it and heading up the steep earthy hillside is a fixed rope, a good indicator. Cross over the wooden fence and gain this rope handrail. Follow it up, then a continuing path left to below the crags. A further rope assists the final rock scramble from the top of a pinnacle to gain the ledge below the cliffs. This rope will be subject to wear and great care should be taken.

❶ Filth Infatuated   8m   5+
Rosemary Conaly 1997
This route climbs the bolted groove to the left of the overhanging face.

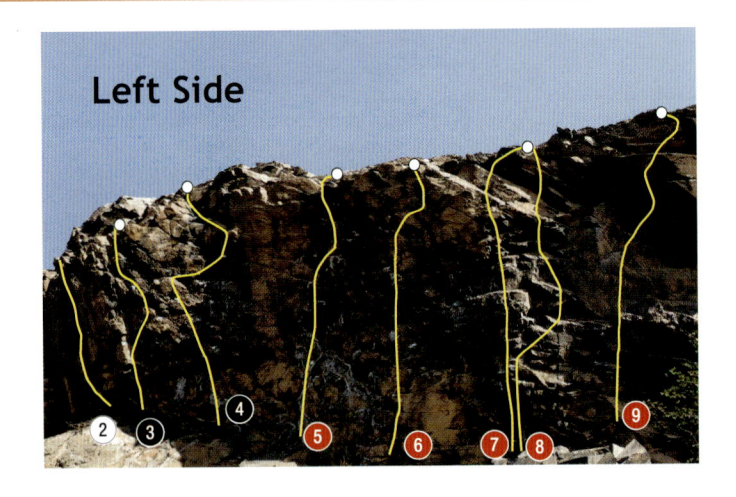

❷ Open Project
Dave MacLeod
The furthest left line of bolts on the overhanging face, finishing into the easier scoop above.

❸ Happiness in Slavery   10m   8b+ **
Dave MacLeod 2004
The faint right-facing groove gives a short and fierce route. Move desperately upwards on poor slopers, toe hooks and undercuts to get established on a triangular hold. Either make a long defeating Egyptian for the jug or make use of the sidepull lumps in between.

❹ Voodoo Magic   10m   8b **
Andy Gallagher 1996
Steep dynamic starting moves lead up to a good triangular hold. Make hard moves right to gain the sloping handrail. Move left to a finishing jug.

Dumbuck

5 Awaken 10m 7c+ ***
Andy Gallagher 1992
The classic of the crag. Powerful moves lead to the obvious spiky jug. A hard move from a sloper gains easier climbing and the amazing 'thank god' finishing jug. Most take the 2nd bolt pre-clipped.

6 Flesh for Fantasy 10m 7c+ **
Cameron Phair 1994
Another excellent sustained climb. A sharp start leads to steeper moves through the bulge.

7 If Six was Nine 10m 7c **
Cameron Phair 1992
Powerful undercutting leads to a tricky rockover onto the ramp.

8 Parallel 10m 7c
Andy Gallagher 1995
The line just to the right of If Six was Nine has a powerful start on small undercuts and a technical finish. Often wet.

9 House of Pain 10m 7c+ **
Andy Gallagher 1996
An excellent varied line through the huge scoop. Tackle the initial technical wall to the sloping diagonal crack and a hard clip. A 'jump around' to a sidepull jug leads into steep moves through the roof. Finish on the right.

10 Dirty Sanchez 10m 7c+ **
Michael Rudden 2001
Start up Gentle Mass Touching, then follow the scoop leftwards with unusual contortions to finish into House of Pain.

11 Gentle Mass Touching 10m 7c *
Andy Gallagher 1992
This climbs the groove and wall right of the scoop. Long moves up the start of the groove lead to a jug on the lip. Continue on good but spaced holds up the wall above.

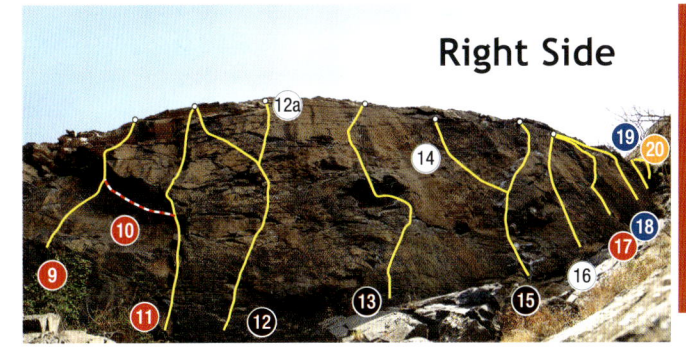

12 Aqua Vitae 10m 8b+ **
Dave Redpath 2012
Tackles the system of increasingly bad undercuts to a finale going left at the top into Gentle Mass Touching at its last bolt. The direct finish remains a closed project.

13 Devastation Generation 10m 8c ***
Dave MacLeod 2004
The small scoop is gained with a hard dynamic move. The crux involves using a small finger pocket and sloping undercut to gain the slot above. Scotland's first 8c.

14 Open Project 10m
Starts up So Be It before making a long span left.

15 So Be It 8m 8a+ ***
Dave MacLeod 2000
The right-slanting ramp is a brilliant power route. Climb the ramp past a jug before making a long throw up right to a big sloper. Holding the swing into the next move provides an entertaining redpoint. There is a

Dumbuck

Dave Redpath on Devastation Generation (8c), Dumbuck (photo Mark McGowan)

project branching off left.

16 Open Project 8m
The direct line just right of So Be It.

17 Second Sights 7m 7c+ *
Dave Redpath 1998
A short hard boulder problem past a small block hold and undercut above.

18 Twister 8m 7a+
Darren Stevenson 1997
A hard move at the start leads to a difficult traverse left on undercuts. A good variation **The Twisted Hip** is to carry on upwards finishing up the next route at 7a ***.

19 Tragically Hip 12m 6c+ **
Jon Jones 1997
A good route which works its way leftwards. A hard start out of the niche overhang leads to good varied climbing above.

20 Breathe the Pressure 12m 6b+ *
Darren Stevenson 1998
A difficult, blind starting move over the bulge leads to pleasant climbing up the slab.

Dunglas - Strathblane

(NS 5749 7895) L64 E348 Alt 120m North-West facing
Maps p15, p27 Diagram p28

This conical volcanic plug is situated 1km east of Strathblane in pleasant open countryside at the foot of the Campsie Fells. The rock is micro-porphyritic basalt with marked hexagonal columns on the north and east faces. It is a great place to visit in the evening from the Central Belt. The sport routes often remain dry even on good days in winter and

Dunglas

RECOMMENDED TASTY BITES
Fish Suppers from Romy's on the A81 in Bearsden (opposite Hillfoot Train Station).

TOP TIPS
This is a great 'after work' crag with easy access from Glasgow.

DIRECTIONS
From Glasgow, take the A81 towards Blanefield, turning east onto the A891 at Strathblane (named Campsie Road and signposted to Lennoxtown). On the left after 50m is Cockalane View. Pass this and after another 50m on the left is a wide parking area in front of a church and cemetery (NS 5637 7935). For a first time visitor, it's worth driving on a few hundred metres to see where the crag is, then returning to the parking area. Strathblane is served by bus from Buchanan Street Station in Glasgow, leaving every couple of hours.

From the east it is possible to loop around Falkirk on the M9, taking the M876 to join the M80 from Stirling and the north. Exit at Junction 4, taking the A803 through Kilsyth, then the A891 through Milton of Campsie and Lennoxtown to reach Strathblane, passing the crag.

APPROACH
Time: 20mins
On the opposite (south) side of the road is a sign saying Public Path, Lennoxtown 4. Head down the path, which then bends left and follows a disused railway line along a cutting. When this opens out, the crag is easily seen on the right. Don't cross the fields early, but continue to a gate in front of the black north face. This is 1km on tarmac so time could be reduced by cycling. The crag is higher up on the right. Please do not approach direct from the A891 or park at the nearby farm as there have been access problems.

There are four lower-offs, referred to in the descriptions as Lower-offs 1 to 4.

midges are rarely a problem. The crag catches the evening sun. The crag stays mostly dry in wet weather, with dripping and weeping only an issue after heavy rain.

A 30m 'wall' rope is adequate as all routes are no more than 15m. Lower-offs are usually in-situ so please leave any krabs or slings in place. Take at least 8 quick draws. Note: All project work on the larger black caves and North Wall has been suspended and lower-offs will be removed. This is due to dangerously unstable rock and collapse of routes.

AMENITIES
The nearby village of Blanefield has some small grocery stores and take-aways. There are supermarkets, petrol stations and takeaways on the A81 as you pass through Bearsden and Milngavie on the way out of Glasgow. In this area, The Burnbrae Hotel (opposite the Allander Sports Centre) does good pub meals.

Dunglas

Dunglas

Central Lowlands

1 Imodium Wall   7a ✶✶
John Watson, Colin Lambton 2009
At the left end of the wall is a ramped pillar; take the leaning wall above this direct to a slopey ramp feature. Step hard left after the 2nd bolt and finish at the apex of the steep green wall and Lower-off 1. Finishing via the crack is 6c.

2 Imodium Crack   6a+ ✶
John Watson, Colin Lambton 2009
The cracked wall from the top of the ramped pillar. Trend right from the pedestal to gain the big crack, then haul steeply up left towards a tiny cave and Lower-off 1. A direct finish is bolted at 6b.

3 Whiplash   6b+
John Watson, Colin Lambton 2009
From the ramped pillar, step right and climb to a tiny triangular cave, then take the black headwall direct trending left at the top to Lower-off 1. Finishing right on Mr Poops to Lower-off 2 is 6b.

4 Mister Poops   6b+ ✶
Colin Lambton, John Watson 2008
The wall and high bulge just right of the base of the ramped pillar, stepping off a raised shelf. The high spike is a red herring! Lower-off 2.

5 Poop Deck   6c+
John Watson, Colin Lambton 2008
Climb the shattered brown wall mid-way along the raised shelf to gain the top of the crack on Bahama Breeze, or finish up Mr. Poops for 6c. Lower-off 2.

6 Bahama Breeze   6c+ ✶
John Watson, Colin Lambton 2008
The obvious ferned crack is climbed up left on juggy holds to surmount a cracked bulge with difficulty to Lower-off 2.

7 Negotiations with Isaac   6b ✶✶
Andy Gallagher 1992
Step off the raised shelf on its right side past a bolt in an embedded boulder to gain the crack for a few moves to a juggy rest at half-height. Step right then take the wall above direct to stretchy last moves to Lower-off 3.

8 The Tanning Salon   7b ✶
John Watson, Colin Lambton 2009
Go direct up to the horizontal crack at the base of Bahama Breeze, then straight through a crux wall sequence to better holds. Finish directly up the wall above just left of The Seam to Lower-off 3.

9 Landward   6b+
John Watson, Colin Lambton 2008
A girdle. Start up Negotiations with Isaac, but travel right across the wall along the two-thirds height horizontal break and finish up Beef Monster to Lower-off 4.

10 Beef Monster   6c+ ✶✶✶
Bruce Kerr, George McIntyre 1989
Start on the small pedestal on the right under the orange steepness. Step up to a horizontal crack, then make crux moves to gain a reluctant finger jug. Yard right to a layaway sequence to reach a rest niche at two-thirds height. Finish up the wall trending right on crimps to Lower-off 4.

11 The Seam   7a+ ✶✶
John Watson, Colin Lambton 2008
Step across from the pedestal of Beef Monster to climb the crack powerfully past the old peg. Gain the rest niche, then finish trending left via a second crux seam crack to jugs under Lower-off 3.

12 Airhead   7a ✶✶
Andy Gallagher 1992
The right-hand bolt-line through the low bulging wall (crux) to gain a line

Dunglas

Kev Gibson making successful Negotations with Isaac (6b), Dunglas (photo Fraser Harle)

of flat holds veering a bit left before finishing up and right through the crimpy Beef Monster headwall to Lower-off 4.

13 The Ring Cycle   7b ★★
John Watson 2009
A super link of the hardest cruxes is a right to left girdle, which gives the longest and pumpiest training route. Start up The Seam, cross hard left through Beef Monster to reach the halfway jugs on Negotiations with Isaac. Climb left past the ferny crack under a steep bulge and through the top wall of Whiplash to Lower-off 1.

CENTRAL LOWLANDS EAST
There are three crags in the vicinity of Edinburgh.

Ratho Quarry - Edinburgh

(NT 1283 7098)   L65 E350   Alt 80m   East or West facing   Map p15

Ratho Quarry re-opened for climbing in 2004, after being closed for a number of years during the building of what has become the Edinburgh International Climbing Arena, or the EICA:Ratho, simply called Ratho by climbers. The open part of the quarry contains three sport climbs and more are planned. These are sheltered, catch the sun and dry quickly all year round. If it does rain then you can always nip inside to sample one of the world's largest and best climbing walls! Details of the EICA can be found in the climbing walls section. Climbing in the outdoor quarry is, as one would expect, free.

AMENITIES
The EICA has a Tiso climbing shop and nearby at Newbridge and Ratho there are pubs, cafes, shops and service stations.

RECOMMENDED TASTY BITES
The EICA has its own very nice cafe from where the antics in the Arena can be viewed.

Ratho Quarry

TOP TIPS
The stability of the dolerite in this quarry has been affected by blasting of the M8 extension immediately to the north. Rock scaling works were carried out during the construction of the EICA but one should still be wary of loose rock, although the sport climbs are generally fine.

DIRECTIONS
The key is gaining the Newbridge Roundabout at the start of the M8 and M9 motorways.
1. From Edinburgh, follow the A8 past Edinburgh Airport to the Newbridge Roundabout. Cross over the motorway and take the B7030 off left, following signs to the EICA Climbing Arena. An access road on the left leads to a large car park (NT 1263 7090).
  If travelling west around the City Bypass, it is slightly quicker to leave at the Calder Junction and take the A71 towards Kilmarnock, following this to the traffic lights at Wilkieston where a right turn to Ratho is also signposted to the EICA Climbing Arena. Pass the road off right to Ratho village then turn right onto the EICA access road.
2. From Glasgow, follow the M8 until just outside Edinburgh, then turn off north at Junction 2 for the M9 to Stirling. Shortly after this, turn off left at Junction 1, which has a sign for the EICA Climbing Arena, to gain the Newbridge Roundabout. Take the first left, the B7030 to Ratho and Wilkieston, and follow the signs to the EICA Climbing Arena as above.
3. Heading south from the Forth Road Bridge, follow the signs for the M8 to Glasgow to join the M9 from Stirling and shortly thereafter leave this at the junction signposted to Edinburgh A8 and Broxburn. On the slip road to the Newbridge Roundabout is a sign for EICA Climbing Arena. Cross over the motorway on the roundabout and take the B7030 off left following the signs to the EICA Climbing Arena as above.

APPROACH
Time: 5mins
Walk toward the EICA but take the service approach. Head down, then up and round to the back of the building where external stairs lead down to the quarry. Outdoor climbing is accepted and it is also possible to approach through the building. Please note that for security reasons the car park is gated and locked at 10pm.

● **The Plums of Ratho   10m   7b ***
Nic Crawshaw 2009
This takes the left-hand line on the east facing wall near the left end of the quarry, quite near the right end of the building roof. Start from a raised ledge perhaps best gained by abseil, not using the building! From the ledge climb the wall by a series of increasingly tricky rockovers and mantels to reach a small overlap where the wall steepens. Make a couple of fierce pulls on small crimps to easier ground and run it out to the belay. The rock is a bit fragile in places.

● **The Grapes of Ratho   10m   6b ***
Ian Taylor 1998
The original line just right of The Plums of Ratho, starting from the same ledge.

● **Wounded Knee   15m   7a+ ***
Ian Taylor, Simon Munro 1994
On the east wall, to the left of the fire escape and facing the building, is a short arete which starts above a huge pile of boulders. Begin on the right side of the arete and at the 2nd bolt, move awkwardly round onto its left side. Move up, then swing back onto the arete to finish on large blocks. The rock scar dates from the first ascent.

Central Lowlands

North Berwick Law Quarry

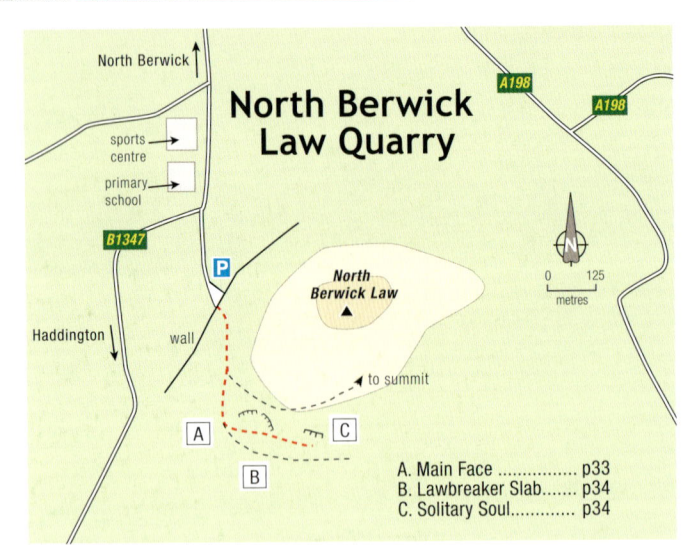

A. Main Face p33
B. Lawbreaker Slab p34
C. Solitary Soul p34

North Berwick Law Quarry – North Berwick

(NT 5540 8398) L66 or 67; E351 Alt 60m South-East and South-West facing Maps p15, p32

This small quarry is situated at the foot of the distinctive volcanic plug of North Berwick Law and it provides a popular sport climbing venue. The routes are short and sharp but give good climbing which is often in the sun and quick drying.

AMENITIES

North Berwick is picturesque seaside town, well geared up for tourists with a good selection of pubs, cafes and places to stay. Milsey Bay has been designated one of Scotland's top beaches and you can watch the seabirds of the Bass Rock live from the Scottish Seabird centre in the harbour.

RECOMMENDED TASTY BITES

Bar meals at The Auld Hoose or The County Hotel in North Berwick.

TOP TIPS

A popular evening venue where long arms are useful. There are also some trad climbs and boulder problems but nothing of any quality.

DIRECTIONS

North Berwick Law's conical shape is obvious from miles around. Coming from Edinburgh, leave the A1 to the north of Tranent and take the A198 to North Berwick. Don't head into the centre but take the signs for Dunbar and Berwick upon Tweed.

Follow this road for 0.6 miles (900m) skirting the centre, then take the B1347 (Law Road) signposted to Haddington. The A198 from the east also gets you to here. Go up Law Road passing the Sports Centre on the right and just past the primary school, turn off left at a sharp bend

Steve Ireland on Necktie (6b+), North Berwick Law (photo Fraser Harle)

North Berwick Law Quarry

with a parking sign The Law and follow a narrow road to the car park (NT 5530 8426).

An alternative, perhaps quicker and more direct, is to turn off the A1 to the north-east of Haddington, at the Abbotsview Junction, then take the A199 and B1347 to North Berwick to gain the car park access road. North Berwick is also served by train in 35mins from Edinburgh.

APPROACH
Time: 5mins
From the car park, walk south (right facing the hill) on the main path around the base of the hill. Ignore a path off left to the summit and continue until a left fork leads past gorse to the quarry.

Most of the climbs lie either side of a corner; on the lighter coloured Main Face, and the darker coloured Lawbreaker Slab to its right.

① Left-Hand Route   8m   6a+ *
Unknown
Three bolts to a lower-off on the higher inset wall left of the Main Face.

MAIN FACE

② Necktie   10m   6b+ *
Bruce Kerr, Rab Young 1989
Gain the left arete of the Main Face and layaway up its right-hand side.

③ Fogtown   10m   7a **
Bruce Kerr, Rab Young 1989
The wall just right of the arete finishes at the same lower-off as Necktie. An extended finish steps right before the lower-off to finish up Law of Gravity without use of the ledge or the arete (7a+).

④ Law of Gravity   12m   7a ***
Rab Anderson 1989
The central line is fingery and sustained. It can be started using the ledge, or better, by a bouldery start on the left which boosts the difficulty slightly.

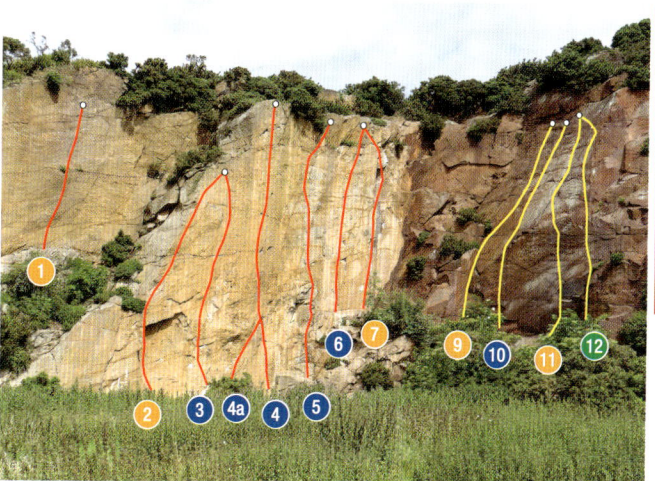

⑤ Jaws of the Law   10m   6c **
Rab & Chris Anderson 1989
The left-hand of three routes starting from a ledge 3m up has some reachy moves.

⑥ Law of the Flies   10m   7a **
Rab Anderson 1989
The central route off the ledge is hard for the short.

⑦ Law and Disorder   10m   6a+ *
Rab & Chris Anderson 1989
The line through the niche at the right-hand side of the wall has a dynamic start.

North Berwick Law Quarry - Lawbreaker Slab

8 Law of the Rings   25m   6c * □
Rab Anderson 1989
A left to right girdle. Start up Necktie, then take the obvious traverse line clipping the 2nd bolts of the routes to Law of the Flies. Follow this to the 3rd bolt, then finish up Law and Disorder. Other links are also possible on the wall.

LAWBREAKER SLAB

9 Darkness Falling   10m   6a+ * □
Calum Mayland, Tom Muirhead 2003
The left-hand route on the red slab is climbed via the corner. An eliminate **The Brazilian** 7a climbs the line without the use of the corner.

10 Igneous Intruder   12m   6c+ ** □
N.Ashton 1993
The second line of bolts. Hard moves gain a crux bulge on smears, leading to an easier finish.

11 Old Law Breaker   12m   6b ** □
Rab Anderson, Chris Greaves, Kenny Spence 1989
The line of ring bolts. Climb onto a ledge to the right of the first bolts then make harder moves to gain the upper slab. A variation climbs to the left of the first bolts at 6b+.

12 Wild Iris   12m   5+ ** □
Calum Mayland 2003
The wall and blunt arete right of Old Law Breaker, finishing at the same lower-off.

13 Solitary Soul   7m   6b * □
Calum Mayland 2000
This two bolt route can be found 170m right of the main area, next to the marking GBH on the rock.

14 Anarchic Law   8m   6a+ □
Calum Mayland 2000

Pete Roy escaping the Jaws of the Law (6c), North Berwick Law (photo Fraser Harle)

Three bolts just right of the arete right of Solitary Soul. Avoid using the arete, which makes it too easy!

Dunbar Crag - Dunbar

(NT 6755 7928) L67 E351   Tidal   North-West facing
Map p15

This sandstone sea-cliff lies 500m west of the harbour in Dunbar. The crag saw a little renewed interest in 2001 and 2002 with the addition of some easier lines, but the rock is soft and sandy and the climbing slightly disappointing. The state of the bolts should be checked before climbing.

AMENITIES
The Cuckoo Wrasse (formerly Starfish Inn) in the harbour does excellent seafood. There are several good chip shops on the High Street.

RECOMMENDED TASTY BITES
A pint of locally brewed Belhaven Best beer.

TOP TIPS
Check the tides before a visit as the crag is tidal!

DIRECTIONS
Dunbar is accessed from the west or south via the A1 and A1087. There are also regular trains from Edinburgh taking around 25mins. Coming in on the A1087 from the direction of Edinburgh, continue to a T-junction near the centre. Turn left into High Street and go to its north end.

Coming from the south on the A1087 also takes you here. Turn left again and you soon reach a road running west parallel to the sea. Follow it for 200m until a road named Bayswell Park is seen on the right, then park on the left opposite this in Lauderdale Car Park (NT 6757 7910). There is also a sign for Cliff Top Trail.

APPROACH
Time: 5mins
Follow Bayswell Park and descend steps to the Cliff Top Trail, where the road turns left. Follow the path left for 40m, then leave it and go out to a rocky headland forming the west end of a big bay. The cliff lies below; descend rightwards past bolts on the cliff top.

● **Hoochie Coochie Man   8m   5+**
Calum Mayland, Deirde MacDonnell 2002
The obvious corner at the left end of the wall.

● **Flown back from Boston   8m   5+**
Calum Mayland, Ben Ridder 2001
The route up the pocketed wall right of the corner.

● **Reaching for the Pilot   8m   6a+ ***
Calum Mayland, Ben Ridder 2001
Climb the reachy wall just right of Flown back from Boston.

● **Aching Arms and Dragging Heels   10m   6c+ ***
Calum Mayland 2001
Follow the overhanging lip using heelhooks. At the end of the lip, crank up and follow pockets up the headwall.

To the right, the rock is very overhanging and the routes rarely attempted.

○ **Open Project**
The left-hand of two lines is reputedly 8a.

● **Celebration Day   12m   7b+**
Gary Latter 1991
The bolts on the right-hand line are in a poor state.

○ **Open Project**
The roof project is reputedly 7c+.

Central Lowlands

Argyll & Lochaber

This section covers a large area but with relatively few sport crags, although it includes many of the best hard routes in Scotland. The Argyll crags start across the Clyde west of Glasgow at Tighnabruaich, the first of five crags on the Cowal peninsula, and heads north up the west side of Loch Lomond. Lochaber covers Glen Coe and Fort William before finishing west of Fort William at Arisaig, on the road to Mallaig.

The Cowal peninsula crags are composed of schist and lie in attractive forest which covers much of this relatively remote area. The two major ones are Tighnabruaich and The Anvil boulder, both home to large roofs with the best routes in the 8s. The Anvil in particular holds Scotland's hardest sport routes, with Metalcore (8c+) and Hunger (9a) taking pride of place. Ardvorlich on Loch Lomond is a lower grade schist crag which is expected to become popular.

Tunnel Wall is a huge overhanging wall of rhyolite at the foot of Buachaille Etive Mòr in Glen Coe with nine mostly 30m routes from 7b to 8a and a controversial history due to its proximity to the mountains. Steall Hut Crag in Glen Nevis has a similar number of even harder and more powerful routes, and with a similarly controversial history. In contrast, three crags near the road west of Fort William were kept very quiet until this guide and so have dodged controversy. Black Crag in particular is unusual, both for being basalt and in this area for having many lower grade routes in its total of 36. The scenery is as beautiful as ever although the equipment is showing its age.

History by Jo George, Dave MacLeod, John Watson, & Rab Anderson

Cowal Peninsula

Sport climbing in this part of Scotland is a recent development, and until this guidebook, many will have been unaware of its existence! The first bolts went in during 1998 but few of these crags have managed to make it into a printed guidebook until now. However, the internet and word of mouth have allowed The Anvil to emerge as one of Scotland's most talked about sport venues of recent years, despite being a long walk from the road.

Michael Tweedley was the first to get development going in the area with Miracle Wall on Loch Eck, developed along with Dave Redpath and Mark Somerville from Edinburgh. This resulted in three excellent little routes which are well worth a visit. Around this time Michael was laboriously exploring the whole area for new sport crags. Michael and Mark Somerville climbed the unusual slate slab at Innellan Quarry beside Dunoon. These routes are very bold without a cool head and some additional trad gear – in fact on one attempt 'Bouncing' Brendan Whitty survived a 25m tumble down the slab ending at the ground due to lack of these!

The really significant development was kept very quiet for a long time. In 2000, Redpath and Tweedley visited the Tighnabruaich area to check out a roadside arete they'd spotted. When they arrived, the local council had blown it to pieces because it overhung the road in a seemingly threatening manner. Instead they explored the steep jungle below the spectacular viewpoint at the Kyles of Bute. Hidden in the

History

Argyll & Lochaber

steep undergrowth and reminiscent of a Jurassic Park set, they stumbled upon several large buttresses including The Kraken, not the mythical sea monster but an intimidating nose of schist with a 12m horizontal underside.

An exciting phase of development kicked off with Jerusalem (6a+) and Moments of Enlightenment (7a+) from Redpath. In 2001 and 2002 several of the best lines fell such as Psychosis (7b+) from Redpath, and Moonbeams and Honey Dreams (7b+) from Mark Somerville. This excellent technical slab unfortunately needs a brush and some more attention to return it to its quality status. Michael Tweedley continued to try the awesome project across the roof which became Elysium (8a), eventually completing the line in 2006. Dave MacLeod was donated another awesome project crossing the Kraken roof to gain the hidden barrel shaped headwall. This resulted in Hand of Andromeda (8a+) in 2003. A published photo of this route sparked much curiosity as to the location of the venue. Dave Redpath took advantage of a dry start to 2004 to wrap up his Kraken project Shield of Perseus (7c+) as well as Event Horizon (7c+), taking the diagonal lip of Savage Slab.

The Anvil on Loch Goil is probably Tweedley's best find yet and has steadily earned its place as Scotland's hardcore sport venue as the remaining projects are being completed. Dave MacLeod opened development with the fine arete of Anvilfire (7c+) and went on to equip most of the remaining projects, most of which are very hard. Not all the lines are up in the 8s though and some of MacLeod's routes such as Hammertime (7b+) are worthy middle grade additions. In the mean-

1. Tighnabruaich....... p40
2. Miracle Wall........... p45
3. Innellan Quarry...... p46
4. The Anvil............... p47
5. The Bastion........... p52
6. Ardvorlich............. p53
7. Tunnel Wall........... p56
8. Steall Hut Crag...... p60
9. Cat's Eye Crag....... p65
10. Ranochan Walls..... p66
11. Black Rock............ p68

time Dave Redpath was studiously working and training for his eventual redpoint of Spitfire (8a+) on the front face. More good additions followed from the main protagonists, but things went to another level with Redpath and MacLeod's epic spring siege in 2007 resulting in Redpath's Fire Power (8b) and MacLeod's Metal-core, Scotland's first 8c+.

Since then, Malcolm Smith has taken an interest in the crag, repeating Body Blow (8b+), along with Alan Cassidy, and Bodyswerve (8c), as well as adding the brutal Smiddy (8b+) and Blackout (8b). In 2010 Malcolm Smith completed the set of roof projects by firstly climbing the central line linking on to Metalcore to give Blood Diamond (8c+), then the even longer and more powerful Hunger, Scotland's first 9a.

Ardvorlich
These walls were originally climbed trad up to about E3 by John Watson, Colin Lampton and G.Foster. As they demanded crux peg placements and had generally poor gear, it became an accepted retro-bolted venue. The left wall was bolted and climbed by Graham Harrison, the right wall mainly by John Watson, who also added a few more bolts and lines to the left wall, as well as ring-bolt lower-offs. Watson later bolted Quarterdome, but finding the project too hard and failing to persuade anyone else to fight through the bracken, has lost enthusiasm for this upper crag. But he still plans to modernise the bolting of Hidden Walls, which should make the venue popular.

Tunnel Wall
The first bolts to reach the Highlands were back in 1952 when Scottish legends, Hamish MacInnes and John Cunningham realised the potential of utilising the steep, seemingly impregnable central wall on Creag a' Bhancair to practise aid climbing techniques. At that time Hamish also believed if they could aid past the lower wall then they may be in with a chance of free climbing the upper wall. However, it was not to be as the pair left shortly after to climb in New Zealand, Antarctica and the Himalaya. Many years later the bolts they placed would become the approximate line of Fated Path. It wasn't until 1958 when Cunningham returned, this time with partner Mick Noon, and the imposing cliff was finally breached with an ascent of the now classic Carnivore (E2). Creag a' Bhancair continued to attract many leading lights over the following decades and many superb trad lines were created finishing with Romantic Reality (E6/7) by Dave 'Cubby' Cuthbertson in 1984.

Then in 1986, influenced by the sport climbing developments taking place south of the border and on the Continent, Cuthbertson, along with the talented youngster Graeme Livingston, aka The Brat, were lured back to the stunning, unclimbed central wall known as the Tunnel Wall. This section of the cliff had been named because of its resemblance to the sidewalls of a railway tunnel and the climbers who subsequently hung out there were likened to the children in the then popular TV series The Railway Children.

In their mind the Tunnel Wall held the prerequisites for a sport venue and so the pair went on to create the outstanding lines of Livingston's Fated Path (7c+) and Cuthbertson's aptly named Uncertain Emotions (7b) in 1986. After Fated Path, sport climbing in Scotland came to the fore and a couple of months later Cuthbertson climbed Marlina on Upper Cave Crag, but using only two bolts and some trad gear. By the following year opinions were still divided but there was enough support for Cuthbertson to add The Railway Children (7c) and Livingston to add Admission (7c+), the hardest so far. Due to the difficulty and time consuming nature of hand drilling bolts, these climbs were sparingly bolted and in part made use of the odd peg and natural gear placement. Fairly soon after, it was the turn of Glaswegian Paul Laughlan to add another fine addition with Tribeswomen (7c+) in the summer of 1990. The routes quickly gained a formidable reputation. At the time, there was a fair bit of controversy over these routes, which came to a head after they were fully bolted by Rab Anderson and Dave Cuthbertson. Various debates were organised and as a result the use of bolts here and in Scotland as a whole were discussed. Since then the dust has settled and although the sport climbs on Creag a' Bhancair have become generally accepted, the Tunnel Wall remains the Scottish sport crag closest to the mountains.

The climbs now see a steady trickle of traffic and a few more have been added. Firstly, in 2002 Dave Birkett linked Fated Path with Admission to give Fated Mission (7c+). Then in 2004 Dave MacLeod produced The Third Eye (7c) and Axiom, the wall's first 8a.

Vector Space (7c+) was added by MacLeod in 2011 and this brought the number of sport routes, on what was at one time thought a seemingly blank wall, to a grand total of nine. All of these climbs on this world class venue are worth three stars or more.

Steall Hut Crag
Back in the '70s Dave Knowles had aided his way across the crack-line which slashed the front face of this small yet impressively steep crag. At A3, in later years it was crying out to be freed. This steepest section of rock remained untouched by the trad climbers until 1992 when visiting climber Murray Hamilton's attention was drawn to Knowles' original aid line. Hamilton, one of the great names in Scottish climbing, was now living in France and with an abundance of sport

climbing on his doorstep, had reached a new level of strength and fitness. Perhaps influenced by sport climbing, or limited time, he climbed the crack in sport style, pre-placing trad gear and redpointing it to give what was undoubtedly one of Scotland's hardest and best crack climbs: Leopold E7 6c or 8a.

Shortly after, Cuthbertson and Malcolm Smith, (both members of the British Competition Team and undoubtedly two of the strongest climbers in the world at that time), along with Edinburgh sport climber Duncan McCallum, turned their focus to the steepest section of the cliff. In 1993, after much deliberation, they made the decision to bolt some lines. Cuthbertson chose a project which started up Leopold then took a direct line up the stunning headwall above. This was a controversial move as it meant retro-bolting the start of Hamilton's line, which although climbed sport style, was lead on in-situ trad gear.

Smith completed his line to give Steall Appeal (8b) with its desperate and reachy boulder problem crux giving Scotland its then hardest sport line. Over the next few years, Cuthbertson worked his line, a projected 8c+, getting to within a few moves of the finishing holds on several occasions. Dave MacLeod was also inspired by the route and by Cuthbertson's efforts and with his climbing improving over the years, his various attempts saw success became a real possibility.

Having moved to Fort William in July 2007 and taking advantage of the dry rock in poor weather, he focused on working the route with its crucial Egyptian. Stolen (8a+) was almost a side issue at the end of the month before success on Ring of Steall (8c+) two days later. In 2010 Dave MacLeod added The Gurrie (8a+), as well as a link from this into Steall Appeal to give The Gurrie Appeal (8b). To bring things up to date, MacLeod has continued activity in 2011 on his now local crag, succeeding on several projects, including The Fat Groove (8a) and its extension Steall Worker (8b+).

Dave Redpath engages in Trench Warfare (7b) at The Bastion (photo Jo George)

West of Fort William

The cliffs along the A830 are set apart from the established climbing areas around Fort William and developments are generally of a more recent nature. Starting in 2006 the cliffs were pretty much developed singlehandedly by Tom Ballard. Black Rock has provided a mainly low to mid-grade venue with routes such as Black Death (6a), Black Jack (6b) and Black Adder (6b+) standing out. At Cat's Eye Crag and the Ranochan Walls there are some good mid-grade routes such as Immaculate Conception (7a+) with a few harder routes thrown in like the fine Swan Lake (7c), Layaway to Heaven (7c+) and Way Out West (7c+).

ARGYLL - COWAL PENINSULA

Bordered on three sides by spectacular sea lochs and in the north by mountain and glen, the Cowal Peninsula is an area of outstanding scenic beauty and cultural heritage. Sandwiched between Loch Fyne to the west and Loch Long to the east, the peninsula extends south into the Firth of Clyde towards the Isle of Bute. The peninsula contains a number of recently developed and important climbing areas.

The Anvil and Tighnabruaich crags are two of the main crags here and both share the same characteristics; hardcore climbing in a beautiful and peaceful setting. Climbing at The Anvil requires a bit of commitment to trying difficult climbs with a long approach. However, the crag rewards the effort with the high quality climbing on offer and routes that stay dry when almost every other crag in this guide would get wet. Tighnabruaich is quite a contrast in that it has an extremely short approach, but shares the quiet ambience of the Argyll area. Miracle Wall at Loch Eck, Innellan Quarry at Dunoon and The Bastion at Loch Goil are the other crags on the peninsula.

Tighnabruaich - Loch Riddon

(NS 000 775) L63 E362   Map p37, p41

This is an adventurous venue with a distinctly wild feel, despite being a roadside crag! It comprises of several craggy buttresses of mica schist on a steep wooded hillside dropping straight into Loch Riddon at the Kyles of Bute. The crags lie directly below a viewpoint stop on the A8003 to Tighnabruaich. The outlook down the Kyles to the Isle of Bute is one of the most picturesque of any crag in this guide. However, it is not a conventional convenience sport crag. The routes are scattered around a series of buttresses and moving between these necessitates a bit of bushwhacking. It does make up for this gripe with exciting routes, the beautiful setting and the fact that it is a good winter venue. In fact, summer is probably the worst time to visit due to midges. If visiting in mid-winter, wait for at least one dry day beforehand.

AMENITIES

The town of Dunoon is geared up for visitors and has several good pubs, restaurants, cafes, a supermarket and B&Bs. Dunoon Tourist Information (08707 200 629) has friendly staff and will phone round accommodation for you. If staying near Tighnabruaich, the village of Tighnabruaich itself has B&Bs and lively pubs.

RECOMMENDED TASTY BITES

The Burnside Bistro in Tighnabruaich.

TOP TIPS

Again, a visit in summer is likely to result in a feast for local midges. The crags catch the morning sun in winter and generally need only one day to dry out.

DIRECTIONS

Since the crag is on the Cowal Peninsula, which is bordered on three sides by sea lochs, the quickest approach from Glasgow or anywhere in the Central Belt or Borders is by ferry from Gourock to Dunoon. Otherwise a long drive of 85 miles (136km) is required from Glasgow via Arrochar. There are two ferry operators departing and landing at different points and times, both at about half-hourly sailings daily. For fares and timetable information check <www.western-ferries.co.uk> or 01369 704452 and< www.calmac.co.uk> or 0800 066 5000. From Dunoon, head north on the A885/A815 then west across the peninsula on the B836 onto the A886 then pick up the A8003 south to Tighnabruaich.

If approaching from the Highlands, it will be quicker to go through Arrochar (A83), then down the west side of the Cowal Peninsula (A815, then A886) to join the A8003 as for the direct approach via ferry from Dunoon and Glasgow. The crags lie below a well signposted viewpoint lay-by (NS 0002 7752) at a highpoint on the road roughly 4 miles (6km) north of the village of Tighnabruaich.

APPROACH

Time: 5 or 10mins
Climb over the fence at the viewpoint tourist map and walk downhill following a jumble of small boulders rightwards. After about 30m in altitude a small path traverses left (facing downhill) to the base of Savage

Tighnabruaich

Slab, 5mins. From this junction continuing straight down and slightly rightwards through trees leds to The Kraken after a further 30m drop in altitude and below a smaller wall, 10mins in total. The pointed nose can be spotted through trees to the left as you walk down. The approach for The Lost World, the large buttress whose top is easily seen from the parking, is detailed under that crag.

The routes on each buttress are described left to right.

SAVAGE SLAB

(NS 0006 7755)   Alt 130m   South-East & North-East facing
Approaching from the left, Savage Slab consists of two broken slabby faces angled from one another by a hanging arete with a steep roof below.

1 Ya Butey   8m   6a+
Mark Somerville 2000
The first route from the approach sits 5m from the left end of the sunny face, and is often dry. No hanger on the 1st bolt.

2 Open Project
The right end of the main slab has an undercut lip and steep roof below. The line through the curving rail will have a desperate start.

The next four routes are on the north-east face, beyond the arete.

3 Event Horizon   10m   7c+   ★★
Dave Redpath 2004
This bouldery line has nice moves following the lip leftwards. Start at the same point as Psychosis on two crimps. Climb leftwards to a jug on the rail and make a short series of hard moves to get established on the slab above. Good holds soon follow.

4 Psychosis   10m   7b+   ★
Dave Redpath 2001
Start at two crimps at head height on the lip. A campus move kicks off a desperate short sequence to gain better holds after a few metres. Easier but technical climbing leads to the top.

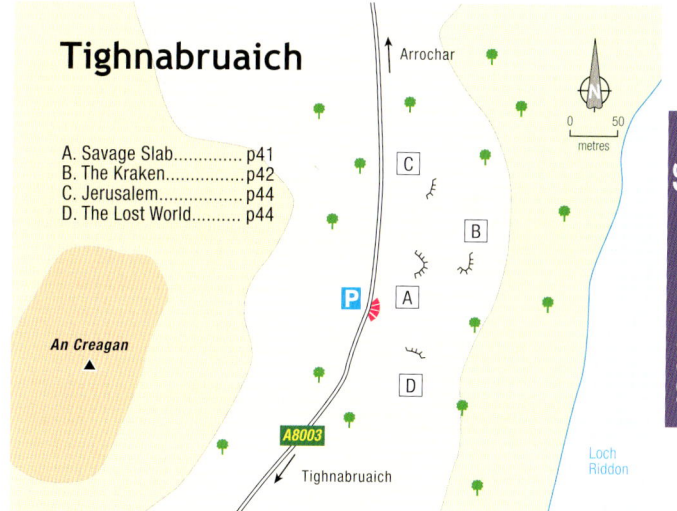

The large slab to the right holds potential of further routes for the green fingered. The next two sport routes sit at the top end of the slab, right of a shallow groove.

5 Bananas in Pyjamas   10m   7b
Mark Somerville 2000
Climb the slab to the right of the shallow groove.

6 Moonbeams and Honey Dreams   10m   7b+   ★
Mark Somerville 2002
This technical slab climb takes the blank looking line of bolts near the right edge of the slab. Very thin and tenuous moves.

Tighnabruaich
A. Savage Slab............ p41
B. The Kraken............. p42
C. Jerusalem............... p44
D. The Lost World........ p44

THE KRAKEN

(NS 0007 7748)   Alt 90m   North-West to East facing
Map p41

This is the main event at Tighnabruaich, dominated by a stunning 12m horizontal roof. The name comes from the legend of a huge invulnerable sea-beast which would devour merchant shipping.

7 Smoke on the Water   10m   7b *
Dave Redpath 2001
Follow the next route up the wall before breaking out left to tackle the short overhanging headwall on hidden finger pockets.

8 Moments of Enlightenment   10m   7a+ **
Dave Redpath 2000
Start at a bolt belay at the left edge of the roof. Climb onto the vertical left wall and climb rightwards with difficulty past an obvious glued crimp. The climbing eases towards the lower-off.

9 Elysium   25m   8a ****
Michael Tweedley 2006
The stunning line climbing the roof directly. From the left edge of the roof, climb the hanging niche in the roof and drop down to jugs (rest); as for Hand of Andromeda. A series of undercuts then lead leftwards to a desperate sequence to pass the hanging ramp feature near the lip. Good holds on the lip lead to the easy upper arete.

10 Apollo   20m   8a+ ****
Dave MacLeod 2006
Weird '3D' climbing through the horizontal groove leading out to the nose of the Kraken. Follow Hand of Andromeda to the start of the headwall but swing left and gain undercuts in the groove which are followed with technical knee-barring to a belay just over the lip.

11 Hand of Andromeda   25m   8a+ ***
Dave MacLeod 2003

Dave Macleod holding the Hand of Andromeda (8a+), Tighnabruaich (photo Cubby Images)

Another stunning line with exciting and varied climbing. From the left edge of the roof, climb the hanging niche in the roof and drop down to jugs (rest), as for Elysium. Move right to a large curvy undercut in a gap in the roof. Use this to gain the thin diagonal crack in the headwall (crux). Climb the crack and its continuation on pockets with more difficulty to the lower-off.

12 Head of Medusa   10m   6b+
Dave Redpath 2004
This starts down and just right of the huge roof, at the left end of the lowest base of the wall and near a chopped rhododendron bush. Step onto the wall from the left corner. Move up through an overlap to a lower-off on the mid-way ledge.

The next two routes are reached by climbing Head of Medusa to its finishing ledge.

13 Shield of Perseus   18m   7c+ **
Dave Redpath 2004
Step down from the ledge and make a desperate move to gain a finger jug on the lip shield. Sustained climbing leads to the hanging groove above and a lower-off.

Tighnabruiach

⑭ **Clash of the Titans 22m 7b ★★**
Dave Redpath 2002
This route tackles the hanging arete above the ledge. Dynamic moves lead to better holds; the easier upper arete can be surmounted on the left via a good pocket.

To the right of the sport routes lies a tall corner capped by a roof, which remains unclimbed.

JERUSALEM

(NS 0008 7755)   Alt 110m   East facing
Map p41

Well to the right of the Kraken is a small wedge shaped crag with a gully in its left side. Approach via the base of the Kraken; traverse right (facing up) first descending slightly, then rising to where Jerusalem can be easily seen. Continue rising to its base, about 80m from The Kraken.

● **Killing in the Name of   10m   7b+**
Dave Redpath 2000
Climb the gully wall into a niche. A hard move above the niche prevents an easy success.

● **Room with a View   15m   6b ★★**
Michael Tweedley 2000
Climb the left side of the front slab past a small roof.

● **Jerusalem   15m   6a+ ★★★**
Dave Redpath 2000
Pull out from the bottom right corner of the front slab on small quartz pockets. Continue up the slab with via some long rockovers.

THE LOST WORLD

(NS 0003 7740)   Alt 120m   North-East facing
Map p41

This is the large buttress seen from the parking, characterised by smooth walls and a long band of roofs. The routes are longer than most in the area and have exciting and varied climbing. It is possible to approach the base of the routes by bush-whacking down and across right for 100m from Savage Slab. However, the easiest approach is to abseil down the routes to start. From the car park, walk south along the road for 50m and drop down through trees to an open area at the top of the wall. Take an extra rope to abseil down to bolt belays at the base of the climbs.

⑮ **Distant Cries   20m   7b+ ★**
Dave MacLeod 2004
The steep wall left of a big leaning arete. The climbing gets increasingly difficult to a technical finale at the capping roof.

Miracle Wall

16 Crouching Tiger   20m   6c+   **
Dave Redpath 2004
The line through the hanging ramp in the capping roof. A technical and interesting lower wall leads to a long reach for a jug at the base of the ramp. From here, easier climbing leads across the ramp and finishing slab.

17 Vanishing Point   20m   7b   **
Dave Redpath 2004
Start at the same belay as Crouching Tiger but climb the wall direct past a hard move. A long reach left to the vanishing point of the roof scoop (crux) gains the easy finishing slab. Good climbing.

Miracle Wall - Loch Eck

(NS 1416 8987) L56 E363   Alt 30m   South-West facing
Map p37

This good little spot provides a small selection of routes on excellent clean mica schist, in a beautiful setting on Loch Eck. A day visit to Miracle Wall would best be combined with Tighnabruaich, Innellan or bouldering in Glen Massan or Glen Croe. It features 10m routes through the steep lower wall and a good finishing slab. The crag is often dry but is fairly sheltered from breezes.

AMENITIES

The nearby Coylet Inn is a 17th century fishing inn. It has excellent bar and restaurant menus and a good selection of real ales, as well as providing accommodation. It is the perfect place to sit outside and enjoy the stunning scenery after a day's cranking. You can even hire rowing boats from The Coylet Inn. If it's wet you can visit the lovely Benmore Botanic Gardens at the base of Loch Eck. The Whistlefield Inn is about 2 miles (3km) north of the crag and provides good bunkhouse accommodation and also serves excellent food.

RECOMMENDED TASTY BITES

Fresh seafood from Loch Fyne at The Coylet Inn.

Mike Tweedley on Room with a View (6b) (photo Jo George)

Argyll & Lochaber

Innellan Quarry

TOP TIPS
The faint hearted might want to lean over the top of the crag and pre-place a sling on the lower-off to make the run-out finishing slab a little less worrying.

DIRECTIONS
From Glasgow the direct approach is via Dunoon by ferry from Gourock (see Tighnabruaich for details). The crag lies some 9 miles (14.5km) north of Dunoon overlooking Loch Eck, above a bend on the A815. This is the road that would be reached coming from the crags at Tighnabruaich. Pass The Coylet Inn and continue for 1km to park in a lay-by on the left, just after some loch side bends and 200m before a bend with a wall on the loch side of the road (NS 1426 8959). This wall can be seen as you approach but by then you may have just passed the lay-by!

From Glasgow the longer approach by road is to take the A82 and A83 through Arrochar and turn off for Dunoon (A815) to reach Loch Eck. Reach a left turn for Ardentinny at NS 1437 9351. Don't take this but continue down the loch side for 2.3 miles (3.8km) watching for a wall which forms a banking left of the road. After another 100m is a left bend notable for having a wall on its outside (loch side). The crag is above this bend. Park in the lay-by on the right some 200m further on. There is room for a couple of cars just nearer the bend and the crag but pulling out requires a lookout passenger. If you reach The Coylet Inn, you have gone too far. To approach by public transport it is best to travel by train or bus to Gourock and take the Western Ferry to Dunoon. From here take the Campbeltown Citylink bus to Loch Eck.

APPROACH
Time: 2mins
From the lay-by, walk north along the road to the bend. The crag is 30m up the tree covered hillside immediately above the north end of the bend.

● **Angels with Dirty Faces   10m   7a+ ** ✓
Dave Redpath 1998
The left-hand bolt line. Climb up to a crack then go right and climb up on quartz pockets to exit onto the slab, heading right for the lower-off.

● **Holyman   10m   6c *** ** ✓
Michael Tweedley 1998
Excellent pumpy climbing on Heuco style pockets in the centre of the wall, followed by some weird moves leading onto the slab and lower-off.

● **Bible Babble   10m   6c** ✓
Mark Somerville 1998
The right-hand line. Climb the wall to a powerful move, then continue up the slab with steady but run-out climbing to the lower-off.

Innellan Quarry - Dunoon
(NS 165 745)   L63 E363   Alt 30m   South-East facing
Map p37
This huge slate quarry just south of Dunoon provides probably the most unusual sport routes in this guide. It is marked on OS maps as Bullwood Quarry. Dominating the quarry face is a massive easy-angled slab reaching almost 90m in length. The slab is angled about 50 degrees and the routes have been very sportingly bolted and are not strictly true sport climbs. The slab dries very quickly after rain and can be climbed on in winter. The routes were originally climbed on trad gear but not reported. Abseil descents are necessary due to the length of the routes.

AMENITIES
The town of Dunoon is geared up for visitors and has several good pubs, restaurants, cafes, a supermarket and B&Bs. Dunoon Tourist Information (08707 200629) has friendly staff and will phone round B&Bs etc for you. If staying near Tighnabruaich, the village of Tighnabruaich itself has B&Bs and lively pubs.

RECOMMENDED TASTY BITES
The Burnside Bistro in Tighnabruaich.

The Anvil

TOP TIPS
Take two half ropes and a rack of small gear including RPs to make the routes feel a little less frightening (but also less adventurous!).

DIRECTIONS
Dunoon is best reached from the Central Belt via the Western Ferry (cheaper) or Calmac (lands closer for walking to the quarry) which leave regularly from Gourock; see Tighnabruaich. There is no need to take a car across, although a day visit is best combined with one of the other crags in the area such as Miracle Wall or Tighnabruaich and then a car is needed. The Quarry lies by the A815 just beyond the southern edge of Dunoon.

APPROACH
Time: 2mins
Climb over a stone dyke on the left to enter the quarry.

- **The Wave** 60m 6a+ *
Mark Somerville, Michael Tweedley 2000
A direct line up the centre of the smooth slab, passing just 5 bolts to a lower-off. Good climbing and rather unnerving!

- **The Edge** 60m 6a *
Mark Somerville, Michael Tweedley 2000
Start as for The Wave then head rightwards to a bolt. Follow obvious thin cracks to another bolt. Now take a good foot ramp which leads to the chain on The Wave. Either take some trad gear with you or leave your brain at the bottom.

The Anvil - Loch Goil

(NS 2054 9551) L56 E363 Alt 110m West-South-West to North facing Maps p37, p47 Diagrams p48, p52

This is another adventurous crag in a remote and quiet location, yet featuring intense and spectacular climbing. The crag is a massive

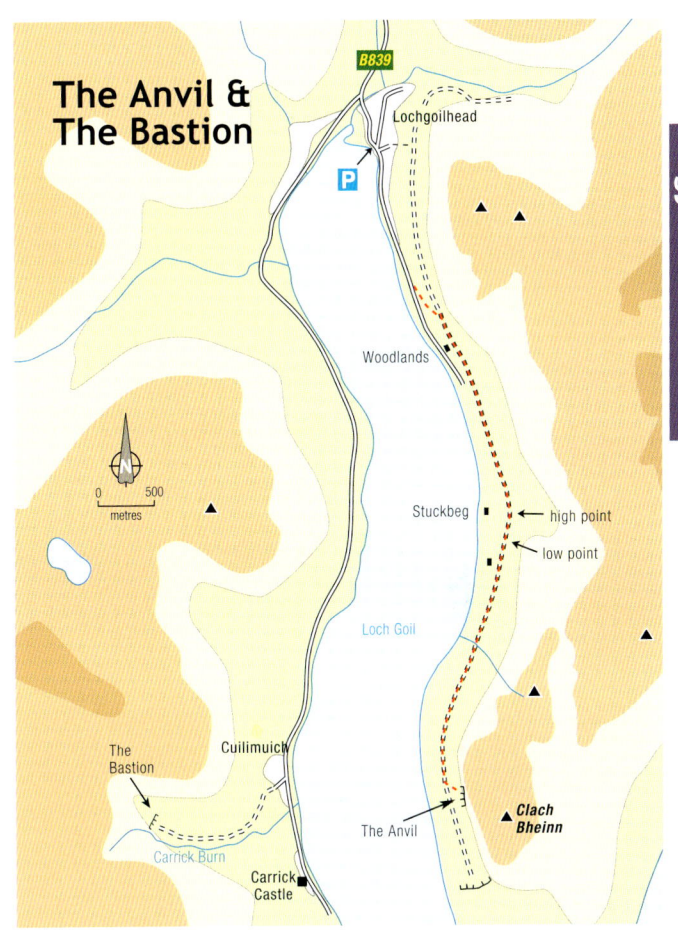

Argyll & Lochaber

48 The Anvil

free-standing 30m high mica schist boulder, roughly shaped like an Anvil and overhung on three sides. It is situated some 6km south of Lochgoilhead in wooded slopes on the east side of Loch Goil. The rock is mostly excellent and clean with rough coarse grained schist. It has some drainage and takes a few days to dry out completely in winter. However, once dry the crag stays dry much of the time and can be climbed on in the rain. Midges can be a problem in summer due to the surrounding forest, but the crag sees lots of sun.

AMENITIES
Lochgoilhead has pubs and cafes and a good shop and Arrochar has shops and a petrol station.

RECOMMENDED TASTY BITES
The obvious large castle on the west side of Lochgoilhead is a holiday complex which has an excellent cafe.

TOP TIPS
Use a mountain bike to make the approach much quicker; bikes can be hired in Lochgoilhead.

DIRECTIONS
From the Glasgow and Loch Lomond direction, follow the A82 to Arrochar and the A83 to the summit of the Rest and be Thankful pass. From here the B828 and B839 lead to Lochgoilhead; 55 miles (88km) from Glasgow. From the other crags on The Cowal Peninsula take the A815 alongside Loch Fyne and cut across via Hell's Glen and the B839. Park in the main car park in the village as some friction has occurred with the locals over parking further on.

APPROACH
Time: 1hr (walking fast) or 45mins with a bike
Walk south along a residential road near the shore of the loch for about 1.5km until a good path leads diagonally up to reach a forestry track. The track leads on down the east bank of Loch Goil. Follow this downhill for 1km, then back uphill for 1km to a fairly level section for 2km.

The Anvil

Now there is a long downhill for about 600m and at its end continue for 200m gently up to a left curve. Here there are some big boulders behind the ditch on the left and look for an orange marker post below them in the ditch (NS 2050 9550). The Anvil lies 30m uphill from the track and is just visible through the trees. The name Carnach Mor on the 1:25000 map roughly translates as the place with the big rock and may refer to it before forestry obscured it. If you end up cycling uphill through a tunnel of pines, you have gone too far.

First reached is a large front face which gives fingery climbing on smooth, gently overhanging rock. This angles left to an even steeper north-west face. Finally this is bounded with the underside of the Anvil presenting a highly impressive 25m roof. The climbs are described left (the roof) to right although you reach the right end first.

THE ROOF

There are three lines of bolts starting from the base and leading to two possible finishes. It is also possible to reach onto the wall at half-height from a convenient boulder and to combine with either finish.

1 Amateur Hacker   10m   6c
Dave MacLeod 2005
Climb round a boulder, then reach across the gap and use a shelf to gain and climb the slanting groove above; balancy.

2 Metalcore   25m   8c+ **
Dave MacLeod 2007
The line of a faint crack on the left side of the roof, followed in its entirety to the apex.

3 Bodyswerve   20m   8c *
Dave MacLeod 2006
Start up Metalcore with some big moves, then climb directly up a faint groove on a series of miserable edges to gain the slanting groove of Amateur Hacker. Finish up this. Perma-dry.

4 Body Blow   10m   8b+ **
Dave MacLeod 2006
Metalcore is accessed by swinging in from the halfway boulder and then via a desperate crimping sequence. Finish up this.

5 Blood Diamond   25m   8c+ **
Malcolm Smith 2010
Start up a faint groove which is the central start. Reach the point where Body Blow swings in, then finish up Body Blow/Metalcore.

6 Blood Fire   25m   8a+ **
Alan Cassidy 2007
Start up the faint groove of the central start but swing right onto the big holds of the right finish. Finish up this.

Dave MacLeod on Hunger (9a), The Anvil (photo David Redpath)

The Anvil

Dave Redpath caught on the Crossfire (7c+) (photo Cubby Images)

7 Hunger   25m   9a   ***
Malcolm Smith 2010
Start up the line of bolts at the right side of the roof but then link left to the left finish (Metalcore). A stunning piece of power endurance climbing.

8 Fire Power   25m   8b   **
Dave Redpath 2007
Start up the right line of bolts, but this time move right to the easier right-hand finish.

9 Heavy Metal   9m   7b
Dave Redpath 2005
Start off the halfway boulder and climb the top half of Fire Power. A wild leap and swing on a jug is the crux.

10 Shadowlands   20m   7c   ***
Michael Tweedley 2006

An attractive diagonal crack in the arete between the roof and the North-West Face. Always seeping at its base but the holds themselves stay dry so don't be put off; this is an excellent route.

NORTH-WEST FACE

11 The Smiddy   15m   8b+   **
Malcolm Smith 2007
The super thin and crimpy overhanging wall branching right from Shadowlands after four bolts. It features a Font 8a crux section.

12 Cowal Crusaders   15m   6c   *
Dave MacLeod 2004
From the base of the face, follow an easy ramp to a big ledge, then finish up a steep groove on big holds (as for Friendly Fire).

13 The Atlantic Strikes Back   15m   7c   *
Dave MacLeod 2007
Climb a small but interesting tapering groove just left of the right arete of the north-west face to the big ledge where Cowal Crusaders is crossed. A tough boulder problem gains a ramp on the wall above. Follow this rightwards to the belay of Friendly Fire.

14 Friendly Fire   12m   7a   *
Richard McGhee 2006
Start up the right arete of the face but after one bolt, follow a crack-line past a hard move to gain the ledge. Continue up the steep groove above on big holds (as for Cowal Crusaders).

15 Anvilfire   12m   7c+/8a   ***
Dave MacLeod 2004
The technical arete formed between the North-West and Front Faces. Pull past a bendy flake and make a thin move to gain better holds. At the last bolt, pull up and rockover onto the left side of the arete with a couple of hard moves to gain the top. Creeping closer to 8a as it continues to spit off climbers.

The Anvil 51

Argyll & Lochaber

Malcolm Smith working what would become Blood Diamond (8c+), at the Anvil. (photo Cubby Images)

The Anvil

FRONT FACE

16 Spitfire 12m 8a+ ****
Dave Redpath 2004
The left side of the smooth wall of the front face gives a classic fingery outing with sustained and technical climbing.

17 Crossfire 17m 7c+ ***
Dave Redpath 2006
A diagonal crack running across the face takes in Spitfire's crux but is not so sustained. Follow the next route (Blackout) for two bolts, then traverse into Spitfire with a tricky move. After its crux continue along the cracks on good holds to the Anvilfire lower-off.

18 Blackout 15m 8b ***
Malcolm Smith 2007
Straightforward climbing leads to a huge sidepull jug. The crux sequence above is heinous but on excellent rock going left into a faint groove. The more direct finish remains an 8c open project.

19 Hammertime 12m 7b+ **
Dave MacLeod 2004
Climb Blackout to just beyond the 1st bolt before heading rightwards. This gives superb climbing on edges and pockets leading diagonally up the wall to meet the right arete at the finishing slab.

20 Nu Mettle 10m 7b **
Dave MacLeod 2004
A devious and technical line climbing a right-trending faint groove on poor holds to join the right arete and the lower-off of Hammertime.

21 Way out West 10m 6b *
Dave MacLeod 2004
The right arete to the lower-off of Hammertime is the crag warm-up, but still doesn't give in easily.

The Bastion - Loch Goil

(NS 175 952) L56 E363   South-East facing   Map p37, p47

Yet another recent find in the quiet corries of Cowal. The crag is actually a large boulder which lies in the pleasant small glen above the village of Carrick Castle on the west bank of Loch Goil. Although the boulder is generally poor for bouldering the south face is steep and of similar character to Myopics Buttress at Dunkeld. One sport route and one project exist at present. Some bouldering exists in the immediate area but the ground underneath is very wet.

AMENITIES
As for The Anvil.

RECOMMENDED TASTY BITES
As for The Anvil.

Ardvorlich

TOP TIPS
This is another good winter and spring crag, which doesn't take much drainage and catches the morning sun. It can be damp during the shortest days when the sun is too low.

DIRECTIONS
If approaching from Glasgow follow the A82 to Arrochar and the A83 to the summit of the Rest and be Thankful pass. From here the B828 and B839 lead to Lochgoilhead. Follow the road down the west bank of Loch Goil to Carrick Castle.

APPROACH
Time: 30mins
From Cuilimuich, just before Carrick Castle village, follow a farm track south-west out of the village which quickly moves into the glen. The boulder lies about 100m beyond the end of the track.

● **Trench Warfare   15m   7b ★★**
Dave Redpath 2004
The left-hand sport route. Gain a resting jug below the roof with a long reach before moving onto steeper ground dynamically or otherwise. This is followed on small but positive holds to a resting place before an easier finish.

○ **Open Project**
The right-hand line breaks through the roof on smaller holds but poorer rock.

ARGYLL - LOCH LOMOND
There is one crag at Ardvorlich on Loch Lomond and although it lies within Argyll, it does stand apart from the other sport crags in this area. Ardvorlich is set amidst beautiful surroundings and with lower grades, it is destined to become popular.

Ardvorlich
(NN 3231 1217) L56 E364   Alt 80m   West facing
Maps p37, p53   Diagram p54

These pleasant and sunny schist walls hide above Ardvorlich B&B on the west bank of Loch Lomond, not far from the head of the loch. The venue is accessible and attractive but with a secluded feel. The walls provide technical climbing on crimps and pockets with grades in the 6s. Some of the bolts were initially placed quite far apart but there are plans to improve the situation. In summer the bracken is forbidding but although the distance through it is quite short, a visit in spring or a dry autumn day is still more pleasant.

AMENITIES
The nearest place for petrol, accommodation and shops is Arrochar.

RECOMMENDED TASTY BITES
The Inveruglas Tourist Information Centre, opposite the Loch Sloy power

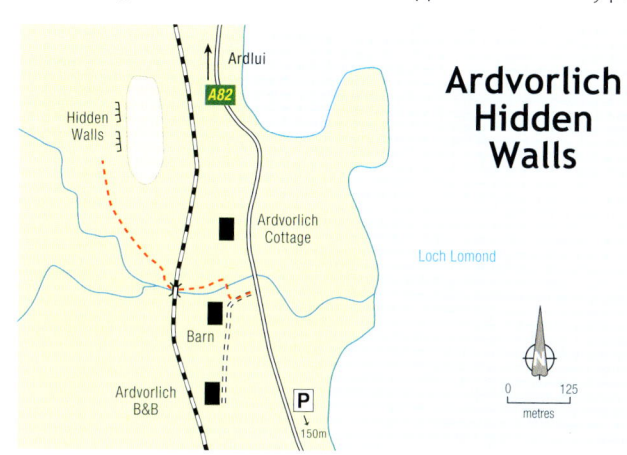

Ardvorlich Hidden Walls

Ardvorlich

station is a fine place to stop for a bite to eat. Located on the banks of Loch Lomond, the views are lovely and the food and drink is simple but good.

TOP TIPS

A long sling and screwgate karabiner are useful for extending lower-offs over the slabby tops; these can easily be collected from the top later. Please leave any in-situ extensions in place, as routes are no longer than 20m.

DIRECTIONS

From the north or south follow the A82 along the west side of Loch Lomond. From the south, about 4 miles (6km) north of Tarbet, is the well signposted Inveruglas Visitor Centre and a big car park on the shores of the loch. Continue north for 1.3 miles (2km) to a small pull-in on the right (loch side). This is 80m before a first sign to Ardvorlich B&B, so you need to be alert or turn back. From the north, it is 2.5 miles (4km) from Ardlui railway station to the B&B. Continue south for 350m from its entrance to the pull-in (NN 3266 1170).

APPROACH

Time: 15mins

Walk 350m north to the Ardvorlich B&B entrance. Go through a gate, then cross a fence on the right after 40m (before reaching a big barn). Cross a stream and follow its right side for about 100 rough metres to reach where the stream passes under the railway. Go under the railway and immediately go back up to beside the railway line. Go round a wall to a small climbers' path which leads uphill to the crag. The walls appear suddenly, facing away from the road. If the stream is in spate or potential access problems develop, it is possible to start 400m north of the B&B, cross the railway by an old footbridge and approach the crag from the north.

HIDDEN WALLS - RIGHT WALL

Routes are described right to left.

**1 Magic Carpet Ride   20m   6b ** **
John Watson 2002
The direct central line, aiming for the very apex of the right wall. Bolts and pegs on this one, hold your nerve! Due to be fully bolted.

2 Snake Eyes   15m   6a *
John Watson 2005
Pull through the central roof and go left to join with Dilemma. Step left and finish up a juggy left-slanting ramp to a sapling, then go right to the lower-off.

3 Dilemma   20m   6a+ *
John Watson 2005
Make the crux quartz pull through a bulge and travel up right through Snake Eyes to finish direct up stepped ledges at the top.

HIDDEN WALLS - LEFT WALL

Routes are described right to left.

4 Lake Lomond   15m   6a ★★
Graham Harrison 2004
After an initial cracked left-curving groove under a sapling, breathe deep and step left onto the superb headwall.

5 Drifting Too Far from Shore   15m   6c ★
Graham Harrison 2004
Start between the groove and a right-facing corner. Take the bulge on the right using cunning. Finish direct up the headwall.

The next two routes are diagonals which use bolts on other routes.

6 Jacksonville Hip   20m   6b
Graham Harrison 2006
A surprisingly independent diagonal line. Clip the 1st bolt on Drifting Too Far from Shore, heading left past The Groove and on past Sinking Feeling to finish in the corner.

7 Race for the Prize   20m   6b
Graham Harrison 2006
Another diagonal line going in the opposite direction. Clip the 1st bolt of The Groove, head right and finish to the right of Lake Lomond.

8 The Groove   15m   6a ★★★
John Watson 2002
The central groove has good juggy climbing to a crux step up to good pockets and an enjoyable final headwall. The holds are there! Mantel the top to lower off.

9 That Sinking Feeling   15m   6a+ ★
Colin Lambton 2002
The tricky left arete to a 1st bolt (pre-clip), then easier to the 2nd bolt, then up to a scooped groove (crux). Step through this and finish up left.

Jo George paddling up Lake Lomond (6a), Ardvorlich (photo Stone Country)

Ardvorlich

Argyll & Lochaber

Tunnel Wall

🔟 Arm Carnage 20m 6c
John Watson 2006
Boulder along the roofed crag at the left and lunge up to a ledge by the 1st bolt. Follow this up and right to step across to join That Sinking Feeling. Often wet.

QUARTERDOME

(NN 3202 1244) Alt 220m South-East facing

A high crag above Hidden Walls has two bolted lines of no special quality and a high quality but hard project without hangers. At the time of writing, the future of the crag appeared doubtful.

APPROACH

Time: 20mins from Hidden Walls
Uphill from Hidden Walls are two walls close together but largely hidden by trees. To their right and at the same height is a clean curving arete but this is not as good as it looks. Head initially towards the clean arete, then go up between it and the two walls before traversing left to the crag. This is obvious on arrival as a huge roofed scoop. The approach is very rough and tedious during the bracken season.

Side Issue 15m 6b
John Watson
Climb the blunt slabby left arete of the scoop via an initial slab to the groove of Godot. Gain higher slabs to step round to the lower-off. All bolts are shared with Godot.

Waiting for Godot 20m 7b
John Watson
Take the left wall of the scoop through a quartz band to the left arete. Step up and back round the arete (crux) to the lower-off (which needs improving).

Endgame Project (open) 15m 8a?
John Watson
The left wall of the scoop direct. Climb the quartz band direct to an undercut overlap. Crimps and pockets lead with increasing difficulty to the top.

LOCHABER

There are five sport climbing venues in the Lochaber area. The first of these is the Tunnel Wall in Glen Coe, then close to Fort William is Steall Hut Crag in Glen Nevis. West on the Road to the Isles and Mallaig are Cat's Eye Crag and the Ranochan Walls at Loch Eilt, then Black Rock overlooking the sea near Arisaig. Between them these venues cover a fabulous cross section of Scotland's scenery from mountain to glen and loch to sea.

Tunnel Wall - Glen Coe

(NN 216 551) L41 E384 Alt 450m North-West facing
Map p37 Diagram p58

The Tunnel Wall is one of Scotland's most impressive sport climbing venues, offering a small number of superb routes in a fantastic mountain setting. It is a striking pink wall which forms part of Creag a' Bhancair, a cliff which is located low down on the western flank of one of Glen Coe's most celebrated mountains, Buachaille Etive Mòr.

The climbs, with one 7b exception, are in the realms of 7c to 8a and are long, sustained and surprisingly intimidating in character. The rock is an excellent quality rhyolite, almost slatey in texture and perhaps something of an acquired taste. All routes are adorned with a profusion of crimps, pinches and sidepulls, and although crux sequences can be complex, stopper moves are rare and therefore the routes are ideally suited for the on-sight. A few of the more recent climbs are a bit run-out in places and some may find a clip-stick useful at the starts.

For best crag conditions, the spring months of April to June are recommended; any later and climbing days will require careful selection as the midge will be making its presence felt! However, pick your days carefully (a breezy day for avoiding midges) and climbing can be enjoyed through to early November, by which time it'll be getting too cold for even the most hardened Scottish climber! The Tunnel Wall dries quickly after rain and due to its steepness climbing is often possible during rain showers, as long as the wind does not blow the rain onto the rock.

Tunnel Wall

Argyll & Lochaber

Dave MacLeod on Axiom (8a), Tunnel Wall, Glen Coe (photo Cubby Images)

Tunnel Wall

The crag catches the sun late in the afternoon making it the ideal choice for an evening's, or half day's cragging.

AMENITIES
The Kingshouse Hotel, 2 miles south of the crag offers accommodation (bunkhouse & rooms), meals and has a bar. Eight miles north of the crag (just off the A82 before Glencoe village), the Clachaig Inn has a climbers' bar offering food, good real ales and accommodation. Further along this same road is the Red Squirrels campsite and bunkhouse. Glencoe and Ballachulish villages have all the usual amenities, pubs, cafes, hotels, B&Bs, campsites, petrol and grocery shops. Ballachulish also has a bank, which opens on Tuesdays and Fridays and the petrol station in Glencoe has a Link machine for cash withdrawals.

RECOMMENDED TASTY BITES
Try the homemade soups, home baking and a good cafe latte from Crafts & Things in Glencoe.

TOP TIPS
With the exception of Uncertain Emotions, a 60m rope is necessary. Come armed with stamina!

DIRECTIONS
By car, follow the A82 to Glen Coe and park in the large lay-by at Altnafeadh (NN 220 563). Heading north, this lay-by is 1.8 miles from the Glen Etive road junction, or if heading south – 9 miles from Glencoe village. The Citylink Glasgow-Fort William bus service also passes the lay-by but you will have to ask the driver politely to stop here, otherwise it's a two-mile hike from the Kingshouse Hotel junction, which is the bus's normal stopping point.

APPROACH
Time: 30mins
From the lay-by, cross the road and follow the wide track over the river to the white cottage of Lagangarbh, which is a Scottish Mountaineering Club hut. Approximately 200m beyond this the path splits; follow the right-hand branch. After a further 10mins leave the path at the first obvious, large boulder on the right side of the path and pick up a narrow track (vague at first) traversing rightwards. Very shortly you will pass another larger boulder at a usually dry stream bed. The path then gently rises under a line of small crags to emerge at the foot of the Tunnel Wall.

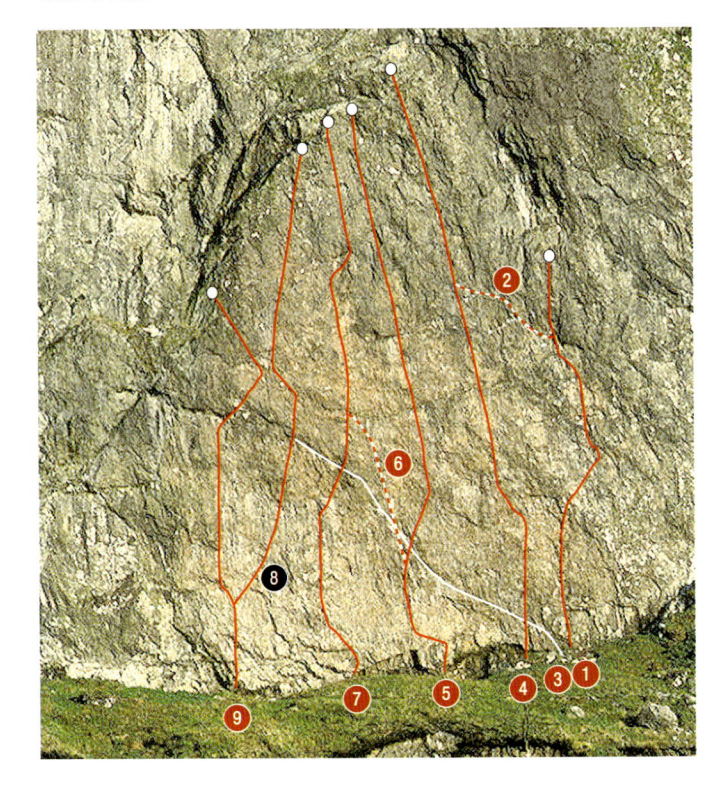

Routes are described from right to left.

① Uncertain Emotions 22m 7b ★★★
Dave Cuthbertson 1986/1988
The first sport route up the right side of the wall gives excellent and varied climbing with two distinct cruxes, a crafty hands free rest and a little sting in the tail for a tired leader – okay three cruxes!

② The Railway Children 30m 7c ★★★★
Dave Cuthbertson 1987
A classic. Follow Uncertain Emotions to the resting niche at two-thirds height. Where that route goes up and right, make a left traverse along the break before launching up the technical crux wall above. If successful, good easier climbing leads to the lower-off.

③ Vector Space 38m 7c+ ★★★
Dave MacLeod 2011
This follows the obvious diagonal overlap running across the wall into a finish up Axiom. Great steady climbing. Longer but without the difficult cruxes of the other 7c+s on the wall.

④ Tribeswoman 28m 7c+ ★★★★
Paul Laughlan 1990
Direct start added in 1995 by Dave Cuthbertson.
The highlight of this superb sustained climb is a technical wall above the 5th bolt. It then joins Railway Children for its crux! The original route started further left and utilised two old bolts – rarely climbed these days.

⑤ Fated Path 30m 7c+ ★★★★
Graeme Livingston 1986
Excellent sustained climbing up the compelling central line. A crux high up regularly spits out tired leaders.

⑥ Fated Mission 30m 7c+ ★★★
Dave Birkett 2002
An excellent and logical combination with a distinctive crux. Follow

Joanna George on The Railway Children (7c), Tunnel Wall, Glen Coe (photo Cubby Images)

Spider Mackenzie getting a grip on Tribeswoman (7c+), Tunnel Wall, Glen Coe (photo Rab Anderson)

Fated Path to the 4th bolt and make some difficult moves before going hard left to join Admission above its crux bulge. A bit run-out in parts.

7 Admission   30m   7c+   ***
Graeme Livingston 1987
Possibly the hardest 7c+ on the wall with the main difficulties found on the lower third. The middle section offers excellent steady climbing to a good rest at the top break. But there is a nice sting in the tail!

8 Axiom   30m   8a   ***
Dave MacLeod 2004
Another great climb taking a parallel line to Admission, just nudging into the realms of 8a. Start up The Third Eye to the 2nd bolt, then break off rightwards with increasing difficulty to a hard section on sidepulls to gain good edges in a faint niche (technical crux). More sustained climbing leads to a decent rest before moving up, then rightwards to another difficult section, then easier ground to finish. Run-out in parts.

9 The Third Eye   25m   7c   ***
Dave MacLeod 2004
The furthest left sport line takes the pale wall and bulge above. Some difficult moves lead to a boss at the 3rd bolt (rest). A sustained fingery section leads to easier climbing on good holds through the bulge, followed by another thin move to gain the big horizontal and lower-off.

Steall Hut Crag - Glen Nevis

(NN 1764 6825)   L41 E392   Alt 270m   North facing
Maps p37, p61   Diagram p63
This infamous venue has the only sport climbing in the Glen Nevis area and is pretty much the stamping ground of the elite! The diagonal cracklines are inspiring and the climbs, once dry, are possible even during heavy rain. The exits of Leopold and especially Arcadia take a long time to dry out, but the lower sections and Steall Appeal are more or less perma-dry. May or September is often the best time to visit. The crag does catch breezes though and is always in shade, so good conditions do occur in mid-summer when the crag is most likely to be fully dry.

Steall Hut Crag

DIRECTIONS
From a roundabout just north of Fort William (on the A82), follow the road up Glen Nevis to the car park at its termination after 10km (NN 168 691). Fort William is well served by public transport, train or Citylink bus from Central Scotland. From here a bus service runs to the Lower Falls of Glen Nevis (does not operate in winter).

APPROACH
Time: 35mins
A stunning 20min walk up the Glen Nevis gorge through some of Scotland's most magnificent scenery leads to Steall Meadow. Continue to the far end of the meadow and cross a wire bridge below Steall Falls. Just across the bridge is the Steall Hut, and the crag is easily seen from behind it. The crag is recognisable by the central cave and diagonal crack-lines with a large brown slab left of the main crag.

1 Diamond Back 20m 6b+
Dave MacLeod 2012
This climb takes the protruding diamond shaped slab at the top left of the main brown slab. Climb the lower slab and pull through the bulge on good holds.

2 Diamond Groove 20m 6a+
Dave MacLeod 2012
Start up Diamond Back but then follow the groove running under the protruding slab and then climb it's right arete to the lower-off.

3 End of the Line 28m 6b+ *
Dave MacLeod 2012
The centre of the big brown slab is taken by **Steelyard Blues**, a now vegetated E2 5b. This line takes the right side of the slab, from the lowest rocks. Climb the lower slab, surmount the bulge and continue up the good open slab to a tricky section on small pockets near the lower-off. It is also possible to start up cleaned ledges on the left, avoiding the initial bulge at 6b.

AMENITIES
Fort William is well geared up for tourists and climbers. Nevisport is the first stop-off for many passing climbers and also has a good and very popular cafe and pub which often has live music in the evenings. Fort William has many B&Bs at competitive prices. There are several independent hostels in the Fort William area – see <www.hostel-scotland.co.uk>. Glen Nevis itself has a good campsite and youth hostel.

RECOMMENDED TASTY BITES
The Hot Roast Company on the High Street precinct serves excellent fresh roast meats on their cafe menu. Pop in for one of their '8a fuelling' meat rolls and a chat with the friendly owner.

TOP TIPS
Unfortunately Steall is among Scotland's most infamous crags when it comes to midges! Come prepared with headgear as repellent is not enough.

Steall Hut Crag

4 Tipping Point 20m 6c
Dave MacLeod 2012
Start just right of the arete at a jug. A tricky boulder problem at the start leads to pleasant climbing up the arete and upper slabs.

5 Dam That River 20m 7b*
Dave MacLeod 2012
Start as for Tipping Point but break out rightwards following the line of the trad route **Lame Beaver** (E7) to the roof. Pull directly through the roof (crux) to a kneebar rest and continue up the wall on small holds to rejoin Tipping Point. To protect the trad section on the lower wall take some wires or clip the third bolt on Tipping Point and pre-place a sling on the bolt after the roof after an ascent of Tipping Point.

6 The Fat Groove 25m 8a *
Dave MacLeod 2011
The long diagonal bomb-bay groove running rightwards to join and finish up Trick of the Tail. Very technical climbing before the back-and-foot rest as it crosses Stolen.

Dave MacLeod steals another route - Stolen (8b), Steall Hut Crag (photo Cubby Images)

7 Steallworker 40m 8b **
Dave MacLeod 2011
An excellent stamina link-up of The Fat Groove into Leopold, with lots of cruxes but lots of core-working rests too; hard. Follow The Fat Groove to the rest in the groove of Trick of the Tail. Pull rightwards over the lip of the roof and traverse right along the lip with difficulty to gain the foot of the rightwards slanting crack of Leopold. Finish up this.

8 Stolen 25m 8b **
Dave MacLeod 2007
A stunning line following the zigzag grooves and headwall with sustained difficulty and excellent climbing. It crosses The Fat Groove as it heads left. Low in the grade.

There are two harder starts to Stolen: the **Left Hand Start** (route 8a on diag.) is an open project, and **Stolen Direct Start 8b/8b+ *** (route 8b on diag. Dave MacLeod 2012). Bouldery climbing on undercuts leads to the back-and-foot rest on Stolen. The start is worth 8b in itself.

9 Trick of the Tail 20m 7b+ *
Mark McGowan 1989
Originally a trad route but retrobolted in 2011 with permission from the first ascentionist. Climb the central recess to gain and follow the big groove left with perplexing moves to gain a no-hands rest in a niche. Either lower off from here (the finishing bulge is often wet) or take some trad gear and break out right to finish as for Arcadia.

10 Maxwell's Demon 25m 8b *
Dave MacLeod 2011
A direct line cutting through the diagonal crack of Arcadia. Pull through the apex of the central cave with difficulty to join Arcadia for a short way. Pull direct out of the crack via an undercut and move right (crux) to gain the finishing crack of Ring of Steall. It starts on bolts, then on in-situ pegs and wires in Arcadia and bolts again at the end. Starting up The Fat Groove and joining Maxwell's Demon at the cave roof nudges it up to 8b+ (**Irn Age** Dave MacLeod 2012).

Steall Hut Crag 63

Argyll & Lochaber

Steall Hut Crag

11 Arcadia 25m 8a ★★★
Gary Latter 1993
Not strictly a sport climb, it follows the left-slanting diagonal crack-line emanating from the central recess. The initial section is common to Leopold and is bolted, the remainder protected by in-situ wires and pegs. Bring a selection of wires and cams for the finishing section which is rarely dry. The route is sustained and technical with the crux leaving Leopold.

12 Leopold 25m 8a ★★★★
Murray Hamilton 1992
The right-slanting crack is one of Scotland's hardest and best crack-climbs. The meat of the route (until beyond the crux) is bolted as part of the route below. A selection of cams and wires is required to protect the upper section. In summer the final 2-3m of climbing is often wet and the route has been climbed in this condition! A difficult pinch move at half-height is the crux. After this, move out right on undercuts to a shakeout. Surmount the shield of rock to regain the line.

13 Ring of Steall 25m 8c+ ★★★★
Dave MacLeod 2007
This desperate but stunning line was attempted over several years in the 90s by Dave Cuthbertson, later resisting attempts by Malcolm Smith and Dave MacLeod before eventually succumbing. Follow Leopold to the poor rest after the crux before breaking out left to gain an undercut on the smooth overhanging wall. A desperate crux section leads to further hard climbing up the diagonal crack and finishing groove.

14 Fighting the Feeling 22m 9a ★★
Dave MacLeod 2012
A more direct finish to Ring of Steall. From the base of the crack beyond its crux, move up right with desperate climbing on tiny edges

15 The Gurrie 20m 8a+ ★
Dave MacLeod 2010
Climb the parallel line right of Leopold with tough moves through the bulge, leading into the finish of Leopold.

Andy Coish on Leopold (8a), Steall Hut Crag (photo Gary Latter)

Cat's Eye Crag

16 Gurrie Appeal 20m 8b
Dave MacLeod 2010
Start up The Gurrie but move rightwards into the finish of Steall Appeal. Low in the grade.

17 Steall Appeal 10m 8b
Malcolm Smith 1993
The line of bolts taking the smooth bulging wall near the right end of the crag. A desperate and reachy boulder problem crux at the 2nd bolt is one of the hardest moves ever done on a Scottish route, especially if you are short!

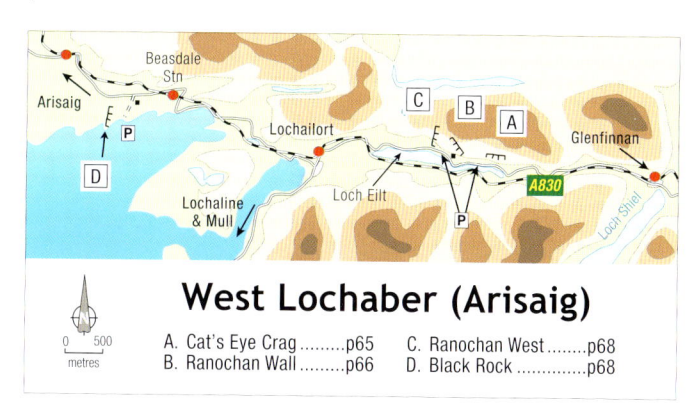

West Lochaber (Arisaig)

A. Cat's Eye Crag p65
B. Ranochan Wall p66
C. Ranochan West p68
D. Black Rock p68

Cat's Eye Crag – Loch Eilt

(NM 8434 8195) L40 E398 Alt 110m South facing
Maps p37, p65

This crag, the nearby Ranochan Walls and Black Rock near Arisaig all lie along the A830 to Mallaig, known as the Road to the Isles. Cat's Eye Crag is the first encountered and takes the form of a prominent prow with a wooded base facing across the east end of Loch Eilt. The rock is compact schist which dries quickly and catches the sun for most of the day. The grey streak of Swan Lake is seen from the road.

AMENITIES

There are pubs/hotels at both Lochailort (Lochailort Inn) and Glenfinnan. The nearest bunkhouses are the Glenfinnan Railway Station Sleeping Car, a very unusual sleeping place, and a bunkhouse at The Glenuig Inn, which is 8 miles (13km) south of Lochailort on the A861. It is best to buy petrol in Fort William on the approach since the closest further west is at Morar. The nearest big shop is at Arisaig.

DIRECTIONS

Head west from Fort William on the A830 towards Arisaig and Mallaig. Pass Glenfinnan and after 4 miles (6km) is the start of the next loch, Loch Eilt. Immediately after a sharp bend the loch is visible, also the crag is seen on the hillside to the right (north); park on the verge on the right (NM 8415 8170).

APPROACH

Time: 10mins
Cross boggy ground and head up left of the crag before traversing right to its base. Scramble up to a tree belay and a paved stance.

FIXED GEAR

As with the other crags in this area, the routes usually finish at a chain which is inadequate for lowering off; the last person should abseil. The public spirited should leave a krab or maillon.

The routes are described right to left.

● Swan Lake 20m 7c ***
Tom Ballard 2007
A grey streak up a slabby wall. Start atop a block. Boulder the initial wall to a rest on a shelf. Undercuts lead to a step right and a no hands rest. Forge up the headwall using sidepulls and crimps to clip the belay from a quartz fin. Bolted from the ground up.

Argyll & Lochaber

Ranochan Wall

Layaway to Haven 15m 7c+ **
Tom Ballard 2007
A cleaned corner to the left is much harder than it looks. Tread carefully otherwise the start will become much harder. Bolted from the ground up.

The blind flake in the slab to the left is a closed project. No hangers or chain in place.

Ranochan Walls - Loch Eilt

(NM 821 823) L40 E398   Maps p37, p65

There are two walls above Ranochan, a house by the road on the north shore of Loch Eilt. The main crag has attitude, is much steeper and feels much higher than it looks from the road. It gets all the sun and any breeze going, so dries quickly. The view over the loch is particularly fine.

AMENITIES
As for Cat's Eye Crag.

DIRECTIONS
Head west from Fort William on the A830 towards Arisaig and Mallaig. Pass Glenfinnan and after 4 miles (6km) is the start of the next loch, Loch Eilt. Immediately after a sharp bend the loch is visible and Cat's Eye Crag is up on the right. Continue for 1.5 miles (2.4km) to the white house of Ranochan. The crags are seen from just before the house, particularly the main crag, which lies above the house and has a long roof at one-third height and a horizontal crack at two-thirds height. Park at the west end of a deer fence which encloses the house. There is a small pull-in for two cars at NM 8200 8225; otherwise park 250m further on at a lay-by. Both walls are visible from the pull-in.

APPROACH
Time: 10mins
Head up the west side of the deer fence by an animal track leading towards Ranochan West, then turn right to the main Ranochan Wall, 5mins, or continue left to Ranochan West.

FIXED GEAR
As with the other crags in this area, the routes usually finish at a home-made chain system which is inadequate for lowering off; the last person should abseil. The public spirited should leave a krab or maillon. Clipping the first bolt is not always easy and using a clip-stick is a possibility.

RANOCHAN WALL

(NM 8214 8230)   Alt 80m   South-West facing   Map p65

The main wall above the house. Some short trad routes come boulder problems have also been climbed at the ends of the crag. The first 3 routes share the same line of bolts so the harder routes may feel like eliminates.

1 Cold Shoulder 9m 6c
Tom Ballard 2006
Boulder a short wall, or jump, to the break. Step left and dynamically take the left arete.

Ranochan Wall

2 Way out West 9m 7c+ *
Tom Ballard 2006
Boulder the short wall to the break. Climb the wall without the help of either arete to a good rail; another hard pull may reach the top!

3 Sneaker Freaks 9m 7b+
Tom Ballard 2006
Boulder the short wall to the break. Step right and scrape desperately up the right arete.

4 Devil's Advocate 12m 6a+
Tom Ballard 2006
The bomb bay like slot with awkward climbing and a tricky finish.

5 Kneed 4 Speed 12m 6c+
Tom Ballard 2006
Attempt to climb the right arete; step right to a chain.

6 Bulldog Drummond 12m 7a+
Tom Ballard 2007
Gain the break via a hand jam and good holds. Step up to an undercut and crimps above; clip the first couple of bolts on Lateral Thinking. Reach a good hold above a rock scar. Span left to holds, then move up and right to a flat one. Clip a lone bolt, making a hard move to stand on the flat hold.

7 Lateral Thinking 15m 7a+ **
Tom Ballard 2006
Start at a small roof. Gain the break and a sloping shelf above to a good hold above the rock scar, then awkwardly layback to a flake. Reach right across the wall to an inset crimp and another above to the second break. A block allows a tricky finish.

8 Esperanza 15m 6c+
Tom Ballard 2006
Climbs the left arete of a wide streaked groove with a burly pinch move. Undercut to vicious crimps and good jugs above to the higher break. A tricky finish up the wall above remains.

9 Chip 'n' Pin 15m 7a+
Tom Ballard 2006
Bridge the wide streaked groove. At the break make a hard series of moves using sidepulls and crimps to reach a flake. More hard moves reach the second break and finish via a curved crack.

10 Goosey Goosey Gander 14m 6c+ *
Tom & Kate Ballard 2006
Mantel a small ledge and stand up to the first break. Rock up to an undercut and step left to a thin undercut and good hold above. Use sidepulls up to the second break, then pull over the bulge using crimps, gunning for better holds to finish.

11 Immaculate Conception 14m 7a+ ***
Tom & Kate Ballard 2006
From the undercut on Goosey Goosey Gander, clip a bolt, pull onto the hanging wall and climb sensationally up with a hard devious move to make the second break. Stand awkwardly to finish up the short easy corner.

12 Running Blind 18m 7a+ *
Tom Ballard 2007
Pre clip the first two bolts on Immaculate Conception. Start under the roof on the right. Take the roof crack next to the right arete past a spike, laybacking through a hard move to reach the second break. Step left to finish via the easy corner.

The glaring line is **An Eilt Wind that Blows no Good** E1 5b. Use a sharp spike to pull into the main corner. The lower-off from When the Wind Blows could be used.

13 When the Wind Blows 15m 6c **
Tom Ballard 2006
Pull sharply over the roof and up to an overlap. Stem left to improving

Argyll & Lochaber

Ranochan West

holds and a hanging flake in a lovely exposed position. A series of tricky moves lands at the top of the corner.

14 Jungle Run   15m   6c
Tom Ballard 2006
Start as for When the Wind Blows. Pull over the roof and up to an overlap. Sharp holds direct up a short crack lead to a horizontal break. A fine pocket is the key to the slabby wall.

Link ups /Traverses

15 Pin Ball Wizard   25m   6c *
Tom Ballard 2007
Follow When the Wind Blows to the top break. Traverse this leftwards to eventually arrive at the chain on Kneed 4 Speed.

16 Pelican Brief   20m   6a+
Tom Ballard 2007
The lowest horizontal from right to left, and back if you enjoyed it.

17 Long and Winding Road   25m   6b+
Tom Ballard 2007
Climb Devil's Advocate to the top of the corner. Step across passing the Kneed 4 Speed chain, traversing the break rightwards to lower off from the top of An Eilt Wind that Blows no Good.

18 Chasing Shadows   20m   7a+
Tom Ballard 2007
A diagonal line from left to right. Start up Devil's Advocate to the lowest break. Move along right to use an undercut and crimps to reach a sloping shelf. Now make a vicious move to get established on good jugs. Span right to a flake and smear across to sidepulls and eventually the break. Continue as for Long and Winding Road.

RANOCHAN WEST

(NM 8197 8247)   Alt 100m   South-East facing   Map p65

There are two walls, a smaller one on the lower left between trees and a diamond shaped wall which is the one seen from the road. Each wall has one line of bolts with a route either side sharing them. The diamond shaped wall also has trad routes.

19 Blue Velvet   8m   6c
Tom Ballard 2006
Climb the left edge of the slab between trees. Step right to finish.

**20 Slip Sliding Away   8m   7b **
Tom Ballard 2006
The very centre of this pale seamed slab. A diagonal seam runs out to leave a slap up and left to another and the top.

21 Lakey Hill   10m   6a+
Tom Ballard 2008
The left side of the diamond shaped wall.

22 Niagara   10m   6b
Tom Ballard 2008
The fine blank looking wall right of the bolts has more holds than appearances would suggest.

The central crack-line is **Wilderness of Mirrors** (E1 5b). The serrated wall between the cracks is **Zambezi** (E3 5c). The widest crack-line is **Pinch Beck** (E1 5b). A thin crack to reach a large break near the top is **Clover Field** (E1 5b).

Black Rock - Arisaig

(NR 6766 8372)   L40 E398   Alt 5m   South-East to East facing   Maps p37, p65

An unusual but substantial basalt crag by the sea offers some good routes in a lovely situation, but the crag and its equipment need some love and attention. However, it is still worth a visit and some of the routes may be worth more stars.

Black Rock

69

Argyll & Lochaber

The crag takes a couple of days to dry after heavy rain, although a few routes are quicker. The underlying rock is solid but there are still occasional hollow blocks and a little scaly rock which should improve quickly with a few ascents; it is recommended that helmets are worn. The routes have had few ascents so be cautious over the grades, although there has been no criticism. Climb cautiously in case of equipment shortcomings, especially on routes 19 to 31.

AMENITIES

As for Cat's Eye Crag.

DIRECTIONS

Head west from Fort William on the A830 towards Arisaig and Mallaig. Pass Glenfinnan, Loch Eilt and Lochailort to reach Beasdale railway station. 1.3km after this, left turn signposted Druimindarroch; this is the second on the left after the station and about 30 miles from Fort William. Go down this road and soon turn left (the second left) down a tiny road when straight on is blocked by a gate. Continue to the road end at the water's edge. There is room for two cars on the verge and more on the beach, although the high tides would seem to reach here, NM 6842 8426.

Black Rock

APPROACH
Time: 15mins
Walk south-west along the coast through two bays until the crag blocks the way. The approach is boggy in places and those wearing trainers will get wet feet.

FIXED GEAR
As with the other crags in this area, the routes usually finish at a home-made chain system which is inadequate for lowering off; the last person should abseil. The public spirited should leave a krab or maillon. Being near the sea, some of the chains are starting to rust but it is hoped that better lower-offs will be placed.

1 Grey Edge   10m   6a
Unknown
The very left end of the wall. Move up steeply before pulling out left on to the left edge. Continue up the edge with feet on the steep wall for a couple of moves to a final slab.

2 Black Sabbath   10m   6b
Tom Ballard 2006
Climb on pockets to a down-pointing tooth. The first bolt is rather high and pre-clipping the first bolt of Grey Edge is sensible, or start that way. From the tooth, reach right to a protruding hold, then move up to a shelf below the capping roof. Finish up Grey Edge.

3 Black Beauty   20m   6b
Tom & Kate Ballard 2007
A high girdle of the left side. Start as for Black Sabbath. Climb up to the 2nd bolt on Black Heart, then traverse rightwards across the wall, clipping more bolts before stepping up to finish at the chain on Black Death (route 13).

4 Black Heart   10m   6b+
Tom Ballard 2006
Start beneath a horizontal flake. Climb up to this and take a parallel line to Black Sabbath, with a technical sequence to reach a chain to the right. Slightly easier if you finish up Black Sabbath.

5 Voyage of the Black Pearl   25m   6b *
Tom Ballard 2006
A full lower girdle of the left side. Start as for Black Heart. Make a rising traverse across the wall following the low natural fold to finish at the chain of Black Jack.

6 Black Adder   10m   6b **
Tom Ballard 2006
A superb starting sequence leads to a diagonal break. Blast directly up the grey streaked wall above direct to reach the chain.

Fiona Murray colourful on Black Death (6a+), Black Rock (photo Andy Nisbet)

⑦ Black Beard 12m 6b
Tom Ballard 2007
A disjointed boss to the faint diagonal fault. Continue to an overlap and escape rightwards to reach the chain.

⑧ Black Friday 12m 6a+ *
Tom Ballard 2006
The gentle bulge and steeper wall above with a technical finish to the same chain as Black Beard.

⑨ Pot Calling the Kettle Black 12m 6a+
Tom Ballard 2006
Start left of a bendy tree. Head diagonally rightwards up a small ramp above the bendy tree to an easing mid-way up the steep wall above. Go rightwards to the chain.

⑩ The Black Pig 12m 6a+
Tom Ballard 2006
Just right of the bendy tree. Climb up to and over a bulging rib to easier ground and a steep finish.

⑪ Unfinished Business 12m 5+
There is a line of bolts starting 6m right of the bendy tree and heading up a shallow groove to end at a single bolt with a blue tape. It is now possible but not pleasant to make a vegetated finish to a tree at the cliff-top.

⑫ Black Dog 15m 6a+
Tom Ballard 2006
A slight left-facing corner low down. Climb until it runs out, then up the wall above to big holds near the top. Move rightwards to finish.

⑬ Black to Black 12m 6a *
Tom Ballard 2008
Start up the wall just right of a more prominent groove to a bulge. Pull through on good holds to follow the line of bolts between two black streaks.

⑭ Black Death 14m 6a+ **
Tom Ballard 2006
Start up the wall just right again and continue up the wall on good holds with the crux near the top.

⑮ Black as Bill's Mothers 10m 6a *
Tom Ballard 2006
Start at a grass patch 1m up. Go up the wall and cracks in a faint groove.

⑯ Black Jack 10m 6b ***
Tom Ballard 2006
Tremendous climbing through the left side of the roofs using a variety of novel pockets. Finish as Black as Bill's Mothers, or I Can't Believe ....

⑰ I Can't Believe it's Not Black 12m 6c *
Tom Ballard 2006
The right side of the double roof. The crux pull is on small holds through the first roof. Continue to a tricky finish. The bolts and hangers were mostly in-situ when the 2006 ascent was made.

⑱ Black Seal of Approval 12m 6b
Tom Ballard 2006
The bulging flake in the concave speckled orange wall, finishing up large stubby blocks.

⑲ Black Mamba 12m 6b *
Tom Ballard 2006
Follow the bolts up the right side of the speckled orange wall. Usually dry?

Next is a mossy section with no routes, then a large tree growing out of the base of the crag. The next routes start just right of the tree.

Black Rock

Andy Hyslop snaking up Black Adder (6b), Black Rock (photo Colin Moody)

20 Blackberry   20m   6c
Tom Ballard 2007
The hangers are not in-situ. Just right of the tree and looks unlikely. Climb the steep wall past an overlap, with reachy moves. Awkward but easy climbing takes you to the base of a deep groove. Break left (Black is Back goes straight up) to beneath the obvious stacked roofs. Go through these and curl rightwards to the Black is Back chain.

21 Black is Back   20m   6c
Tom Ballard 2007
The hangers are not in-situ. Start as for Blackberry, just right of the tree and looks unlikely. Climb the steep wall past an overlap, with reachy moves. Awkward but easy climbing takes you to the base of a deep groove (Blackberry now goes left). Climb the headwall using good hidden holds direct to the chain.

22 Black Hawk   30m   6b+
Tom Ballard 2007
Start just right of the tree. Follow a right-trending fault to reach and continue along Black Holes of Calcutta. Bold at the start.

23 Black Eyed Peas   20m   6c *
Tom Ballard 2006
A central line up the steep wall with a good rest beneath a curving overlap. Step up to this and continue above to a tree with slings. Seven bolts, but only 5 hangers in place.

24 Black where we Belong   20m   6c *
Tom Ballard 2008
Climb up the initial steep wall which gradually eases to provide a rest at half-height. The crux is passing the smooth bulge using small holds before romping the final headwall to the tree with slings.

25 Black for Good   20m   6b+
Tom Ballard 2007

Black Rock

Pass the large flange on the right to a diagonal overlap. Move left to a flake in a bulge, pull over this to good holds trending left up the wall to reach the tree with slings.

26 Black in the Day   18m   6b *
Tom Ballard 2006
The pillar and the wall above to reach and pass a narrowing and continue to a handrail at the base of a blank wall. Keep to the left of the bolts using good holds to reach a chain left of a small prow.

27 Black Again   25m   6b
Tom Ballard 2007
Take Black in the Day to the 3rd bolt. Break diagonally left to clip the 4th bolt on Black for Good. Continue to the overlap on Black Eyed Peas. Pull over, clipping the bolt up right, traverse left to the chain on Black is Back. An adventurous outing.

28 Black Magic   18m   6c *
Tom Ballard 2007
Climb Black in the Day to the good handrail at the base of the blank wall. Move up a faint groove and attack the blankness, keeping to the right of the bolts with a long reach to gain jugs.

29 Black Holes of Calcutta   20m   6b+
Tom Ballard 2007
Start up Black in the Day until past the 3rd bolt, then sidle rightwards above the bulging upward curving overlap. The grade is uncertain.

30 Black Power   18m   6c *
Tom Ballard 2007
The shallow groove right of the pillar to the roof bulge. Pull over to continue rightwards in a fine position to the chain of Black in Time.

31 Black Velvet   15m   7a
Tom Ballard 2007
Past the pillar and under the roofs. Bridge the golden corner to a faint ledge. Take the roof using large sloping holds finishing direct past a spike to the Black Holes chain. The 5th bolt is hard to clip.

32 Black in Time   15m   6c
Tom Ballard 2007
Climb Black Velvet to the 3rd bolt. Step right and move up to a hidden pocket. Move powerfully to the lip and groove, pulling over with trouble to reach a tantalising jug beside the chain.

ATONEMENT WALL

(NM 6764 8379 - top)   Alt 30m   South facing

Follow a slight path uphill from the right side of Black Rock. Go under a fallen tree and across to the side of an obvious twisted pinnacle. The wall lies behind it. Scramble down into the slot to start. All equipped with stainless steel bolts and hangers. Clean and dries quickly.

33 Bend it like Beckham   8m   6a+
Tom Ballard 2008
The slanting crack moving right to a ring lower-off.

34 The Hole   8m   7a+ *
Tom Ballard 2008
From the lowest point of the wall. Step left to a flake and climb direct to a ring. There is a hard move to finish!

35 Atonement   8m   7b+ *
Tom Ballard 2008
From the lowest point of the wall, climb direct to a tree and sling.

36 The Duchess   6m   6a+
Tom Ballard 2008
Move left to an inverted ramp and short crack to a tree and sling.

Argyll & Lochaber

Stirlingshire to Perthshire

This is the heartland of Scottish sport climbing and being near the big cities, may see as much action as the other areas added together. Most of the crags are mica schist outcrops in this beautiful wooded region of Scotland. These crags come in all shapes and sizes from short steep and punchy (as seen at Glen Ogle, Weem, Stronachlachar and Strathyre), to long and steep at Dunkeld. There are also several easier angled venues such as Rockdust, Dunira and Lower Lednock which have yielded varied and intricate climbs.

However, three venues stand out as being very different to the rest. The long vertical escarpment at Bennybeg is great for beginners and unique in offering very friendly roadside climbing from 2 to 6a. Newtyle Quarry is an even more unique climbing experience with dry tooling, huge roofs and intricate slabs. The Sport Wall at Upper Cave Crag is probably the most famous sport crag in Scotland and its classic stamina outings Marlina (7c), Hamish Ted's (7b+) and Silk Purse (7c+) are a rite of passage for all serious sport climbers in Scotland.

However, the newer and less well known crags are very likely to gain just as much notoriety in the coming years. Inversnaid and Stronachlachar have surely the most stunning outlooks of any of the crags in this guide if not in the country! These crags also have a genuinely wild feel and a day spent there definitely feels like you are really getting away from it all. Only the noise of cars across Loch Lomond from Inversnaid reminds you that civilisation isn't too far away. In this way the crags exemplify Scottish sport climbing in general; solitude, natural beauty, variety and a break from the sameness of limestone sport crags.

History by Dave MacLeod

The sport crags described in this chapter represent the meat of Scottish sport climbing, both in terms of quality, popularity and numbers of routes. Upper Cave Crag at Dunkeld has a long history as a forcing ground for technical rock climbing standards on the Highland crags, so it is no surprise that Perthshire's sport climbing history started on its impending central wall. These early developments were controversial as ever and occurred in a piecemeal fashion with routes using minimal bolts and natural gear.

In July 1986 Duncan McCallum climbed a mixed trad and bolt route from Squirm Direct, via what became the Marlina crack, to a lower-off in the middle of the wall. In August Dave Cuthbertson added more bolts to the wall and utilised this lower-off, when he created the logical route up the steep wall to give Marlina (7c). In September this was fully bolted and climbed by a slightly different line, as followed today, by Steve Lewis. At the same time the obvious former aid line up the smooth right side of the wall and the headwall above the Marlina crack was climbed by Murray Hamilton's Fallout. This line was subsequently linked more directly in 1987 by Graeme Livingston and named Silk Purse (7c+).

The Sport Wall rapidly became popular and

History

remains so today with many climbers using the routes for training. During the early '90s Graeme Livingston made an impressive solo ascent of Marlina. In 1992, Duncan McCallum, along with Johnny May and Rab Anderson enhanced the quality of the place even further by climbing a logical alternative finish to Marlina's lower wall, taking the steep arete above the base of the crag. Hamish Teddy's Excellent Adventure (7b+) became a popular classic straight away and is now one of the most climbed sport routes in the country. At the nearby Myopic's Buttress, The Vibes (7c) had to be re-bolted twice following removal of the bolts by the ever present objectors to sport climbing.

The crag-ridden slopes on either side of the Highland trunk road through Glen Ogle held curiosity for passing climbers for years but had been largely ignored. In 1992, Paul Thorburn and others finally investigated the crags and recognised their potential as a significant sport climbing venue, being short but very steep.

Rab Anderson completed the first routes at The Diamond; Metal Guru (6c) and Children of the Revolution (7b) whilst Thorburn worked on Off the Beaten Track (8a), finally completing this superb test piece in 1993. During this year, the best lines fell to Anderson, McCallum and company. Routes such as Chain Lightning (7b+) and Spiral Tribe (8a) were climbed, while Iain Pitcairn concentrated on his project which eventually became Digital Quartz (8b).

Dundee climbers Neil Shepherd and George Ridge moved the development into top gear, with new routes spreading to the other Dark Side buttresses and to the Sunny Side in May 1994.

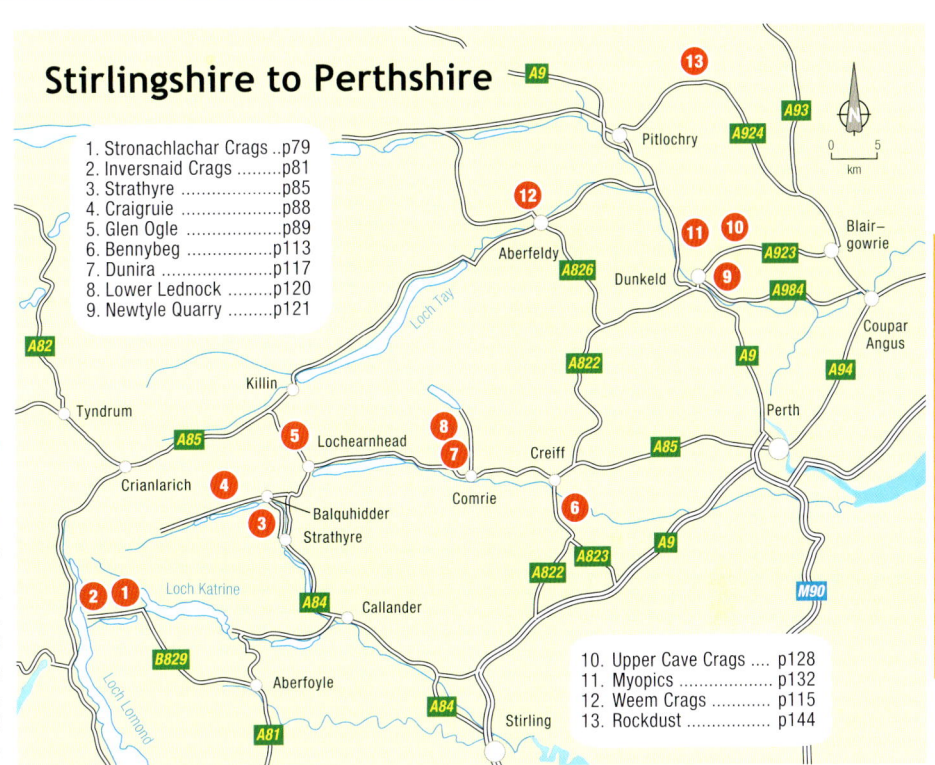

Stirlingshire to Perthshire

1. Stronachlachar Crags ..p79
2. Inversnaid Crags p81
3. Strathyre p85
4. Craigruie p88
5. Glen Ogle p89
6. Bennybeg p113
7. Dunira p117
8. Lower Lednock p120
9. Newtyle Quarry p121
10. Upper Cave Crags p128
11. Myopics p132
12. Weem Crags p115
13. Rockdust p144

Shepherd's classic Scaramanga (7a+) remained unrepeated for years because it lay just a little further from the road than the lower crags. The Sunny Side crags provided a welcome change from the steepness and intensity of the Dark Side and many quality easier lines were opened by Shepherd and Ridge such as Hot Chocolate (6b) and The Greenhouse Defect (6b). At the end of 1994, the main activists began looking into other sport venues and so the wave of development which had produced over 100 routes in the space of three years came to an abrupt end.

History

Malcolm Smith on Spiral Tribe (8a), The Diamond, Glen Ogle (photo Rab Anderson)

The development of many Scottish sport crags has occurred in this staccato fashion with intense periods of development (reflecting the enthusiasm of the activists), followed by long periods of quiet while attention switched to new crags. So when Paul Thorburn discovered Strathyre Crag in late 1993, it only took until May 1994 for Rab Anderson to equip and bag all the main lines to produce another quality venue with a good range of mid-grade (7a to 7c) routes such as Electrodynamics (7a) and Static Discharge (7b).

Unfortunately the bug didn't seem to catch on at the nearby Craigruie near Balquhidder which featured two rather lonely sport routes from Thorburn and Ridge. Scope remains here for further quality new routes.

The next venue to get the new route blitz, again previously largely ignored by traditional developers, was the numerous buttresses in the woods above Weem, overlooking Aberfeldy. This time it was George Ridge along with Neil Shepherd, Colin Miln, Isla Watson and Janet Horrocks who developed the place at lightning speed over the course of spring 1997. The Weem crags stand out as one of Scotland's best venues due to their sheltered climate and quick drying walls. Add to this the fact that there is an excellent resource of low to mid-grade climbs (5+ to 7b), all in a beautiful setting and it is not surprising that the crags have succeeded in gaining steadily in popularity where Glen Ogle has failed to. The best of the routes here such as The Republic of Scotland (7a+) by Miln, and The Screaming Weem (7b) by Ridge are becoming known further afield as modern classics.

The small wall of Stronachlachar High Crag,

Isla Watson on Highland Cling, (6b) High Crag, Stronachlachar (photo Colin Miln)

spectacularly perched high above Lochs Katrine, Arklet and Lomond, was one of the crags near the east side of Loch Lomond to be equipped by the enthusiastic team of Colin Miln and Isla Watson. Colin's route My Own Private Scotland (6c+) sums up the quiet and wild character of the area. This wall and the wooded outcrops above the road junction catch any sunshine that's going. This means they are often dry in the winter months when high ferns and midges are absent and most other venues remain wet.

Indeed, development of the string of outcrops on the east side of Loch Lomond at Inversnaid, so often stared at from the west side by passing climbers in their cars, kicked off in late October with Wild Swans (6b+) by Isla Watson. The smooth slab yielded several more good technical

History

Janet Horrocks making a Confession of Faith (6c) at Weem (photo Colin Miln)

lines, especially Dark Skies (6c) from Colin Miln. Attention moved to the furthest crag north of Inversnaid; Crystal Crag, so named because of the strange white crystalline patina covering the smooth wall. This patchy covering provides a rash of small crimps, giving a series of long and sometimes devious routes. The classics here are undoubtedly the longest ones, Fear and Self Loathing (7a+) and Age of Aquarius (7a) from Miln. However, the shorter routes on the right-hand side really pack it and are surely some of the hardest to on-sight in this guide at these grades! Of these, Watson's Far From the Malham Crowds (7a) is the best and again, the name says it all. Late in 2004, Dave MacLeod cleaned up the abandoned project at the left end giving a very fingery 7c; Been Caught Stealin'.

In 2000, attention turned back to the wooded crags at Stronachlachar especially the G-Spot, a huge boulder very well hidden in the trees. The slabby wall here, like Wild Swans Buttress provides a welcome break from the short, steep and vicious routes typical of mica schist sport climbing. George Ridge got in on the act with the perplexing Venga Boys (6c+), but the classic here is Hideous Kinky (7a) from Miln and Watson; a precarious slabby groove on great rock. An excellent little project waited until 2004 to be completed by Dave MacLeod and Ric Waterton; a 7c slab!

The 'all then nothing' nature of the development at the crags didn't help with nurturing lasting popularity beyond the initial interest, however, some new faces did appear on the scene to take up where the main players had left off. Dave Redpath developed Mirror Wall in Glen Ogle in 1997/8 with routes like Blind Faith (7b) and a range of easier routes. Once fully developed by Ridge and Horrocks, this wall became one of the best on the Sunny Side. Rab and Chris Anderson showed renewed interest in the Sunny Side, producing a large batch of new routes on Creag nan Cuillean and several new buttresses.

Over on the Dark Side, Mark Garthwaite just beat Mike Lauder to the first ascent of a fine arete project high on the hillside at Concave Wall. Arms Limitation (7b+) was separately claimed by both climbers and has rightly become one of the most popular mid-grade routes in the glen. The central Concave Wall project was first bolted and attempted by Dave Redpath but later abandoned. This eventually fell to Dave MacLeod in 2004 after much effort to give Snipe Shadow (8b). MacLeod also polished off several other abandoned hard projects in the area such as Cease Fire (8a+) on the Diamond and Solitaire (8a+) on Bond Buttress, as well as making the long awaited repeat of Digital Quartz (8b).

Rockdust near Pitlochry saw the first routes opened in 1999. This venue gave Colin Miln, Isla Watson and Calum Mayland long vertical and

A sunny day at Bennybeg (photo Alan Halewood)

Stirlingshire to Perthshire

interesting climbs at amenable grades such as 21st Century Citizen (6b+) and French Onion Soup (5+). Rab and Chris Anderson tied up a few remaining lines in 2003 to consolidate the ever increasing numbers of quality lower grade sport routes in this area.

Still at the lower end of the difficulty scale, another completely new venue near Crieff, the long escarpment of Bennybeg was comprehensively developed in 2003 by local climber Scott Muir to finally give Scotland an extensive, accessible low grade (2 to 6a) venue such as those seen on the continent. Despite the usual initial controversy over this development, the crag has become very popular with queuing for routes seen on sunny weekends! During 2004 Muir continued to unearth new lower grade venues which had previously been ignored, developing Lower Glen Lednock and Dunira with a large haul of routes between 5+ and 6c+. Lower Lednock was debolted in 2007 after the discovery that some routes had been trad climbed, but after trad climbing there failed to become popular, it was agreed the bolts could be replaced.

Totally different but even more controversial were the sport climbing developments in Newtyle Quarry in 2003. Scott Muir saw the dripping wet, partially bolted, chipped and abandoned project in the back of the unbelievable 'Tube' cave as having potential for use as a training route for winter/mixed climbing in the same style as dry tooling mixed routes on the continent. The crucial difference was that the route would be a summer dry tooling route, climbed using ice axes and crampons, with no ice or snow in sight. Muir completed the project to give a 40m pitch of continuous roof climbing! Too Fast, Too Furious (M12) is certainly one of the most unusual and striking routes in Scotland.

Also in The Tube, Dave MacLeod, ate up yet another abandoned project; Hurlyburly (8b). This completely manufactured roof climb was originally created by Iain Pitcairn and Paul Thorburn in the early '90s but saw off attempts to redpoint it. MacLeod returned soon after his redpoint and soloed the route – possibly the hardest solo of a sport route in the UK at the time. Just down the hill, the Happy Hooker Wall was opened by Muir for tooling routes with Va Va Voom (M8), sparking a blaze of popularity and activity in the new discipline led by an enthusiastic band of activists including Paul Diffley, Dave Brown, Fiona Murray and Michael Tweedley. Newtyle is now home to a diverse range of routes from bold trad, sport climbing and dry tooling disciplines and is vastly more popular than it was in the past, firm evidence if any was neetded that such different styles can develop sensibly and co-exist happily providing great climbing for everyone.

The intensity of development at almost all the crags in this chapter has meant that not many gaps have been left open for further development. The future expansion of sport climbing in Perthshire probably lies in the development of new crags, of which there are several suitable for sport climbing and these have been eyed up by local climbers for some time. A notable exception to this is the buttresses surrounding Craigruie near Balquhidder. With a continuing band of enthusiastic activists out snooping around the glens, it seems likely that news of another whirlwind of new routing won't be too far away.

Dave Cuthbertson warming up with a Short Circuit (6b), Strathyre (photo Rab Anderson)

STIRLINGSHIRE

The crags in this area all fall within the eastern part of the large Loch Lomond & The Trossachs National Park and comprise two groups. The first group lies beyond The Trossachs to the north-west of Stirling and is made up of the Inversnaid Crags on the east side of Loch Lomond and the Stronachlachar Crags on the west side of Loch Katrine. The second group lies to the north of Stirling, on the edge of the National Park, and is made up of Strathyre Crag at Strathyre, then Craigruie at Balquhidder and last but not least, the extensive crags either side of the road through Glen Ogle at Lochearnhead.

Stronachlachar Crags - Loch Katrine

L56 E364   Map p75

This collection of small crags lie on the steep wooded slopes of Garradh, above the tiny hamlet of Stronachlachar on the western side of Loch Katrine. The area offers short sport routes on good, clean mica schist in a spectacular setting with views along Loch Katrine and Loch Arklet. The crags are a real suntrap and take little drainage and can be climbed on all year round. In summer it can be hot but The G-Spot is rather sheltered and can suffer from midges. A visit can be combined with the Inversnaid crags.

AMENITIES

Aberfoyle is a popular tourist village with shops, cafes and pubs. The Inversnaid Hotel has a large bar and serves meals in summer. There is a good cafe, The Snaid, at the top of the hill descending into Inversnaid. Aberfoyle has a good tourist information centre (08707 200 604) which will help you arrange accommodation in the area.

RECOMMENDED TASTY BITES

Bar meals at The Forth Inn on Aberfoyle Main Street.

TOP TIPS

Visit in the colder months to avoid midges, bracken and to catch some winter sunshine! The crags dry out very quickly with any sun.

Stronachlachar
A. G-Spot p80
B. Chasm Buttress p80
C. High Crag p81

DIRECTIONS

From Glasgow follow the A81 then the A821 to Aberfoyle. Take the winding but picturesque B829 and follow this for about 11 miles (17km) to the T-junction just before Stronachlachar, between Loch Arklet and Loch Katrine. Turn left and park by squeezing off the road at a couple of possible places (not the passing place). One is at NS 3930 0971.

From other directions, reach Aberfoyle from the M9 at Stirling by initially following the main A84 north-west, then A873 west to join the A81 coming down from Callander on the A84 to the north.

From the T-junction, two adjacent buttresses can be seen near the top of the wooded area. The right-hand one has no routes at present, the left-hand one is Chasm Buttress. The G-Spot lies hidden in trees directly below Chasm Buttress. High Crag lies well up and left of the wooded crags.

G-SPOT

(NN 3909 1017)   Alt 280m   South facing

This hidden little wall is actually a giant boulder with good rock. A nice alternative to the steep and thuggy climbing normally associated with mica schist sport, offering technical off-vertical climbing.

APPROACH

Time: 20mins

The best approach is up the left side of the woods, as for High Crag. When approximately 50m below Chasm Buttress (which can be seen poking out of the trees), traverse into the woods at what looks like a logical place and continue a short way until the huge boulder is found, probably just above where you arrive. The forest is full of hidden gaps between boulders covered in vegetation; watch those ankles.

1 Rhumba al Sol   12m   6a
Isla Watson 2000
The left-hand arete has good climbing but is a little mossy due to the adjacent tree.

2 Hideous Kinky   12m   7a *
Colin Miln, Isla Watson 2001
Climb the blank scoop, then teeter up the thin wall above to an easy finishing niche.

3 Venga Boys   12m   6c+ **
George Ridge 2000
Climb the right to left diagonal groove with technical moves to pass the initial roof. Good climbing to the same lower-off as Hideous Kinky.

4 El Mundo Fanatico   12m   7a+
Colin Miln 2000
Follow Venga Boys to the top of the groove, then step right to a technical finish up the headwall above.

5 Live-in Skin   12m   7c **
Dave MacLeod, Ric Waterton 2004
Start up Venga Boys but pull rightwards through the initial groove on crimps to a thin diagonal crack. Step right and climb the thin technical wall (crux).

CHASM BUTTRESS

(NN 3909 1021)   Alt 310m   South facing

The left-hand of two adjacent steep walls seen from the road has one route at present and potential for more lines at all grades. It is so named because of the huge chasm at its base formed by a fallen boulder.

APPROACH
Time: 20mins
Approach as for High Crag until level with the buttress, then contour across to it.

Unnamed 15m 7b+
Unknown
The only line on the wall at present, taking the grossly leaning wall left of centre. A very deceptive move gains the ledge below the roof. Above the roof, pumpy and blind climbing leads to a sting in the tail.

HIGH CRAG

(NN 388 102)   Alt 430m   South-South-West facing

APPROACH
Time: 40mins
Walk directly up the steep bracken slope on the left-hand (east) border of the woods. The crag lies above and left of the top of the woods. It is recognisable as a clean square wall sitting on top of a larger dark rectangular wall which is lichenous. It is bigger than it looks.

1 Raksasha 6m 7a
Colin Miln 1997
The extended boulder problem at the left end. From the slopers on the lip, pull slightly left to jugs. Tough.

2 High and Mighty 6m 7b+
Dave MacLeod 2004
Another tough bouldery line just to its right on tiny crimps to the same lower-off.

3 Lady of the Loch 10m 6b *
Isla Watson 1998
The line of small hidden pockets. Pleasant climbing.

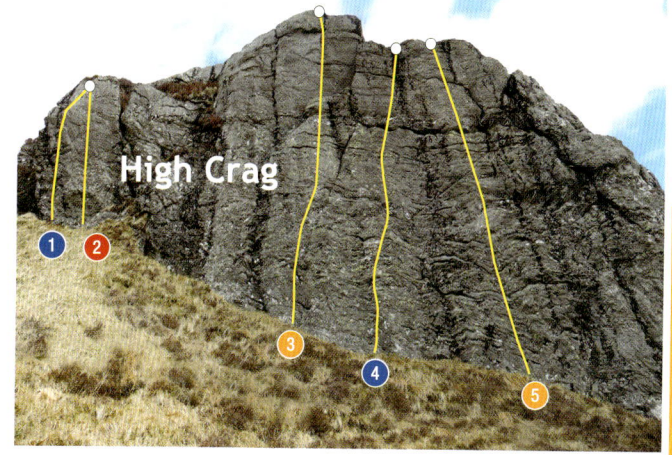

4 My Own Private Scotland 10m 6c+
Colin Miln 1997
The sustained central line has a nasty crux at the top on slopers to gain the finishing jugs above the lower-off.

5 Highland Cling 10m 6b *
Isla Watson 1997
The furthest right line of bolts on the face gives pleasant wall climbing.

Inversnaid Crags - Loch Lomond

L56 E364   Maps p75, p82

This section describes the series of mica schist outcrops on the east bank of Loch Lomond, accessed from Aberfoyle and the B829 at Inversnaid. These outcrops are well seen from the A82 running up the west side of Loch Lomond at Inveruglas. The area has a wild and quiet feel and all the crags feature spectacular views onto the loch. The crags are west

Inversnaid

facing and steep and can often be dry and sunny during the autumn/winter months, and are more easily approached when the bracken is down. Most of the buttresses have been developed as sport venues, providing a good resource of quality climbing. The crags are described running northwards from Inversnaid. The area suffers much less from midges than Glen Ogle or other more sheltered venues. There are good boulders in the area but little is written up. There are no topos because the crags are in trees.

AMENITIES
As for Stronachlachar.

RECOMMENDED TASTY BITES
As for Stronachlachar.

TOP TIPS
The crags feature very blind climbing with some very well hidden holds, particularly on Crystal Crag. If you want to avoid frustration, send your partner up the route first to get the holds chalked for a flash attempt.

DIRECTIONS
From Glasgow, follow the A81 and A821 to Aberfoyle. Take the B829 for about 15 miles (23km) past Stronachlachar Crags, alongside Loch Arklet to Inversnaid and park at the Inversnaid car park at the road end by the pier (NN 0370 0889).

From other directions, reach Aberfoyle from the M9 at Stirling by initially following the main A84 north-west, then A873 west to join the A81 coming down from Callander on the A84 to the north.

APPROACH
Time: 20mins

Walk northwards from Inversnaid along the West Highland Way for 550m to reach a boat shed. Keep to the lochside path for 350m until you reach a wooden bridge, then 20m beyond this follow a good path with wooden steps uphill to a wooden bench. Just beyond the bench the path passes through a low stone wall with a tree and old ruin on the left

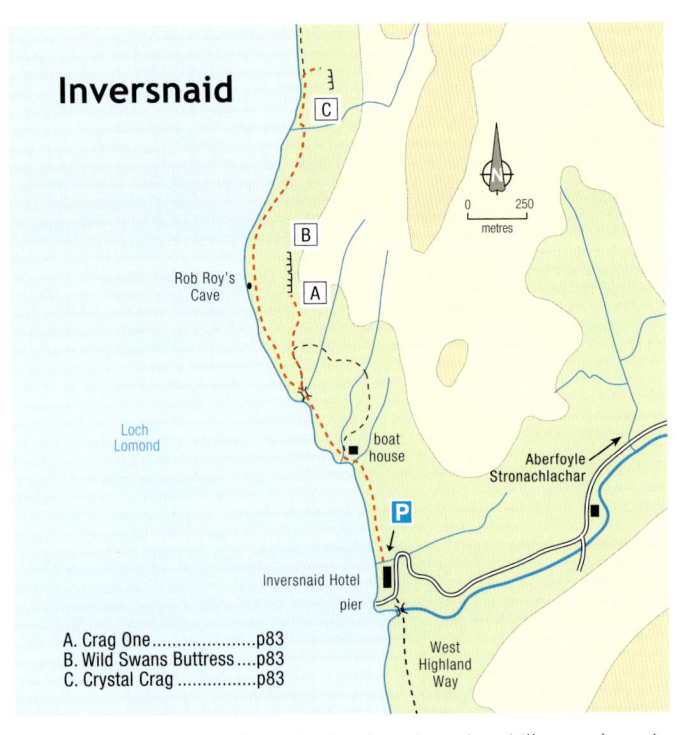

A. Crag One....................p83
B. Wild Swans Buttress....p83
C. Crystal Crag................p83

– NN 3338 0981. From this point, head northwards uphill towards a mix of small outcrops and boulders to reach a small plateau. Now head north, traversing the steep hillside above the loch -don't go up to a bigger plateau. Follow a sheep path beneath the line of crags. First reached is Crag One with a distinctive large overhang. Next reached is Crag Two with an even bigger overhang. Continue towards Crag Three which is much less obvious but then descend northwards to a slabbier crag behind a big tree – this is Wild Swans Buttress.

CRAG ONE

(NN 333 100)   Alt 120m   West facing

● **Hobble   10m   7a+**
Colin Miln 1997
A short and bouldery route near the right end of the crag, just left of a tree

○ **Open Project**
A good looking line on the steep pocketed wall 5m left of Hobble.

The next two buttresses running northwards, Crags Two and Three, have several bolted projects which have been abandoned.

WILD SWANS BUTTRESS

(NN 3332 1018)   Alt 110m   West facing
This crag offers fingery climbing on good quality schist with a pleasant outlook towards the loch. It lies just beyond and at a slightly lower level than Crag Three. Routes are described left to right.

● **The Ridge   10m   6c**
Colin Miln 1998
Traverse leftwards to the arete (crux), then move up to easier climbing. The hangers were missing in 2011.

● **Dark Skies   10m   6c ***
Colin Miln 1997
A fingery and blind start leads to a faint groove and better holds above.

● **Wild Swans   10m   6b+ ****
Isla Watson 1997
The central line on the pocketed wall with excellent rock.

● **Moonlight Sonata   10m   6b ****
Isla Watson 1998
Start at the right end of the wall. Trend leftwards to join the final section of Wild Swans.

● **Wild Goats   10m   7b**
Dave MacLeod 2004
Start up Moonlight Sonata. From a finger pocket immediately above its 3rd bolt, climb the smooth wall above on tiny crimps, trending slightly right to a flat hold. Finish into the scoop above.

CRYSTAL CRAG

(NN 3356 1095)   Alt 100m   West facing
This crag lies further to the north and provides several good longer routes which give sustained fingery climbing on unusual quartz edges. The long approach is worth it for the climbing, the views and the relative absence of midges. Again, the crag is best visited in the spring and autumn and it stays remarkably dry.

APPROACH
Time: 50mins
Follow the West Highland Way as for Wild Swans Buttress but continue northwards along the path, passing Rob Roy's Cave. Further along, 200m after crossing a bridge, you will be forced to squeeze between two large boulders and a tree on the path. At this point (NN 3340 1090), climb steeply and trending slightly leftwards through the woods to reach the crag. It lies high in the trees but not on the hillside above. The crag can be recognised by a smooth lower quartzy wall capped by stepped overlaps; there is a big patch of ivy at its left end.

To combine with Wild Swans Buttress, a direct line from there is likely to be very rough and not recommended. Going directly downhill to the West Highland Way and joining the regular approach takes about 30mins overall.

It is best not to approach the climbing directly from underneath, wet and awkward, but head up to the left side of the crag and locate a

Inversnaid

spacious gearing up spot below an obvious slab. The climbing can then be accessed down and right to the ledge below the routes.

🔴 **Been Caught Stealin'   15m   7c ***
Dave MacLeod 2004
This climbs directly up the smooth wall at its left end on tiny holds to boldly join the next route; it needs another bolt. The ivy has encroached badly on to this route and some serious cleaning would be needed before an ascent.

🔵 **Fear and Self Loathing   15m   7a+   ***
Colin Miln 1998
An excellent outing. Break out left from the lower section of Age of Aquarius and make a fingery traverse leftwards to gain the upper wall. This eventually leads to better holds.

🔵 **Age of Aquarius   15m   7a   ****
Colin Miln 1998
Another superb route. Technical moves on sharp holds lead to a ramp. Trend leftwards up this until it is possible to break out onto the finishing wall.

🔴 **Purgatory   12m   7b ***
Colin Miln 1999
Start up Age of Aquarius but climb directly over the roof above (crux). Move left above the roof to the Age of Aquarius lower-off.

🔵 **Roadkill Recipes   10m   7a ***
George Ridge 1998
Start by a small tree. Climb up and right through an overhang. Technically the warm-up route of the crag but pretty tough all the same!

🔵 **Ruby Slippers   10m   7a+**
Janet Horrocks 2000
Pleasant climbing up the lower wall leads to a blind crux below the overhang.

Jules Pearson dancing up Ruby Slippers (7a+) (photo Neil Shepherd)

🔴 **Rebel Without Applause   10m   7b**
Colin Miln 1998
Gain a rising ledge, then move up to a quartz boss. Use this to gain the tricky headwall via a very blind crimpy sequence. Desperate to on-sight!

🔵 **Far From the Malham Crowds   10m   7a ****
Isla Watson 1999
Thin and technical climbing near the right-hand edge of the wall. Again, desperate to on-sight.

Strathyre Crag – Strathyre

(NN 5550 1925) L57 E365   Alt 190m   South-East facing
Maps p75, p85   Diagram p87

This crag is situated on a small afforested hillside above the back road between the villages of Strathyre and Balquhidder. It lies just off the main A84 north from Stirling and is easily seen to the west of this road about a mile north of Strathyre. Despite its diminutive appearance it is a steep compact buttress of quality mica schist which yields a surprising number of sustained and powerful little climbs, with a couple of technical nasties such as Bridging the Gap thrown in for good measure.

The crag's left side and surroundings receive the sun from early morning through to the early afternoon, although the main wall is sufficiently steep to lose it just before midday. For best conditions, choose a warm breezy day. After heavy rain weeps are likely so allow a few days to dry out.

AMENITIES
Strathyre village has Maggie's Cafe, several B&Bs, a hotel (open to the public), pubs, petrol, the village shop and a large caravan & camping park (open March to October, 01877 384285).

RECOMMENDED TASTY BITES
The Inn at Strathyre serves good food and the steak pies from the Scotch Oven in Callander are not to be missed!

TOP TIPS
Both strong arms and fingers are helpful. Don't forget the midge cream and head net during the summer months.

DIRECTIONS
From the south follow the A84 through Callander, then alongside Loch Lubnaig until you reach the village of Strathyre. The same road gets you here from the north and is joined from the east by the roads alongside Loch Tay or Loch Earn.

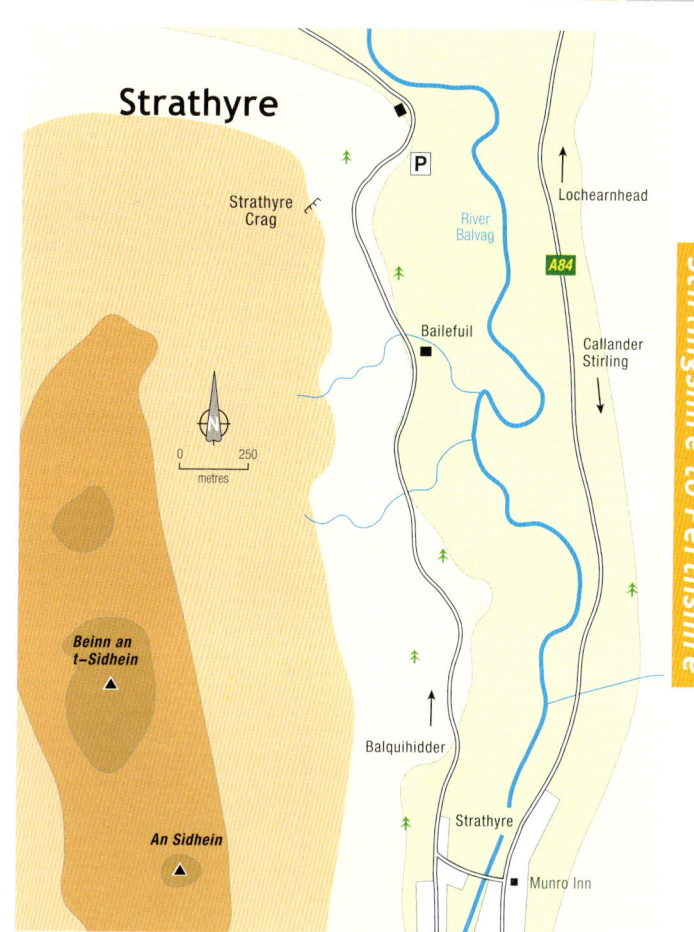

Strathyre Crag

Once in the village keep an eye out for a small road junction immediately opposite the Munro Inn. The sign for the Inn is small but the required road is the only west turn in the village. Head down this narrow road, over a humpback bridge, and at the first split, turn right, signposted Balquhidder. From this junction drive on for 1.3 miles (2km) and look out for a clearing in the trees on your left, about 200m past the entrance to the Strathyre Outdoor Centre. The top of the crag is visible on the hillside above this clearing. The best spot for parking is 250m beyond the clearing where there is a pull-off on the right opposite a forestry track (NN 556 194).

APPROACH

Time: 10mins
Walk back along the road and head into the wood on the left side of the clearing where a vague path can be found which leads up rightwards above the clearing through a small break in thick trees. Pass a broken lower crag and continue uphill with some faith (it's not far) to emerge from the trees. A traverse right leads to a hollow at the base of the main crag. It is easy in the spring but in summer the bracken at the foot of the crag can be over head-height!

1 Power Sink   10m   7b
Rab Anderson 1994
The short wall to the left of the prominent arete is short and to the point.

2 Electrodynamics   10m   7a *
Rab Anderson 1993
The pumpy arete – just keep going!

3 Bridging the Gap   10m   6c+ *
Rab Anderson 1994
The prominent corner-groove gives a fine exercise in technique which is more awkward than it looks!

4 Short Circuit   10m   6b **
Rab Anderson 1993
The hanging groove right again gives steep climbing on good holds; the warm-up.

5 Crossed Wire   10m   6a+
Rab Anderson 1996
Start as for the previous route but at the 1st bolt swing round to the right and follow a curving groove to finish at a lower-off to the right.

6 Clam Chowder   10m   7a *
George Ridge 1994
Climb the wall to the right to a ledge, then cross the previous route and go straight up the thin wall above.

7 High Tension Lead   10m   7c *
Paul Thorburn 1994
Climbs the crimpy wall to finish up Static Discharge.

8 Static Discharge   10m   7b ***
Rab Anderson 1993
The classic of the crag. Climb directly up the wall to gain the crack; follow this for a short way then up the easier headwall above. A little more difficult for the short.

9 New Power Generation   10m   7c **
Alan Cassidy 2008
Follow the line of bolts just right of Static Discharge to a slab, rock over and find a crux just before the lower-off.

10 Cracking the Lines   10m   7b *
Rab Anderson 1994
Climb the obvious crack from its base to finish up Static Discharge. In other words, the short person's version!

Strathyre Crag 87

Stirlingshire to Perthshire

11 All Electric   10m   7b+ **
Rab Anderson 1996
The direct line from the base of the crack, sharing 2 bolts then trending rightwards near the top to finish on the lower-off of Circuit Breaker.

12 Circuit Breaker   10m   7b *
Rab Anderson 1994
The short, steep leaning wall eases in its upper half. An entertaining start!

13 Power Surge   10m   6c *
Rab Anderson 1993
The leaning wall and scoop. A stiff pull at the start leads to easier climbing. Finish direct to the lower-off.

14 Spark Thug   10m   6b
Rab Anderson 1994
Going up the corner to a ledge is more awkward than it looks!

Craigruie

Colin Lambton feeling the Power Sink (7b), Strathyre Crag (photo Stone Country)

To the right of the main crag is a short wall with the two following routes.

15 Circuit Bored   7m   6c
Neil Shepherd 2001
The left to right traverse.

16 Bloody Shocking   6m   6b
George Ridge 2001
A tricky little move may stop some in their tracks.

Craigruie - Balquhidder

(NN 4973 2033)   L51 or L57 E365   Alt 250m   South facing   Map p75

This steep mica schist crag lies near the west end of Loch Voil on the lower slopes of Creag nan Speireag. There are only two routes at present but here is scope for more. The rock is smooth but a little soft.

AMENITIES
As for Strathyre Crag.

RECOMMENDED TASTY BITES
As for Strathyre Crag.

TOP TIPS
Combine a visit with Strathyre Crag or take a drill and do some new routes!

DIRECTIONS
Take the Balquhidder turn off from the A84 at the Kingshouse Hotel north of Strathyre. Follow the road past Balquhidder and Rob Roy's grave until the crags appear on the right above the settlement of Craigruie. Park at a wide track entrance (despite the no parking signs nearby) at NN 5038 2019. From Strathyre Crag, continue along the minor road to Balquhidder and join the direct route.

APPROACH
Time: 20mins
Go up the wide track to an industrial shed and just before it, cross a fence into a field. Cross the field diagonally left to the top right corner of a forest. The crag is now seen beyond a slabby arete which is the closest crag. Go past its base, still diagonally uphill to reach the crag, which is characterised by a flat wall which gets steeper to the left. There are established trad routes on the buttresses above Rhuveag, a few hundred metres further west.

Glen Ogle

● **An Dialtaig** 15m 7b+
Paul Thorburn 1992
This is the only route on the steep left side of the wall. Climb carefully to a high 1st bolt and finish with powerful moves through the bulge.

○ **Open Project**
An abandoned line up the centre of the blank, less steep section.

● **Dirty Deeds** 10m 6a+
Rick Campbell 1993
This is a sparsely bolted line up the right side of the wall, and with some hangers missing.

GLEN OGLE - LOCHEARNHEAD
L51 E365   Maps p75, p89

Glen Ogle is a small but important glen which runs northwards from the village of Lochearnhead. It is the route taken by the main A84 as the major means of access to the Highlands from Stirling, 30 miles (50km) to the south, and Perth 35 miles (60km) to the east. At one point a railway which connected through to Oban ran through the glen, as can be seen by a fine 12 arch viaduct which is now part of a popular cycleway and walkway. On a visit to the far flung reaches of her Empire,

Queen Victoria likened Glen Ogle to the Khyber Pass, through the Hindu Kush mountain range! Perhaps not as grand, Glen Ogle does have its finer points though and of interest to the climber are numerous crags lining either side of the glen. On the west side of the road those of the Dark Side are readily seen sitting above the former railway whilst those on the east or Sunny Side lie directly above the road and are more difficult to see.

AMENITIES
Lochearnhead has a selection of pubs and restaurants. The Inn at Strathyre does good food. The main stopping place for food for visitors from the Central Belt tends to be Callander, which is well geared up for tourists and even has a small climbing wall (see Introduction).

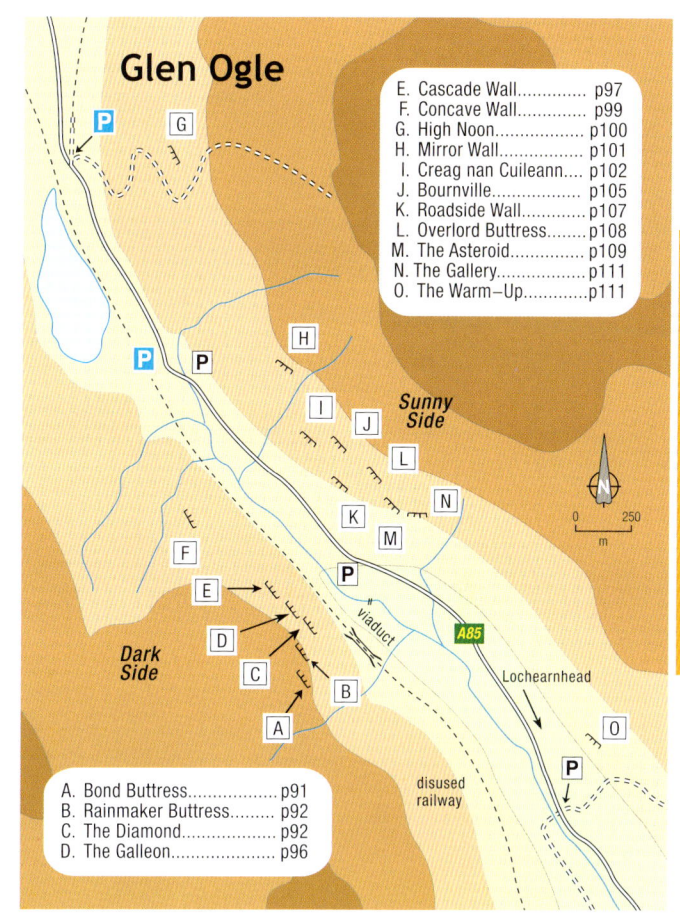

Glen Ogle

E. Cascade Wall............ p97
F. Concave Wall............ p99
G. High Noon................ p100
H. Mirror Wall............... p101
I. Creag nan Cuileann.... p102
J. Bournville................. p105
K. Roadside Wall........... p107
L. Overlord Buttress....... p108
M. The Asteroid............. p109
N. The Gallery............... p111
O. The Warm–Up............ p111

A. Bond Buttress............ p91
B. Rainmaker Buttress.... p92
C. The Diamond............. p92
D. The Galleon.............. p96

Stirlingshire to Perthshire

Glen Ogle Dark Side

RECOMMENDED TASTY BITES

The Snack Van at the top of the glen is an excellent place to re-fuel after a hard day on the bolts.

DIRECTIONS

From the south, follow the A84 north through Callander to Lochearnhead and continue north into Glen Ogle. From Perth and the east, take the A85 west alongside Loch Earn to Lochearnhead and turn right into Glen Ogle. The road west along Loch Tay from the A9 between Dunkeld and Pitlochry leads to Killin then onto the A84 at the north end of the glen.

Glen Ogle Dark Side

The sun starved hillside on the west side of Glen Ogle is littered with steep mica schist crags, holding a high concentration of sport routes. Since its development in 1993 and subsequent rather tongue-in-cheek label of 'Scotland's premier sport climbing venue' many of the routes have remained slightly neglected, although a hardcore of devotees has continued to visit. This is a shame because many of the routes are very good.

With the exception of Bond Buttress, the climbs are short, steep and devious. They give good, intense climbing and there is an abundance of routes at all grades. The hillside acts like a sponge and it takes several days for the crags to come into good dry condition. In summer the midges can be awful, so pick your days. The best time of year to visit is during a sustained dry period in autumn or spring, or on a windy day in summer. The crags only catch the sunshine until 10am, so early starts are a good idea. Many of the routes have a rather high first bolt which can be stick-clipped.

Most of the crags lie up and right of the obvious viaduct halfway up the glen. The buttresses are described running northwards up the glen. All the climbs have been described left to right on their respective crags.

TOP TIPS

The key to making the most of Ogle is strategy. It is best to visit on windy days for good conditions and lack of midges. If the wind is low,

Glen Ogle Dark Side
A. Bond Buttress p91
B. Rainmaker Buttress....p92
C. The Diamond p92
D. Buzzard Wall p95
E. The Raven.................p95
F. The Underworld p95
G. Galleon Wall p96
H. Cascade Wall.............p97
I. Far Beyond p98
J. Down Under..............p99
K. Concave Wall............p99

go to the most exposed buttresses, such as Bond or Concave and come prepared with a head net. The bolts are quite old so take care; those on slow drying routes are particularly inclined to be suspect. A number of the lower-offs have old krabs and maillons so it might be useful to take something else along.

DIRECTIONS

From Lochearnhead (see above) the road climbs through the glen towards its summit. Park at a pull-off on the left at (NN 5710 2674), just above the top arch of the old railway viaduct on the other side of the glen. This is just south of a bend and easily missed if concentrating on the traffic. If this pull-off is closed for any reason, drive up towards the summit and just after the road bends sharply to the left after a small bridge, park in a lay-by on the left (NN 5621 2759). From here the old railway line, now a cycle and walkway, can be used to approach the crags. This is also the quicker approach to Concave Wall. Traffic moves fast on the road through the glen and care should be taken in crossing the road

Glen Ogle Dark Side

on foot and in pulling out from any of the parking areas. Try to park to avoid exiting across the line of oncoming traffic.

APPROACH

From the pull-off opposite the viaduct, head downhill and cross the burn by a wooden bridge which can be seen from the parking spot, then go up and under the top arch of the viaduct; 6mins. From the alternative upper lay-by, drop down through trees onto the old railway line and follow it down the glen to the top end of the viaduct; 15mins. See individual crags for approaches from here.

BOND BUTTRESS

(NN 5692 2622)　Alt 420m　East facing　Map p89

This buttress is unusual for Glen Ogle, featuring long and exposed routes. It takes a little longer to approach than the viaduct crags but it's definitely worth it and is more exposed to breezes and morning sunshine than the lower crags. The crag does suffer from some seepage and although the routes are good and are given their original stars, they may not be as clean as they were.

APPROACH

Time: 30mins

From the top end of the viaduct, break rightwards uphill towards the nearest crag, The Diamond. Follow sheep paths leftwards under Rainmaker Buttress to gain open hillside. Walk directly uphill to reach the tall buttress.

① Open Project
Just left of the huge arete is a bulging groove which was bolted some 10 years ago but remains unclimbed.

② Solitaire 20m 8a+ *
Dave MacLeod 2003
The huge blunt arete meeting the Scaramanga groove at its top. A flake leads to a small ledge. Launch up the arete with a very sustained sequence on tiny crimps and a mono-pocket, moving slightly left just below the break. From the break, easier climbing leads to the final section of Scaramanga.

③ Scaramanga 20m 7a+ *
Neil Shepherd 1993
The line of the crag, staying cleaner and drier. Climb the big flake/groove on good holds to a resting ledge below the roof. A technical section leads leftwards to a difficult swing onto the arete.

④ Boldfinger 22m 7a *
Dave Redpath 2003
A superb varied route. Follow the Scaramanga groove to the ledge. Break out right through roofs on big holds to gain the superb pockety headwall. This leads with sustained interest to the top.

Stirlingshire to Perthshire

Glen Ogle Dark Side

RAINMAKER BUTTRESS

(NN 568 262)   Alt 350m   North-East facing   Map p89

This rather adventurous buttress lies directly above the viaduct, up and left of The Diamond. It is a large white wall with a large overlap near the top. There is continuous dripping water from the top of the crag in all but drought conditions, but the routes remain dry most of the time.

APPROACH

Time: 20mins

From the top end of the viaduct, break rightwards uphill to the nearest crag, The Diamond, then follow sheep paths leftwards until underneath the wall. Scramble up a steep vegetated ramp to gain a large ledge below the climbs. An old rope remains in place on the ramp; do not trust it.

The End Justifies the Means   15m   7b+ *
Dave Redpath 1998
This route climbs the centre of the wall via a triangular scoop to reach the right side of the big overlap. Start from a detached boulder below the scoop. Gaining this is very bouldery. Follow quartz pockets to slopers under the overlap. Pull through the overlap with pumpy climbing to the lower-off.

Power Shower   14m   7b+ *
Dave MacLeod 2003
The bolt-line right of The End Justifies the Means. A straightforward start leads to a hard crux section to gain a standing position above the overlap. Easier but sustained climbing leads to the lower-off.

THE DIAMOND

(NN 5687 2653)   Alt 300m   North-East facing   Map p89

Many of the Dark Side crags are formed as a line just up and right of the viaduct. The Diamond is the closest of these.

APPROACH

Time: 15mins from the pull-off

From the top end of the viaduct, break rightwards uphill to reach the crag. For the other crags, traverse rightwards from The Diamond.

The Diamond is probably the best and used to be the most popular crag in the glen, with a large number of routes at a good spread of grades. It seeps after prolonged wet periods, but once dry it can be climbed on during wet weather.

1 Midge Patrol   12m   6b *
Chris Anderson 1993
A pleasant little route which is steeper than it looks; a good warm-up.

2 Open Project
A short bouldery line up the smooth black wall.

3 Open Project
Another short bouldery wall.

4 Easy Over   12m   7a **
Rab Anderson 1993
Good climbing up the steep pocketed wall to the ledge. Above this, jugs lead through the roof to an easy finishing slab.

5 Digital Quartz   15m   8b *
Iain Pitcairn 1994
Gain the quartz boss, move slightly left and make a series of desperate crimpy moves to gain the ledge and a sit-down rest. The upper wall is 7c and is climbed to the right of Children of the Revolution to a shared lower-off; don't blow it here!

6 Cease Fire   15m   8a+ **
Dave MacLeod 2001
Climb the short lower bulge to the diagonal fault. Launch directly up the wall above on crimps to a stopping place. Small finger pockets lead to the top break (crux) and the chain.

Glen Ogle Dark Side

7 The Link 15m 7c+ *
1994
Climb the first two bolts of Cease Fire and then finish up Digital Quartz.

8 Spiral Tribe 15m 8a ***
Duncan McCallum 1993
From the 1st bolt of Children of the Revolution, climb the steep wall above with great moves and increasing difficulty to a crux last move.

9 Off the Beaten Track 15m 8a ***
Paul Thorburn 1993
Excellent climbing up the right side of the wall. The crux is at mid-height on small pockets.

10 Children of the Revolution 18m 7b *
Rab Anderson 1992
The original route on this wall is a wandering line which gives good climbing. Start in the black, often wet scoop under the arete of Chain Lightning. Follow the diagonal fault running leftwards across the face to the ledge and cave. Pull through the roof just left of Digital Quartz and make technical moves (crux) to good holds and a shared lower-off.

11 Chain Lightning 15m 7b+ ***
Rab Anderson 1993
Superb moves up the right arete, easing towards the top. Pre-clip the 2nd bolt to prevent a knee-capping!

Stirlingshire to Perthshire

The Diamond

Glen Ogle Dark Side

12 One in the Eye for Stickmen   15m   7a *
Neil Shepherd 1993
A line of resin bolts following the steep slopers just right of Chain Lighting.

13 Old Wives' Tail   15m   6b *
Neil Shepherd 1993
The crag warm-up taking the corner-ramp. Good climbing.

14 Metal Guru   15m   6c ***
Rab Anderson 1992
The thin crack on the vertical wall right of the main face. The climbing gets increasingly difficult towards the top.

15 Open Project
The blank looking wall between the cracks.

16 Gross Indecency   15m   7c
Rab Anderson 1993
A hard lower wall using a flake leads to the ledge. From here climb the steep wall just right of the large off-width crack.

17 Trossachs Trundler   10m   7c
Malcolm Smith 1993
A perplexing bouldery line of resin bolts climbing through the V feature. Lower off from the ledge.

18 After the Flood   12m   6c *
George Ridge 1993
Another line of resin bolts. A steep start leads to an awkward finish. The lower-off is frustratingly hard to clip.

19 Arc of a Diver   12m   6c **
Rab Anderson 1993
Again, a steep start leads to the ledge. The crux is on the headwall.

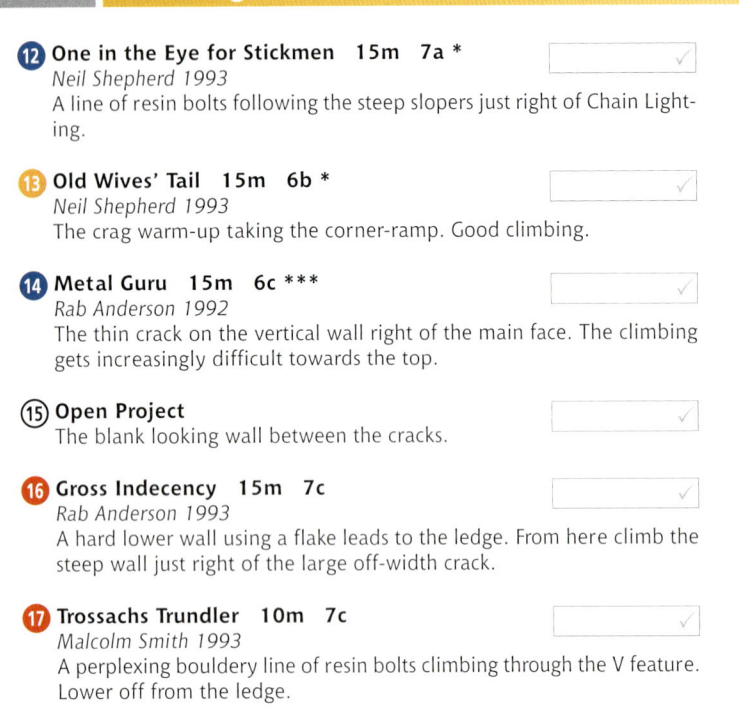

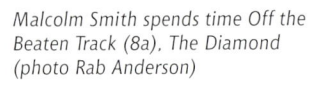

Malcolm Smith spends time Off the Beaten Track (8a), The Diamond (photo Rab Anderson)

Climbing Raspberry Beret (6b+), The Diamond in the kind of troos you'd find in a secondhand store (photo Rab Anderson)

20 Climb and Punishment   12m   7b+
Rab Anderson 1994
This one is bouldery before and after the ledge!

21 Wristy Business   10m   6c+ *
Rab Anderson 1993
Climbs the cleaned groove to the ledge followed by the deceptive wall above.

Glen Ogle Dark Side

22 Raspberry Beret 10m 6b+ *
Chris Anderson 1993
The nicely featured wall starting from the ledge.

23 Ship Ahoy 8m 6b
Chris Anderson 1993
The wall at the far right end of the crag gives slightly scrappy climbing.

BUZZARD WALL

(NN 5684 2657) Alt 310m North-East facing

This small roofed buttress lies 50m right of the end of The Diamond and at a slightly higher level. Buzzards have nested here in the past. Please avoid disturbing them.

Cut Loose 8m 7a+
Rab Anderson 1993
The central line takes the widest section of the roof using the flake.

Hang Free 8m 7a+
Rab Anderson 1994
The line through the V shaped roof to the right.

THE RAVEN

A steep wall that lies directly above Buzzard Wall.

The Edge of Ecstasy 8m 6c *
Neil Shepherd 1994
Climb the left side of the arete, taking the slab.

Rush 8m 7a **
Neil Shepherd 1994
The right side of the arete, following a crack for part of the way.

Raving Lunatics 8m 7b *
Neil Shepherd 1995
A powerful sequence right again.

Recreational Chemistry 8m 6c+
Neil Shepherd 1995
A short and thuggy route leading to the same lower-off as Raving Lunatics.

THE UNDERWORLD

(NN 5682 2663) Alt 295m North-East facing

This crag is 60m right of The Diamond, on the lowest tier of rock, and directly below The Galleon wall. The routes are tiny and are best described as bolted bouldering.

Carsonagenic 6m 6a
George Ridge 1994
Climb the left-hand line, starting direct to avoid the choss on the left.

Open Project
Very eliminate and thin climbing.

Hanging out on the Smalls 6m 7a **
George Ridge 1994
Superb thin and crimpy climbing, over all too soon.

Under Where? 6m 6b
George Ridge 1994
There are good holds if you can find them!

XX 6m 6c
George Ridge 1994
A flaky start leads to thin climbing above.

Satan's Slaves 6m 6a
George Ridge 1994
Again, poor rock at the start leads to better stuff above.

Maniaxe 6m 6b
Andrew Banks 1993
A boulder problem start to get to the 1st bolt.

Stirlingshire to Perthshire

Glen Ogle Dark Side

- **Under Mind   6m   6b+**
George Ridge 1994
Start from the cave at the right end. Gain a large protruding hold, then go up to even better holds.

THE GALLEON

Alt 305m   North-East facing   Map p89
The continuation of The Diamond, 60m right of it and above The Underworld. It is reached by traversing across the grass slope from its right edge. Although it is the slowest of the cliffs to dry out, some of the routes are great.

- **Weigh Anchor   8m   6b+**
Rab Anderson 1994
The wall left of a hanging corner in the roof with the crux through the roof.

- **Frigging in the Rigging   8m   6c ***
George Ridge 1994
Easy climbing up to the roofed corner, then a horrible thrutch.

- **Slave to the Rhythm   8m   7a+ ****
Rab Anderson 1993
Start right of the corner. Climb the bulging wall on ever worsening holds to the lower-off.

- **Rum Ration   8m   7a+ ***
Duncan McCallum 1993
Climb to the roof left of a groove come niche, then go right into the groove. Move up and back left to the lower-off.

- **Blithe Spirit   8m   7a *****
Rab Anderson 1993
Once dry, the right-hand side of the groove gives a brilliant route.

Duncan McCallam earning his Rum Ration (7a+), The Galleon (photo Rab Anderson)

Glen Ogle Dark Side

🔴 **Get a Grip** 8m 7b *
Rab Anderson 1993
The next line gives fingery climbing towards the top.

🔵 **Eat Y'self Fitter** 8m 6c **
George Ridge 1993
The line of jugs and staple bolts to the big staple bolt lower-off. A great and popular wee route.

🔵 **Infinite Gravity** 8m 7a+ *
Neil Shepherd 1994
A crimpy boulder problem through the roof at the start leads to slightly easier climbing.

🔴 **Fight Fire with Fire** 8m 7c **
Neil Shepherd 1993
Another crimpy and powerful start, easing slightly above; good climbing.

🔵 **Waiting for a Train** 8m 6c *
George Ridge 1993
Steep and short with good holds, following a left-slanting crack.

🔵 **The Pack Horse** 8m 6c ***
Neil Shepherd 1993
The pocketed overhanging wall gives excellent thuggy climbing on jugs.

🔵 **Horrid** 8m 6c
Roger Maguire 1993
The scoop at the right end of the wall is fingery.

Beyond this, just before the gully separating this wall from Cascade Wall, the crag gains height and gives the following two slabby routes, which may need re-cleaning.

🟡 **Don't Pass Me By** 10m 6a+
Neil Shepherd 1994

A welcome break from the steepness of the rest of the routes.

🔵 **The Guilt Trip** 10m 6c **
Andrew Banks 1993
The bulging wall guarding access to the slab succumbs to reckless crimping.

CASCADE WALL

(NN 5667 2669) Alt 305m North-East facing Map p89
This steep buttress lies 20m right of The Galleon and at the same level. Again, it takes a while to dry out, but the best routes dry quickest. A lower tier is Down Under.

🔵 **Hive of Industry** 6m 7a+
Neil Shepherd 1993
The very short and very steep left arete has one desperate move. A tough on-sight!

🔴 **Gotta Sin to Be Saved** 8m 7b *
George Ridge 1993
Climb the steep wall direct to the lower-off of Paradise Road.

🔵 **Paradise Road** 9m 6c *
George Ridge 1993
The obvious left-slanting line has a bold 3rd clip.

🟡 **Short Sharp Shocked** 10m 6a+ ***
Janet Horrocks 1993
The left edge of the wide diagonal crack is probably the most climbed grade 6 in the glen. It still gives weak arms a fright though!

🔵 **The Age Old Problem Rears its Ugly Head** 10m 7a
Neil Shepherd 1994
Hard moves through the overhang and headwall.

Stirlingshire to Perthshire

Glen Ogle Dark Side

Havering Skate 10m 6b+ *
Neil Shepherd 1994
The groove, arete and crack.

Open Project 10m
The next section of cliff stretching rightwards to the waterfall is only usually dry in mid-summer.

Speedfreak 10m 7b *
George Ridge 1993
From a big pocket, gain a mono-pocket and use this to gain a line of good edges leading to the lower-off.

Cauldron of Spite 10m 6c *
Chris Anderson 1994
From the big pocket low down on Speedfreak, move up and right to a horizontal, then gain the quartz boss. Easier ground leads back left to the lower-off.

Stone Junky 10m 6c
Rab Anderson 1993
Follow a diagonal crack to two-thirds height, then step right and climb the wall above direct.

Dirt Digger 10m 6b+
Rab Anderson 1993
The line through a lower continuation of the diagonal crack gives good climbing.

That Sinking Feeling 10m 7a
Rab Anderson 1994
The steep left arete of the wall underneath the waterfall.

The finishes of the following two routes can be wet but the water tends to drip out from the wall. They still need dry conditions.

Debt of Pain 10m 7b
George Ridge 1994
A line just right of the arete.

The Drowning Pool 10m 7b
Rab Anderson 1993
Lies just left of (or in) the waterfall.

FAR BEYOND

Alt 305m North-East facing

The continuation of Cascade Wall, beyond the waterfall. It is characterised by a prominent square-cut roof, the right end of which forms a steep groove. It has become neglected but would be better if the routes got more traffic and the remaining projects climbed.

Submersion 6m 7a+
Rab Anderson 1995
Just right of the waterfall, all too similar to The Drowning Pool.

The next four lines of bolts are open projects, some of which look good, and very steep.

Far Beyond Driven 6m 6b+ **
George Ridge 1994
Climb the steep wall using various contortions.

Driven to Distraction 6m 6b+ *
George Ridge 1994
Start right of the arete. Climb to the left edge of a large block, then continue up and left.

Hyper Hyper 6m 6b
George Ridge 1994
Climb to the right end of the block, then follow a crack to the lower-off.

DOWN UNDER

Alt 290m North-East facing
Another small wall lies directly below Cascade Wall.

- **The Bends** 8m 7a+ **
  Rab Anderson 1993
  The centre of the leaning wall features a peculiar square hold. A hard start for the short.

- **Open Project**

- **Nitrogen** 8m 6b+
  Neil Shepherd 1994
  Climb direct to the second roof, then go up and left to the lower-off.

CONCAVE WALL

(NN 566 266) Alt 360m North-East facing Map p89
This isolated crag lies up and right of the Viaduct Crags and is well seen from the large lay-by on the left (NN 5621 2759), recognisable by the very steep right arete. The routes are short but certainly pack a lot in! It catches a northerly or easterly breeze very well and can give cool, midge free conditions when the viaduct crags are midgy.

APPROACH
Time: 20mins (30mins from the pull-off opposite the viaduct)

From the upper lay-by on the left (NN 5621 2759), head down to the old railway line and follow it down to NN 5662 2696, from where the crag is also visible (especially when there are no leaves on the trees). Go straight up to the crag. The crag can also be approached from The Diamond by traversing right under all the crags until it can be seen above.

- **Embrace my Weakness** 8m 7c+
  Dave Redpath 2003
  Move up ledges and gain a line of pockets. These lead to a hard sequence on edges to gain the finishing jug.

- **Snipe Shadow** 10m 8b **
  Dave MacLeod 2004
  The central blank concave wall. Technical climbing on finger pockets leads to a desperate crux section near the top.

- **Arms Limitation** 14m 7b+ ***
  Mark Garthwaite 1999, equipped by Rab Anderson
  The superb and exposed right arete. It gives technical climbing in its lower half, followed by some big moves higher up.

- **Northern Exposure** 15m 7a+
  Dave Redpath 1998
  Start up the arete, just beyond the thin section, pull right and pull awkwardly through a roof. More blind and awkward climbing leads up the off-vertical wall above to a lower-off.

PROJECT CRAG

(NN 574 249) East facing
High on the hillside and separated from the other cliffs, this crag has been ignored despite being equipped over a decade ago. It lies at the top of a huge boulder field and has a huge horizontal roof in its centre. The rock on some of the equipped projects is quite poor. However there is some good rock and potential for some good routes that would be worth the walk.

It can be approached from directly below, but the easiest approach is to park at the large lay-by on the west side of the road at the head of the glen (NN 5621 2759) and walk under Concave Wall, traversing the hillside to reach the crag in 40mins.

Glen Ogle Sunny Side

The east, or sunny side of the glen is a very different experience to the Dark Side. The crags see lots of sun and dry quickly. They also tend to be less steep, often featuring vertical fingery climbing on edges and pockets, with intricate moves.

These crags are also exposed to a westerly breeze and in summer they tend not to be as midgy as those on the other side of the glen. On a sunny dry day in winter, the crags can often be a pleasant place to climb. The crags are described running southwards from the parking area at the top of the glen. All the routes are described running left to right.

TOP TIPS

Due to the sunny aspect, the crags are climbable more often than most people think in the autumn and winter months. Also, the highest buttresses such as Mirror Wall sit at a relatively high altitude and have an open aspect so can be a good place to escape greasy conditions lower down in mid-summer. A number of the lower-offs have old krabs and maillons so it might be useful to take something else along.

DIRECTIONS

See Glen Ogle introduction for directions to Lochearnhead. North of here the road climbs through Glen Ogle passing the various parking areas with the crags lying on the hillside to the east immediately above the road. They are not as easy to identify from the road as those on the opposite side of the glen.

Traffic moves quickly on the road through the glen and care should be taken in crossing the road on foot and in pulling out from any of the parking areas. If possible try to park to avoid exiting across the line of oncoming traffic, which may entail a turnaround at the head of the glen, at the lochside layby or the snack van layby, either before, or after the day's climbing. The relevant parking place is described under each crag.

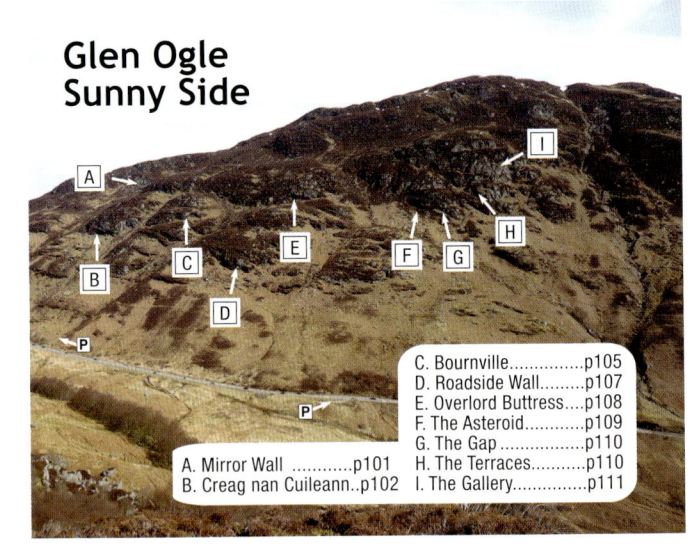

Glen Ogle Sunny Side

A. Mirror Wall p101
B. Creag nan Cuileann..p102
C. Bournville...............p105
D. Roadside Wall.........p107
E. Overlord Buttress....p108
F. The Asteroid............p109
G. The Gap p110
H. The Terraces...........p110
I. The Gallery...............p111

HIGH NOON

(NN 5637 2830)   Alt 430m   South-West facing   Map p89

This isolated crag lies at the head of the glen and is reached from the large lay-by where the snack van resides. It sits immediately above the forest and is hidden until you reach it. The routes give fingery vertical wall climbing, with honeycombed pocketed rock near the top.

DIRECTIONS

Park beyond the head of the glen, on the east side of the road, in the main car park for the snack van and picnic area (NN 5588 2839).

APPROACH

Time: 15mins

Glen Ogle Sunny Side

Ignore a track to the picnic area. Follow a forestry track past a locked gate with a walkers' gate to its left until after some hairpins, it reaches the top of the forest. There are obvious crags above but it is not these. Follow the top of the forest left (north) for 200m and the crag is immediately above.

There is a trad line taking the left side of the face, through a diagonal crack **All Change** (E4 6a).

● **The Ariel Man   10m   6c+ ****
Mike Lauder 1998
The line takes the left edge of the wall. A hard move gains the grooved arete, after which the groove is followed into the pocketed wall above.

○ **Open Project   10m   7c**
1998
The line in the centre of the crag will give a very bouldery start leading to much easier climbing. No hangers.

● **Electric Sunday   10m   6c**
Dave Redpath 1998
The right-hand bolted route on the wall, starting just left of the gully (no bridging!). Climb to the pod then go left into the honeycomb pocketed top wall.

MIRROR WALL

(NN 5692 2755)   Alt 500m   South-West facing   Map p89
One of the best crags on the sunny side of Glen Ogle, with immaculate pocketed rock. It is very quick drying and gives fingery climbing.

DIRECTIONS

For Mirror Wall, Creag nan Cuileann and Bournville, park in either of two lay-bys at a bendy section of the road, on either side of a bridge just south of the largest parking area with the snack van which resides at the top of the glen. Of these, the bigger tarmac lay-by is on the west side of the road just north of the bridge (NN 5621 2760). The smaller but slightly nearer one to the crags is immediately on the south-east side of the bridge at NN 5636 2750; the approach is described from here.

APPROACH
Time: 25mins
There are sheep tracks, but these can be difficult to find in summer due to high bracken. Mirror Wall is the northernmost crag accessed from here and it sits much higher on the hillside than Creag nan Cuilean, which can be seen on looking down the glen. Cross the fence and follow a rising traverse southwards across the hillside first to one electricity pylon and then to the next one. Head up right to a burn which forms a shallow valley, then climb its left side and continue to the crag which is now visible ahead. Some may prefer to continue on the path come sheep track to Creag na Cuileann, then head up to the cliff from the left side of this crag; longer but less bracken and less of a flog.

1 Munrobagger   15m   6b+ **
George Ridge 1998
A shallow corner and wide crack which shapes the left side of the wall.

2 Blind Faith   15m   7b *
Dave Redpath 1997
A line of red hangers. Make a series of hard moves on two-finger pockets to gain a small pod. Continue with less difficulty. Shared lower-off with Munrobagger.

3 Take a Hike   15m   7a **
Janet Horrocks 1998
The first line of staple bolts following the line of a thin crack up the left side of a shield of rock in the centre of the wall.

4 Cony the Calvinist   15m   6c **
Dave Redpath 1998
Climb the shield of rock to attain a standing position. Keep hunting for pockets in the top wall.

Stirlingshire to Perthshire

Glen Ogle Sunny Side

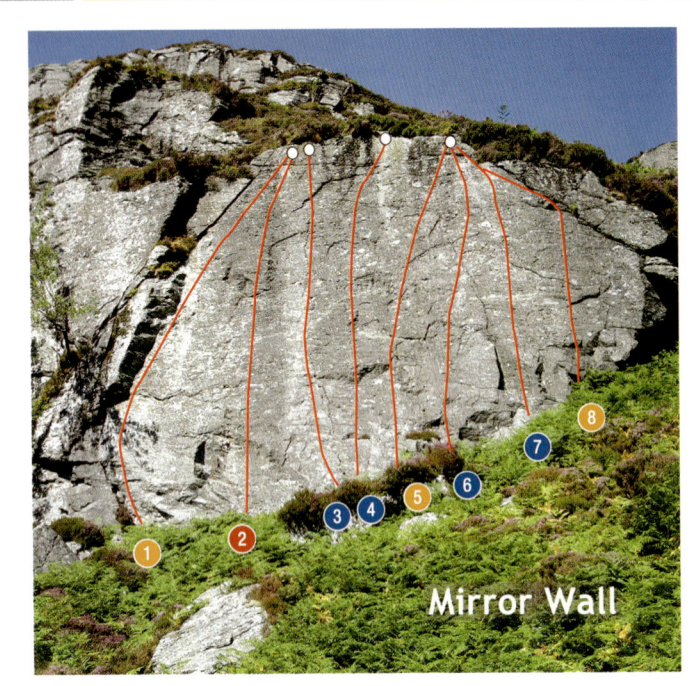

**5 Fat Eagles Fly Low   15m   6a+ ** **
Janet Horrocks 1998
The best of the easier routes on the wall gives enjoyable climbing following the second line of staple bolts up the thin ragged crack-line to the right of the shield of rock.

6 Retribution   15m   6c+ *
Dave Redpath 1998
From the right end of the ledge, climb the wall through the diagonal crack.

7 Bad Religion   15m   6c *
Dave Redpath 1998
The triangular scoop and thin looking wall above.

8 Carry On Up the Corbetts   15m   6a+
George Ridge 1998
The rightmost climb finishes at the same lower-off as Fat Eagles Fly Low, converging with the previous routes at the top.

CREAG NAN CUILEANN

(NN 568 272)   Alt 370m   South-West facing   Map p89   Diagram p104, p105

There are a number of sport routes on this originally traditional crag. It is the largest crag on the hillside and is split by a low roof. Apart from Idiot Wind which lies at the left end of the crag, the sport routes are grouped together at the right end of the crag to the right of **Poison Ivy** (E3), a prominent crack splitting the wall right of the central fault.

DIRECTIONS

Park at either of two lay-bys at a bendy section of the road, on either side of the bridge just south of the largest parking area with snack van which resides at the top of the glen. A bigger tarmac one is on the west side of the road just north of the bridge (NN 5621 2760). A smaller but slightly nearer one to the crags is immediately on the south-east side of the bridge at NN 5636 2750; the approach is described from here. An even lower pull-off saves 5mins but is less safe to use as it lies close between two bad bends (NN 5657 2723). Creag nan Cuileann can be seen from the bridge on looking down the glen.

APPROACH

Time: 15mins
Cross the fence to reach a pylon then pick up a path, which can be difficult to find in summer due to high bracken, and traverse to the next pylon. From here rise gently up the hillside following the path

Glen Ogle Sunny Side

across a stream, around the hillside and on to a rowan tree visible on the skyline. A short ascent past large boulders gains the right end of the crag.

1 Idiot Wind 10m 7b ★★
Rab Anderson 1998
At the far left end, 5 bolts to a lower-off. Brutal moves lead to a shake out, before a few tricky moves to finish.

To the right there are six trad routes on a long wall above roofs.

2 Fight or Flight 15m 6c+
George Ridge 1998
The roof and wall just right of a left-slanting crack which lies near the right end of the long wall above roofs.

3 Slaphead 15m 6b+
George Ridge 1998
The roof and bulge immediately right of the blocky chimney.

4 Fat Chance 15m 6c ★
George Ridge 1998
The short thin crack in the roofed bulge just right of the shallow blocky chimney.

5 Fight the Flab 15m 6c+ ★
Rab Anderson 1998
Climbs the roof left of Let it All Hang Out, then the short, blunt slabby nose. Approach from the right as for Let it All Hang Out. Take great care with the block under the line; do not stand on the left-hand/lower block.

6 Let it all Hang Out 15m 6c+ ★
Rab Anderson 1998
Climb the roof close to its widest point and continue up the slab above to a lower-off in the trees.

Ian Cropley managing to Hang On! (6c), Creag nan Cuileann (photo Rab Anderson)

Glen Ogle Sunny Side

7 Happy Campus   15m   6c
Rab Anderson 1999
The roof right of Let it all Hang Out to quickly join and finish up this.

8 Hang On!   15m   6c *
Janet Horrocks 1998
The small roof and featured wall just right of the previous route.

9 Step on It   15m   6a
George Ridge 1998
Start right of Hang On! and move up left into it for a finish.

10 Life in the Fat Lane   15m   6b+ *
Rab & Chris Anderson 1998
The short but steep crack right of Step on It, just before the crag turns the edge. The lower-off is on the heather ledge, beyond the rowan tree.

Just to the right, around the edge and facing down the glen is a small buttress with a short arete and leaning sidewall which contains the following routes.

11 Chasing the Bandwagon   16m   6a *
Colin Miln 1998
The line left of the arete is a pleasant introduction to the climbing here.

George Ridge – Reaching the Limit (6c), Creag nan Cuileann, Glen Ogle (photo Rab Anderson)

Glen Ogle Sunny Side

the mid-height ledge.

15 Having a Little Flutter   15m   6c *
George Ridge 1998
The lower wall to the right of Dazed and Confused leads to a pokey finish to the left of the thin crack in the headwall.

16 Kinmont Times   10m   6a+ *
George Ridge 1998
The right to left-slanting diagonal crack cutting across the other routes on the recessed section of wall to finish on the left edge as for Dazed and Confused; direct to the lower-off is 6c.

17 Ceuse Jimmy   15m   6c *
George Ridge 1998
Start up the diagonal crack of Kinmont Times and climb the obvious thin crack in the headwall; save something for the last moves which are also a bit pokey.

18 Lichen Virgin   15m   6a+ *
Janet Horrocks 1998
The hollow flake, wall and groove bounding the recessed section of wall. It shares a first bolt with Kinmont Times.

19 Loose Living   15m   6a *
George Ridge 1998
The obvious groove leads to a lower-off shared with Ghost Trail.

20 Ghost Trail   15m   6b+ *
Rab Anderson 1998
The white streak at the extreme right-hand end of the crag; a little gem.

BOURNVILLE

(NN 5698 2715)   Alt 390m   West facing   Map p89   Diagram p107

12 Reaching the Limit   15m   6c *
Rab Anderson 1998
The line on and just left of the arete, sharing the first two bolts and the lower-off of Chasing the Bandwagon.

13 Clutching at Straws   15m   7a *
Rab Anderson 1998
Just to the right is this leaning sidewall and arete, aptly named!

Up the slope to the right, is a wall which faces directly towards the road; the main, left-hand part of the wall is slightly recessed. There is a small tree lined ledge cutting across the wall at mid-height.

14 Dazed and Confused   20m   6a
Janet Horrocks 1998
The route on the left edge of the recessed section uses the tree to gain

Stirlingshire to Perthshire

Glen Ogle Sunny Side

This crag lies about 100m beyond the right end of Creag nan Cuileann, at a slightly higher level. It is another vertical wall covered in little pockets and is recognisable by its chocolate brown colour. It is a nice little venue and although the grades are all fairly similar, the more you do the harder they feel! Some of the lower-offs are single bolt.

APPROACH
Time: 20mins
Approach via Creag nan Cuileann; a sheep track leads up and across right from the foot of Ghost Trail.

1 The Dirty Dozen   8m   6a
Isla Watson, Colin Miln 1998
The furthest left line on the wall.

2 It Ain't Over till it's Over   8m   6a+
George Ridge 1998
The next line just to the right through a thin crack.

3 Coward of the County   8m   6a+
George Ridge 1998
Climbs a slightly darker coloured streak.

4 Half Covered   8m   6b *
Neil Shepherd 1994
This line is unfortunately split by a ledge and it finishes up a white streak.

5 High and Dry   8m   6b
George Ridge 1998
This finishes through a small overlap at the top of the crag.

6 Chocoholics   8m   6a+
Neil Shepherd 1994
The bolts just left of a thin crack in the centre of the crag.

Chocoholics (6a+) and Karen Latter, Bournville, Glen Ogle (photo Gary Latter)

Glen Ogle Sunny Side

Start just left of a small but obvious niche at ground level and follow another line of staples. Nice moves on pockets and edges, with one thin move near the top.

12 Voodoo Ray   8m   6c
George Ridge 1994
The fourth line of staples starts just right of the niche. Climb the pocketed wall until forced to use the arete. Using the arete is precarious; climbing the wall direct is rather blind!

The following crags are located further right from the main Sunny Side cliffs and although they can be approached from there, they are normally approached from below using the pull-off at (NN 5710 2674) opposite the viaduct.

ROADSIDE WALL

(NN 5703 2710)   Alt 340m   South-West facing   Map p89
This wall is the lowest of the crags. It lies below and to the right of Creag nan Cuileann and Bournville, up and right of the left-hand of two pylons when seen from the parking spot opposite the viaduct.

APPROACH
Time: 10mins
Head direct.

**1 Don't Fight the Feeling   10m   6b *
George Ridge 1994
Climb the barrel shaped wall in the centre of the crag; lower-off shared with the next climb.

2 Rock is Dead   10m   6b
George Ridge 1998
Climb just right of a chimney, through a bulge and up the right side of the barrel shaped wall; shared lower-off.

7 Fingers of Fudge   8m   6b+
Neil Shepherd 1994
Going through a tiny overlap at the start, this is the next line to the right.

**8 Sudden Alchemy   8m   6b *
Janet Horrocks 1994
The highest line on the crag follows a line of resin staples.

9 Hot Chocolate   8m   6b *
Neil Shepherd 1994
The line up the brown streak has thin moves on perfect rock.

10 Sorry Tess   8m   6b *
George Ridge 1994
There are a couple of thin moves between the 1st and 2nd bolts of a line of staples, then much more user friendly holds.

11 The Greenhouse Defect   8m   6b *
George Ridge 1994

Stirlingshire to Perthshire

Glen Ogle Sunny Side

APPROACH
Time: 20 or 25mins
Either direct from the parking spot opposite the viaduct (20mins) perhaps via climbing on Roadside Wall, or from the parking areas further up the glen and walking past Creag nan Cuileann and Bournville (25mins total).

1 Restless Souls   10m   7a **
Chris Anderson 1995
The left side of the buttress looks easy, but it is very steep. A long reach helps.

2 Open Project
Follow Restless Souls to the 2nd bolt, then go right and up.

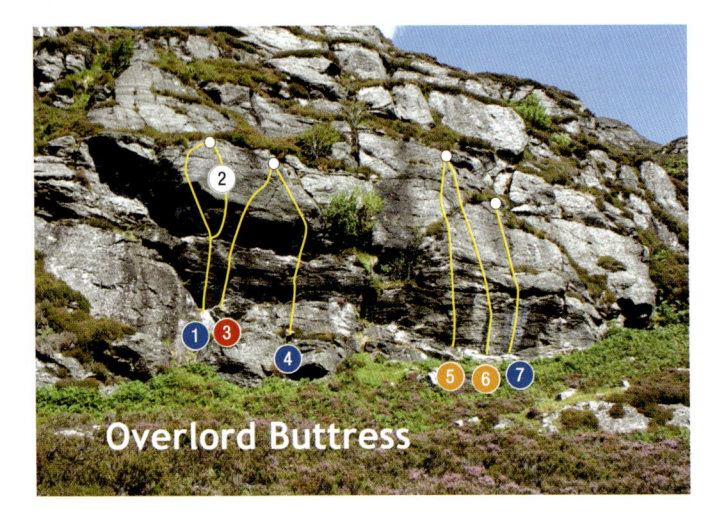

Some 10m right are two routes up a slabby wall above a roof.

3 Dark Skies   8m   6b
George Ridge
Climb up to and round the left end of the roof, then up the left edge of the slabby wall before moving right to a lower-off shared with the next climb.

4 Hold the Press   10m   7a *
George Ridge 1995
Boulder up to beneath the small roof, pull over and climb the right edge of the slab; shared lower-off.

OVERLORD BUTTRESS

(5714 2710)   Alt 420m   South-West facing   Map p89

This is the steepest of the Sunny Side crags. It lies above Roadside Wall, up and right of Bournville, from where it can be seen 5mins walk away.

❸ Overlord   12m   7b *
Rab Anderson 1994
Steep and powerful climbing, finishing right via the diagonal crack to a shared lower-off with Overkill.

❹ Overkill   10m   7a+ **
Rab Anderson 1994
The right side of the wall is also steep but has generally good holds, if you can find them!

❺ Over the Top   10m   6b+ **
Rab Anderson 1994
Good varied climbing, from very steep to slabby, with the crux somewhere in between.

❻ Pushover   10m   6b+
George Ridge 1998
Best done with an all out jump for the jug!

❼ Pullover   10m   6c
Rab Anderson 1996
Climb left of the first two bolts, or right (slightly harder), and pull over awkwardly onto the slab. Either lower off beneath a heathery ledge or continue left and up to the lower-off of Over the Top.

The next group of the cliffs, The Asteroid, The Gap, The Terraces and The Gallery, lie further right on the area of craggy hillside to the left of the obvious streamway which descends to a bend in the middle of the glen.

THE ASTEROID

(NN 5728 2704)   Alt 400m   South-West facing   Map p89   Diagram p110
This is a black slab well right of Overlord Buttress, at a slightly lower level. There are four pleasant routes on lovely waterworn rock on the left half of the slab. There are only two bolts per route and lower-offs have

Colin Lampton experiencing Overkill (7a+), Overlord Buttress, Glen Ogle (photo Rab Anderson)

Glen Ogle Sunny Side

double bolt hangers linked with tat. They are all around the same standard and some might scrape 6a. There is more scope and with some work, this could be a nice little venue.

APPROACH

For this, The Gap and The Terraces, head up from the mid glen pull-off just above the viaduct on the opposite side of the glen (NN 5710 2674). Approach direct (20mins) or via Roadside Wall, or 5mins from Overlord Buttress (30mins from the top of the glen).

1 Mars 10m 5+
Ross Hutton 2000
The leftmost line finishes by moving right in a very runout position to the lower-off of the next route.

2 Trojan 10m 5+
Ross Hutton 2000
More direct to the same lower-off.

3 Jupiter 10m 5+
Ross Hutton 2000
Start briefly up a right-slanting crack before climbing diect.

4 Starboard 10m 5+
Ross Hutton 2000
The rightmost line crosses the diagonal crack.

THE GAP

(NN 5731 2702)   Alt 400m   South-West facing

This lies 30m right of the right end of The Asteroid and is a small clean quick drying wall hidden in a recess.

5 Beggar's Banquet 10m 6c+ *
George Ridge 1994
Climb to the quartz, pull through the overhang and continue up the wall above.

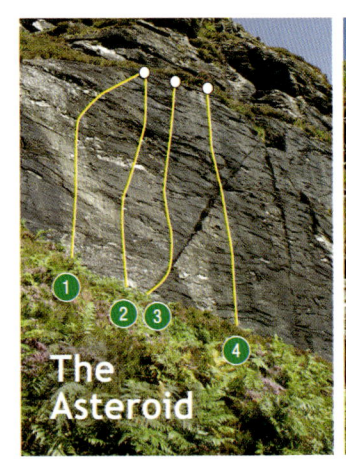

6 Chimera 10m 6b+ *
Janet Horrocks 1994
From the quartz, go right then move up to the ledge. Precariously bridge up the shallow groove to the lower-off.

THE TERRACES

(NN 5736 2703)   Alt 410m   South-West facing

This cluster of crags lies 100m to the right of The Gap. Walk rightwards across the hillside from The Asteroid, below a more broken area of rock, to where a terraced crag can be seen sloping rightwards and down. This is home to a couple of routes at its top end.

7 Saturation Point 12m 6b+ **
Dave Redpath 1998
This line takes the wall at its highest point. Move up the wall into the break. Traverse this leftward for a few moves before pulling out of the overlap, and continuing up the slab above. A mono move awaits.

Glen Ogle Sunny Side

8 Saturation Right-Hand   10m   6a+
Dave Redpath 1998
Start as the previous line. This time continue directly through the overlap.

Continuing down from the terrace across a broken area the last area of rock culminates in a short steep arete.

9 Northern Exposure   8m   6b+
Richard Fielding 1994
The left side of the steep arete leads past 2 bolts and over the top to a 2 bolt lower-off linked with tat.

THE GALLERY

(NN 5740 2703)   Alt 430m   South facing   Map p89
This gently overhanging and quick drying pocketed wall lies above The Terraces.

APPROACH

Either via The Asteriod and the rest of The Sunny Side, or direct from the mid glen pull-off opposite the viaduct, passing right of the main rocks and up steep broken ground before traversing left under the top tier. It can be difficult to spot from below. Look for the clean ear shaped patch of rock above and left of an exposed area of quartzite, 25mins.

From The Terraces, go left and over the top of the Saturation Point lower-off, then traverse right on a sheep path which leads directly there, 1min.

10 Mona Sleaza   10m   6a+ *
Chris Anderson 1994
The left side of the wall through a diagonal crack.

11 Modern Tart   12m   6b+ *
Rab Anderson 1994
Through the left side of a small arched overlap, then up a thin crack-line to lower off as for Art Attack.

12 Art Attack   14m   7a+ *
Rab Anderson 1994
The centre of the lovely smooth pocketed wall.

THE WARM-UP

(NN 5812 2612)   Alt 300m   South-West facing   Map p89
This isolated buttress lies some distance south of the main group, not too far above the road and almost at the base of the glen. It is the biggest visible piece of cliff and has a grassy terrace beneath it. The outlook is pleasant and there is enough to go at to make a visit worthwhile. Take some hangers and complete the lines!

Stirlingshire to Perthshire

Glen Ogle Sunny Side

The Warm-Up

APPROACH
Time: 15mins
Park at the first big pull-off on the right driving northwards into the glen (NN 5797 2567). This is around a bend beyond the last house and below the first crags seen on the east side of the glen. Walk up a track, then go left and ascend the hillside to the crag; short but steep and fairly brutal, this might be the warm-up!

① Open Project
At the left end of the crag and at the right end of a prominent capping bulge is a line of bolt studs without hangers

② Unknown
A line of 5 bolts 2m to the right leads to a twin ring lower-off.

The following routes are 6m right of the line of 5 bolts.

③ Ultraviolet   10m   6b+ *
Neil Shepherd 1994
Climb the bulging wall, then trend right to a shared lower-off with the following route.

④ Outshined   10m   6a+ *
George Ridge 1994
A shallow groove joining Ultraviolet at its 3rd bolt.

Some 15m right is the next wall, with a prominent right-diagonal crack.

⑤ Open Project   10m
Direct from the start of the diagonal crack – one stud, no hanger is readily visible.

⑥ Burnt Offerings   10m   6b+ **
George Ridge 1994
Follow the diagonal crack to near its end, then go direct to a lower-off.

⑦ Face the Heat   10m   7a **
Neil Shepherd 1994
Climb directly up the wall on small pockets to the same lower-off as Burnt Offerings; very crimpy.

⑧ Infrarete   10m   6b+ *
Neil Shepherd 1994
The arete, of course!

The following routes are 10m right, beyond a grassy break.

⑨ Project
A line of studs leads to the same lower-off as the following route.

⑩ Under the Same Sun   10m   6b+
Neil Shepherd 1994
Starting from the rock scar, make thin moves up the slab.

⑪ Burn Baby, Burn   10m   6a+
George Ridge 1994
Climb the hanging groove to the slab, then tackle the overhang above.

⑫ **Burn it Up 10m 6b+**
George Ridge 1994
An eliminate up the wall to the right. Find that mono-pocket and crank!

⑬ **Open Project**
Complete except for two hangers.

PERTHSHIRE
This is another large area with a diverse selection of crags composed mostly of schist. The exception is the small and immensely popular quartz-dolerite volcanic dyke next to the road at Bennybeg outside Crieff. At nearby Comrie is the more remote and quieter Dunira, plus the longer middle grade routes of recently rebolted Lower Lednock. To the east overlooking the River Tay there is the slate of Newtyle Quarry, an unusual roadside dry-tooling and sport climbing venue. Also in the Tay valley, on splendid wooded hillsides, are the fine schist crags at Craig a' Barns at Dunkeld and Weem near Aberfeldy. The section concludes with Rockdust Crag near Pitlochry, another schist crag with a lovely open outlook to the hills.

Bennybeg - Crieff
(NN 863 188) L58 E368 Alt 40m South-South-East facing
Maps p75, p113 Diagrams p114, 116
Bennybeg is a very accessible, friendly and relaxing place to climb all year round, with 27 well bolted low grade sport routes. At present, grades range from 2 to 6a and the close and well-considered spacing and placing of the bolts, especially on the easier grades, has meant that they are appropriate for beginners and kids. Some of the lower-offs were replaced in 2011. As well as the ease of access and its sheltered and sunny aspect, another of the cliff's attractions is that it is situated 2mins from a cafe.

The crag is a volcanic dyke made of quartz-dolerite which catches the sun all day until early evening. Muthill and Crieff are well sheltered by the Ochils, Ben Chonzie and Ben Vorlich, meaning that it is often surprisingly dry even when pouring in the central belt. The crag dries rapidly after rain and it is possible to climb even in light showers.

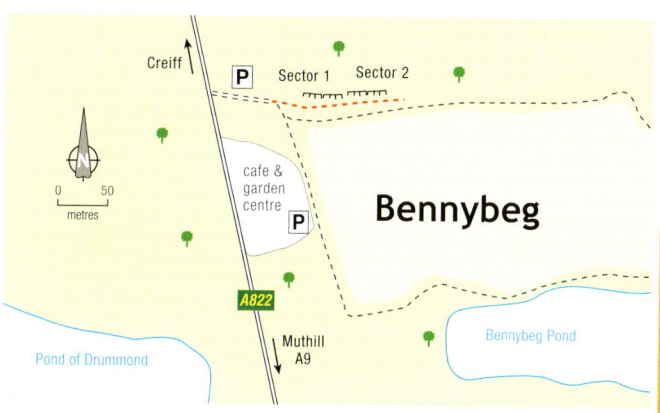

The Bennybeg area is managed by a charitable trust for the good of the community and the conservation of the wildlife and special site of scientific interest. The ponds to be found at the top end of the nature trail that Bennybeg Craig sits on are an SSSI for aquatic plant life. Perth and Kinross Ranger service help maintain the area as well as look after the nature trails, benches and path clearance. The landowner, Drummond Estates and local businesses recognise the value of the crag for climbers and are tolerant of climbers. Special attention should be paid to the cleanliness of the area and even litter dropped by the public should be removed so as the blame does not fall on climbers – that includes cigarette stubs.

AMENITIES
Crieff has all the amenities of a good sized town and is only 5mins by car from the crag. Muthill similarly has a few pubs, a post office, petrol station and tea room. Drummond Castle and stately grounds are amongst the most impressive in the country. The Red Grouse experience, Crieff Hydro, Drovers Experience and Stuart Crystal Factory offer good local options if it rains. At Bennybeg itself, there is currently the Ceramic Experience offering tea and coffee, a kids' play area and ceramic paint-

Bennybeg

ing for kids and adults, beside this is the Old Smithy and a comprehensive Garden Centre. Being located next to the crag, this makes Bennybeg an attractive venue for those with families and any non-climbers.

RECOMMENDED TASTY BITES
The Ceramic Experience, or Bennybeg Cafe can be walked to between routes – what more can you ask for! The Muthill Village Hotel provides Real Ale, also good bar and a la Carte meals.

TOP TIPS
Newcomers beware – the seeming abundance of huge holds belies their often rounded and frictionless properties. Combined with the steep nature of the crag, little in-cuts, cheeky side-pulls and bulges, Bennybeg can and will give a sneaky, but thoroughly good pump.

DIRECTIONS
Bennybeg lies a little to the north of the A9 dual carriageway between Stirling and Perth, from where it is easily accessed using the A822 Braco to Crieff road, which is joined by the A823 from Gleneagles a little further east on the A9. The crag is located roughly mid-way between Muthill and the outskirts of Crieff, about 1 mile from each. From Crieff, the A822 road is signposted to Stirling.

Bennybeg and the crag are marked on the OS 1:50000 map. Look for a road sign to Bennybeg, which leads into the car park for Bennybeg Smiddy, Bennybeg Plant Centre and Ceramic Experience Cafe. The crag is situated in the adjacent field and is visible from the road. The landowner has asked climbers to park on a prepared area off a small track which leaves the A822 150m towards Crieff from the main car park. This track is easily missed as it is gated and drivers are distracted by a road sign to Templemill, which is to the north of the track. The parking area lies directly in line with the end of the crag on the other side of the gate. If this is full, then ask in the cafe and it will be acceptable to park there.

APPROACH
Time: 30secs
The routes have been described in two sectors from left to right, starting with the first and lowest section reached as you approach from the car park.

SECTOR 1
The first clean rock is near a big tree at the cliff base.

① Route One   8m   3+ *
Unknown
A crack-line just left of the big tree.

② Route Two   8m   4+ *
Unknown
The wall right of the big tree and just left of a wide crack system.

③ Bill and Benny the Flower Pot Men   8m   3 **
Rory Howett 2003
The wide crack system, climbed on good polished holds.

4 Bennydorm   8m   5 *
Scott Muir 2003
Climb the next crack to the right and which runs out at half-height, then the short wall above.

5 Driven round the Benny'd   8m   5+ *
Scott Muir 2003
Superb wall climbing.

6 Benny and the Banshees   8m   4 *
Scott Muir 2003
An out of balance move right will either have you screaming or rocking to the top.

7 Benny Hill   8m   5+ *
Scott Muir 2003
Deceptive, but very enjoyable wall climbing

8 United Colours of Bennyton   8m   3 **
Rory Howett 2003
The major line of weakness, almost a chimney, right of Benny Hill is excellent.

9 Scorchio   8m   5 **
Unknown
A thin crack-line right of the chimney.

10 Route 10   8m   4 **
Unknown
A crack and wall, starting in brambles.

11 Benny Goodman – King of Swing   20m   5 **
Howard Tingle, Mark Powell 2011
Start up Route 10 to the obvious mid-height break. Move left and follow a rising diagonal line which is the higher of two breaks, clipping bolts on other routes, to finish up Bill and Benny the Flower Pot Men (or Bennydorm if damp). Nice climbing for a quiet day.

SECTOR 2

12 Benny's Groove   10m   2 *
Scott Muir 2004
An obvious groove just left of the arete which starts the largest section of wall. Scotland's easiest sport route. Good holds and a few plants.

13 Beggars Belief   10m   4 *
Unknown
Immediately right of the arete.

14 New Beginning   12m   5 *
Scott Muir 2003
A great introduction to the harder routes at Bennybeg. Start 20m right of the previous route at a small bush 3m up. Climb the first line of bolts up the main section of wall with sustained interest.

15 Beguile   12m   5 **
Scott Muir 2003
More good wall climbing immediately right leads to an exciting finish.

16 The Spanner   12m   5 *
Scott Muir 2003
Join Benny's Black Streak at its 3rd bolt and finish up this.

17 Benny's Black Streak   12m   5+ **
Scott Muir 2003
The evil black wall climbed direct is excellent and leads to a sprintable finish.

18 Lady Willoughby   12m   4 ***
Scott Muir 2003
An elegant wander up the wall and shallow groove to the left side of the tree overhanging the crag. It is probably the classic of the crag.

Bennybeg

19 Beg to Differ 12m 5+ *
Scott Muir 2003
Start as for Lady Willoughby to the 1st bolt. Gain the obvious hanging plaque from the left and crank to the top on good but spaced holds.

20 Beg'tastic 12m 5 *
Scott Muir 2003
Sustained wall climbing just before the grassy break in the crag.

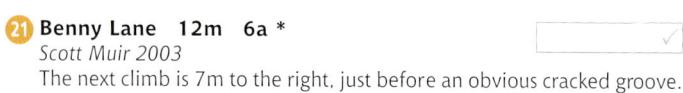

21 Benny Lane 12m 6a *
Scott Muir 2003
The next climb is 7m to the right, just before an obvious cracked groove.

22 Ally's in Wonderland 12m 3+ ***
A.Muir 2003
A magical trip up the cracked groove leads to a tree

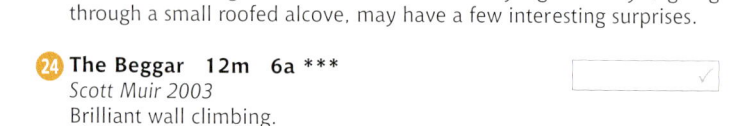

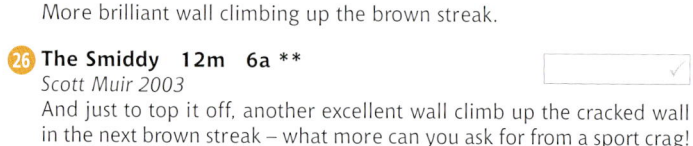

23 The Beg Issue 12m 4 *
Scott Muir 2003
Or not such a Big Issue! The wall immediately right of Ally's, going through a small roofed alcove, may have a few interesting surprises.

24 The Beggar 12m 6a ***
Scott Muir 2003
Brilliant wall climbing.

25 Beggar's Banquet 12m 6a **
Scott Muir 2003
More brilliant wall climbing up the brown streak.

26 The Smiddy 12m 6a **
Scott Muir 2003
And just to top it off, another excellent wall climb up the cracked wall in the next brown streak – what more can you ask for from a sport crag!

㉗ Begone 12m 5 *
Kieran Kelly 2003
The last route on the crag climbs up and left to the lower-off on The Smiddy.

㉘ Beg Pardon 30m 5+ ***
Kieran Kelly, Scott Muir 2003
A truly antisocial outing, but one of the best routes here! Climb to the 2nd bolt on New Beginning, step down and traverse right passing the 3rd bolt on Benny's Black Streak. Step up and clip the 3rd bolt on Lady Willoughby and continue past Beg'tastic to a lone bolt beneath the large overgrown crack in the middle of the sector. Keep traversing right, clipping the 4th bolt on Ally's in Wonderland, to the last bolt on The Smiddy. Climb straight up to the lower-off with relief.

Dunira - Comrie

(NN 7428 2466) L51 or L52; E368 Alt 300m South facing
Maps p75, p117 Diagram p118

Dunira is located to the west of Comrie and Crieff, above the main A85 from Perth to Lochearnhead and Glen Ogle. The climbing at Dunira is superb and the cliff is a suntrap making climbing possible all year round. The view down the Strathearn valley is to die for and makes the relatively long walk (for a sport crag) totally worthwhile. The crag has a good variety of low to mid grade routes giving varied climbing. Solitude is guaranteed and the big boulders below the crag may provide some good problems with a scrub.

Dunira is the obvious wedge shaped crag above the tree line, visible from the long overtaking straight as you leave Comrie heading west. The climbing has steep rock and big holds when needed in the lower grades and good quality, crimpy wall climbing on the harder routes. On these harder routes, 'thank god jugs' tend to arrive just when everything starts going wrong. The crag dries very quickly due to its exposed nature. Several of the easier routes were debolted in 2010 but the bolts were replaced in November 2012; there is therefore a mixture of older expansion bolts and new stainless steel glue-ins

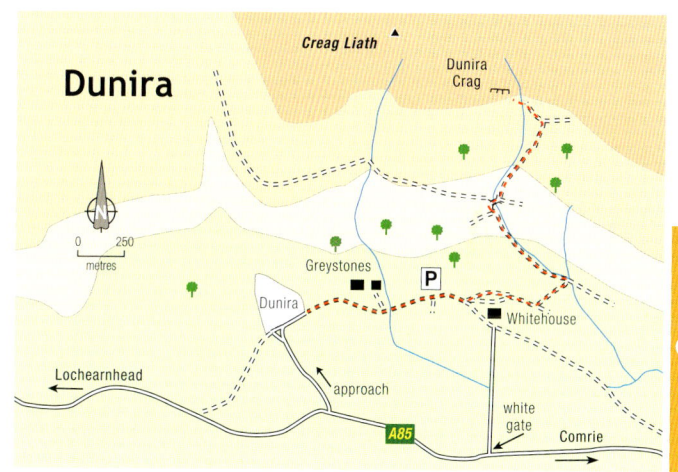

It is essential for good relations to be kept with the landowner so follow the directions to the crag closely please.

AMENITIES
Comrie offers all necessary amenities, banks, cafes, grocery stores, petrol. Also worthy of note is the Comrie Cancer Club Shop which often has some nice second hand climbing items, including the occasional hard to find books like Extreme Rock!

RECOMMENDED TASTY BITES
Tullybannocher Cafe just outside Comrie is the nearest pit stop going east, offering a good selection of homebakes and eats, in a friendly atmosphere. In the other direction, the Clachan Cottage Hotel at Lochearnhead is probably the best watering hole for climbers heading back west.

TOP TIPS
Bring a tartan rug, binoculars, Cheese and Wine. A change of base layer

Dunira

is recommended for the warm-up approach.

DIRECTIONS

Approaching from Perth along the A85 or north along the B827 to the A85, head through Comrie; as you pass the village exit signs hit your mileometer and continue for exactly 2.3 miles (3.7km). Take a single-track tarmac road on the right with a small sign for Dunira. If you go too far, you'll find a track cutting back right and with a similar sign (see approach from west). Follow the tarmac road for 500m to a crossroads, turn right and continue along the tarmac road running into a dirt track (often pot holes). After about 200m from the last house, there is a wide entrance on the left where a track cuts back left uphill; park here without obstructing the entrance; if in future the landowner objects, go back to the houses (NN 734 238). Please do not drive beyond this. The landowner has no objection to climbers, just cars.

From the west, pass through St Fillans and just after Kindrochet take a track with a small signpost for Dunira which leaves the A85 on the left. There is a gatehouse on the left of the turn off. Bump down this pot holed disaster or better and preferable, continue for 600m further along the A85 to the access as above.

APPROACH

Time: 30mins

Leave the car park heading east along the same road. The landowner has requested that anyone with a dog should please keep this on a lead until well on the hill. Just before reaching Whitehouse itself the road forks left along a public right of way (not signposted as such) and heads uphill to bypass Whitehouse. Continue for 600m, then come back left along the track as it doglegs back on itself above a field, now heading north-west and following a small stream. Take a right fork (NN 742 242) to cross the stream by a wooden bridge. A new track now forks left and follows the right (east) bank of the stream. From the end of this new track, cross the stream and pick up the vague path that contours to below the crag. Then fight your way steeply up through bracken (easy in the spring and winter, up to head height in mid-summer!) for about 150m to the crag, which is bigger than it looks from below.

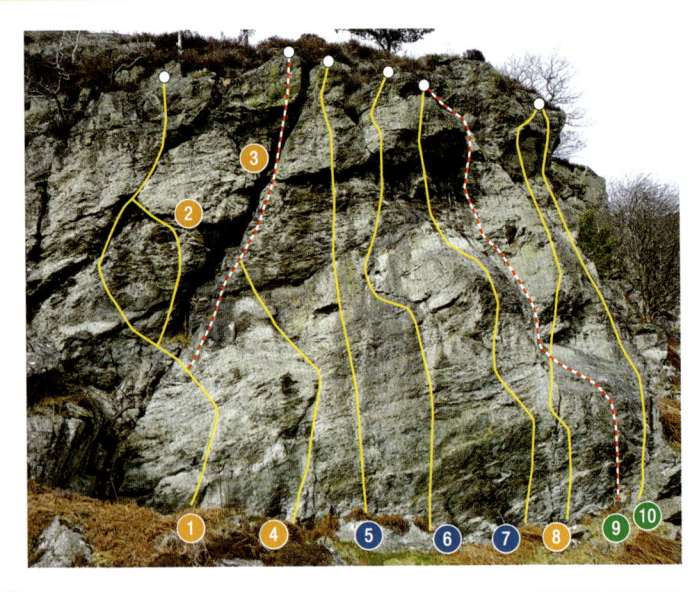

1 The Whitehouse   18m   6a+ *
Scott Muir 2004
From the flake at the left end of the crag, make a tricky move to gain its top, then traverse out left along a handrail. Stand up on the high ledge to gain the left to right break and then don't stop till the top. Good although escapable!

2 Whitewash   18m   6b
Scott Muir 2005
A short savage eliminate, tough for 6b! Start up Whitehouse, then climb directly on small sharp holds to gain the break as above.

3 Twenty Shilling Woodworm   18m   6a *
Scott Muir 2004

Start up Whitehouse, passing the rotten stump at the base of the steep diagonal break. Swing like a king up the break to the top before the rot sets in. Worth every penny!

4 George's Bush   18m   6a **
Scott Muir 2004
Climb the excellent flake-crack to join and finish up Twenty Shilling.

5 Glen Bolt'achan Big Gun's   18m   6c **
Scott Muir 2005
A great fingerlickin' direct son of a route that shoots its barrel right at the very end. Climb the wall direct on magic edges.

6 The Fort Dundurn Gurner   18m   6c+ **
Scott Muir 2004
The next line of bolts right should make most folk grimace. A sharp little number heading for the undercut flake at mid-height, then finishing through the small overlap and crack above. Wobble right to finish.

7 Dunira or Die   18m   7a **
Scott Muir 2004
Either you do this or you don't. No prisoners taken. The excellent steep and crimpy lower wall leads to a fortunate rest below the roof. From here, pull up and left, before (possibly!) returning right to a rocking finish. The route of all evil.

8 Dun Moan'in   18m   6b
Scott Muir 2005
The superb overhanging crack leads to a slab. Climb the next short wall on flakes and layaways to a final slap. Stroll up to the roof and pull through to an exciting finish. The very last moves can get a bit dirty but one bolt remains to protect this.

9 Tullybannocher Tea Room   18m   5 **
Scott Muir 2004
A truly delightful trip up the right to left line of weakness passing

Susan Jensen on the steep 6a holds; George's Bush, Dunira (photo Andy Nisbet)

Lower Lednock

through the roofs at the top with ease and in time for Tullybannocher's finest tea and cakes.

10 Strathearn Shangrila 18m 4+ **

Scott Muir 2004

On the edge of all things great! Climb the rounded arete direct to a tantalising finish and a view to savour.

Lower Lednock - Comrie

(NN 7614 2409)   Alt 200m   South-East facing   Map p75

Glen Lednock should be renamed the Glen of Tranquility! A rather grand name, but one fitting of a Glen that has an approach to a Munro, 3 star traditional routes, 3 star sport climbs and 3 star boulder problems on two contrasting types of rock, quite an achievement for a place that was once called 'a bit of a backwater' for climbers. Hopefully this beautiful area will now receive the attention it deserves.

The routes were bolted by Scott Muir in 2004, then the bolts removed in 2007 because of doubts as to whether the crag was suitable for sport climbing, particularly as some of the lines had previously been trad climbed. However it didn't become popular as a trad venue, so it was agreed the bolts could be replaced. This rebolting had not taken place when this guide went to print, so route descriptions are based on the original descriptions and should only be taken as a general guide. For further details see the SMC website <www.smc.org>.

The sport routes are on a buttress of excellent steep schist, mostly overlooked as development of traditional routes took place further up the Glen. Only on closer inspection does the crag reveal its true secrets in the way of roofs, grooves and amazing height. The very quick access and superb views across to Ben Chonzie make this a memorable place to climb especially with the blazing morning sun to warm and the natural water spring at the base of the crag to enjoy.

The cliff dries quickly after rain and provides climbs up to 28m. The routes are sustained with the cruxes often on the steepest rock, roofs and bulges giving a great feeling of exposure for a single pitch venue. Some bolts may be slightly hidden from below or in slightly strange places because the rock is at times too dubious for placing bolts in. The crag was extensively cleaned, but care should be taken, with the odd loose hold still possible. The climbing is particularly good for the grades!

AMENITIES

Comrie offers all necessary amenities, banks, cafes, grocery stores and petrol.

RECOMMENDED TASTY BITES

Tullybannocher tea room just outside Comrie is the nearest pit stop going east, offering a good selection of eats and friendly atmosphere. In the other direction, the Clachan Inn at Lochearnhead is probably the best watering hole for climbers heading back west.

TOP TIPS

The sun leaves the crag in the early afternoon. Bring a 60m rope and plenty of draws.

DIRECTIONS

Take the A85 east from Lochearnhead or the A85 west from Perth to reach Comrie. It is also possible to take the B827 that turns of the A822 just after Braco to reach Comrie more directly from Stirling. From the centre of Comrie, continue along the A85 (signposted Crianlarich) past a right angle bend to the right, then at a subsequent right angle bend to the left, leave the A85 and go straight on. There is a small sign for Glen Lednock beside the Deil's Cauldron Restaurant. Follow this single track road uphill through bends and forest for 1.8 miles. The crag is unmissable as the first obvious and nearest piece of rock on the left. There is a single parking spot beneath the crag (NH 7626 2426), opposite a passing place and 50m before a track which cuts back left and has a green signpost for Kindrochet 'Maam Road'. If you reach this track, turn and go back as there is no parking or turning for a while. If the parking spot is full, go back towards Comrie for 300m where another car can be parked beside a footpath. It is possible that the gate to the track will stay open and cars could then be parked easily just behind it.

APPROACH

Time: 5mins
Cut up on to the Maam Road track and follow it for 50m just past a small stream. Go directly up to the crag, hopefully via a small path through the bracken.

🟢 **Zombie Nation   28m   5+ ***
Climb the arete at the left edge of the crag directly to a tree and tricky mantelshelf. Climb the wall above on the left.

🟢 **Clairvoyant   28m   5+ ***
Climb the tricky initial wall immediately to the right, then the crack above which gives access to a ramp running up left. Finish up Zombie Nation.

🟠 **Quidditch   25m   6a ***
This is really a more sustained and direct finish to Clairvoyant. Climb Clairvoyant to the ramp. Pull across the steep wall above and right, by way of a left to right handrail. This gains the groove and hanging slab left of The Deil.

🟠 **The Deil   25m   6b ***
Right again is a lower wall. Climb this to a shallow corner and undercut flake. At the top of this, attack the steep wall directly and head for a triangular shaped roof high up. Pull through this directly to the top. Excellent.

🟢 **The Road to Hell   30m   5 ***
A fantastic wander up the crag! Climb the open groove right of The Deil to a cracked block, which once climbed up and left, gives access to the obvious easy angled left-slanting ramp. Follow this to finish up Zombie Nation.

🟠 **Cauldron of Fire   25m   6a+ ***
The base of the wall now steepens. Climb the crimpy lower wall to broken ground. Head up and left to climb the airy left edge of the black wall by cracked blocks and cracks. Pull onto the hanging ramp above and break through the overhang on good holds. Climb the left edge of the large upper wall.

🟠 **Black Magic   25m   6b+ ***
Start up Cauldron to the broken ground. Climb bulging ground in the black wall just to the right of the last route to gain the hanging ramp with difficulty. The seemingly impossible roof above is committing, exhilarating and surprisingly easy once you find the key! Climb the excellent wall above directly.

🟠 **Harry Snotter   25m   6b ***
Right of the smooth wall is a broken groove. Follow this to easy ground and the black wall. Climb the black wall to the right of Black Magic heading for the snotter of rock that hangs out of the roof at the right edge of the big upper wall. Use the snotter to gain the wall above before your arms blow and climb directly in a sensational position to the top.

🟠 **Witch Hazel   25m   6a ***
Right again, the broken wall gives access to the right end of the black wall. Pull through a cracked groove in this to climb the open chimney right of Harry Snotter. Pull back left onto the upper wall and climb this to the top.

🟠 **Resident Evil   30m   6a or 6b ****
If you've not yet had enough, this best seconded route should give you an exposed and devilish trip across the steepest ground on the crag. Start up Witch Hazel, grovel along the upper hanging ramp and finish up The Deil at 6b or Quidditch at 6a depending on how your arms or head now feel!

Newtyle Quarry - Dunkeld

(NO 045 413) L52 or L53; E379   Maps p75, p122
This unusual slate quarry is located just off the main A9 some 12 miles (20km) to the north of Perth where the towns of Birnam and Dunkeld

Newtyle Quarry

Newtyle Quarry Dunkeld

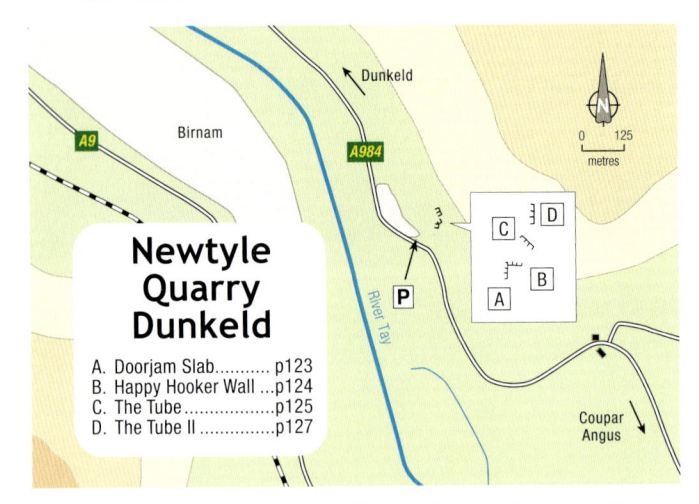

A. Doorjam Slab............ p123
B. Happy Hooker Wall....p124
C. The Tube..................p125
D. The Tube II p127

span the River Tay. It was originally a trad venue known as Birnam Quarry but the steep walls were ignored until sport and dry tooling routes were developed and the correct name of Newtyle Quarry is now used. The recent sport developments here have created a significant, if controversial renewal of interest in the quarry. Since the quarry is situated just outside Dunkeld, a visit to the quarry can therefore be combined with the Dunkeld crags. The routes do tend to seep in winter, or prolonged wet periods, although this is irrelevant for the dry tooling routes. However, once dry, the rock climb Hurlyburly remains dry in all weathers. Midges are rarely a problem.

The trad, sport and tooling routes co-exist nicely and represent one of the most diverse cragging experiences at a single crag anywhere! However, this has only been possible with careful development and respect for the existing climbs in the quarry. It is strongly urged that no dry tooling or bolting should take place on existing trad or sport routes and new routes should be equipped following thorough consultation with local activists.

DRY TOOLING ROUTES

Tooling at Newtyle is a great experience which many have enjoyed since the routes were established in 2003. The developments were broadly accepted providing existing lines were not damaged and the routes give excellent climbing on previously ignored areas of rock which are generally too loose for worthwhile rock climbing. They have been given 'D' grades, reflecting an an ascent using modern ice tools and crampons on dry rock with no expectation of ice forming at any time (although you never know...). On the routes in The Tube, heel-spurs are helpful to make the best of any rests, although these are frowned upon on the continent these days. The routes are climbable all year round and in all-weather conditions.

While this is sport climbing, care should be taken to avoid the obvious dangers of climbing at your limit wearing lots of spikes. Leaders and belayers need helmets; the rock is loose and axes are frequently dropped. It is acceptable to have the first or sometimes second bolt pre-clipped before a lead. Be careful clipping as falls are very sudden, often head-first, and the ground isn't too far away! Many of the routes have drilled hooks. Do not alter these or add more. Clean technique is important to avoid damaging the small hooks (not to mention body parts!). If hooks become damaged then let one of the first ascentionists know at <www.scottishclimbs.com>.

AMENITIES

There is a Tiso outdoor shop at the roundabout to the north of Perth. The quaint Perthshire town (there's a cathedral, so city is perhaps more appropriate) of Dunkeld offers all the usual amenities – grocery stores, cash machine (in the village square), cafe, pubs, chippy, hotels, B&Bs. The adjoining village of Birnam has a petrol station. In Dunkeld, the Taybank (the name tells you where it is) 'Scotland's musical meeting place' is a favoured apres climb haunt.

RECOMMENDED TASTY BITES

The Birnam Post Office tearoom (1km from Dunkeld village) is a must for connoisseurs of home baking. Order the platter of homemade cakes or scones, pot of tea (made with real tea leaves) and homemade lemon curd or jam – then try not to eat the whole platter or you'll never get up those climbs! Palmerston's cafe in Dunkeld is also recommended, as is the Scottish deli, Menzies of Dunkeld who do great sandwiches and ice cream.

TOP TIPS
Don't knock the dry tooling routes until you've tried them! DT is an excellent climbing experience which has gained an enthusiastic following. There's a lot more to it than just yarding.

DIRECTIONS
Turn off the A9 at Dunkeld. If heading north (from Perth), and just after the second stretch of dual carriageway, don't take the Dunkeld, Birnam signed loop road unless going to the Birnam Post Office tearoom. Instead, take the next road off right, signed to Coupar Angus and Blairgowrie; this goes through Dunkeld. If heading south, this same turn-off is signed to Dunkeld. Continue past the Birnam road (despite the old name for the crag) and cross the bridge over the River Tay, then turn immediately right to follow the A894 Coupar Angus road down the side of the river. After 1.3 miles (2km), on emerging from the trees, the small Dean's Park housing estate is located on the left with its entrance just beyond. This is a wide tarmac entrance, just round a bend, but since the Dean's Park sign faces slightly away it's easy to miss. If you go round a big left bend to where the ground on the left flattens out, then you have gone too far. Parking is a bit of a problem at the time of writing. One or two cars can be squeezed onto the verge to the right (south) of the Dean's Park entrance by the old gate at the quarry entrance. The grass verge on the other side of the entrance to Dean's Park is another option. Please do not park on the road to the houses.

APPROACH
Time: 1min 30secs
Pass 5m to the right of an old gate right of the entrance to Dean's Park and follow a path up right under the slate slope to the first area, Doorjam Slab.

DOORJAM SLAB

(NO 0454 4120)   Alt 100m   West facing
This is the rock seen on the left when the path levels off. It is characterised by a forked lightning finger crack on the left and a low roof on the right. Routes are described from left to right starting with the slabby left arete.

1 Give Me Sunshine   12m   6c+ *
Ian Taylor 2001
This pleasant slab climb follows a line of bolts just right of a big arete. An excellent exercise in high rockovers. Unfortunately the route gets dirty and needs a serious re-clean.

To the right is the thin crack of **Spandau Ballet** (E2 5b). Right again is the low roof.

Newtyle Quarry

② Pulliscious   10m   D5+   *
Scott Muir 2003
This route starts on the left of the roof and climbs rightwards to join and finish up Roofiliscious. A powerful lock near the start adds an extra punch to its parent route.

③ Roofiliscious   10m   D5+   *
Scott Muir 2003
This climbs directly over the roof to gain the steep wall above.

④ Grooviliscious   10m   D4   **
Scott Muir 2003
A pleasant route taking the slabby groove right of the roof with thin moves. A great introduction to dry tooling, without the need for big arms!

⑤ Bonzai   10m   D4   *
Fiona Murray 2003
A line of red bolts lead up the slab right of the groove to join Grooviliscious just below the lower-off.

HAPPY HOOKER WALL

Alt 110m   North facing
This is the overhanging wall which runs up the slope round to the left of Doorjam Slab. Routes are described from left (top) to right. It can be very difficult to spot the hooks on an on-sight ascent; an abseil inspection to place the draws and spot hooks is recommended before a flash attempt.

⑥ A Mind of Metal   15m   D7+   *
Paul Diffley 2003
This follows the left border of the wall. Start 1m right of the corner and climb the crack until it is possible to break out onto the wall and climb straight up a white strip passing several bolts to a chain.

Happy Hooker Wall

⑦ Insane in the Membrane   10m   D9   *
Dave MacLeod 2003
The hair-line crack gives thin climbing on marginal hooks in its central section, with easier climbing on curious red pockets leading to tricky finishing move using a lunge or pinch move to gain the ledge. Lower off from the bolt at the ledge.

⑧ Happy Hooker   10m   D7   **
David Brown 2003
Starting at a flake, this follows the blue bolts up the widest of the parallel cracks. Big moves between positive hooks.

⑨ Va Va Voom   10m   D8   ***
Scott Muir 2003
This superb pumpy line follows the right-hand crack before breaking onto

the steep headwall above. Technical moves low down and a sting in the tail.

⑩ The Sting   10m   D8 **
Michael Tweedley 2003
The groove in the arete just to the right. Technical and blind climbing leads to a tricky top section common with Va Va Voom. Pre-place a sling or a long draw for the bold third clip.

THE TUBE

(NO 0458 4129)   Alt 120m   South-West facing (ish!)

This unusual cave reaching into the earth is home to some of Scotland's most unusual climbs! Hurlyburly was entirely manufactured with drilled slots to create a superb series of moves. The other two lines were the first of their kind in Scotland to be climbed in dry tooling style in summer. The short hanging left arete of the cave entrance is taken by **Gone in 60 Seconds** (E7 6c).

APPROACH

From Happy Hooker Wall, head up left on a small path, briefly down, then up to the mouth of the cave (about 100m total).

⑪ Hurlyburly   18m   8b ***
Dave MacLeod 2003
The left-hand bolt-line. Start at the highest point it is possible to reach the rock (further bolts extend down into the dusty depths). The climbing is very sustained and powerful but with no desperate cruxes, the smooth manufactured pockets giving great moves.

⑫ Good Training for Something   18m   D12- **
Will Gadd 2007
The central, often wet crack-line is very sustained until an unlikely and cramped rest in a niche allows some respite before pulling into Too Fast Too Furious to finish.

Newtyle Quarry

Sam Clarke making it through the Hurlyburly (8b), Newtyle Quarry (photo Mike Mullin)

⑬ **The Torch Lite   20m   D11 ***
Malcolm Kent 2007
The very steep, long and blank area left of DTS Spirit, provides a sustained addition to the cave. Finish at a lower-off in the dark pod of Too Fast Too Furious. The line going all the way to the top will be mega!

⑭ **DTS Spirit   14m   D12 *****
Jeff Mercier 2011
The short and super powerful line to the left of Fast and Furious. Start from a sidepull just left of Fast and Furious and move leftwards on huge moves before joining that route for one move above the 7th bolt. Continue back leftwards to finish at the Fast and Furious lower-off.

⑮ **The Big Bad Wolf   35m   D12 *****
Greg Boswell 2012
Start up Fast and Furious (next route), swing left into the stein pull on DTS Spirit, then climb this for one big move. Swing left into the core hole on Torch Lite, then climb this to the point where it heads right at the top. Swing left into the crack of Good Training For Something and climb this swinging right into the pod of Too Fast Too Furious. Follow a line of bolts up and left through the headwall to the right of Hurlyburly, then rock up onto the slab and follow this up and right to a lower-off. Do not use any holds on Hurlyburly, although the route is far enough away that it will not be a problem.

⑯ **Fast and Furious   14m   D10 *****
Scott Muir 2003
The most popular route and a modern test-piece, located at the back of the cave. Follow the obvious scratches up drilled holes to the orange lower-off shared with DTS Spirit.

⑰ **Too Fast Too Furious   35m   D11+ ******
Scott Muir 2003
One of the world's hardest dry tooling routes at the time of the first ascent. Climb Fast and Furious and push on, all the way across the cave roof, taking in some wild and wacky climbing on the way. The crux is

probably the end of the hanging ramp, but there is hard climbing throughout.

⑱ Frankenstein   35m   D13 *
Greg Boswell 2012
Climb DTS Spirit to the last clip, move up and left from the stein-pull to follow the two big undercut flakes via more stein-pull moves to reach Torch Lite. Follow this route to where it moves right at the top and tackle the roof of the cave directly via huge moves. Follow the hairline crack up the triangular rock shield to finish as for Big Bad Wolf (no using the crack of Good Training For Something, left, or the resting pod of Too Fast Too Furious, right, at the top). Fight the pump and follow the hairline crack to reach the leftwards traverse of Big Bad Wolf and finish up this.

⑲ French Connection UK   35m   D12 *
Adam Russell 2012
Climb DTS Spirit into the top of Too Fast Too Furious

THE TUBE II

(NO 0458 4131)   Alt 140m   West facing
Some 30m in height directly uphill from The Tube is another buttress with a clean slabby face and slanting lip below on the right.

● El Ringo   16m   6a+ *
Fiona Murray 2004
The direct line taking the left side of the slab, giving pleasant climbing.

● Dance into the Groove   18m   6b+ **
Michael Tweedley 2004
Climb the central shallow groove until a few balancy moves lead rightwards to the chain.

● Like a Virgin   18m   6c *
Michael Tweedley 2004
Start as for Dance into the Groove. At the 2nd bolt, traverse right across a corner and climb the left side of the arete. Make a tricky move round the arete to gain better holds and the chain. Very balancy.

○ Open Project
The arete direct through its steep lower section.

○ Hammerhead and the Quarryman   15m   D9 **
Michael Tweedley, Paul Diffley 2004
The slanting lip and continuation to a chain round a tree.

Greg Boswell about as un-traditional as you can get on Frankenstein (D13), Newtyle Quarry (photo Mhairi Roberts)

Upper Cave Crag

Upper Cave Crag - Craig a' Barns - Dunkeld

(NO 0188 4383) L52 or L53 E379   Alt 220m   South-West facing   Maps p75, p128

Craig a' Barns is a densely afforested hill lying immediately to the north of the picturesque and historic town of Dunkeld, just off the A9 some 12 miles (20km) to the north of Perth. It is a craggy hillside that contains a number of cliffs which have long been a popular traditional climbing venue. Upper Cave Crag lies deep in the woods towards the right side of the hill. The lovely Perthshire countryside which surrounds Dunkeld is at its most beautiful during the autumn and this together with the temperature, makes it a particularly good time for climbing here. The wooded slopes of Craig a' Barns are criss-crossed by pathways that date back to 1773 and it is a popular and peaceful environment much enjoyed by locals and tourists alike, as well as outdoor enthusiast such as cyclists, walkers and climbers.

Cave Pass is the valley in the middle of the Craig a' Barns hillside and to the right of this the wooded slopes contain two surprisingly big and compact buttresses of mica schist. These are the Upper and Lower Cave Crags, the upper of which can be seen poking out above the trees whilst the lower is practically hidden below. At the foot of Lower Cave Crag is Lady Charlotte's Cave, a folly which was constructed by the 3rd Duke of Atholl in 1774 for his wife Lady Charlotte Murray and the feature that has given rise to the crag's name (as well as the classic trad E5 on Upper Cave). This cave provides a good, if somewhat drafty, shelter complete with fresh running water, fireplace and chimney!

Lower Cave Crag has in the past featured two short, yet worthwhile sport climbs but the bolts were chopped and the climbs have remained that way ever since. There are some great trad climbs here and this is one venue where many people do bring a rack and combine both trad and sport.

As with many Perthshire venues, Dunkeld is blessed with a dry climate and while the rest of the country is being swept by bad weather, the Cave Crags are often basking in the sunshine. The impressive wall of Upper Cave Crag remains dry for much of the year and its overhanging nature provides shelter during periods of rain or light showers.

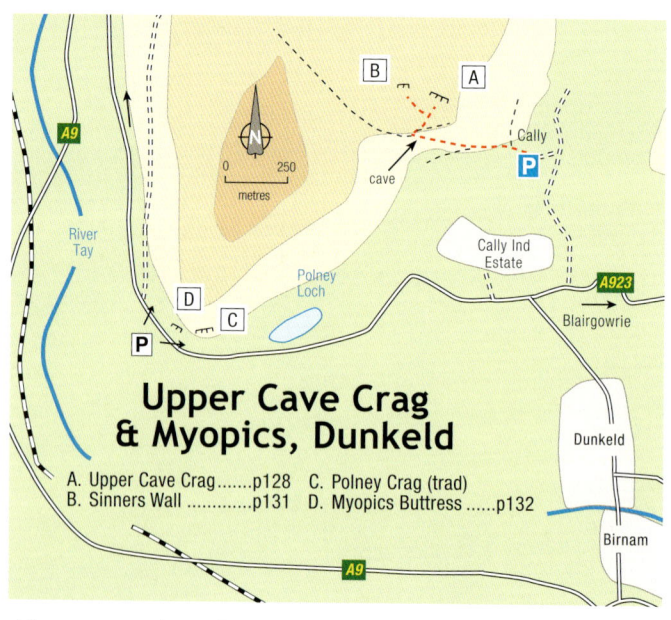

Upper Cave Crag & Myopics, Dunkeld

A. Upper Cave Crag.......p128   C. Polney Crag (trad)
B. Sinners Wall ....p131   D. Myopics Buttress p132

After more prolonged periods of wet weather however, the lower sections begin to weep, rendering the starts near impossible for mere mortals!

AMENITIES
As for Newtyle Quarry.

RECOMMENDED TASTY BITES
As for Newtyle Quarry.

TOP TIPS
There is some good bouldering here. Classics are traversing the foot of

Upper Cave Crag

the crag and the start to Morbidezza, the rib at left end of the Sport Wall. The overhanging wall starting next to the cave approximately 20m further right from the Sport Wall provides a gentle warm-up.

Although it's traditional to boulder out the starts at least once, a clipstick or a bouldering mat can be useful as there is a hard move before the high first bolt of both lines.

DIRECTIONS

Turn off the A9 at Dunkeld. If heading north (from Perth), and just after the second stretch of dual carriageway, don't take the Dunkeld, Birnam signed loop road unless going to the Birnam Post Office tearoom. Instead, take the next road off right, signed to Coupar Angus and Blairgowrie; this goes through Dunkeld. If heading south, this same turn-off is signed to Dunkeld. Cross the fine Thomas Telford bridge over the River Tay and drive all the way through Dunkeld towards the hillside beyond, then take the first road off to the right, signposted Blairgowrie (A923).

After 150m, take the second turn on the left, the first being for Cally Industrial Estate. This second turn is a rough estate track which has a small sign for the Atholl Estates Cally Car Park 0.5km. Follow this track into the forest then turn left to reach this large car park (NO 024 437).

APPROACH

Time: 15mins

From the notice board, follow a path uphill and which bends left to split after 40m. Take the left and traversing path. After 250m slightly rising is a junction where the path splits; keep to the right on a small yet well worn path. After 230m is a fallen yew tree which has to be crossed (Lower Cave Crag sits above) and 50m beyond this, after crossing a stream (occasionally dry), the path splits. Cut back on the rough right fork to reach the stream where it issues from Lady Charlotte's Cave; Lower Cave Crag now lies ahead.

For Upper Cave, don't cross the stream here but go steeply uphill on a slight path, then break off right and cross the stream just above large boulders. A small path now leads steeply up the slope with the crag soon becoming visible on the right.

Stirlingshire to Perthshire

Upper Cave Crag

Pete Roy enjoying the feel of Silk Teddy (7c), Upper Cave Crag (photo Fraser Harle)

Upper Cave Crag is split into two halves. The left-hand half contains the Sport Wall which is situated towards the right-hand side of a long gently overhanging wall of quality rock, in parts almost limestone-like in appearance. All the routes, variants and combinations rank with the best in the country and come highly recommended. Stamina is the name of the game here. The routes were rebolted in 2010 with stainless steel bolts. Sinners Wall is a small buttress offering a cluster of short routes between 6b and 7a and is located a short distance up the slope to the left of the main crag.

SPORT WALL

There are two starting lines of bolts which lead to various interconnected routes above. The obvious feature is a thin diagonal crack running up right to left in the wall's upper half. Many variations and eliminates are possible for those who have the established lines wired.

1 Marlina   17m   7c **
Dave Cuthbertson 1986
The left-hand line of ring bolts trending left then right past a handrail to the 5th bolt at the bottom of the crack. Climb the crack to where it fades and make a hard move up and left to a lower-off chain. Sustained climbing with the redpoint crux at the top.

Marlina Extension (Rab Anderson) has a bolt up and right of the lower-off which enables the climb to be extended to the Silk Purse lower-off. This is easier than the climbing below but a bit more control has to be exercised to continue! A more sustained alternative (7c) is to climb Marlina to its last but one move and instead of going left to the belay, head up the finish of the Silk Purse.

2 Ultima Necat   16m   7b+ **
Mark McGowan 1987
Another quality route which should gain in popularity since its rebolting. Start as for Marlina and climb to the 3rd bolt, then where that route trends right, go up and left with difficulty to gain spaced but better holds leading past some bolts to the Marlina lower-off.

Upper Cave Crag

3 Hamish Teddy's Excellent Adventure 20m 7b+ **
Duncan McCallum, Johnny May, Rab Anderson 1992
Justifiably the most climbed route of this grade in Scotland and affectionately known as Hamish Ted's. Climb Marlina to its 5th bolt at the start of the crack before continuing up and right to a stopping place below the hanging arete. Climb this with a blind move and continue in a great position on the edge of the prow to a lower-off below the capping overhang.

4 The Silk Purse 20m 7c+ **
Graeme Livingston 1987
This climbs the right-hand line of ring bolts to finish up the flying groove above the top of the crack on Marlina. A sustained and fingery lower section culminates in a hard move left past the 4th bolt, then left past a 5th bolt to join Marlina at the handrail. Gain the crack and climb it till it fades then step right into the pumpy final grove, climbed initially on sloping sidepulls and poor footholds; the redpoint crux! Gain the middle of the three lower-offs.

5 Silk Teddy 18m 7c *
Dave Cuthbertson, Rab Anderson 1990s
As the name implies this is a combination of Silk Purse and Hamish Ted's. Climb Silk Purse to its 4th bolt then continue above through a shallow niche past 2 bolts to gain the upper section of Hamish Ted's. The original line followed Silk Purse to its junction with Marlina but with the addition of the bolts in the niche it is now climbed direct, giving the straightest line on the wall. The original line is best for those building towards a Silk Purse redpoint.

SINNERS WALL

(NO 0186 4386)   South-West facing
This wall is located up the slope, 50m or so to the left end of Upper Cave Crag, from where it is visible. A clip-stick is useful.

**1 Sinners Paradise 15m 7a *
Rab Anderson 2003
The leftmost line. Start up easy ground then step left and make a difficult move to gain the crack over the bulge. Easier (but no less steep!) climbing leads to the top.

**2 Six Fours-les Plages 15m 6b
George Ridge, Chris Ridge 1995
Start up the crack then break out left and over the bulge on good holds. Steeper than it looks!

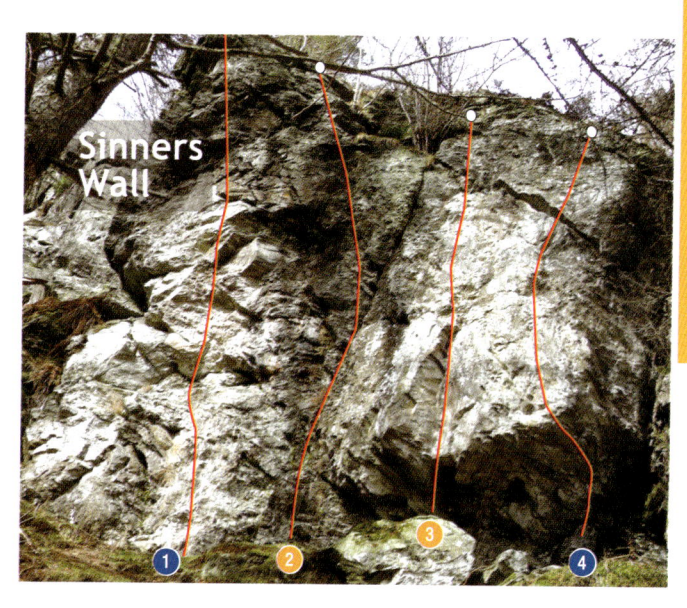

Stirlingshire to Perthshire

Myopics Buttress

3 Fear of the Dark   10m   6b *
Janet Horrocks, George Ridge 1995
An undercut bouldery start leads to better holds and easier moves leading to the top.

4 Father Figure   10m   6c *
George Ridge, Chris Ridge 1995
The right-hand line. Another bouldery start leads to interesting but easier climbing.

Myopics Buttress - Dunkeld

**(NO 0097 4310)   L52 or L53 E379   Alt 150m   South-West facing
Maps p75, p128**

This short but viciously overhanging crag lurks in the woods at the left end of the Craig a' Barns hillside to the west of Dunkeld. It sits just above the old A9 where it passes around the left side of the popular trad cliff of Polney and it provides a suitable playground for muscle bound thugs. Though it can sometimes be surprisingly breezy, the sheltered and overhanging nature of the crag permits climbing in the rain. A small cave in the rocks about 200m to the north provides a good traditional doss.

AMENITIES
As for Newtyle Quarry.

RECOMMENDED TASTY BITES
As for Newtyle Quarry.

TOP TIPS
Go equipped with strong arms!

DIRECTIONS
Turn off the A9 at Dunkeld. If heading north (from Perth), and just after the second stretch of dual carriageway, don't take the Dunkeld, Birnam signed loop road unless going to the Birnam Post Office tearoom. Instead, take the next road off right, signed to Coupar Angus and Blairgowrie; this goes through Dunkeld. If heading south, this same turn-off is signed to Dunkeld. Drive all the way through Dunkeld. On meeting the right turn for Blairgowrie (A923) and Upper Cave Crag, continue on, signed Pitlochry, Inverness (A9). The crag is 0.9 miles (1.4km) from this turning. After passing a small lochan on the right side of the road, look out for Polney crag up on the right and on a long right-hand bend in the road just after the crag, bump up the kerb to park on a grassy verge on the right. The closer you are to a track off right and a gate signposted Keep Clear, the more directly under the crag you are. It might be better to turn the car here before parking. One car can be squeezed in close to the gate but don't obstruct the entrance to the track. Please note that this parking spot is on a bend and it's perhaps worth using a passenger to guide you out.

Es Tressider spends time on the Chopping Block (7b), Myopics Buttress, Dunkeld (photo Adrian Crofton)

Myopics Buttress

APPROACH
Time: 1min
Head directly uphill to the crag, which is visible from the road.

1 Phantom   15m   7a+
Unknown 2000s
This is the leftmost line, to the right of the crack taken by the trad climb **Myopic's Corner Direct** (E2 5c). Poorer rock. Take the left end of the roof system, then go steeply through the bulge to finish rightwards.

2 The Chopping Block   20m   7b *
Neil Shepherd 1996
Climbs directly up to and over the lower left-hand break through the bulges in the front face of the buttress; impressive.

3 The Vibes   20m   7c **
Ian Cropley 1991
Climb the right-hand rib onto the wall, then trend rightwards and up with difficulty before moving leftwards through the break in the roof to a blind exit.

4 Granola Head   20m   7c *
Duncan McCallum 1990
The 1st bolt has been flattened; stick-clip the 2nd. Climb the steep initial wall with a powerful move to gain the tapering groove above. Take five before tackling the short steep headwall above.

5 Vibe Heads   20m   7b+ ***
Unknown
This excellent combination starts up The Vibes, then crosses over and finishes up Granola Head.

6 Unnamed   15m   7a
George Ridge 1996
Start from a higher platform on the right and climb a slight rib, short and nippy.

Weem Crags - Aberfeldy
(NN 843 501) L52 E386   Maps p75, p134

These popular crags are located in the Tay Valley to the north of Dunkeld, amidst beautiful, ancient woodland overlooking the villages of Weem and Aberfeldy. A collection of half a dozen crags of good quality mica schist offer a surprising variety of climbing, each with its own distinctive character.

Weem Rock, Aerial and Secret Garden Crags are ideal venues for the lower to middling grade climber, with over thirty well bolted routes from 5+ to 6c+. Those looking for something a little more testing should visit The Sidewall at Weem Rock where overhanging climbs on relatively big holds can be found – something of a rarity in Scottish climbing. By contrast the short crimp nasties at Hanging Rock and Easter

Weem Crags

Weem Crags

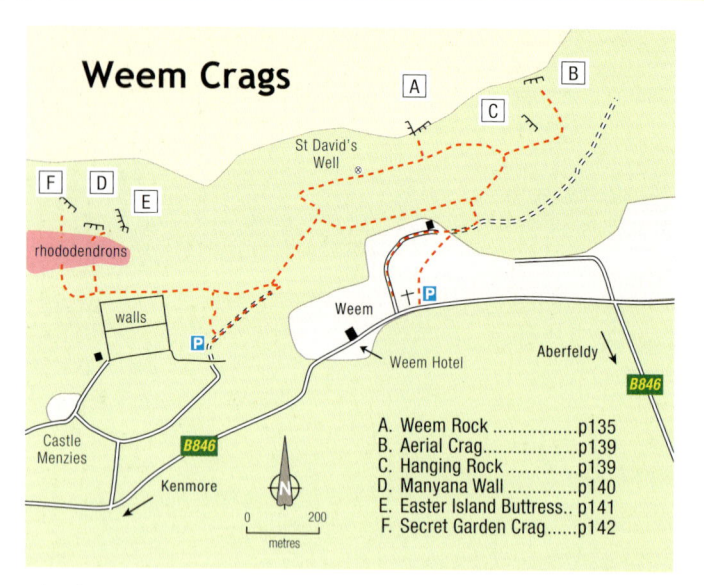

A. Weem Rock p135
B. Aerial Crag p139
C. Hanging Rock p139
D. Manyana Wall p140
E. Easter Island Buttress .. p141
F. Secret Garden Crag p142

Island Buttress are sure to test your finger strength.

Given the area's stable climate, sunny aspect and the quick drying nature of the rock, most of the walls here do dry quickly, although not quick enough to be described as a winter venue. The Main Wall at Weem Rock dries much slower due to seepage. It should be noted however, that while the canopy of trees surrounding the crags provide shelter from bad weather, equally it can make for hot and humid conditions during the summer months. Unusually midges are not a big problem at Weem, however the place is instead plagued with an abundance of ticks!

Of final note, the woods are alive with flora and fauna so please respect your surroundings, stick to the paths, and keep an eye out for the intriguing wood sculptures hiding in the woods. The woods are a designated (SSSI) for a rare flower, the Sticky Catchfly, *Lychnis viscaria*; a delicate flower with bright rosy red petals, which is only known to exist at 12 sites in Scotland and Wales. It can be found on the some of the vegetated parts of the crags and care should be taken not to damage any.

AMENITIES

Aberfeldy has everything a climber should need – hotels, pubs, traditional tearooms, cash points, bank, supermarket, petrol, Munros Outdoor Shop (sells climbing gear and chalk), a campsite and a bunkhouse <www.adventurers-escape.co.uk> in Weem itself. If that's not enough there is also the Aberfeldy whisky distillery, a working watermill and white-water rafting nearby.

RECOMMENDED TASTY BITES

The Pantry tearoom in Aberfeldy serves up a good pot of tea and fresh homemade baking. For evening grub the chippy in the square is recommended – particularly the haddock in breadcrumbs. The nearest watering hole is the Weem Hotel (in Weem) which has been refurbished and as well as the usual fare also offers snacks, lunches, real ale, teas and coffee.

TOP TIPS

For a tick free visit, make sure you don't leave clothes lying around and do a tick check at the end of the day! A rope bag is recommended for the dusty ground.

DIRECTIONS

Weem Crags are sited on the north side of the Tay Valley close to the village of Aberfeldy, some 30 miles (48km) north-west of Perth, and are easily accessed from the A9. Heading north or south on the A9, turn off at Ballinluig and follow the A827 west for 9 miles (15km) to Aberfeldy. Drive through the centre of the village and at the traffic lights look out for the B846 signposted to Weem; the Black Watch Inn is on the corner of the junction. This junction can be gained from the west via the A827 Loch Tay road, or from the south via the A822 & A826 Sma' Glen road. Follow the B846 over the humpback bridge across the River Tay and around the bend into the village of Weem.

For Weem Rock, Aerial Crag & Hanging Rock, park in a car park immediately before the church (the first building on the right in Weem) – NN 8440 4979. For Secret Garden Crag and Easter Island Buttress, go through Weem and turn right at a sign for Weem Forest Walk and Castle Menzies, then turn immediately right for the Forest Walk car park (NN 8399 4970). To switch areas, either walk for 10mins on the Forest Walk (see map and details below), or drive round.

WEEM ROCK

(NN 8443 5012)   Alt 200m   West and South facing

This is the largest of the Weem Crags and offers 23 routes from 5+ to 7b. It features two contrasting facets, an overhanging west facing sidewall and an off vertical south facing front face. The climbs on the Sidewall are steep and pumpy on generally good holds, while those on the frontal Main Face to the right are thin and technical and will certainly test your trust in footwork. Some of the climbs on this cliff are amongst the best of their type in the area.

APPROACH

Time: 15mins

From the Weem church car park, walk up a road on the other side of the church for 150m to reach a house named Tigh na Sgoill. Don't follow the road to a private house named Tressour Wood; instead turn right along a wide grassy path. Follow this for 60m, then turn left onto a small path which breaks up the hillside. Where it meets the main path after 40m, turn right and head uphill, around a big left turn hairpin bend at 200m and on for another 100m, up then slightly down. Ten metres before some steps up take a vague and unobvious path, especially when overgrown in spring/summer, which leads up the steep hillside over rocks, fallen trees and nettles to the base of the crag.

To go to the Secret Garden area from Weem Rock (perhaps because this is wet), regain the main path and turn right up the steps. Follow the main path mostly traversing and going past St. David's Well until the path descends. Go down, ignoring a left fork which goes back towards the car, until at a left hairpin not far above houses, there is a path right from the

Sadie Renwick on High Pitched Scweem (7b), Weem Rock (photo Cubby Images)

Weem Rock

point of the hairpin. This joins the normal approach and leads to the walled garden, 15mins plus 10mins to the crags.

The Sidewall

This dries more quickly than the Main Face and is not as affected by rain, however the slab beneath the wall can seep and something to keep the feet dry for the take-off might be useful. The climbs are described from bottom to top, right to left.

**1 The End of Silence   15m   7b **
Colin Miln 1997
A crimp fest up the lower wall quickly eases to give easier enjoyable climbing to the top.

Next is a bottomless corner-crack capped by a roof, the most prominent feature on the wall **The Last Temptation** (E2 5c).

**2 Last Gasp   15m   7a+ **
Gary Latter 1997
Follow The Screaming Weem to its 5th bolt, then traverse hard right to the steep arete and move up to the flake. Follow staple bolts up the arete, which eases higher up.

3 The Screaming Weem   18m   7b *
George Ridge 1997
The route left of the left arete of the bottomless corner is a pump fest! Superb climbing with a distinct crux sequence between the 2nd and 4th bolts, however, don't relax too much for gaining the upper headwall can prove tricky. The difficult direct start is commonly avoided by coming in from higher up on the left and then stepping right to clip the 2nd bolt.

4 High Pitched Scweem   15m   7a **
Neil Shepherd 1997
It's steep and it's pumpy! Gain a ledge on the slab by scrambling up left onto it, or once dry climb the slab and corner itself, bolt on the sidewall. Fingery moves lead to a crux gaining the upper wall, then a jug fest up

the headwall to gain a lower-off left of the arete. One of the best of its kind in Scotland.

5 One Pig One   15m   7b *
Neil Shepherd 1997
From the ledge in the corner move up into a hanging corner, then fight on using pockets and sidepulls followed by better holds to the top.

6 Every Last Drop   15m   7b
Rab Anderson 1997
Similar climbing to the right-hand routes but not as good with some dubious rock. Climb One Pig One to its 4th bolt, then pull up left to climb the furthest left line of bolts. The route is currently overgrown and the hangers have been removed.

Main Face
Diagrams p137, p138, p139

7 The Real Mackay   18m   6a+ *
Dougie McKay 1997
This climbs the slabby arete between the Sidewall and the Main Face. After a tricky start, pleasant climbing follows. Nearing the top the angle eases and although the climbing is easier, be prepared for a bit of a run-out and some loose rock.

8 The Long Good Friday   20m   6c+ **
Isla Watson 1997
Start 5m right of the arete and climb the long wall, crossing through a series of overlaps. Thin, balancy and continually interesting climbing.

9 Confession of Faith   20m   6c ***
Janet Horrocks 1997
An excellent sustained climb taking a direct line up the centre of this section of wall. Make thin moves to gain a very welcome sidepull under the larger overlap. Blind and tricky moves soon lead to easier ground. A good exercise in footwork with a technical crux; sustained.

Main Face, Left

10 Manpower   20m   6b *
Dave Pert 1997
A short, tricky and sometimes dirty slab is climbed to the gain the overlap and intermittent crack-line above. Sparsely bolted, with a high 1st bolt. The crux move feels a little intimidating with the last bolt at your feet. Varied and interesting climbing.

11 Boomhead   20m   6a+
Neil Shepherd, George Ridge 1997
The route has a contrived direct start over a bulge. This can be avoided by moving left to the arete, then back right. Higher up, turn a roof on its right, then move back left and go up a wall to the top. Watch out for loose rock and a tricky, poorly protected move to finish.

12 Staring at the Sun   18m   5+ *
George Ridge 1998
This climbs the edge overlooking the central groove and although a bit

Stirlingshire to Perthshire

Weem Rock

broken it is still worthwhile. The first bolt is very high; clip it from a good hold round to its left and take care. The initial overhang has good holds.

13 Soup Dragon   18m   6a *
Janet Horrocks, Isla Watson 1997
A fingery start is followed by varied climbing.

14 Scooby Snacks   18m   6a+ *
George Ridge, Dave Johnson 1997
Another crimpy start leads to easier moves. The angle kicks out near the top so make sure you have some strength left!

15 One Step Beyond   18m   6a+ *
Isla Watson, Colin Miln 1997

Climbs a crack and steepening wall above; the crux is saved for last! Shared lower-off with Scooby Snacks.

16 Down to the Last Heartbreak   18m   6a+ *
Isla Watson, Colin Miln 1997
Start as for the previous route, then step right after the 2nd bolt. A tricky move near the top.

17 The Trial of Brother Number 1   18m   6a *
Colin Miln, Isla Watson 1997
A dirty slab leads to more pleasant climbing and an interesting crux move to gain the lower-off!

18 Lapdancing   18m   6b *
Rab Anderson 1998
A dirty start leads to the arete, then climb up to and over the roof above. Be careful of loose rock at the top!

19 The Llama Parlour   15m   6c *
Janet Horrocks, George Ridge 1997
Climbs the thin, crimpy wall left of the steep corner. The difficulties aren't quite over when you get to the top of the wall; either go left over the roof, or move right to the lower-off on the next route.

20 The Protection Racket   12m   6a+ *
D.Johnson, George Ridge 1997
Good bridging up the corner is followed by a tricky move to gain the lower-off.

21 Lighten Up   12m   6a *
Rab & Chris Anderson 1999
Climb a broken flake 2m right of the corner and move back left, finishing leftwards to lower off .Climb a broken flake 2m right of the corner, then pass the bulge on its right and move back left, finishing leftwards to lower off. The route is quite tricky to strip on lower; it may be easier to second.

Main Face, Centre

Aerial Crag - Weem

Main Face, Right

22 Crowing at the Enemy   10m   6b *
Rab Anderson 1998
Start right of the flake and tackle the slight arete and wall above. Proves more awkward than it looks.

23 Bark Bacherache   10m   6b+
Rab & Chris Anderson 1999
The last climb on the crag; don't use the tree.

AERIAL CRAG

(NN 8460 5021)   South facing   Alt 300m   Map p134
This cliff is situated high on the hillside and visible from the car park, high on the right. Aerial receives plenty of sunshine with great views of the surrounding countryside. The crag characteristics are typical of the area with a projecting front face and steep sidewall. The only two sport routes climb the attractive front face, while a steep sidewall to the left contains a brace of good trad lines.

APPROACH
Time: 30mins
The approach is complicated and there is no real path to follow. The simplest way is to follow the approach to Weem Rock as far as the hairpin bend, then head uphill, diagonally right, in a north-easterly direction, aiming for a huge beech tree at 30m. Contour rightwards from here, soon passing a 3m high rock wall and later a cluster of pine trees on the left (100m from the beech tree). The crag lies directly uphill from here. Reach a rocky boulder slope leading to broken rocks. Turn these rocks on their left to gain a mossy lower wall below the crag, which is hidden from here. Continue on their left before traversing right to the wall, which is just where the steep hillside begins to level off.

Kissing the Witch   10m   6b *
Janet Horrocks 1997
The line of bolts to the right of the arete, taking the bulge direct.

Static in the Air   10m   6c *
George Ridge 1997
Climb the left-slanting crack-line and fingery wall to the same lower-off. Keep out of the obvious crack at the start.

HANGING ROCK

(NN 8459 5012)   Alt 190m   South-West facing   Map p134
Hidden amidst moss covered boulders and enclosed by forest is the little crag of Hanging Rock. You may be forgiven for thinking you've stumbled into the enchanted forest of Narnia, but despite its similarity to the setting in that well known CS Lewis book, there are no unicorns, centaurs or fauns...and better still no wicked White Witch! The crag

Stirlingshire to Perthshire

Hanging Rock - Weem

resembles a giant boulder and although the routes are generally very short, they are of a very fingery and bouldery nature.

APPROACH
Time: 15mins
Follow the approach for Aerial Crag as far as the huge beech tree at 30m. From here look up left for a group of huge beech trees and reach them after another 40m. Pass to the right of a small outcrop into pines. Go through the pines rightwards and the crag is seen beyond some large boulders, 5mins from the hairpin.

1 Remanufacture   10m   7c+ **
John Gaskins 2003
The left-hand line on the wall has a very bouldery crux on small crimps leading to a slightly easier finish.

2 Crushed by the Wheels of Industry   10m   7a+ *
George Ridge 1997
Start just to the right of the crack. Hard moves lead to the thinner crack; fingery.

3 The Chemical Generation   10m   7b **
Colin Miln 1997
Climb the pumpy layback flake to join the crack, then finish direct via some thin moves.

4 Alien Artefact   10m   7b *
Neil Shepherd 1997
Very thin and bouldery climbing with long reaches to link pockets and edges.

5 The Glass Ceiling   10m   6c
George Ridge 1997
Climb the steep, wide crack on the right side of the wall, then traverse left to a large pocket on Alien Artefact and finish up that route.

MANYANA WALL
(NN 8379 4988)   Alt 180m   South facing   Map p134
The smallest of three crags in the western group but the easiest to find in what can be a jungle of rhododendrons. It is described first as it is useful in finding the others. This is a more recently developed crag which gives a less crimpy climbing style than its neighbours.

APPROACH
Time: 10mins
From the Forest Walk car park, don't take the main path right but follow a rougher zigzag path uphill through the forest to a junction. Take the left fork for 100m to the start of the high stone wall of the Menzies Castle walled garden. The right fork leads to Weem Rock via St David's Well. Now follow the wall to its far end.

The three crags in this area are above here, just beyond a rhododendron thicket. This grows quickly but is often cut back, so the best line

Easter Island Buttress - Weem

may change. From the west end of the wall, head directly uphill for 3mins. When the rhododendrons have been cleared, the crag is visible from the wall.

🟠 **Tomorrow Never Comes   12m   6b ***
Neil Shepherd 2007
The left arete of the buttress; nice climbing on excellent rock.

🟠 **Sometime Soon   12m   6a ***
Derek Armstrong 2007
The central line; another good route.

🟢 **Don't Do Today what you can do Tomorrow   11m   5+**
Neil Shepherd 2007
The furthest right line. Not as good as the other two but routes at this grade are not exactly thick on the ground here!

EASTER ISLAND BUTTRESS

(NN 8382 4990)   Alt 180m   West-South-West facing   Map p134

This small buttress offers a handful of short pumpy and crimpy climbs, similar in style to those on Hanging Rock but not as steep. The base of the crag has become a little overgrown but regardless, several of the climbs come highly recommended. For those looking for quality fingery routes it is certainly worth a visit. The crag gets the sun for much of the day.

APPROACH
Time: 10mins

In early spring and late autumn the crag can be seen from the walled garden, however in summer it is completely obscured by the woodland canopy. Head to Manyana Wall and just below it, traverse right for 30m. If the Manyana Wall route is overgrown, it is easier to head direct from the start of the wall, following a small path which rises uphill to the crag.

Easter Island Buttress

Stirlingshire to Perthshire

Easter Island Buttress - Weem

Neil Morrison face to face with President Shhean Connery (7a), Easter Island Buttress, Weem (photo Rab Anderson)

The routes are described from right to left.

1 Right in the Face   10m   6b *
Rab Anderson 1997
Climb the right arete to The Republic of Scotland lower-off.

2 The Republic of Scotland   10m   7a+ **
Colin Miln 1997
Starting left of the arete, good holds soon give way to crimps and a final hard move just below the belay. A good crimpfest!

3 President Shhean Connery   8m   7a *
Colin Miln 1997
Crimp your way directly up the wall to The Republic of Scotland lower-off.

4 Left on the Shelf   12m   6c *
Rab Anderson 1997
Climb left-slanting cracks to the shelf, then go over the small roof to finish up the slabby wall above.

5 Motion Sickness   12m   6c+
Unknown
Climb the leftmost line, then break up left around the roof and climb the top wall on its steep side. Shared lower-off with the previous route.

SECRET GARDEN CRAG

(NN 8374 4993)   Alt 200m   South-West facing   Map p134

Secret Garden differs from the other crags at Weem, being closer to limestone in character. The crag is worth a visit in its own right and offers a variety of interesting routes for the intermediate climber. Two large fir trees overlook the crag and these provide some shelter and protection from the rain. This, together with its quick drying nature, make it an ideal crag to visit if the weather is unsettled. The cliff catches the afternoon sun.

Secret Garden Crag - Weem

APPROACH
Time: 15mins
Approach as for Manyana Wall to the far end of the Menzies Castle walled garden. Continue through an ivy covered tree-arch and on for some 20m before heading directly uphill (sometimes a small path). Keep left of Manyana Wall (if visible) and find a break in the rhododendrons which leads (at the time of writing) under a fallen tree and just left of a huge flat-topped rock to slightly more open ground from where the crag is seen up left. If you are near a stream which flows through the rhododendrons, you are some 30m too far left. The stream runs up to Stream Wall but is not a good approach.

1 100 Ways to be a Good Girl   10m   6b+
Janet Horrocks 1997
Climb the limestone-like grey streak at the left end. Slower to dry.

2 Batweeman   10m   6b+ **
Isla Watson 1997
A nice line up the corner and technical wall above. A distinct crux move near the top can be made easier by careful footwork!

3 Forbidden Fruit   15m   6c **
Isla Watson 1997
A good varied climb up the cracks and overlaps. Climb up on sloping holds past a small roof, then pass the left end of the midway overlap to gain a ledge and continue up the crimpy wall above.

4 The Missing Link   20m   6c+ **
Isla Watson 2000
A contrived link-up but good climbing. Climb the bottom half of Faithless over the roof, step left and climb the top half of Forbidden Fruit.

5 Faithless   15m   6c+ **
George Ridge 1997
Follow a diagonal seam to the roof, then pull through this to finish direct, or a little easier just to the right.

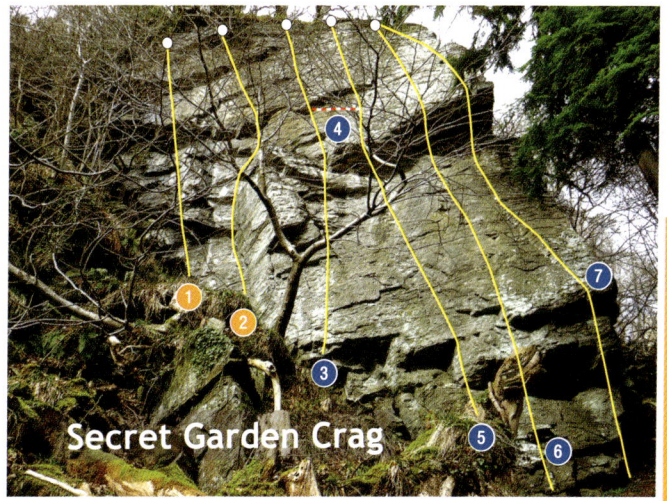

6 The Watchtower   15m   6c+ **
Colin Miln 1997
Climb the lower, thin slabby wall making a tricky move just beneath the roof. Pull steeply over the roof and finish up the wall above on small but good holds.

7 Caledonia Dreaming   15m   6c **
Neil Shepherd 1997
Follow the thin crack just left of the arete all the way with dynamic moves through the roof.

8 Don't Knock the Block   13m   6a+ *
Janet Horrocks 1998
The first line on the right-hand sidewall is a little green now. A tough, fingery start gives way to easier climbing up the edge to the ledge, finishing up the left headwall to top.

Stirlingshire to Perthshire

Caledonia Dreaming (6c), Secret Garden Crag, Weem. Climber Neil Morrison (photo Rab Anderson)

9 Brass Monkeys 8m 6a+ *
George Ridge 1997
A bouldery start is followed easier climbing up the wall.

STREAM WALL

This is located 30m to the left of Secret Garden Crag. Its left-hand end, as its name suggests, has a stream running over the top of the crag. On the right-hand side there is just one route.

● Justice 10m 7a *
Colin Miln 1997
Climb the steep wall to gain the hanging crack.

Rockdust Crag - Pitlochry

(NO 0307 6414)   L43 E387   Map p75
This crag, actually named Creag na Cuinneige, is set well back from the road on the open hillside overlooking Glen Brerachan, on the A924 between Pitlochry and Blairgowrie. It is a peaceful spot with an open outlook and great views. The rock is yet another variety of mica schist, generally vertical and undulating in nature, with a few bulges and undercut sections thrown in for good measure! There is a Lower Crag, then up and to its right is a higher Main Crag which is much the better of the two.

ENVIRONMENTAL CONSIDERATIONS

The tenant farmer, who runs the SEER (Sustainable Ecological Earth Regeneration) Centre, and the landlord are happy to tolerate low impact climbing on their land. If you have time to spare it may be politic to visit the Soil Remineralisation Demo gardens or buy some seasonal produce – or just say hello – after all the crag is named after the crushed rock they use to increase soil fertility!

AMENITIES

The nearby popular tourist town of Pitlochry has all amenities, such as pubs, B&Bs, hotels, camping, shops, filling station, supermarkets and

Rockdust Crag

Lower Crag

Main Crag

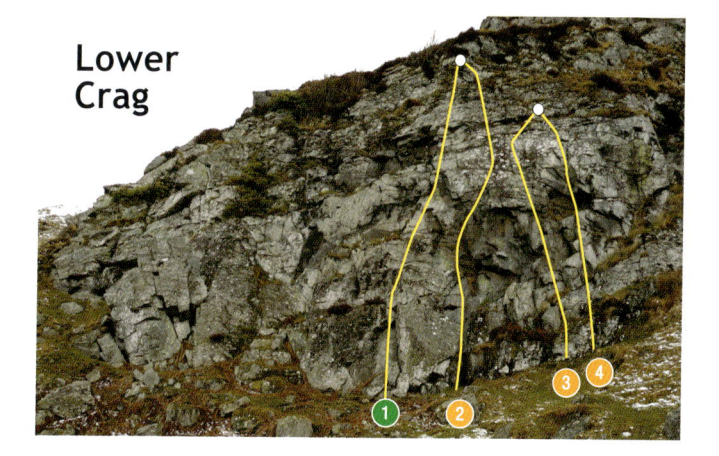

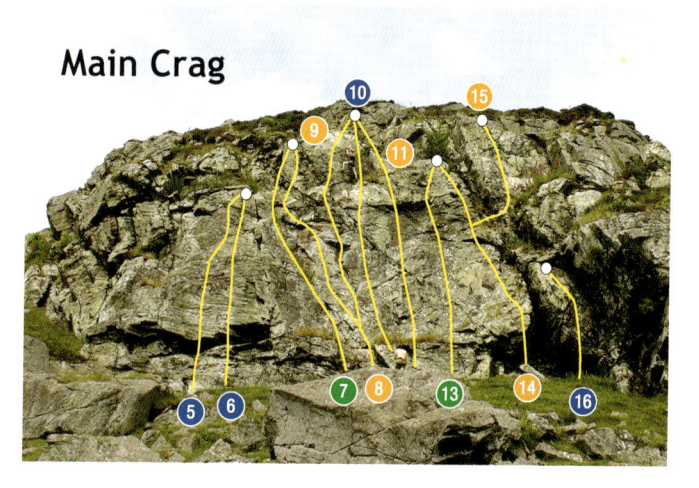

Munro's outdoor shop which sells chalk and guidebooks.

RECOMMENDED TASTY BITES
Lots of places to eat in Pitlochry, however the Moulin Hotel on the road to the crag is recommended for good food and the beer from its micro brewery.

TOP TIPS
The southerly aspect ensures plenty of sunshine, so pack the sun cream, take a picnic and enjoy.

DIRECTIONS
Heading north or south on the A9, exit at Pitlochry. Drive into the town centre and take the A924 signed to Moulin, Blairgowrie and Braemar. Continue uphill past the Co-op supermarket and from the Moulin Hotel, follow the road for 6.8 miles (11km) to reach the SEER Centre car park next to the road (no sign in 2011). This is just after the entrance to the farm and before some sharp bends; park at the far end (NO 0255 6374). The crags are clearly visible in profile on the hillside beyond. A mobile telephone transmission aerial is located below the Main Crag.

APPROACH
Time: 15-20mins

Cross a rusty gate just east of the car park and walk diagonally across the field towards the top of the trees then go through a gate and shortly thereafter ascend the hillside and go through another gate. Continue above and either step over a fence to reach the Lower Crag, or go right and through a gate. Please shut all the gates properly. To reach the main crag head up the steep slope to the right.

LOWER CRAG
(NO 0302 6408)   Alt 360m   South-South-East facing

1 Millennium Madness 16m 5+ *
Isla Watson 2000
Start to the left of a large detached flake and climb to a lower-off at the

Stirlingshire to Perthshire

top of the crag. A surprisingly pleasant route on some excellent holds with the top wall being more positive than it first appears.

② Virtual Life   16m   6a+ *
Colin Miln 2000
Start to the right of the large detached flake and climb a groove. Another good line through surprisingly steep ground. Shared lower-off with Millennium Madness.

③ Sending the Wrong Signal   12m   6b
Colin Miln 2000
Climb to a bolt in a groove, then break out left and climb the wall to a lower-off just above the break. The tricky section is short lived.

④ Cat Scratch Fever   12m   6b
Calum Mayland 2000
Wear long sleeves and trousers on this one! Start just right of the previous route, gain a recess and climb a groove above to a shared lower-off. Graded 5+ if you step right and climb right of the crux groove.

MAIN CRAG

(NO 0307 6414)   Alt 390m   South-South-East facing
Described from left to right, all the climbs are well bolted and have double ring thread through lower-offs. There are some trad climbs here. At the time of writing, the hangers on the first bolts of Moulin Rouge, Quiet Revolution and French Onion Soup had been removed, possibly since peregrines had been using the ledge at the top. However, this was only as a feeding station and not a nest site and had not occurred in any previous year. Until replaced the bolts can be used by placing a wire over the bolt stem, but are not unreasonably bold without.

⑤ Downshifting   12m   6c *
Isla Watson 1999
The leftmost route. Stiff fingery moves at the start lead to easier climbing. Pass to the left of the top bolt to gain a small triangular roof, then go up right to the shared lower-off. A more direct finish can be made using small crimps as for Twilight Shift (6c+).

⑥ Twilight Shift   12m   6c+ *
Colin Miln 1999
Again some fingery moves to pass the initial bolts. Finish directly to the right of the top bolt on small crimps to reach the shared lower-off, or cop out right to use the crack (much easier).

⑦ Rubrique   18m   5
Rab & Chris Anderson 2003
Climbs the rib on the left of the left-slanting fault in the centre of the crag, moving right across the top of the fault to reach the lower-off shared with Cabaret.

⑧ Cabaret   18m   6b+ *
Rab & Chris Anderson 2003
An eliminate just left of 21st Century Citizen to reach a lower-off shared with Rubrique. Start at the foot of the fault and climb just to its right.

⑨ 21st Century Citizen   20m   6b+ **
Colin Miln 1999
The best line on the crag. Start as for the previous route then move right to weave up through steep walls and bulges. A short traverse gains the lower-off. Sustained but never too desperate.

⑩ Moulin Rouge   20m   6c **
Rab & Chris Anderson 2002
A direct line between 21st Century Citizen and Quiet Revolution, sharing the lower-off of those routes. Slightly contrived in the lower half, but soon leads to good sustained climbing with some tricky moves to finish up the right edge of the tower.

⑪ Quiet Revolution   20m   6a+ *
Isla Watson 1999
After a tricky start the climbing eases off for a bit before tackling a

Rockdust Crag

small roof to gain a ledge by a block (care). From the ledge, finish up left to the 21st Century Citizen lower-off.

12 Tribute 20m 6a+ *
Rab Anderson 2003
The prominent left-slanting diagonal crack is gained by the first 3 bolts of the next route and followed to the lower-off on Rubrique. The crux is on Moulin Rouge. You might be better having someone second this on a top rope to strip it!

13 French Onion Soup 14m 5+ **
Isla Watson 1999
Named after the excellent dish served up at the Moulin Hotel. Climb through the diagonal crack (as for Tribute) and at the 3rd bolt avoid difficulties by moving left, then back right. Good and interesting climbing; keep something in the bag for the top!

14 Gimme Shelter 14m 6a *
Calum Mayland 1999
Start from the top of the boulder on the left of the cleft. A few tough initial moves lead to pleasant, easier climbing up the wall above and a lower-off shared with the previous route.

15 Egyptiana Jones 20m 6a *
Isla Watson 2000
Follow the previous route to its 3rd bolt, then trend right and cross the fault to finish up the nice wall above. Be careful with loose rock in the fault.

16 Wandering Minstrel 8m 6c+ *
Calum Mayland 1999
The short line up the overhanging arete on the right of the cleft certainly gives you its money's worth! Easier if climbed on the right (6c).

Stirlingshire to Perthshire

John Lyall having a Quiet Revolution (6a+), Rockdust (photo Andy Nisbet)

Angus

Angus can realistically claim to be the spiritual home of sport climbing in Scotland. The area has enjoyed a steady year on year increase in numbers of sport routes since the first were recorded in 1983. The result of this is that no area other than Angus can boast to having more sport routes than trad ones. The areas continued popularity has doubtless benefited from the excellent local climate and the absence of those twin terrors, the midge and the tick.

Sandstone predominates in the area with the harder angular variety in the quarries giving a slightly reach dependant style, whilst the softer rounded rock at the coast and at Kirrie Hill gives a more gritstone like experience. The esoteric venue of Elephant Rock adds an unusual volcanic crag to the mix and also provides climbing in a beautiful surrounding, whilst the Red Head is home to the most outrageously positioned sport route in the country.

In recent years the area has fallen back from the cutting edge of the grading scale. However there are plenty of routes of all standards, ranging from a 'Sector d'Initiation' at the Arbroath Sea-Cliffs to ferocious grade 8s at Balmashanner, to keep most people occupied for many a season.

History by Neil Shepherd

In overall climbing terms sport climbing is a fairly recent development in the North-East. The area was always a staunch bastion of traditional climbing and the close links to the nearby mountains tended to reflect that. Not surprising then that the start of sport climbing required the arrival of a group of climbers who were not tied to the traditional allegiance. Coupled with a selection of suitable crags in the Angus quarries the scene was set. With the passing of nearly 30 years from the first free climbing protection bolt being placed at Legaston Quarry in 1983, to the present situation, where there are several hundred sport routes across the region, it is probably fair to say that the area's sport climbing has truly come of age.

Legaston Quarry was the first crag to be recognised as having sport potential and in 1982 the first clip-up route was created with Armygeddon (5+), albeit using pegs rather than bolts. Further pegs were then placed but regular visits to an increasingly bolted Peak District made the placement of the first local bolt inevitable and in December 1983 it went in! The route had to wait for drier weather though and Driller Killer (6c) didn't come into being until early in 1984.

The placement of the first bolt in the area was not without incident however with Murray Hamilton, at the time residing in Kirriemuir, removing the hanger and Neil Shepherd replacing it on several occasions. Eventually either common sense prevailed or the protagonists grew tired and the route became established.

1985 saw further routes appear with bolts forming the main protection though they were not at this stage true sport climbs. In particular Shepherd opened up the big wall of Forbidden Buttress with the aptly named No Remorse (6c+). Hamilton was quickly in for the second ascent and then he recruited John 'Spider' MacKenzie to make a bolt free lead. After discussion the trio decided the bolts were justified and remained in place. Interestingly enough it wasn't long before both Murray and Spider had upped sticks and moved to France to sample among

History | 149

other things the high standard sport climbing available there!

Attention switched the following year to Balmashanner. At first enthusiasm and strength were lacking but eventually Shepherd cleaned and bolted what was to become Savage Amusement (7b) and others cleaned and top-roped the line of Hell Bent for Lycra. At Legaston the route of the crag was climbed, Spandex Ballet. At the time sporting an E5 grade it had only two peg runners so didn't immediately fit into the 'true sport climb' bracket. July of 1987 saw the theft of all the in-situ gear at Legaston. What the perpetrator of this act gained other than a bagful of old pegs and caving hangers is unclear, but it was undoubtedly the catalyst for a change in attitude towards protection for the locals. Luckily the climbing manufacturers had picked up on the inadequacy of the old caving bolts and Petzl and Mammut bolts began to appear like a rash!

During 1988 most local eyes were focused on Balmashanner. In June, 17 year old Dave Douglas led the first route to breach 'the wall' with Hell Bent for Lycra (6c+). Other routes then fell quickly to both Douglas and Shepherd, ranging from E3 to E5. The grades given to these routes reflected the sparse in-situ gear at the time. The climbs at this stage could not be regarded as proper sport routes.

Balmashanner kicked off early in 1989 with Start the Fire (6b+), the first full clip-up being climbed on the 3rd of January by Shepherd, warmed by a large bonfire. Over at Legaston, Grant Farquhar and Douglas both repeated Spandex Ballet (7a+), taking advantage of the bolts which had replaced the pegs. Finally,

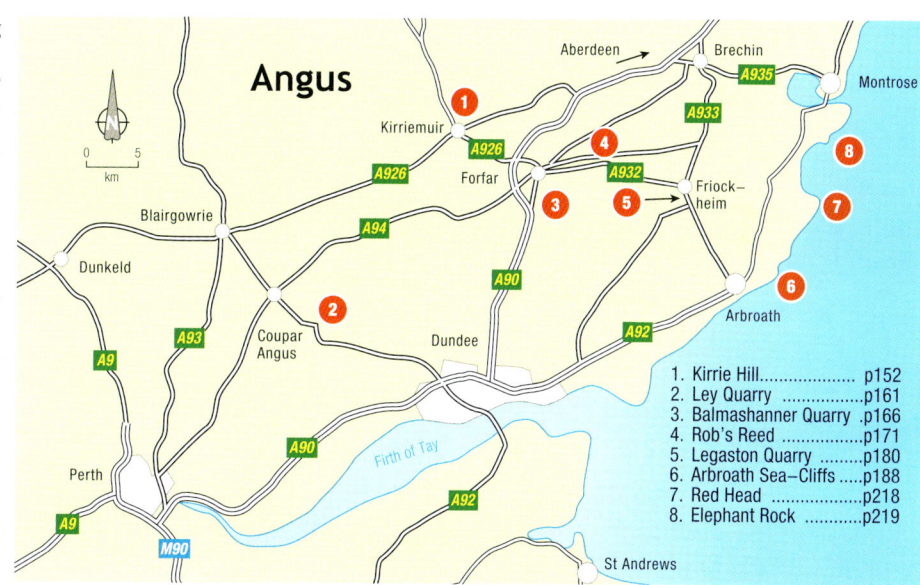

1. Kirrie Hill..................p152
2. Ley Quarry p161
3. Balmashanner Quarry .p166
4. Rob's Reed p171
5. Legaston Quarry p180
6. Arbroath Sea–Cliffs p188
7. Red Head p218
8. Elephant Rock p219

unknown 15 year old Stuart Cameron showed the shape of things to come by making the second ascent of Savage Amusement.

In 1990 there was little new route activity, but the popularity of both quarries increased. The in-situ equipment was improved and multiplied, particularly at Balmashanner. However, before the rains arrived in autumn, Grant Farquhar and Stuart Cameron both redpointed the open project at Balmashanner to give Gravity's Rainbow (7c+), at the time one of the hardest sport climbs in the country.

A year later Cameron unleashed his full power and added The Niche (8a+). By 1992 The Niche had become a training route for Cameron and Malcolm Smith with each climber running laps on it! Cameron was thus forced to up the ante again and on a far from perfect evening in July 1992, he established his Merchant of Menace (8b).

The same year also saw the beginning of development at a new venue, Ley Quarry near Coupar Angus. For the next four years this was to provide the enthusiastic team of George Ridge and Shepherd with many new routes in a sheltered location. The years of 1993 and 1994 were probably the most productive period in Scottish sport climbing to date. All across the country climbers had invested in Hilti drills and were putting them to good use; Ley and the Arbroath sea-cliffs were no exception.

As 1984 had been the golden year for Legaston Quarry, so 1994 proved to be the same for Ley. Ridge got the ball rolling with the difficult Holy Water (7b) the same day as Shepherd added the technical Magic Thumb (7b). Other fillers in were then added but as the 'worked out' signs were going up most attention turned to the coastline. Less than a mile from Shepherd's front door the sea-cliffs at Arbroath were exploited with ruthless efficiency. Lines such as Jeff Ross's The Krab (6b) were showing the potential and it wasn't long before Ridge had pushed up the difficulty with Pilgrim's Progress (7a). Late on, an excellent year of development was rounded off with one of the areas best routes The E'evil Dead (6c) at the Needles E'e.

Controversy however was never far away and, as a result of the bolting of coastal rock both in Angus and further north, a meeting was convened in Aberdeen to discuss and draw up guidelines for future development. This resulted in lively but sensible debate and an expression of local democracy led to the drawing up of a distinctly different set of guidelines to those proposed by the Mountaineering Council of Scotland at an earlier meeting in Glasgow.

With coastal guidelines in place 1995 was at best a year of filling in at the Angus quarries, thankfully not literally! Shepherd added Legaston's hardest route Charred and Damned Desire (7b+) to Rotten Wall and the long dry summer allowed Ridge to climb his Babylon Wall project to give She Conceives Destruction (7a). At Balmashanner, Shepherd returned to the fray later in the year, after recovering from a broken finger, with the hard Made to Suffer (7b+).

Most of the available rock however was at the Arbroath sea-cliffs and the new routing became frenzied with whole walls being developed. Various climbers were tackling more audacious lines. Ross's Peem Machine (6c+) in particular showed the way for the next generation of routes on more inhospitable terrain. Prospecting for new lines went on through the winter and into early 1996 enabling the main activists to start the year's new routing early on. The Haven was rediscovered from the trad days of the early '80s and the usual suspects were joined by David Pert and Aberdeen based Neil Morrison in developing its walls very quickly. Eventually even stalwart members of the Aberdeen traditional scene arrived, with climbers found to be enjoying the unique style of the climbing at Arbroath and not a nut in sight!

Away from the coast, 1996 saw Shepherd add some of the final routes to the area's quarries. Balmashanner received Tales of Creation (8a), certainly the hardest addition in the area since the Cameron years. Strangely enough, 1997 did not see any notable sport climbing activity in the North-East at all. As it turned out nearly all the main activists were busy at the new mecca – Weem in Perthshire! This could possibly be regarded as the calm before the storm.

Out looking for potential bouldering in January of 1998, Pert and Shepherd almost literally stumbled across Elephant Rock. The bouldering proved uninviting but realisation quickly dawned that the crag was in fact solid and of an inspiring height and steepness. During 1998 and 1999 the crag was practically worked out with Shepherd not surprisingly setting the pace as the crag was barely 15mins from his front door! Morrison and fellow Aberdonian John Wilson were also active, often repeating the routes as fast as they were put up and adding their own also.

Balmashanner also saw some notable repeats when Ed Morgan did the second ascent of Tales of Creation in 1998 and Ian Cropley accounted for the overdue third ascent of The Niche in 1999 reckoning it to be as hard as the infamous 'Magnetic Fields' at Malham Cove.

The first year of the new millennium saw most of the remaining lines at The Elephant climbed. Legaston Quarry also received a final burst of development when Shepherd completed the last lines on Rotten Wall.

Good summer weather and the return of Jeff Ross to the fray led to an explosion of routes at the Arbroath sea-cliffs in 2001 with around 50 new additions. Many routes were repeated by visitors such as Dave Douglas and Mike Reed. At Elephant Rock, Shepherd rounded off the crag's development with its hardest route, Alien Breed (7b+).

The dire summer of 2002 meant new routing was slow. In between the rain however Ross added one of the best routes to Arbroath with The Siren (6c). Bolts also finally arrived at the highest sea-cliff in the area, Red Head. Shepherd cleaned and climbed the huge hanging arete to give Cock o' The North (6c), without doubt the most outrageously placed sport route in Scotland.

A good summer doesn't always follow a bad one but 2003 was certainly good. Plenty of new routes were added at Arbroath, mainly the work of Ross and Shepherd, with the long overlooked Non-Tidal Wave being practically climbed out.

The most news worthy activity of the year however was going on at Balmashanner. During the summer several repeats were made of Tales of Creation and The Niche before Dave MacLeod finally picked the plum of the second ascent of Merchant of Menace, 11 years after it was originally climbed. Third and fourth ascents quickly followed from Gary Vincent and Alan Cassidy to show that the next generation had well and truly come of age.

Things continued in the same vein early in 2004 with Ross and Shepherd adding further routes to the sea-cliffs. Alas an unfortunate abseiling accident suffered by Jeff Ross whilst prospecting a new line applied the brakes to this prolific team. The following year a strong student from Poland studying at Dundee, Tomek Kazimierski, firstly picked off the old Grotesque project (7b) before sending Shepherd's long standing project in the Mermaid's Kirk. This magnificent but rarely dry line, Ossian, gave the sea-cliffs its first 8a. Shepherd opened up a couple of new walls at Grannies Garrett and Dickmont's Den but enthusiasm was in short supply.

Away from the coast, the big news in 2005 was Scott Muir's rediscovery of Rob's Reed just outside Forfar. The crag had been visited by locals in the early '80s for aid practice (just like nearby Balmashanner) but had become forgotten. Scott had just finished equipping the short routes on the left wall at Balmashanner and quickly saw the potential to exercise his drill further. Working in secrecy he quickly added a dozen good routes to

Iain Macdonald pebble pulling on Parental Guidance (6b), Arbroath (photo Neil Shepherd)

the crag's right end. Muir's departure from Forfar early in 2006 prompted him to let Shepherd and Ridge in on the venue, but only Shepherd showed enthusiasm. After a final brief flurry at the sea-cliffs with Kazimierski it was full steam ahead at Rob's Reed.

Initially working alone, Shepherd was then joined by an old school friend, Ken Edwards who was returning to the area, and new routes were added in large numbers through the rest of 2006. As the season that year drew to a close a discussion on the internet forum of scottishclimbs.com prompted Shepherd to take a close look at the obvious crag on Kirrie Hill. Looked at by every man and his dog, often literally as it's a popular dog walking spot, the soft sandstone had discouraged much practical exploration.

Joined by Edwards the initial enthusiasm of 'let's do a couple of routes and see how it goes' stretched on through the remarkably warm and dry winter into the following year with a tally of more than 50 routes equipped and climbed by the end of April 2007. Local activists Iain Macdonald, Ken and Ronald Henderson worked tirelessly to get the crag tidied and routes added whilst Edwards and Shepherd regularly placed over 80 bolts in a day. The sunny aspect of the crag and its family friendly facilities and grades created the area's and possibly the country's most popular sport climbing venue.

Later in 2007 saw the opening of the ultra steep Dirty Harry's Cave at Rob's Reed and through 2008 and 2009 the remaining lines were gradually climbed. A second wave of exploration at Kirrie Hill by Mark Cashley and the Hendersons added another clutch of routes in 2009 and early 2010. There is still much rock to climb in Angus and whole walls yet to open on the Arbroath coast so the final chapter in Angus sport climbing has not been written yet.

Kirrie Hill - Kirriemuir

NO 3915 5456 (left end) to NO 3927 5463 (right end)   Alt 165m   South-South-East facing   Maps p149, p152

Kirrie Hill is an extensive quarried outcrop on the eastern outskirts of the pleasant country town of Kirriemuir. It has a great outlook over the Strathmore Valley and is both sheltered and sunny in equal measure. All year round climbing is possible as seepage is rare and indeed the bulk of the original development was carried out between December 2006 and the end of April 2007. It will be found to be particularly family friendly with a park, a Peter Pan themed Neverland play area and toilets located conveniently beside the parking above the crag. The crag sports a wide variety of grades but is a rare sport venue in that a good number of the climbs are 6a or below.

The rock is a softish sandstone and does require careful handling in places. However, on the well established lines this has become less of a problem. No stars are given to avoid over popularity damaging the starred routes but in terms of choice, 'what you see is what you get'.

AMENITIES
Kirriemuir has all the facilities of a small town, including a petrol station and take aways, but no supermarket. Forfar is the nearest big town.

RECOMMENDED TASTY BITES
The 88 Degrees Cafe, 17 High Street, Kirriemuir comes highly recommended as a coffee shop with hand made chocolate, cheeses, cakes, drinks and simple meals.

TOP TIPS
Sun cream is useful and a very soft brush can be handy on some of the sandier holds.

DIRECTIONS
Approaching from Kirriemuir town centre, follow brown tourist signs for Camera Obscura (or simply Visitor Attractions). After many turns, there is a right turn into West Hill Road, then another right turn into a small tarmac road. Follow this uphill to its end at a tarmac parking place in front of the cemetery and the Neverland play area.

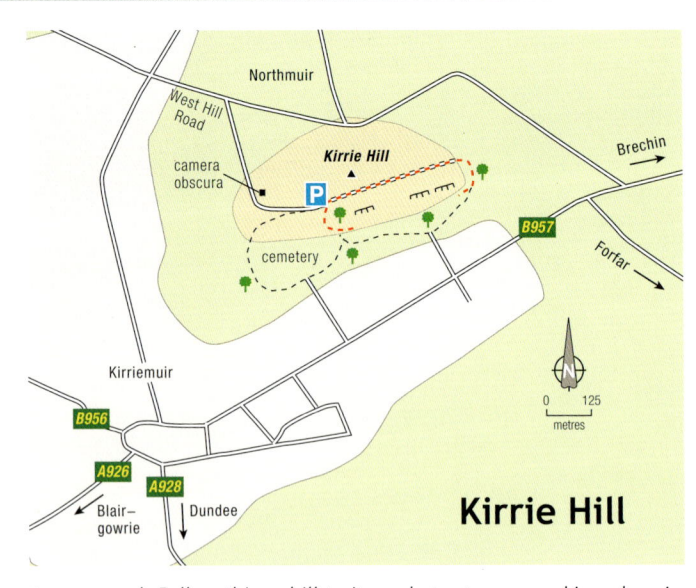

Coming from the A90 Dundee to Aberdeen road, the route most will take to get here, leave at the Forfar/Kirriemuir junction and take the A926 towards Kirriemuir. Continue through the village of Padanarm to reach the hamlet of Checkiefield. Turn right here up an unclassified road to reach the B957 at a T junction. Turn right onto B957 then quickly take a left to Northmuir. Follow this road uphill and round to the left. As the road reaches the top of the hill the park will be seen ahead. Continue ahead on West Hill Road, then turn left and drive up to the parking.

APPROACH
Time: 3mins
From the east end of the parking area, walk along the track past Never-

Kirrie Hill

land, then head downhill beside the cemetery wall on a prepared footpath which is signposted Kirriemuir Path Network; Town Centre. At the bottom take a path off left (not down towards the houses) and traverse into the open and the crag.

The crag is divided into three distinct areas, Left, Centre and Right. Each of these areas is further subdivided. From the approach the first area reached is the Left, also known as The Bay.

LEFT - THE BAY

This area of rock is set back from the rest of the crag and is a natural suntrap. The rock runs to overlaps and ledges on the left side and more continuous steepness at the right end.

Sleepy Hollow

The left end of The Bay deserves its name, and although almost into the trees, it provides good climbing on solid rock.

① Unenforced Layoff   14m   5
Derek Armstrong 2007
Climb awkwardly over two overlaps but a surprising choice of holds eases the pain!

② Mushroom Heads   14m   5
Neil Shepherd 2007
Fairly straightforward climbing, leading directly to a shared lower-off with Unenforced Layoff.

③ Another Green World   14m   6a
Ken Edwards 2007
A parallel direct line, with good moves up the groove on excellent rock.

④ Spirits Drifting   14m   6a+
Ken Edwards 2007
Harder climbing over the overlap at 5m, then some fine moves directly up the slab above.

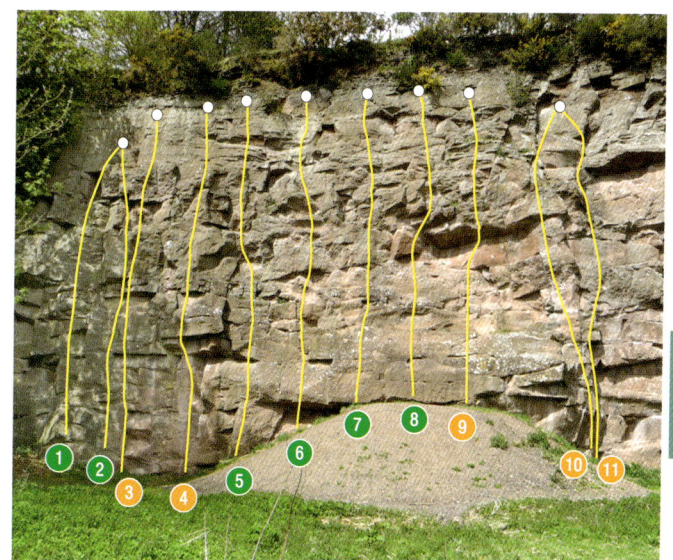

⑤ Becalmed   13m   4+
Ken Edwards 2007
Do as the name suggests on this enjoyable outing. Follow sandy coloured hangers on good holds.

The Mound

An aptly named section of the wall where the routes start from a mound built up against the rock face.

⑥ Sombre Reptiles   12m   5+
Ken Edwards 2007
A tricky start can be avoided by coming in from the right, then climb directly on good but hidden holds.

Kirrie Hill

10 Hard Labour 13m 6a
Ken Edwards 2007
Starting halfway down the mound's right edge, skirt the twin overlap to the right, then trend gradually up and left to finish out right at a lower-off.

Main Wall

This forms the right side of The Bay, from the base of the mound to the far right corner, and contains a selection of harder routes.

11 Dogmatic 15m 6a+
Ken Edwards 2007
Tricky climbing in the shallow corner and above, but it eases with height. A shared lower-off on the right with the next two routes.

12 Caned and Unable 15m 6c
Ken Edwards 2009
An eliminate line just right. Hard fingery moves over the first overlap lead to easier climbing and thank god holds that reduce the impact of the second overhang. A blinkered approach helps!

13 Paws for Thought 15m 6b
Ken Edwards 2007
Another thin start, but persevere and better holds appear. The juggy roof is crossed at its widest point.

14 Thorny Issue 15m 6b+
Ken Edwards 2007
Some fine thin climbing up the slab left of a mid-height bulge. Finish direct.

15 All Chalk, No Traction 15m 6c
Ken Edwards 2007
Excellent climbing up a pillar leads to a bulge. Pull over and climb the fine slab to a shared lower-off with Thorny Issue.

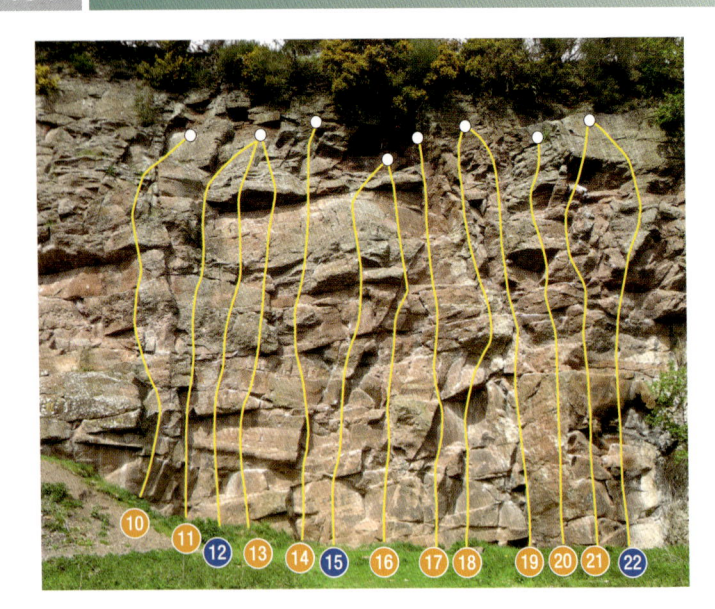

7 On the Up 11m 5+
Ken Edwards 2007
A more technical line.

8 Mound over Matter 11m 5+
Ken Edwards 2007
From the peak of the mound, climb to the left end of the overlap. Pass this on good holds to the top.

9 Grassy Knoll 11m 6a
Ken Edwards 2007
A harder route which takes the centre of the overlap. A short sharp crux!

Kirrie Hill 155

16 Boarding Party 14m 6b
Ken Edwards 2006
A deceptive start up the innocuous groove to the right of the pillar. Easier above to a lower-off below a capping roof.

17 Dubh be Dubh 15m 6a+
Ken Edwards 2006
Go up the left side of the black slab to tricky moves left and up. Continue direct to reach the high lower-off on the sidewall.

18 The (Beach) Ball of Kirriemuir 15m 6b+
Neil Shepherd 2007
Direct up the black slab to grapple with the beach ball itself. Pull directly over to fine laybacking up the overhanging prow.

19 Let there be Rock 15m 6a+
Neil Shepherd 2007
The large left-facing corner leads direct to a fun squeeze-chimney and a lower-off shared with the previous route.

20 Bon the Edge 15m 6b+
Neil Shepherd 2007
Climb the sharp arete, easier than it looks, before tackling the crux overhang above.

21 Whole Lotta Kirrie 15m 6b+
Neil Shepherd 2007
Go up an obvious short crack to the ledge, then directly through confusing bulges on awkward holds. Cross the final roof to a shared lower-off with Black int' Back.

22 Black int' Back 15m 7a
Neil Shepherd 2007
The hanging flake is gained delicately before powerful climbing turns the overhang above (hidden bolt). An easier finish leads to a shared lower-off.

Pete Trudgill doing the Dubh be Dubh (6a+), Main Wall, Kirrie Hill (photo John Trudgill)

Kirrie Hill

㉓ Pharmacist's Apprentice 8m 6b
Ken Edwards 2009
Start easily until a long reach up and right provides the crux; continue on good holds.

㉔ Crystal Myth 8m 6b
Ken Edwards 2009
Steep but balance required. Is that a mantelshelf I see above half-height? Lower-off on the right shared with Chasing Dragons.

㉕ Chasing Dragons 8m 6c
Ken Edwards 2009
Thin and technical climbing. Easy in the grade.

㉖ Tim'rous Beastie 8m 6a
Mark Cashley 2009
A steep start eases off after the slab is gained. Mice climbing!

㉗ Sonsie Face 8m 6a
Adam Wilson 2009
Another slabby route where cunning will see you through.

㉘ Glaikit Folly 8m 5
Helen Greig 2009
The warm-up of the sector. Pleasant climbing almost into the trees.

CENTRE

From the right end of The Bay, walking out for 30m brings the next run of crag into view. This area is divided into four distinct zones each with its own character. It contains both the easiest and hardest Kirrie has to offer!

Sector Recreation

The area to the right of the tottering arete. The rock may still need to be treated with caution.

Sector d'Initiation

A fine slabby area of good rock with just a few overlaps thrown in for interest sake.

㉙ Screwless 10m 3
Ken Henderson 2007
The easiest route at the crag and very nice climbing.

Kirrie Hill

33 Joining the Debt Set 11m 6b
Neil Shepherd 2007
Another easy start but the overlap proves taxing despite good rock.

34 On the Never Never Land 11m 6a+
Neil Shepherd 2007
Once again the start can lull one into a false sense of security. The crux lies near the top.

35 La Plage 9m 4
Ron Henderson 2007
To the right of the broken section lies this pleasant left-facing corner.

36 Hill Billies 11m 3+
Neil Shepherd 2007
The left edge of the next slab gives more fun climbing.

37 The Hill has Eyes 11m 5
Neil Shepherd 2007
Go up the easy shelves to a perplexing crux groove.

Black Wall

The slabby rock of the last sector steepens remorselessly into the hardest sector at the crag. Black is the colour of the rock and black is often the mood after an encounter with big Slim Pickins!

38 What Every Woman Wants 12m 7a
Neil Shepherd 2007
A steep start on good holds leads to 'the perch' From here puzzling moves gain a good pocket in the bulge. A hard pull brings sloping holds and then (if you're lucky) the lower-off into reach.

39 Where there's Muck, there's Brass 12m 6c+
Neil Shepherd 2007
A bouldery start over the overlap, then better holds to a bouldery finish up the thin crack.

30 Kirrie on Regardless 10m 3+
George Ridge 2007
Another fine easy climb which is not without interest. Finish at the lower-off for Screwless.

31 Spent 11m 6a
George Ridge 2007
A bit more effort required on this one, not as easy as it looks.

32 Badly Overdrawn Boy 11m 6a+
Neil Shepherd 2007
An easy start leads to a short but intense crux, then easier again to a lower-off.

Kirrie Hill

40 Slim Pickins   12m   7b
Ken Edwards 2007
Head and shoulders above the rest of the routes here for difficulty. A hard start, hard middle and yes a hard finish. Move left at top to share a lower-off with the previous climb.

41 Dig Deep   11m   6c+
Ken Edwards 2007
A powerful start to good holds but the crux is reserved for gaining the lower-off, easier for the tall.

Sector Fat Boys

The next sector is featured with overlaps and slabs which provide interesting and often thought-provoking climbing.

42 Ginger's Jewels   12m   6b+
Iain MacDonald 2007
The roofed nose to the right of the crumbling fault-line. It has a well positioned crux on the upper roof.

43 Beat the Bulge   12m   6b+
Ken Edwards 2007
Delicate climbing picking its way through the bulges.

44 Weighty Issue   12m   6b
Ken Edwards 2007
Starts easily enough and just gets harder! Avoid the temptation of the cop-out to the left higher up.

45 Gut Feeling   12m   6b+
Ken Edwards 2007
A good quality route on decent but hard to locate holds.

46 Touch too Much   12m   7a
Ken Edwards 2007
The test piece of this sector with the crux tackling the obvious hanging arete above an overlap. Graded for a direct ascent; it is easier but fairly pointless to detour left at the crux!

47 Xmas Xcess   12m   6a+
Neil Shepherd 2007
Climb the groove to the overlap which is skirted to the left via some testing moves for this grade.

48 Serious Beef   12m   6c+
Neil Shepherd 2007
Worth shedding a few pounds for! Go up the hard groove to breach the roof direct. Still hard moves await up the slab above.

49 Fat of the Land   12m   6b
Neil Shepherd 2007
Another eliminate line which does offer some nice climbing on good rock.

Kirrie Hill

Get out the blinkers again!

50 Fat Boy Slims 12m 4+
Neil Shepherd 2007
Don't worry though you won't have to! This pleasant left-facing groove is a delight to climb.

51 Monkey See, Monkey Do 12m 6b+
Neil Shepherd 2007
Steep and easy to start but quite hard getting onto the less steep upper section.

52 The Zoo 12m 6a+
Neil Shepherd 2007
The thin groove can be a bit sandy but the rock is better higher up. A shared lower-off with the previous climb.

RIGHT

The next sector lies 20m to the right, past a broken area of rock. The routes here are sheltered and fairly close together. Can be prone to midges on still summer evenings!

53 Walking the Plank 13m 6a+
Neil Shepherd 2007
Start in the right-facing corner, then break out onto the buttress to the left. The closer you get to the end the more precarious it gets!

54 Crocodile Corner 13m 5+
Neil Shepherd 2007
The big corner in its entirety, crux at 10m. Good climbing if you don't bite off more than you can chew.

55 By Hook or By Crook 13m 5
Neil Shepherd 2007
The wall just right of the corner, easier than it looks and popular. Good holds all the way to a final strenuous pull to gain the lower-off.

Piotr Wisthal on Dig Deep (6c+), Black Wall (photo Angus Clark)

Pete Trudgill on Let there be Rock (6a+), Main Wall (photo John Trudgill)

56 Smee Day 13m 5
Neil Shepherd 2007
More surprising climbing at the grade and very enjoyable. Skirt the large roof at the top on its left side and share a lower-off with the previous climb.

57 Wings would Help 13m 6a+
Ken Edwards 2007
Brown coloured bolt hangers mark out this route. A scoop provides interest early on and the roof at the top is crossed direct on good holds to the right of the bolts.

58 Flyboy 13m 6b
Ken Edwards 2007
An angular start leads to the first small roof and some tricky climbing. The upper roof is skirted to the right.

Kirrie Hill

62 Peddle Power 13m 6a+
Ken Edwards 2007
Good climbing up the open groove leads to a steep finish to a juglet up and left of the lower-off.

63 Done and Dusted 13m 6b
Neil Shepherd 2007
An easy blocky start leads to more demanding climbing as height is gained.

64 Curtain Call 13m 6a+
Ken Edwards 2007
Similar but slightly easier than the previous route.

65 When Annabelle met Tinkerbelle 12m 6a
Helen Greig 2009
Start in a small alcove 2m left of the natural left-trending fault-line. Head straight up to join the crack for a final push to the lower-off.

66 El Captain 12m 5+
Mark Cashley 2009
Go straight up the face just left of the fault-line, cross through this to a platform on the right. Climb a right-trending conglomerate crack to a slab and up to a lower-off.

67 El Boa 12m 6a
Mark Cashley 2009
Start at the foot of the left-trending fault-line. Climb this direct in its entirety using bolts from routes to either side. Finish at the lower-off of When Annabelle met Tinkerbelle. The rock is soft in the fault-line and may be loose.

68 Kirrie Sutra 12m 5
Mark Cashley 2009
Starts just right of the fault-line. Climb up following a small arete to a ledge, then take a thin curving crack-line through a conglomerate band

59 Wrong Turn 13m 5+
Ken Edwards 2007
The obvious looming roof is passed to the left and then as the upper slab steepens, better holds are gained.

60 True Path 13m 6a
Ken Edwards 2007
Climb the blocky rib then the arete to the left. The lower-off is partially hidden over bulges at the top.

61 Seeing the Light 13m 6a+
Ken Edwards 2007
Fine climbing with increasing difficulty. An airy finish over the top bulges on good holds.

(take care). From the last bolt, head directly to lower-offs shared with El Captain.

69 Awe! 12m 6a
Mark Cashley 2009
Start under an eye-catching projecting roof with an obvious borehole. Climb directly over the roof, then through further overlaps to a lower-off on a blind slab. Two very long quick draws recommended.

70 Stiff Little Fingers 12m 6b
Mark Cashley 2009
Start 1m right of Awe. Climb an eliminate line up the wall left of the corner. Avoid the use of holds in corner or it's only worth 6a.

71 Markerhorn 10m 4+
Mark Cashley 2009
Follow an obvious corner-line to the lower-off. Do not go above the lower-off as there is loose rock.

72 Grand Jorassic 10m 5
Mark Cashley 2009
Climb the wall immediately right of the corner clipping bolts to your left to the lower-off on Markerhorn.

73 Ruthosaurus 8m 3+
Mark Cashley 2009
Well into jungle for this one. Start right of a tree close to a wall. Follow the dinosaur heads to gain the lower-off. Watch out for dinosaur eggs!

74 Stegosaurus 9m 4
Mark Cashley 2009
From right of the tree deep into the lost world, climb the humped spikes of the Stegosaurus back, passing through the band of dinosaur eggs, and continue through to the lower-off.

Ley Quarry - Coupar Angus

(NO 2572 3772) L53 E380 Alt 140m South-East facing
Maps p149, p162 Diagram p164

Ley Quarry lies hidden in a peaceful woodland setting a few hundred metres from the Dundee to Coupar Angus road. The quarry walls form a natural suntrap and they are well sheltered from prevailing winds. The sandstone is fairly hard but lack of exposure to the elements can leave some of the less well travelled routes feeling sandy. Most of the climbing lies on the main back wall of the quarry above a pool. Thankfully the forward thinking quarrymen left a nice ledge system which provides easy access to the climbs. Belay bolts have been installed at intervals along the ledge to reduce the danger of falling into the pool, though it does occasionally happen! So keep your inoculations up to date and wear a life jacket if you can't swim!

All the routes have been equipped to a high standard using resin bolts and in-situ lower-offs. Overall, the crag has a continental atmosphere and deserves its nickname of 'Le Quarry'. Unlike the other sport quarries, the walls here face south and do not seep. This means that year round climbing is possible and in early spring the place can be scorching when more exposed crags are damp and cold.

AMENITIES
Coupar Angus has a limited range of shops. For climbing related supplies then Dundee will need to be visited.

RECOMMENDED TASTY BITES
The Red House Hotel in Coupar Angus is worth a visit for good pub grub and a decent beer.

TOP TIPS
If you cannot swim bring some water wings. You might find sun tan cream useful here as well.

DIRECTIONS
From Dundee, follow the A923 Coupar Angus road. Just past the straight

Ley Quarry

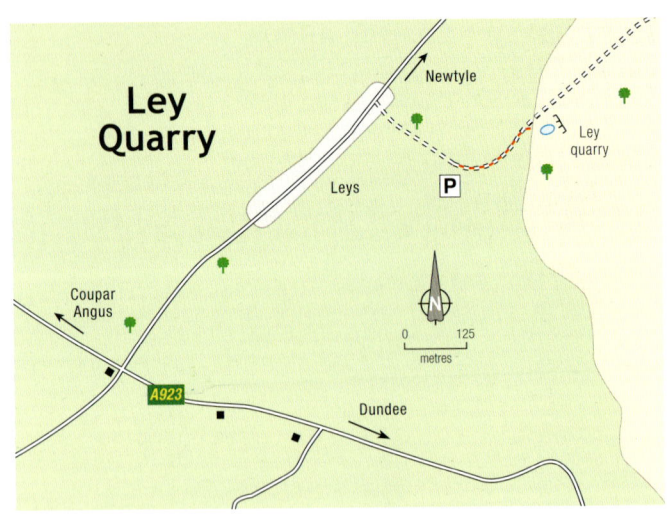

after the road descends from the S-bends of Tullybaccart, there is a crossroads; turn right here towards Newtyle. From the north, or from Perth, gain this point by heading to Coupar Angus and taking the A923 to Dundee. Ignore the first left turn to Kettins and Newtyle and continue for 1.3 miles (2km) to take the second left turn to Newtyle. After 0.4 miles (700m), just after various cottages in Leys itself and before a farm on the right, turn right up a narrow track with a high central grass strip. This leads to a water board reservoir. Park here with care and consideration (NO 2562 3766).

APPROACH

Time: 1min
Follow the track which bends round leftwards past a locked gate and then take the right fork into the quarry. Relations with the landowner have always been amiable, but a specific request was made that visitors do not bring dogs to the quarry.

BOULDERING WALL

On entering the quarry this is the first bit of rock encountered on the left. It offers some good problems but takes a while to clean up due to its sheltered nature. It is also popular for warming up. There are two excellent traverses and the main problems are fairly obvious though there are a few hard eliminates as well.

SMALL WALL

This is the higher right-hand continuation of the bouldering wall. Popular, as it has short easy routes with no water beneath! There are staple lower-offs for all routes which will need to be threaded. The routes are described from left to right.

1 Rotweiller 7m 4
Neil Shepherd 1994
Easy climbing but the finish can be dirty due to inconsiderate top-roping.

2 Scarred for Life 7m 6a
George Ridge 1994
The tall will find this route a lot easier.

3 Magic Pockets 7m 6b *
Jeff Ross 1993
Takes the middle of the wall; short sharp and very popular.

4 Pit Bull 7m 4
Neil Shepherd 1993
Climb the right side of the wall.

5 Cat Scratch Fever 7m 4
George Ridge 1994
The dirty looking corner has quite nice climbing and a good example of iron age bolting!

Ley Quarry

6 April's Arete   10m   3+
Neil Shepherd 1994
One of the easiest sport routes in Scotland. Perhaps! Start part way down the slope at the end of the wall.

POOL WALL

This is the left-hand side of the main quarry wall. From Small Wall, scramble down the steep bank and traverse round to gain the ledge system above the pool. The difficulty of access depends on whether the tide is in! More than one person has taken an early bath here so care is justified! The routes are described as approached from left to right.

7 Easy Ley   10m   6a+
Neil Shepherd 1995
The first line right of the dirty corner.

8 Nectar   10m   6a+ *
Janet Horrocks 1992
Interesting, varied and quite sustained. The final move to the chain is a bit of a stretch.

9 Dropping like Flies   20m   6b
Dave Douglas 1992
A girdle at two-thirds height. Totally anti-social! Climb Nectar to the third bolt, then traverse away right along the break to finish up Not the Risk Business.

10 Nirvana   11m   7a+   *****
George Ridge 1992
Thin fingery climbing leads to an easier upper half. The route of the crag.

11 Five Magics   11m   6b+   ******
Neil Shepherd 1992
Another good, sustained wall climb. It's not over till it's over!

Alasdair Goodmanl having a Barrel of Laughs (7a), The Waterfront, Ley Quarry (photo Tom Russell)

Ley Quarry

⑫ Footfall 10m 6a *
Neil Shepherd 1992
The original route here is a good introduction to clipping bolts and the stretchy moves so common in the sandstone quarries. The old quarry bolt needs threading or a very wide gate krab to clip.

⑬ Not the Risk Business 11m 6c
Neil Shepherd 1992
This fingery route is not so serious but technically a lot harder than the more famous route of almost the same name.

Ley Quarry

14 Drowning by Numbers 12m 7a *
George Ridge 1993
The slab to the right is hard to start and thankfully easier now at the finish.

15 Darkmoon Rising 12m 6b *
Neil Shepherd 1993
Starts from a slightly lower ledge, and proves a shorties' nightmare up the groove.

16 Twilight Zone 10m 7a
George Ridge 1994
More thin climbing up the white wall just right. Can be dusty and is found by most to be in the 'harder than it looks' category.

17 Fishing for Compliments 10m 6b
Neil Shepherd 1994
But unlikely to catch any, as this route is often dirty.

18 Caught in the Act 10m 6b
Neil Shepherd 1994
Interesting climbing makes this an enjoyable climb.

19 Traditional Imperfections 10m 6a *
Neil Shepherd 1994
The last route on the Pool Wall and one of the easiest. Climb directly over the nose of the overhang and finish pleasantly up the slab.

THE WATERFRONT

This is the name for the right-hand side of the Pool Wall. It is best reached by walking around the right-hand side of the pool. It can also be reached by a continuation of the ledge traverse from Pool Wall but the water below is deep! There is now a collection of fine fingery routes here. Most of the climbs are bolted down to low ledges at the waterside but in reality most people start from the higher ledge and avoid the easy and sandy lower sections. The lengths of the routes are given from the higher ledge, on which there are bolt belays. The rock on this side of the wall is steeper and thus even more sheltered than that on the left. This means that routes which don't get a lot of traffic, usually the hard ones, can be a bit sandy through lack of weathering. However, the advantage of the extra shelter will be clearly felt if the rain comes on!

The routes are again described from left to right, as they would be approached if the ledge traverse was continued.

20 Making the Grade 8m 7b
George Ridge 1994
A route which packs a punch and is often underestimated. From the left end of the high ledge, climb directly with a hard section in the middle.

21 Pool of Despair 9m 7a+ *
Neil Shepherd 1994
The line past an obvious pocket. Some powerful lock-offs; the short may well find it more like 7b.

22 Leyed to Rest 9m 7a
Neil Shepherd 1995
A low crux requires forceful climbing. It relents a bit after the 2nd bolt.

23 Barrel of Laughs 9m 7a **
George Ridge 1998
Some skilled 'quarrying' has produced a highly enjoyable route. Good training.

24 Haul or Nothing 9m 7b+ **
Neil Shepherd 1994
Probably the hardest route at Ley. Some of the sandier holds have been reinforced with resin and this has made the route feel a little easier. Leaving the ledge requires hard crimping and this continues all the way to the lower-off.

25 Holy Water 12m 7b *
George Ridge 1994
It is usual to start this route from the ground rather than the ledge.

Balmashanner Quarry

Sustained and reachy wall climbing. Avoid the temptation to leave the route at half-height to rest in the groove of Life's a Beach if you want to receive the blessing!

26 Life's a Beach 14m 6b *
George Ridge 1993
The shallow groove is more sustained than it looks. Technique rather than finger strength is required to ensure you don't get sand kicked in your face!

27 Fat Man Starts to Fall 11m 6b *
Neil Shepherd 1994
Determined climbing is needed to ensure you don't do the same! Go easily up and right to a precarious position under the headwall. Some fingery moves then lead to the chain.

28 Magic Thumb 10m 7b *
Neil Shepherd 1994
Another real finger test. Climb easily to a mantelshelf, surmount this and reach some good pockets below the final slab. Use the small flake up and right and the magic thumb to make the hardest individual move on the crag and reach the chain.

Balmashanner Quarry - Forfar

(NO 4545 4862) L54 E389 Alt 150m North facing
Maps p149, p166

This quarry thoroughly deserves its reputation as one of Scotland's most intense sport climbing venues. It faces due north and is situated on Balmashanner hill just south of Forfar. There is climbing on both of its walls. The left-hand is a small, vertical bouldering wall whilst the right wall is much bigger and steep! How the quarrymen worked at this angle is mind-boggling, or is the whole thing just leaning over more each year? The routes provide excellent climbing which is steep and athletic. The crag outlook is limited so don't bring the family for a picnic! Unless they like to crank really hard between their sandwiches of course....

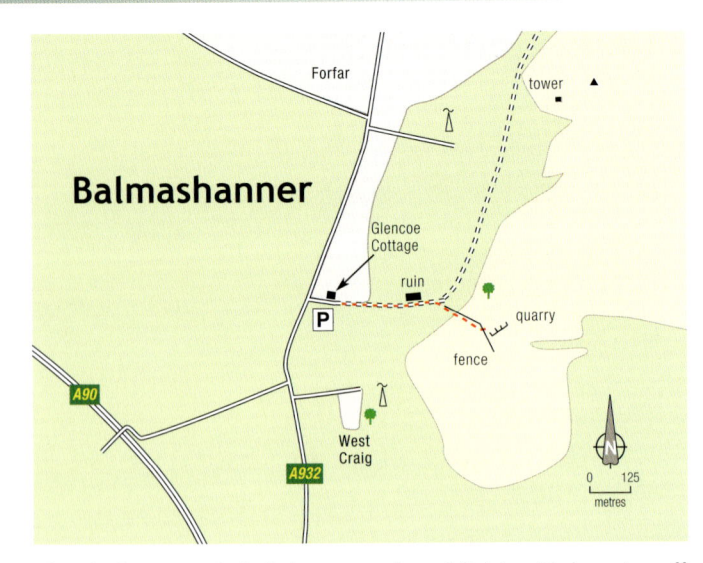

The climbs are entirely bolt protected, and finish with lowering off points just below the top. Please do not remove any of the in-situ gear as it is essential, especially at the top. Though most of the routes have seen some chipping prior to their first ascents, further chipping of these routes will definitely not make you any friends among the locals.

The rock at Balmashanner Quarry is a very compact sandstone, similar to that of nearby Legaston Quarry, although horizontal breaks are less common. The owner of the quarry is happy for climbers to use the crag at their own risk and sometimes comes by to watch the action. Please try to keep the profanity to a minimum, though this can be difficult when falling from the last move on Gravity's Rainbow!

AMENITIES

Food and money in Forfar. A reasonable choice of pubs and carry out establishments means no one should go home hungry.

Balmashanner Quarry

RECOMMENDED TASTY BITES
Lochland's garden centre tearoom does good soup and snacks at a fair price and is only a few hundred yards from the crag.

TOP TIPS
In addition to your strongest pair of arms, bring a patient belayer!

DIRECTIONS
The quarry is situated due south of Forfar, just off the A90 between Dundee and Aberdeen.

Approaching from the south (Dundee) on the A90, take the first junction signposted to Forfar. Follow the road for just over 0.5 miles (800m) until a track on the right signposted Glencoe Cottage is seen. This is between the first and second of the modern houses. Turn onto this track and park almost immediately alongside the hedge (NO 4496 4869). Please do not obstruct any access, as the locals are friendly at present. From the north (Aberdeen), on the A90, it is best to carry on round the Forfar Bypass to turn off and continue as above. There are speed cameras on both approaches along the A90.

APPROACH
Time: 10mins
Follow the track up the hillside past a ruined cottage on the left to reach a sharp left turn. Here, go right through a hole in the dyke and skirt the field following the fence. The top of the quarry is visible over to the left. Climb over the fence and locate the easy descent to the quarry floor. A good appreciation of the crag's angle can be gained by following the fence until level with the face and looking left!

The routes are described from left to right. All of the climbs are protected by in-situ gear, and many of the original bolts have been replaced by resin bolts. Due to the steepness of the crag, it is a good place to train, with Hell Bent and Half the Battle being particularly popular for this. Once the crag is free from seepage it remains dry during the heaviest rain. On humid summer nights however greasiness can make things difficult and a bit of a breeze is to be welcomed.

LEFT WALL
This is the shorter, more open wall sporting an enormous, seemingly detached flake at its left end. These routes provide nice, fun packed, extended bouldering and warm-up to the main courses at Balmashanner. At the extreme left end, the wall forms an arete and around this, the first route can be found in the corner. At the time of writing there has been some infilling of the left side of the quarry and this is starting to affect the starts of several routes on this wall.

① Dennis the Menace   8m   6b *
Scott Muir 2005
Climb the short corner to the roof and employ some fast foot trickery

Balmashanner Quarry

to overcome the overhang and pull onto the slab above.

2 Desperate Dan   8m   6a+
Scott Muir 2005
Start just left of the arete and slap wildly for a good hold – if you get it climb the arete to the top.

3 99 Flake   8m   4
Scott Muir 2005
Climb the obvious curving flake.

4 Ice Scream Wall   8m   6b *
Scott Muir 2005
The obvious thin seam immediately to the right of 99 Flake, finishing at its lower-off.

5 The Balmashanner Bomb Shell   8m   6c *
Scott Muir 2005
Start just to the right of Ice Scream and pull up left to a sidepull near that route. Thin technical moves lead back right and can perhaps allow better holds to be reached.

6 One Can Dan   8m   6b
Scott Muir 2005
In the middle of the wall is a shallow stepped corner running from left to right. Start up this and then break out onto the wall on the left. Finish at the lower-off on Bomb Shell. The line of this route is very uncertain.

7 Mini the Minx   8m   6a *
Scott Muir 2005
Climb the shallow left to right stepped corner in the middle of the wall.

8 Rat Race Face   8m   6b
Scott Muir 2005
Climb the tricky wall to the right; lower-off as for the route above.

MAIN WALL

North facing   Diagrams p168, p170, 171

Situated at a lower level, this is the main feature of the quarry. Continuously overhanging, it is particularly steep at its right end where it is also at its highest.

9 Syes don't Matter   8m   6b
George Ridge 1996
A fun, rising hand-traverse starting on the very left arete of the wall. Gain the traverse by a dyno and traverse quickly rightwards to gain the lower-off of the next route.

10 Sye of Relief   8m   6b+
Neil Shepherd 1995
Climb into the small niche and then break out left to gain a lower-off.

Balmashanner Quarry

11 Digital Sclerosis   40m   7b+ *
David Douglas 1989
The full low-level bouldering traverse of the right wall from left to right, studiously avoiding the resting ledge below Hell Bent by hand-traversing below it. Finish on the starting holds of The Niche. For a there and back award yourself 7c+ and a hearty slap on the back!

12 Firestarter   11m   6a+
Scott Muir 2005
The obvious fault-line running up and left into the hanging niche. Gaining this is tricky.

13 Delivery Man   12m   7a+
David Douglas 1989
The smooth wall right of Firestarter is short and powerful. There are no guarantees that this one will be delivered first time!

14 Start the Fire   12m   6b+ **
Neil Shepherd 1989
The warm-up! Climb the big open corner, fairly sustained climbing with no real crux to a lower-off on the left.

15 Made to Suffer   12m   7b+
Neil Shepherd 1995
The name says it all! Follow the thin crack with hardly a jam in sight directly to a lower-off.

16 Savage Amusement   12m   7b ***
Neil Shepherd 1988
This route gives excellent and powerful climbing. Easier in its upper reaches.

17 Putting Shame in your Game   12m   7c *
George Ridge 1998
The line of well crafted pockets up the pillar just right of Savage Amusement. Suffers more from humidity than the other routes here.

Luke Fairweather getting some Savage Amusement (7b), Main Wall, Balmashanner (photo Angus Clark)

Balmashanner Quarry

Right of this the next obvious feature is a huge flake which splits the upper half of the wall. Worryingly, this now provides the finish for the next two routes.

18 Manifestations   12m   7b *
Neil Shepherd 1989
The local test piece of its grade up the smooth wall directly below the flake. A hard left-hand variation is possible to gain the mid-height ledge (7c). The crucial pocket is prone to seepage.

19 Rat Attack   13m   6c+
Neil Shepherd 1988
The original route to reach the huge flake. Takes the thin flake-crack with difficulty to a junction with Manifestations. Finish up this.

20 Tales of Creation   13m   8a *
Neil Shepherd 1996
The line of staple bolts directly up the face of the flake. Hard at the start, the middle and also at the finish. The tall will find the final crux moves a bit easier.

21 Hell Bent for Lycra   12m   6c+ **
David Douglas 1988
An excellent climb directly up the shallow groove. The last move to the jug below the chain usually proves to be the crux.

22 Le Bon Vacance   13m   7a
Neil Shepherd 1988
This one is a little bit more technical but not so sustained as Hell Bent. Worthwhile.

23 Half the Battle   14m   7a *
Neil Shepherd 1992
Another pumper with the crux at the top! This is another popular training route.

24 The Comfort Machine   15m   6c+ *
Neil Shepherd 1992
Climb to the 3rd bolt on Half the Battle, then hand-traverse the lip of the cave. Follow the pumpy ramp rising rightwards past two more bolts to the lower-off.

25 Off the Couch   14m   6c
Neil Shepherd 1996
The direct start to Comfort Machine. The rock is not very good.

Rob's Reed | 171

28 The Niche   14m   8a+   ***
Stuart Cameron 1991
The essential Balmashanner examination has a very low pass rate! Excellent but extremely powerful climbing.

29 Merchant of Menace   14m   8b   **
Stuart Cameron 1992
The final hard line on the crag and undoubtedly the hardest. The sloping nature of many of the holds can make this route very condition dependant.

30 Balmashanner Buttress   14m   4+   *
Scott Muir 2005
The defining corner at the right end of the wall actually gives some enjoyable easy climbing. A variation leaves this route after its 2nd bolt and climbs the wall to its left **Chein** 6b. No hangers are in place and a further line of staple bolts, just to the left in close proximity to the Merchant, are not on the route.

Rob's Reed - Forfar

(NO 488 523) L54 E389   Alt 120m   South facing   Maps p149, p172

Rob's Reed is a quarried escarpment on Pitscandly Hill to the east of Forfar. It lies partly hidden from view in a woodland setting with flat grassy areas at the foot of the crag. The place is a natural suntrap and is often well sheltered from prevailing winds. This makes climbing here possible all year round.

The rock is fairly hard sandstone, interspersed with bands of conglomerate. This gives a completely different feel to the climbing in comparison to the other sandstone crags in the area. A steady approach seems to give the best results but even still, the odd pebble will be found that lets you down! Thuggy, gung ho climbing will inevitably end in tears! Nervous leaders might feel happier elsewhere but the drawbacks of the rock are more than outweighed by the absorbing climbing and the year round nature of the crag.

26 The Essential Balmashanner   15m   7c   *
Neil Shepherd 1992
Not without merit this route is useful as a stepping stone for those working up to the next route. Climb Gravity's Rainbow to its 4th bolt, then step left to finish up the ramp of Comfort Machine.

27 Gravity's Rainbow   15m   8a   *
Grant Farquhar, Stuart Cameron 1990
Finger wrenching moves on unnatural holds eventually lead past 6 bolts to the lower-off. Good climbing but whoever thought of chipping a finger jam?

Rob's Reed

IMPORTANT NOTE
The crag and the surrounding hillside is home to a population of Red Deer and the landowner has given permission to climb here with the proviso that the deer are not disturbed and that no access is allowed from 1 September until 31 October each year for the rut.

AMENITIES
Forfar has a McDonalds, filling stations and a decent range of shops. For climbing related supplies then Dundee or Arbroath will need to be visited.

RECOMMENDED TASTY BITES
The famous Forfar Bridie from Saddler's bakery in the East High Street of Forfar is real crag food. None of this namby-pamby, wholemeal, health conscious stuff here!

TOP TIPS
Shorts and T-shirts but climbers of a nervous disposition should bring a helmet.

DIRECTIONS
Forfar lies just off the main A90 dual carriageway between Dundee and Aberdeen (speed cameras). From the south, north and west, exit the A90 and drive through Forfar following signs for Arbroath (A932) initially, then take the B9113 Montrose road. Follow this for about 2 miles (3.2km) passing (but not taking) firstly an unsigned turning to Myreside where the crag is clearly visible up on the left, then a quarry entrance on the right. Turn off left by a house, signposted Wemyss Farm.

Reach this same point from Arbroath and the east by following the A932 Friockheim to Forfar road for 3.4 miles (5.5km) from Friockheim. A road on the right signposted Brechin and Pitkennedy is followed for 0.9 miles (1.5km) to a crossroads with the B9113 where a left turn gains the Wemyss Farm road end in 2.5 miles (4km).

Now, follow the farm road uphill through the farm buildings taking great care (20mph) and avoiding the sheepdogs! A sharp left bend leads up to the parking area, off the road on the left at the next switch-back (NO 4934 5228). Important: Do not park on the tarmac at all, even partly, since the large turning area is required for long farm vehicles. Please do not obstruct the local users, as their goodwill is relied on for access.

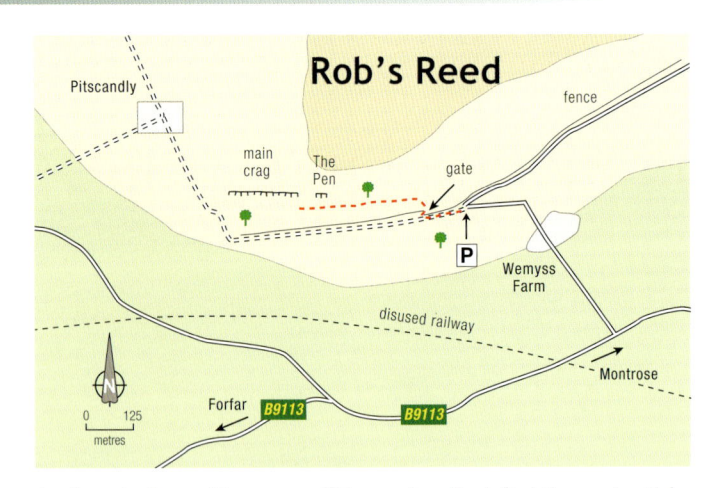

APPROACH
Time: 10mins
From the parking follow a track westwards for 50m to a gate in the deer fence on the right. It is hoped to provide a ladder stile here in the future but at present please take great care not to damage the gate whilst avoiding the fence on either side. The gate has a live electric fence on either side so please take care; more than one person has had a nasty shock from touching the wrong place. The gate itself is not electrified. Head directly uphill following a well worn track to a level area. Turn left here and continue with a couple of undulations, keeping the broken outcrops on your right. After about 70m, the sheltered bowl of The Pen is passed on the right. Another 180m further on, the ground starts to

slope down and a larger crag becomes visible on the right through the trees. Make directly for this and the right end of the main crag comes into view at NO 4890 5231.

All the routes have been equipped to a high standard using varied styles of bolts. All routes have lower-offs and going to the top should be avoided at all costs as the rock deteriorates above the lower-offs. It might be regarded as advisable to wear a helmet here but climbers should make up their own minds as to whether they think it necessary or not.

THE PEN

(NO 4910 5232)   Alt 130m   South-East facing

A recently developed and very sheltered bowl is reached first from the approach and is 180m before the main area. The lower part of the wall is hidden but a shiny lower-off is the most obvious sign. The routes are based around a shallow left-facing corner which lies between a roofed corner on the left and a big damp corner on the right.

1 Spider Pig   15m   7a+ *
Ken Edwards 2010
The wall left of the corner to a high lower-off.

2 Swine Flew   15m   6b
Ken Edwards 2010
The corner itself leads to hard moves out and left to reach the lower-off on the previous route.

3 Harry Trotter   10m   6c *
Ken Edwards 2010
The wall right of the corner to a lower level lower-off.

MAIN AREA

Diagrams p173, p175

The first section of the main area is the highest and has the most open aspect. All routes are described from this end of the crag, from right to left.

4 R n D Dubz   15m   6a *
Neil Shepherd 2010
The easier-angled buttress which sits forward from the line of the crag. Enjoyable climbing.

5 Loose Cannons   16m   6c
Neil Shepherd 2010
Climb the steep and roofed corner. The crux is turning the little lip. Follow the groove up and right to join R n D Dubz a couple of bolts short of the shared lower-off.

Rob's Reed

6 Beyond the Call of Nature   14m   7a
Neil Shepherd 2006
A hard bouldering start leads to the respite of the groove; a little loose in its upper part.

7 Going through on Aggregate   16m   7a **
Neil Shepherd 2006
This climb of two halves is easily recognized by its pink bolt hangers. The vertical, sustained lower wall leads to a thuggy roof which is crossed in a great position to an airy finish.

8 Power Flower   15m   6c *
Scott Muir 2005
An interesting route which was named as a result of an unfortunate meeting between a visiting Italian lady and the electric fence! The lower cracks lead to thin wall climbing, then the route trends leftwards to share a lower-off with the next climb.

9 High Voltage   13m   6b+   **
Scott Muir 2005
A thin start leads to quality climbing up the thin crack.

10 Burning Desire   16m   6c
Scott Muir 2005
Rubber arms or very technical climbing overcomes the start of this route and leads to the easier but sustained upper wall. Care is required with the rock on the final few feet.

11 Fire in the Hold   16m   6a+
Scott Muir 2005
A good stiff start leads again to a sustained and sometimes friable upper section.

12 Squeal like a Piggy   16m   6b
Derek Armstrong 2006
Another stiff start leads to an easier upper wall; still slightly friable in the upper third.

Dave Cowan on High Voltage (6b+), Rob's Reed (photo Gary Latter)

Rob's Reed

Another excellent easier route. A nice mixture of sandstone edges and pebble pulling.

16 Forfaraway 12m 6b *
Scott Muir 2005
Thin climbing through the conglomerate band gives the meat of this route.

17 D.I.V.O.R.C.E 14m 6c *
Scott Muir 2005
A technical and stretchy start. As with many of these routes, it's not over till it's over!

18 Leonardo da Pinchy 15m 6c+ *
Scott Muir 2005
Gain the jug at the bottom of the pod; relish it because there are few more! Blind and sustained climbing leads eventually to a rising leftward traverse to the lower-off.

**19 Deer Hunter 14m 6c+ *ND
Scott Muir 2005
A puzzling start provides the hardest climbing on this route but the groove is pumpy and blind.

ELDERS WALL AREA

The continuation of the main wall is noted as it begins above the old elder stumps and has more screening from trees in front.

**20 Pitscandly Chainsaw Massacre 15m 7a *ND
Neil Shepherd 2006
The first of a trio of similar high quality lines on well cleaned rock. Keep left of the upper groove to avoid loose rock.

21 No Respect for your Elders 15m 6c+ **
Neil Shepherd 2006
One of the best routes here and has a perplexing crux, though thankfully that obvious pocket is as good as it looks!

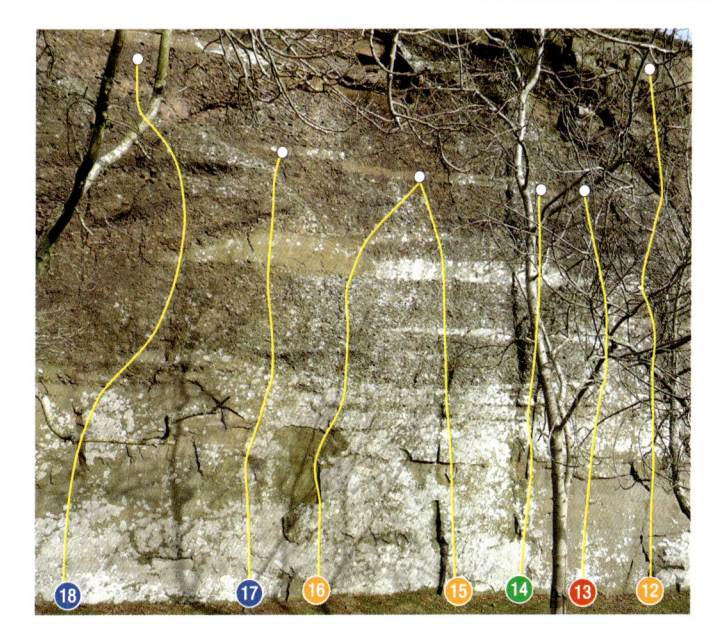

13 Rectified 12m 7b
Neil Shepherd 2010
The oft-looked blank wall to the right of Horny Deer. A profusion of tiny holds and truly technical moves lead to better edges, then a perplexing move off a good pocket brings easier ground to hand.

14 Horny Deer 12m 5+ *
Scott Muir 2005
Good climbing and the inevitable warm-up at this end of the crag.

15 Italian Stallion 12m 6a *
Scott Muir 2005

Rob's Reed

㉒ Fretting over Nothing   15m   7a+ ★★
Neil Shepherd 2006
The hardest of the trio and a good long reach helps, though flexibility can get the reach impaired through the difficulty. Reasons to fret include a contorted mantelshelf on the upper wall.

㉓ Need for Speed   15m   6c
Scott Muir 2005
Another hard start, with fingery climbing in and around the thin seam. Easier above the 3rd bolt.

㉔ Closed Project   15m
Julie Pearson
Please respect the equipper's efforts. There is a line of old bolts close on its left, but they stop halfway up the cliff.

㉕ Autobahn   12m   6c+   ★★
Scott Muir 2006
A good route with varied clmbing. Start up the initial crack-line to gain the conglomerate band. The twin cracks are tricky to gain and harder to climb!

㉖ Grand Theft Auto   12m   7a+   ★
Scott Muir 2006
Easier to start than the previous route but harder and more sustained once into the conglomerate and the upper crack.

㉗ Gatecrashers Galore   12m   7b
Neil Shepherd 2006
A hard route on slightly friable rock in its middle section. More often walked past than probably any other route on the crag! Awkward start then full on moves through the pebbledash gains the big smiley jug. Reach right to the lower-off and remember to walk on by next time!

㉘ One Foot in the Door   12m   7a   ★
Neil Shepherd 2006
Easier and on better rock, this route gets more traffic though is still not a pushover.

㉙ The Uninvited   12m   7a+   ★
Neil Shepherd 2006
A hard bulging start leads to a good shake, then thin climbing on hard to spot holds in the upper section.

CENTRAL SECTION

Diagram p177

This is the short central section of the crag which contains a fine mix of climbing styles. With a couple of thick mats some of these could almost be boulder problems. Do not fall into the trap of complacency though as short doesn't always mean easy!

Rob's Reed

33 Short Haul 7m 7a
Ken Edwards 2007
The bulge is approached by a traverse in from the right and overcome with some monstrous undercutting.

34 Get Shorty 7m 6c+ *
Ken Edwards 2007
A desperate slab start. From the finger edge gain the mono up and right and crank through to better holds. Short and sweet!

35 Welcome to the Big Pocket 10m 6c **
Ken Edwards 2006
A crag classic. A thin slab start from the left gains the pocket of the name and here an elegant mantel or a hideous struggle gains better holds in the block overhang above. The headwall is an anticlimax but make sure you don't come off as you will not want to climb the start again....!

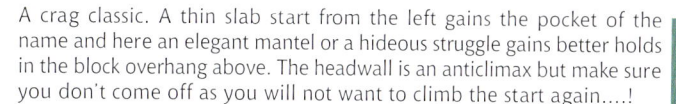

36 Grasping the Nettle 10m 6c
Neil Shepherd 2006
A bit of a conundrum here. Although realistically the same grade as the last route most people find this one comparatively easy!

An undeveloped section of rock leads leftwards to the next sector which is easily recognised by some huge overhangs.

SECTOR CARAVAN

Diagrams p178
This area of the crag has some roof climbing at its right side leading to steep slabs on its left.

37 Totally Trashed 8m 7b *
Neil Shepherd 2009
Hard moves over the roof right of the obvious corner of Trailer Trash. Sustained hard climbing might leave you as the name suggests! Long legs are an advantage here.

30 Sold Short 7m 6c *
Neil Shepherd 2007
The hanging arete gives better climbing than its short length would suggest. Well worth the effort.

31 Closed Project 7m
Neil Shepherd
Please respect the equipper's efforts.

32 Closed Project 7m
Ken Edwards
Please respect the equipper's efforts

178 Rob's Reed

(38) Trailer Trash 9m 7b *
Neil Shepherd 2006
Gain a standing position above the lip of the huge roof under the big corner and it's in the bag. Getting there though is a gymnastic nightmare!

(39) Dennis Caravan 12m 7b *
Neil Shepherd 2006
Another big roof to overcome at the start. A treat for the thugs amongst us. As with the last route it may be found to be easy in the grade.

(40) End of the Road 12m 7a+
Neil Shepherd 2007
A slightly smaller but still substantial roof to overcome at the start gives the meat of the route. Careful pocket and pebble pulling above will see it in the bag.

(41) Snail's Pace 12m 6c
Neil Shepherd 2007
The thin seam come crack-line is gained by some nice moves.

(42) Head of the Queue 12m 6c *
Ken Edwards 2007
The more obvious crack climbed with a lot more difficulty than would at first appear.

Rob's Reed

43 Towed in the Hole   12m   7a
Ken Edwards 2007
A thin start leads to a thin middle, then easier enjoyable climbing above.

44 Good Boy Jo Jo   10m   6b+ *
Iain McDonald 2007
Another technical start, then fine moves on good but sparse pockets.

DIRTY HARRY'S CAVE

Diagrams p178, p179
This feature should be fairly obvious to all. The perfect pick-me-up if you were at all disappointed with the size of the overhangs in the last sector!

45 Make my Day   10m   6a *
Neil Shepherd 2007
The right-hand arete of the cave itself and the warm-up at this end of the crag. Always climbing up and right, head to a lower-off shared with Good Boy Jo Jo.

46 Dirty Harry   12m   6b *
Neil Shepherd 2007
Another fine easy route. Starts just left of the previous climb to gain the groove, then airy and spectacular climbing up and left above the lip to gain the lower-off.

47 The Enforcer   11m   7b **
Neil Shepherd 2007
If one roof isn't enough this climb takes in three! Start a couple of metres into the cave. Climb the double roof. The crux is the short wall below the next overhang. Cross this final overhang to gain a handy lower-off. Low in the grade.

48 The Reinforcer   13m   7c ***
Neil Shepherd 2009
The Enforcer's big brother. Climbs through the multiple roof stack to the left of Enforcer. Eventually reach a lower-off near the top of the crag.

49 Dead Pull   13m   7b+ **
Neil Shepherd 2010
Slow to dry but gives a fantastic roof trip when fully dry. The line of resin ring bolts mark the line, a reasonable shake out is available at the lip of the first big roof.

50 Climb and Punishment   13m   7b ***
Ken Edwards 2009
Brilliant roof climbing on the caves left wall. Technically the big brother of Car Pit Baggers I suppose! Watch those fingers in the shot hole pockets!

Legaston Quarry

51 **Car Pit Baggers** 12m 7a+ **
Ken Edwards 2007
Towards the left side of the cave, a belter of a route! Steep and powerful to breach the initial roof then the technical crux followed by an enjoyable but still not easy upper wall.

52 **Skullduggery** 12m 6c *
Ken Edwards 2007
A line parallel to the previous route gives an easier companion. Climb up the steep groove and thug through the bulges. The upper wall is still sustained right up to the lower-off.

53 **The Sheep of Things to Come** 11m 6b+
Neil Shepherd 2007
This gruesome bulging groove marks the end of the cave proper. All over when the big corner is reached.

54 **Little Bo Peep** 8m 6b
Iain McDonald 2007
The steep grooved nose. Short but intense and offers better climbing than would at first appear. Worth doing.

Legaston Quarry - Friockheim

(NO 5895 4862) L54 E382   Alt 50m   West and North facing   Maps p149, p180

This extensive quarry lies north of Arbroath, near the village of Friockheim, just off the main A933 Arbroath to Brechin road. It provides a useful sport climbing venue for Dundee and the surrounding region and is especially popular in the summer evenings when time is too limited to travel to more distant crags. The quarry is sheltered and the main walls benefit from afternoon and evening sun.

Unfortunately the local farmer sometimes uses the quarry floor as a dumping ground and piles of stones and other farm debris are often present in the place. It is usually kept well clear of the walls and during the summer is cloaked in a natural screen of vegetation. During the winter months the quarry can be particularly grim but several routes are often dry almost all year round.

The rock is very compact sandstone which was used extensively for local building. Horizontal breaks and pockets are common and this tends to give a reachy style of climbing, the 'Legaston Rockover' being a useful technique on many routes. On the less popular climbs the rock can be dusty and sometimes lichenous but in the main it is solid and clean.

Almost all of the sport climbs have lower-off points at the top, an increasing number of which require threading with the rope and it is important that climbers are confident in their own ability to perform this safely before embarking on these routes. If top roping these routes it is important that climbers use their own karabiners rather than running the rope through the fixed gear, this will greatly prolong the life expectancy of the fixed gear, and hopefully those using it!

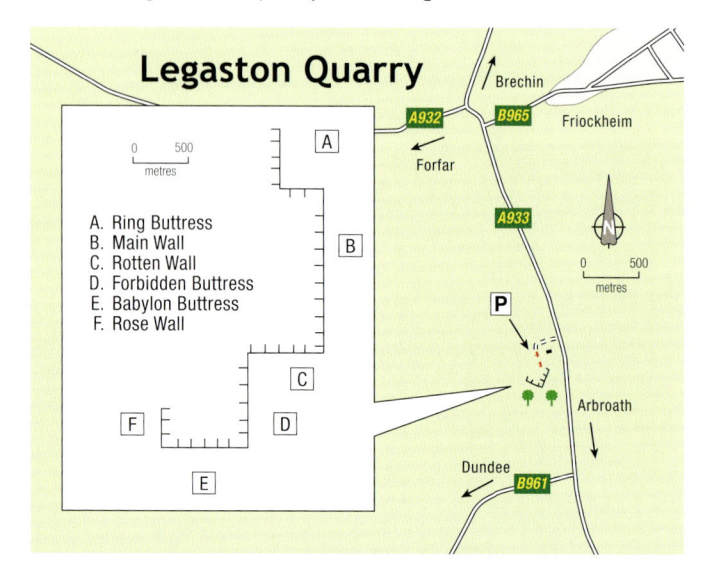

Legaston Quarry

A. Ring Buttress
B. Main Wall
C. Rotten Wall
D. Forbidden Buttress
E. Babylon Buttress
F. Rose Wall

At present it is obvious that the same old routes are getting all the traffic. This means that many good quality routes such as Weasel on Rose Wall and the Babylon Buttress routes, when dry, are becoming overgrown. It isn't far to walk to these routes and it's worth asking yourself whilst on your umpteenth ascent of Between the Lines if it's not time to try something different!

AMENITIES
Provisions can be purchased in nearby Friockheim. Some climbing supplies can be obtained in Arbroath either at Basecamp or Outdoor Action.

RECOMMENDED TASTY BITES
Trumperton Forge Tearoom or The Hamlet Tearoom; both in the nearby village of Letham, to the west.

TOP TIPS
Take care when leaving the parking spot as traffic comes down the hill from the right at high speed.

DIRECTIONS
Approaching from the south via Arbroath, follow the A933 for 5 miles (8km) or so to pass the B961 off left. This road is signposted to Redford & Newbigging and since it leads to Dundee, it is an option for those coming from that direction. Continue down the hill on the A933 for another 0.35 miles (600m) and just round the bend at the bottom of the hill, turn off to the left to park on the right, at the start of a rough track leading to a cottage, NO 5895 4995.

Approaching from the north it is best to leave the A90 at Brechin and follow the A933 towards Arbroath. After a junction on the left to Friockheim, continue 0.4 miles (700m) to the end of a long straight where there is a cottage. The quarry lies in the wooded hillocks behind and to the right of this cottage. Park on the right, at the start of a rough track. The A923 from Forfar to Friockheim is also an option with the crags at Rob's Reed, Balmashanner and Kirrie Hill all being close.

When parking please take note of the sign and try to maintain a reasonable distance from the cottage to preserve the good relations presently enjoyed with the residents. Remember you are parking on their land. These relations will be helped if dogs are not brought to this crag and the language is kept clean. The owner of the quarry has made a special request that climbers leave Fido at home.

APPROACH
Time: 2mins
Walk along the track past the cottage, round a locked gate and through the trees into the quarry.

The climbing is divided into six separate buttresses; these are described from left to right. The routes are also described from left to right on each buttress.

RING BUTTRESS
(NO 5896 4861)   West facing   Map p180
This is the buttress partly obscured by trees on the left side of the quarry. Named after the prominent iron ring at its top, it receives a good share of afternoon and evening sun. The buttress does not suffer from seepage and often remains in climbable condition all year round.

On the left section of the buttress are two converging wide cracks. The left is Very Difficult and the right Severe, with an eliminate VS 4c between them.

1 The Killing Fields   10m   6a
Brian Tilley 1985
An eliminate up the wall keeping right of the wide crack to a shared lower-off.

2 Armygeddon   10m   5+ *
Neil Shepherd 1982
A full-height thin crack. A low crux bulge leads to easier climbing.

Legaston Quarry

**③ Driller Killer   10m   6c **
Neil Shepherd 1984
Good climbing up the smooth wall right of the previous route, technically challenging with a fingery crux.

④ Trial by Dimension   10m   7a
Unknown 1995
A very eliminate route which is even more reach dependant than the norm at this crag!

⑤ Flight of the Mad Magician   10m   6b **
Neil Shepherd 1984
Driller Killer's easier companion, with sustained wall climbing on better holds. Most people elect to lower off the huge iron ring but be warned it is not UIAA approved!

⑥ Seconds Out   10m   5+
Graham Woodfine 1984
The obvious thin seam on the right of the face is quite awkward in the middle and has a long reach at the top.

MAIN WALL

(NO 5895 4860)   West facing   Map p180   Diagram p183
The obvious long back wall of the quarry contains a varied selection of routes. The right-hand section is usually green all winter but the steeper left side can often be found dry all year round.

⑦ Ratbag   12m   6a
Chris Flewett 1984
Superseded by the next route though still worth doing; shared lower-off.

The next two routes have lost a few feet at the start after some excavations were carried out in 1997. Care should be taken as this has left some potential for decking out whilst clipping their second bolts.

⑧ Hunt the Ratbag   12m   6b *
Miles Bright 1989
A direct on Ratbag and better climbing. Climb directly, via a series of difficult reaches, to the lower-off on Ratbag. High in the grade.

⑨ Death is the Hunter   12m   6b+ **
Neil Shepherd 1984
A good wall climb and again stiffly graded. Sustained climbing on small edges gains bigger breaks before finishing awkwardly at the lower-off beneath the tree.

⑩ Sweet Revenge   15m   6a **
Graham Woodfine 1984
An excellent trip; the gear placments are all still there if you want to savour the flavour of the first ascent.

Legaston Quarry 183

11 Junk Man Blues   12m   6a+ *
Dave Johnston 1992
The parallel line just right of Sweet Revenge to a lower-off.

12 Between the Lines   12m   5+ *
Neil Shepherd 1984
A popular route with enjoyable and strenuous climbing. It now has an independent start just right of the last route. Continue direct to a lower-off.

13 Bomber   12m   6a+ *
Neil Shepherd 1984
A nice slab leads to a strenuous crux over the obvious square-cut roof.

14 Brian the Snail   12m   6a
Neil Shepherd 1985
Non-descript climbing up the next smooth section of wall.

15 Brian the Snail Direct   12m   7b
Neil Shepherd 1985
A very difficult but eliminate boulder problem start to the original route.

Legaston Quarry

Gain the small flake on the original line by very technical climbing. If this route doesn't feel desperate then you are either off route or going very well! Rarely repeated in true fashion.

16 The Rocking Stone   12m   4+   *
Unknown 1983
The re-cleaned and bolted fault-line gives excellent and easier climbing.

17 March of Dimes   12m   6a
Malcolm Cameron 1985
The first route on the right side of the wall. An awkward bulging wall provides the archetypal one move wonder.

18 Shoot to Kill   12m   5+   *
Neil Shepherd 1983
Good balance is required climbing up the shallow scoop. Pulling out of the scoop is the crux. With only 2 bolts in its length it feels a bit run out.

19 Overkill   12m   6b   *
Neil Shepherd 1984
Short and sweet. The meat of the route is the middle tier and thin crimping is the dish of the day! Shared lower-off with the next route.

20 Desperate Measures   13m   6b
Neil Shepherd 1984
A companion route to Overkill. Keep left of the bolt, or easier (5+) using holds right of the bolt.

21 Fire at Will   13m   4+
Neil Shepherd 1983
Easier climbing up the wall right of the staircase.

The next routes lie on the big slab at the right end of Main Wall. They have been cleaned from under a dense carpet of moss but are all on very sound rock. They deserve to become more popular. Increased popularity would also have the beneficial effect of stopping the moss growing back.

22 Walking the Straight Line   13m   4+
Neil Shepherd 1984
Enjoyable climbing direct to a twin staple lower-off.

23 Ain't no Rolling Stone   13m   4+
Neil Shepherd 1996
And it certainly gathers moss.... Another easy sport route which deserves more traffic.

24 The Rack   14m   4+
Brian Tilley 1984
The third line on this slab starts by some faint paint marks and climbs directly to a lower-off shared with the next route.

25 Lemon Squeezy   14m   4+
David Pert 1996
The last line on the slab before the overgrown and unsurprisingly unclimbed corner.

ROTTEN WALL

(NO 5893 4865)   North facing   Map p180   Diagram p185
This wall now sports several routes. The newer routes are on slightly friable rock but are cleaning up well with traffic. The effects of the 1997 landscaping are particularly noticeable here with the appearance of a deep pit below Hell's Bells taking its start down in the general direction that the name suggests!

26 The Golden Shot   13m   6b+   *
Neil Shepherd 1986
Good sustained climbing up the extreme left-hand side of Rotten Wall. Start on the ledge on the left and pull right onto the wall, continue almost directly to the lower-off. The direct start is 7a and a well hard boulder problem in its own right.

Legaston Quarry

30 Hell's Bells 15m 6c ★★
Jeff Ross 1989
A companion route to the previous one, with another very hard start. Now starts from the pit and feels harder as a result.

31 Fire Down Below 15m 6a+
Neil Shepherd 2000
The line of gold coloured hangers rising from the base of the pit. Good climbing.

32 Demolition Man 14m 5+
Neil Shepherd 2000
The next line of gold coloured hangers at the far side of the pit. Easier to start using the first hold of the next route but a dyno to leave the deck is also acceptable.

33 The Big J 13m 6b
Neil Shepherd 2000
A small route with a big character! Climb easily up to the big chipped J; use this and some pockets to reach the half-height ledge and finish up the next route.

27 Charred and Damned Desire 13m 7b+ ★
Neil Shepherd 1995
A candidate for the new crag test piece it has not been affected with the lowering of ground level. A stick-clip however makes good sense now!

28 The Hunting Swan 13m 6b+
Neil Shepherd 2000
An indirect start to the next route joining it above its crux. Not as good as the original start but maybe a little easier.

29 First to Fall 13m 6b+ ★
Neil Shepherd 1984
You may no longer be the first but you sure won't be the last! A hard and fingery start is the sticking point for most people.

34 Rocket's Secret Machine 13m 7a ★
Neil Shepherd 2000
An excellent boulder problem start and a hardish move on the upper wall make this route fairly tough. Only really spoiled by the resting ledge available in the middle.

35 Everything Must Go 13m 6a
Neil Shepherd 1996
And most of it did! An easier line just left of the arete with staple bolts. Quite enjoyable climbing but needs more traffic.

36 Edge of Darkness 16m 6a ★
Neil Shepherd 1986
Climb the obvious sharp arete at the right-hand end of the wall, first on

the left face for 8m, then swing right to holds on the arete; 3 bolts to a choice of belay stakes at the top.

FORBIDDEN BUTTRESS

(NO 5892 4859)   West facing   Map p180

This buttress runs parallel to Main Wall and forms the left side of a small square extension to the quarry.

The left side of the buttress contains some traditional climbs. The wide crack just right of the arete is **Purple Haze** (VS 4b). The next crack is **Night-Time Sorrows** (VS 4c). The corner-crack to the right is **Virgin Crack** (VD) and the layback crack leading left into the top of Virgin Crack is **Kiss of Death** (VS 4b). The sport routes are found on the smooth wall to the right and are the best at Legaston. Ground level has risen a couple of feet here since the first ascents which may have left the spacing of the first bolts feeling a bit odd.

37 Direct Access   15m   6c *
Neil Shepherd 1994
Supersedes the old trad route **Mr. Access**. No longer a mere variation on No Remorse it still shares one hold at half-height with that route though using it with the opposite hand (hint!)

38 No Remorse   15m   6c+ ***
Neil Shepherd 1985
Probably the quarry's best route. Sustained and technical wall climbing. A reasonable rest is available just above half-height. Lower-off up and right shared with the next route.

39 Spandex Ballet   15m   7a+ ***
Neil Shepherd 1986
The harder companion to No Remorse gives excellent climbing, rather desperate for the short. Gain and climb the shot hole to a semi-rest. Continue on pockets until an extended Legaston Rockover up and right gains small finger holds. Cross the overlap directly and reach the lower-off.

BABYLON BUTTRESS

North facing   Map p180

This buttress forms the back wall of the small square extension. The name stems from the fact that it once resembled the hanging gardens. Lack of traffic on some routes is seeing a return of vegetation, however, please don't be scared to clean some of this off! Unfortunately the wall gets a lot of drainage and takes longer to dry out than Creag an Dubh Loch and is usually seeping for nine months out of twelve! Once dry, however, it provides several good routes on the best rock in the quarry. The excavations of 1997 have left a superb landing for the bouldering wall at the right end and the excellent low-level traverse is not nearly as scary as it used to be! The starts of most of the right-hand routes are now excellent boulder problems in their own right and much more difficult. The gradings have been revised to reflect this.

Legaston Quarry

(40) Open Project
1995
A line of bolt studs marks this out. It only seems to dry about once every 10 years so any prospective first ascentionist will have plenty of time to get fit!

(41) She Conceives Destruction   14m   7a
George Ridge 1995
Another rarely dry pitch, but at least it comes into condition more often than its left-hand neighbour! A carefully crafted route which, unusually for this crag, proves easier for those short on reach.

(42) Aerodynamic   14m   7b *
Neil Shepherd 1986
A desperate route climbing the thin seam splitting the smooth upper half of the wall by a very explosive sequence, pause only to clip the bolt runner in mid-flight! This route takes a long time to dry. The obvious direct start has been climbed, but is rarely dry.

(43) Lymphomaniac   13m   6a
Neil Shepherd 1985
Worthwhile when clean but does tend to get a bit overgrown.

(44) Roxanne   18m   4 *
Neil Shepherd 1985
A rising diagonal traverse which takes in some fine positions to finish at the lower-off on Necrosis. Clip as many bolts as you can reach as you go!

(45) Diss!   13m   6b
Neil Shepherd 2001
A route squeezed in to utilise the excellent boulder problem start.

(46) Nymphocyte   13m   6b+ *
Neil Shepherd 1984
Good climbing up the central groove after a hard problem start. Lower-off shared with the next route.

Walter Taylor getting Sweet Revenge (6a), Main Wall, Legaston (photo Brian Duthie)

Legaston Quarry

**47 Playing with Fire 13m 6c ** **
Neil Shepherd 1984
An excellent route with varied climbing. Thin in places but hidden jugs in others.

**48 Les Morts Dansant 13m 7a ** **
Neil Shepherd 1985
A technical eliminate up the obvious overhung corner and headwall above. The crux is usually found to be the start for those under six feet tall.

49 Necrosis 13m 6a *
Neil Shepherd 1984
Good climbing up and over the roofed nose.

ROSE WALL

East facing   Map p180
This is the wall facing Forbidden Buttress and running at 90 degrees to Babylon Buttress. Pleasantly it catches the morning sun. Unfortunately it is rather neglected and would benefit from more traffic.

50 Exodus 12m 5
Neil Shepherd 1985
Feels a bit squeezed in, but gives enjoyable climbing with plenty of bolts. Follow the gold coloured hangers directly to a twin ring lower-off.

51 The Weasel 12m 6a+ *
Neil Shepherd 1985
An enjoyable little route which should be far more popular.

52 Remain in Light 12m 6b+ *
Ken Clarke 1986
This eliminate climbs the obvious right arete of the buttress. A hard move past the first bolt leads to better holds on the arete proper. Continue direct. The ethical and the masochistic will avoid the holds in the corner to the right.

Arbroath Sea-Cliffs - Arbroath

L54 E382   Maps p149, p189, p191, p207

These are the sandstone sea-cliffs running north from the busy coastal town of Arbroath. They extend more or less unbroken for several kilometres between Arbroath and Lunan Bay though all of the climbing at present is located in the first kilometre or so as reached from Arbroath. The style of the climbing is due in part to the easily eroded nature of the sandstone and also to the dipping nature of the strata. Rounded and sloping holds predominate and give the area an almost gritstone like feel, though pockets and pebbles also make for some interesting moves. The rock along the length of these cliffs varies from near collapse in some places to outstandingly solid in others. In general the routes are concentrated in the good areas! The sandstone is quite porous so its softness is much more noticeable after rain and the area might best be avoided if there has been a lot of rain. However, though caution should be taken at all times, there have been very few problems with loose rock reported so far but take care with pebbles!

The sea-cliffs at Arbroath are not quite the natural phenomenon that they at first appear. Whilst other sea-cliff areas in the North-East have very visible and intrusive signs of quarrying, the cliffs at Arbroath don't. However, they have also been quarried and on a fairly large scale. Unlike their counterparts further north which have historically recent quarrying with its attendant industrialisation, most of the quarrying here was carried out from the middle of the twelfth century onwards. This is thought to have waned towards the time of the industrial revolution, but by this stage a huge amount of rock had been removed. The full extent of the quarrying can be seen when viewed from above the routes at The Rut. The cliff-top is an area of specific interest and many uncommon and even rare species of plants and wildlife can be found here. Some areas have a SSSI designation and the areas beyond the Mermaids Kirk are also part of the Seaton Cliffs Wildlife Reserve managed by the Scottish Wildlife Trust. It goes without saying that climbers should act in a responsible manner and avoid damaging the clifftop environment in any way.

This area gives some tremendous sport climbing in an atmosphere and

Arbroath Sea Cliffs 189

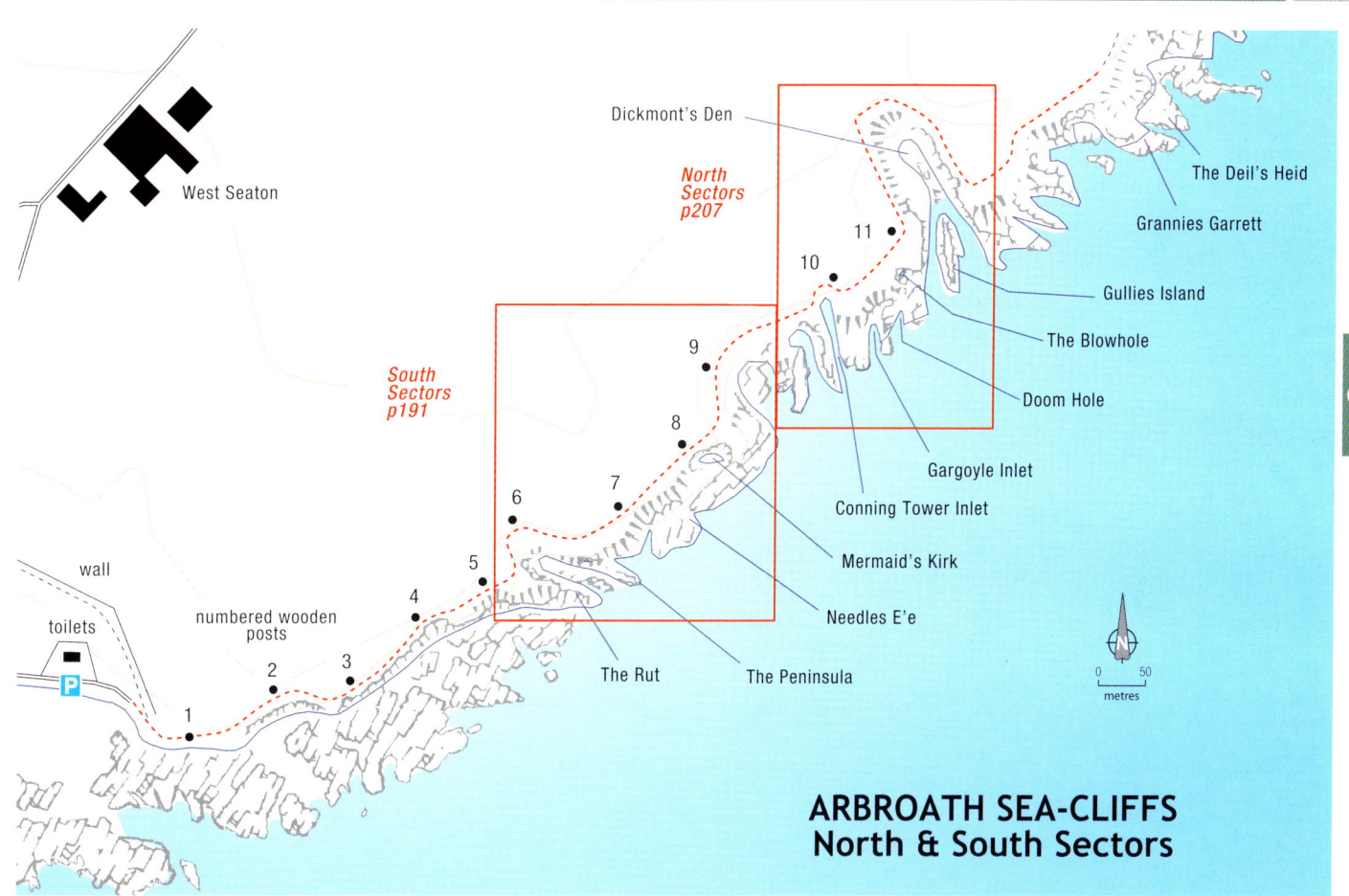

**ARBROATH SEA-CLIFFS
North & South Sectors**

West Seaton

Dickmont's Den

North Sectors p207

South Sectors p191

The Deil's Heid
Grannies Garrett
Gullies Island
The Blowhole
Doom Hole
Gargoyle Inlet
Conning Tower Inlet
Mermaid's Kirk
Needles E'e
The Peninsula
The Rut

numbered wooden posts

wall
toilets
P

Angus

style unique in Scotland if not the U.K. The style of the climbing has been described as "adventure sport climbing". Unlike the usual Scottish sport climbing areas which have lower-off points and fairly easy access the routes at Arbroath often involve committing abseils and in many cases the second has to follow removing the draws. The adventure however does not extend to minimalist bolting and most routes should be found to be adequately equipped.

There are few problems with seabirds or nests and unlike some of the other well developed sport climbing areas in Scotland there are no ticks or midges! The weather in this part of the country is also a bonus having one of the countries lowest rainfall figures and plenty of sunshine. Welcome to the Costa Arbroath!

Balancing this on the downside however, are the usual sea-cliff problems of greasiness and tidal access which can make some areas hard to get in the correct condition. This seems to sit well however with the overall adventure feel. Generally speaking, a dry and breezy day will see many routes in a climbable state. Some of the more recessed lines, especially on the north and north-east faces may take a north-easterly wind to thoroughly dry. Where this is particularly problematic it is mentioned in the text.

The area contains several projects. Active projects will normally be marked with tape round some of the staples or hangers missing. Please respect the effort someone has already put into equipping and cleaning a project which is active. For anyone interested in further development it should be noted that the minimum acceptable standard for fixed gear on these cliffs is stainless steel retained with resin adhesive.

AMENITIES

The pretty coastal town of Arbroath has most facilities and an outdoor shop, Basecamp, where chalk and various items can be obtained.

RECOMMENDED TASTY BITES

Marco's fish and chipper overlooking the harbour is good but being popular, may involve a wait.

DIRECTIONS

From everywhere except the North-East, reach Arbroath by dual carriageway from Dundee, whose ring road makes this approach easiest, even from the Inverness direction (A9). From the north-east use the A90 via either Montrose (A937 & A92), or Brechin (A933).

In Arbroath, there are signposts to Victoria Park and Cliffs now on nearly all of the major routes into the town. Follow these heading towards the harbour initially until the long promenade park, known as Victoria Park, is reached. Drive out to the far end of this and park in the vicinity of the path leading up onto the cliff-top, NO 6583 4113. There are public toilets here and at least one if not more in-situ ice cream vans. The number of ice cream vans can often be used as a reliable weather indicator!

APPROACH

Time: 7-15mins

See each area for a detailed approach description. The cliff-top path is part of the Seaton Cliffs Nature Trail and the numbers on 1m wooden posts along the path for the nature trail provide useful reference points for the climbing areas. The posts are every 100m from the end of the car park and labelled AS01 to AS05, but then only the number 6 upwards. Eight figure map references are also given in case the posts are removed or vandalised.

THE RUT

(NO 6635 4121 - base)   Non-tidal   South-West Facing
Map p191   Diagram p192

An area of short routes on good rock with some varied bouldering. The base of The Rut itself slopes downwards in the line of the strata to the sea and this means care should be taken when bouldering here. Facing the sea, the left wall has an enjoyable selection of very short routes which offer some fun climbing and are nearly always dry. The ease of access and the fact that they can be combined with some excellent bouldering makes this area worthy of a visit. Generally the routes are non-tidal although in a rough sea it can be atmospheric, not to mention

Arbroath Sea Cliffs

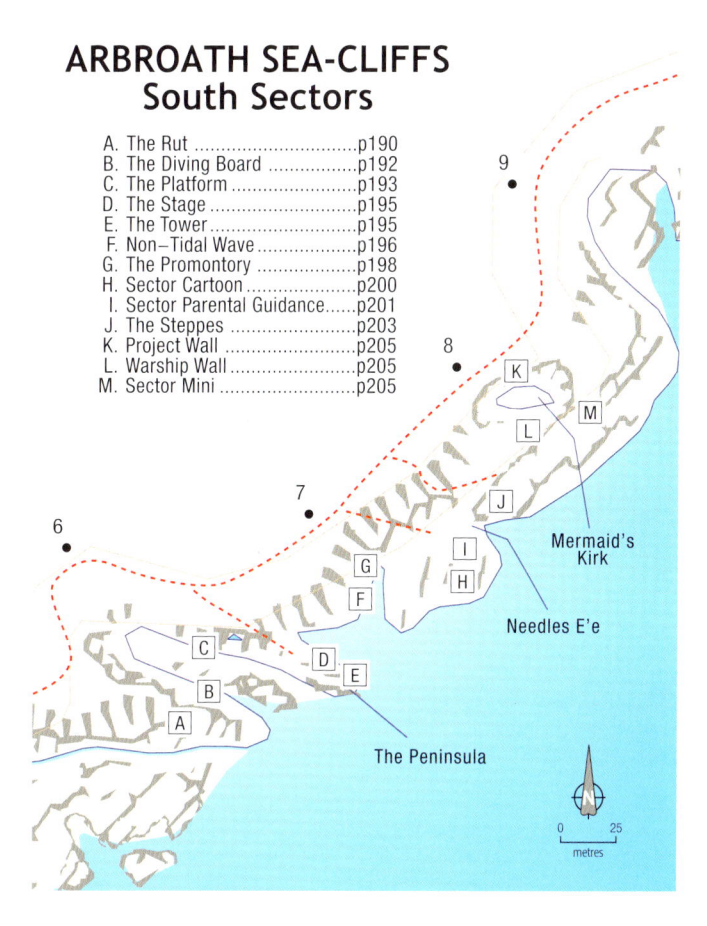

ARBROATH SEA-CLIFFS
South Sectors

A. The Rut p190
B. The Diving Board p192
C. The Platform p193
D. The Stage p195
E. The Tower p195
F. Non–Tidal Wave p196
G. The Promontory p198
H. Sector Cartoon p200
I. Sector Parental Guidance p201
J. The Steppes p203
K. Project Wall p205
L. Warship Wall p205
M. Sector Mini p205

dangerous! There are two staple belays on the flat area above the routes. Some of these routes started life as top-rope problems before being soloed showing that the currently fashionable practice of head-pointing is nothing new!

APPROACH

This is the first developed area encountered when following the cliff-top path north-eastwards from Victoria Park. From the end of the car park, follow this path for 500m to post AS05 where there is a seat and bench. This is at the point where the path cuts slightly inland round the first of the really deep inlets. Follow a very eroded path in a deep rut carefully down the southern side of this inlet to reach a flat area of rock platform well above the sea.

The routes are described from left to right, facing the wall.

1 Stag Night 5m 5+
Neil Shepherd 1982
The furthest left route.

2 Strut yer Stuff 5m 6b
Neil Shepherd 1995
Fingery and technical to gain the top.

3 Burning with Anxiety 6m 6b+
Neil Shepherd 1995
The hardest route here feels a bit squeezed in and has a boulder problem type crux to reach the top from the break.

4 Road Rage 6m 6a+ *
Neil Shepherd 1982
A really nice series of moves using the deep pocket on the upper section.

5 Flaked Out 7m 5 **
Neil Shepherd 1981
The obvious hanging flake. The best route here and an excellent small climb which deserves traffic.

Arbroath Sea Cliffs

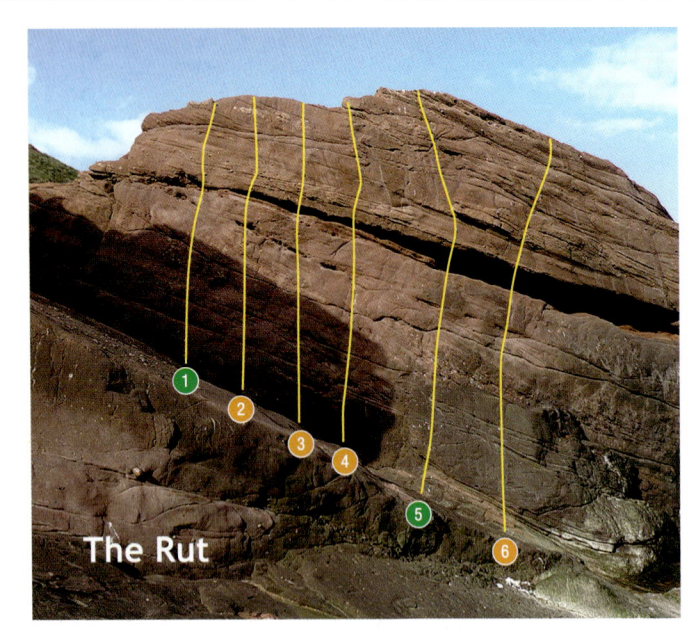

⑥ Stuck in a Rut   7m   6a
Neil Shepherd 1995
More delicate in nature than the previous routes.

THE DIVING BOARD

(NO 6636 4123 - top)   Tidal   North facing   Map p191

The northern boundary of the area of rock above The Rut falls steeply into the deep inlet to the north. Below the steepest section of this wall lies a small tidal ledge known as The Diving Board. At lowish tide it can be clearly viewed from the other side of the inlet above the Platform. There are two routes here up the impending wall, both of which give superb steep climbing when in condition. The face unfortunately is prone to greasiness and requires dry conditions, preferably with a good north-easterly breeze bringing it into condition.

APPROACH

Approach is by abseil from the belay staples above The Rut. Care should be taken to keep a swing going on the way down as the wall is very overhanging.

● In at the Deep End   12m   7a *
Neil Shepherd 2001
Climb easily out left from the Diving Board before blasting straight up the grossly overhanging wall on surprising holds.

● Take the Plunge   11m   6b+ *
Neil Morrison 2001
The line directly above the belay ledge proves to be quite sustained and pumpy.

THE PENINSULA & THE TOWER

(NO 664 413)   Map p191

The next area of climbing lies on the north side of the deep inlet marked on the path with the number six. It consists of a narrow peninsula which ends in a narrow neck beyond which is a squat tower of rock. At present there are four separate faces with climbing in this area.

GENERAL APPROACH

Follow the cliff-top path past Post 6 and continue round the deep inlet for approximately 50m until the path starts to head north-eastwards and runs parallel to the sea again. Immediately on the right a grassy path slopes gently down to a steep eroded section. Descend this with great care, as there is an unexpected big drop to the left side, to reach the large flat area which makes up the top of the peninsula. Belay stakes and multiple bolts are located here.

Arbroath Sea Cliffs

The Platform

**(NO 6639 4125 – top)   Partially Tidal   South facing
Map p191**

This is one of the best walls in the area and forms the south facing side of the peninsula. It receives a lot of sunshine, even in winter and is mainly free from seepage so can usually be relied upon to be in condition. The routes towards the right end are tidal and the whole platform itself can be sea washed and should be regarded as tidal in high seas. There are numerous bolts and a couple of old stakes to belay on above the routes. When belaying above the left-hand routes numerous bolts will also be found near the cliff-top. It is advisable to use as many of these as you can or belay back at the abseil anchors! Some of the routes here now have lower-offs and more may be equipped in this way in the future.

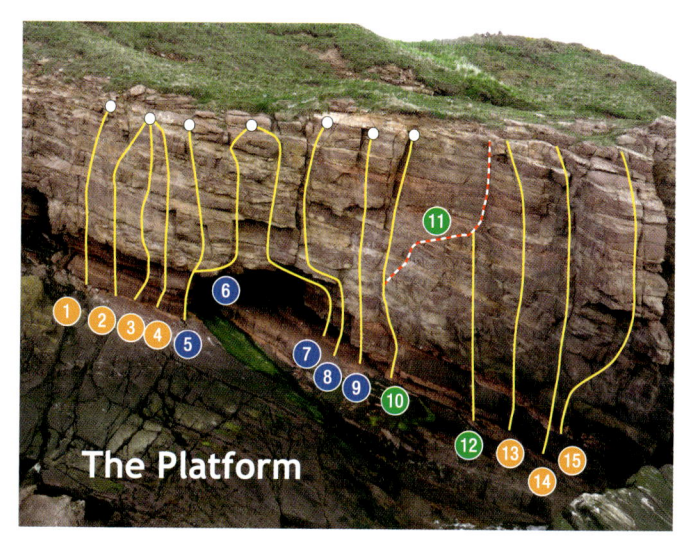

APPROACH

Most usually by abseil, either from the bolts and the twin stakes (which are becoming corroded) above the left-hand routes, or from the bolts and wedged stake for the right end. In bigger seas or at high tide, abseiling down the opposite side of Peninsula can be sensible – this effectively takes you down to The Backstage.

From the left end and facing the wall the routes are:

1 Smokies   10m   6b+ *
George Ridge 1995
A local delicacy and a tasty route as well!

2 Ride 'em Cowboy   10m   6b+ **
George Ridge 1995
Similar but slightly easier climbing. Another thuggy start and delicate finish.

3 Waves of Emotion   11m   6b+ *
George Ridge 1995
Try not to get too overcome as this is the easiest of this similar trio.

4 Parson's Nose   12m   6b *
George Ridge 1995
More good climbing and a little less powerful than the last route.

5 Caught Red-Handed   13m   6c **
George Ridge 1995
Another quality route which is quite a bit harder than those further left. Gain the hanging nose from the front gymnastically. Further acrobatics lead slightly rightwards and up the gently impending wall.

6 Impaled on the Horns of Indecision   15m   6c+ *
Neil Shepherd 2001
Slightly more sustained than the last route.

Arbroath Sea Cliffs

A through cave separates the left-hand routes from the right-hand ones and leads through to The Backstage. When conditions are dry and at low to mid tide, it is possible to traverse through this cave and eventually round to the Non-Tidal Wave and the Needles E'e.

The routes on the right of the cave are again described from left to right.

7 Cast Adrift on the Ocean of Uncertainty   16m   7a+ *
Neil Shepherd 2001
The first line starts at a sandstone coloured bolt hanger. Pull up and left to gain a very strenuous hand-traverse below the roof. Turn the roof and gain a poor rest on a small ledge (try facing out). Pull over the roof above and finish directly with further pumpy climbing.

8 At the Crossroads of Destiny and Desire   14m   7a **
Neil Shepherd 2001
The short overhung corner with two closely spaced bolts leads to the right end of the roof. Make a strenuous finger traverse left along here to gain the big hanging groove proper. Strenuous climbing up this leads to another pumpy top-out. A sustained route of quality.

9 Foundering on the Rocks of Obsession   12m   7a
Neil Shepherd 1994
One of the few routes at Arbroath to have a lower-off point, but many will find that reaching it requires a great deal of effort! The short rib must be climbed delicately to gain a flake and then a rest below a small roof. Pull over this, crux, to finish up a small hanging groove.

10 Seaside Special   12m   5
Neil Shepherd 1983
Another route with a lower-off as trying to top-out is loose and dangerous.

11 Original Route   16m   3+ *
Neil Shepherd 1983
Quite enjoyable and has provided a useful escape route in the past.

12 Direct Start   14m   5+ *
David Mckelvie 1983
Pulling out of the small overhung corner at the start is the crux. Climb the delicate wall to gain the final corner of the parent route.

13 Climbers Wear Platforms   15m   6b
George Ridge 1994
An enjoyable route up the wall. Start in the little groove and climb the delicate wall directly. Keep an eye on the tides or the belayer will need more than platforms to keep dry feet.

14 Towing the Line   16m   6a *
George Ridge 1995
The huge defining groove gives good climbing.

15 Rubbin' Salt into the Wound   15m   6b+ **
Neil Shepherd 2004
Takes the large nose directly. Intimidating but surprising holds help when needed most!

The Platform Lower Tier

Walk up The Platform to where it narrows to a ledge and descend carefully to the left to almost sea-level. The wall on the right is The Lower Tier. There is a pair of belay staples in place above the finishing ledge at its left end.

In with the In Crowd   9m   6b+
Neil Shepherd 2004
The only route at present, follow the line of pods and pinches arising from the huge fault. Sustained and interesting climbing.

The Backstage

(NO 6639 4125 - top)   North facing

This is the north face of The Platform. It has a dark forbidding character and is grossly overhanging in its entirety. The routes require very

Arbroath Sea Cliffs

specific conditions to be climbable and a good north-easterly wind helps.

APPROACH
This is best through the cave from The Platform.

The routes are described as they are reached from the cave.

🔵 **Swimming against the Tide of Tradition 14m 6c+ ***
Neil Shepherd 200
The first bolt line. Climb with some difficulty to the lip where a final tricky move leads to easier climbing and eventually a lower-off.

🔵 **Out of the Red and into the Black 12m 7a ***
Neil Shepherd 2004
The roofed lower section is easier on this route but gaining the slab is hard and the upper groove is difficult for the short.

There is a good bouldering traverse left to right along the length of the roof under these routes at about Font 7a.

The Stage

(NO 6639 4125 - top)   North-East facing   Map p191
This is the wall at the end of the peninsula, which faces The Tower across the gap. Two obvious ring bolts will be seen in the slab at its top, which is 8m from the top of The Platform and The Backstage. The rock on this wall requires some respect and it can be greasy if conditions are not right. There is scope here for further routes but a lot of cleaning would be required.

APPROACH
Follow the Peninsula to its junction with The Tower at a bad step and descend a steep gully which cuts down leftwards beneath the wall. This can often be greasy and care needs to be taken. The routes are described left to right when facing the wall and can be well scrutinised from the descent gully.

🔵 **First Night Nerves 9m 6c**
Neil Shepherd 1981
The ominous crack hanging over the descent gully. It is often greasy and should ensure it never becomes a crowd puller!

🟠 **Shore Beats Working 10m 6b**
George Ridge 1995
What doesn't! But you would need to try it and make up your own mind. This is the slightly easier and more enjoyable route in the centre of the wall.

The Tower

(NO 6641 4124 - top)   North facing   Map p191
Another north facing wall which provides some very good climbing on generally solid and often beautifully pocketed rock. Once again it requires specific breezy conditions to dry it out. Unfortunately for the majority of the time it will be found to be greasy. The rock at the top of some of these routes requires care. Belay bolts are in place well back to the left on the top of the Tower. There are two semihanging stances to allow belaying under the more left-hand lines.

APPROACH
Go down the descent gully as for The Stage, but at the base of the gully step up rightwards onto a small triangular ledge with a belay bolt.

The routes are described right to left on this wall starting with the route directly above the triangular ledge.

🟢 **1 Wall of Hate 8m 5**
Neil Shepherd 1980
The narrow tapering wall above the belay ledge. Good climbing, if a little squeezed in.

Arbroath Sea Cliffs

The Tower

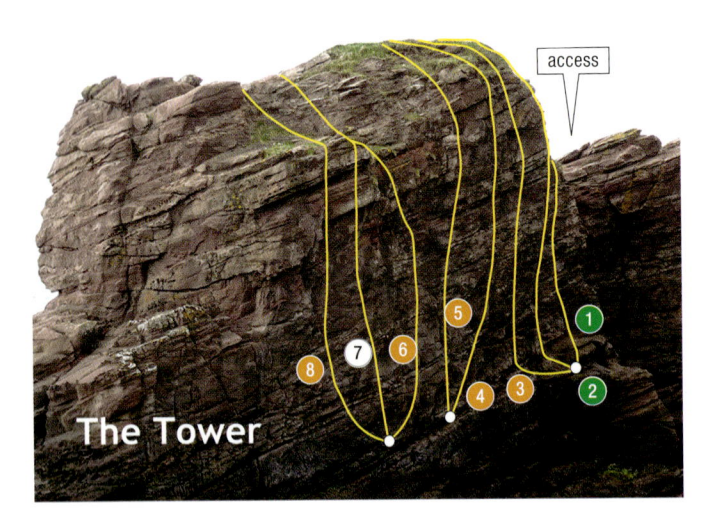

② Meaty Hefts 10m 4 **
Neil Shepherd 1980
Brilliant, fun crack climbing. Enjoy the meaty hefts whilst posing for the crowd watching from the cliff-top, just hope they don't call out the rescue team! Clip the bolts of Wall of Hate to the right.

③ Declaration of Intent 12m 6a *
Neil Shepherd 1994
From the ledge a big step left gains the line. Interesting wall climbing on a series of pockets and other erosion features leads to a hardish move at the top.

④ The Krab 12m 6b *
Jeff Ross 1994
Enjoyable fare when in season and probably the best route on the wall. Traverse down and left to gain the first semihanging stance on the wall. Fairly close to the previous route to start with but a harder and more sustained proposition.

⑤ The Selfish Shellfish 12m 6a
Neil Shepherd 2001
From the same stance a line of staples rises into a final small groove. Climb the wall directly with a long reach in the middle, then good moves up the final groove.

⑥ Ukranian Mermaid 12m 6a
Jeff Ross 2001
The next line can be started at either of the two semihanging stances. Climb the wall easily to a harder finish over the bulge at the top.

⑦ Open Project – no hangers

⑧ Screamin' Demon 10m 6a
Jeff Ross 2001
From the second hanging stance follow the leftmost line of hangers. Friable rock at the top, which is also where it's a little run out!

NON-TIDAL WAVE & PROMONTORY

The following two walls lie on the back wall which lies between the peninsula ending in The Tower and the Needles E'e area. On a first visit, head beyond the cliff and go down towards Needles E'e on an eroded path from immediately before Post 7, then turn right and traverse an exposed slab to reach a large dipping platform of rock. This lies opposite, so you can look directly across at the walls to locate their tops, from where an abseil approach is made.

Non-Tidal Wave

(NO 6642 4129 - top) East facing Map p191
Diagram p197

This awesomely steep but short wall lies 50m north of The Tower and is aptly named. It curls upwards and outwards in fairly equal measure.

Arbroath Sea Cliffs

There are belay staples in the flat rock platform above the wall. The obvious scope for a series of hardish routes here has been realised at last. The crag stays dry in rain but can be affected badly by early season seepage and is prone to greasiness in humid weather due to its sheltered position.

APPROACH

From the main cliff-top path, take a very indistinct path 50m after Post 6. Head across the slope following the faint path to a flat area which lies above the wall and has several belay staples. It is probably best to abseil from a belay bolt and staple running the rope down the central groove (the route Brain Wave) or the big corner at the left end as you face out to sea (the route 7th Wave).

Alternatively an approach is possible via the steep gully just beyond the wall's north end. This has a fair bit of loose rock and is often wet. In anything other than totally dry conditions it is treacherous and not to be recommended. In dry conditions it is also possible to traverse round from The Platform via The Backstage.

All of the routes apart from Wave Escape and 7th Wave have lower-offs.

① Wave Escape   14m   3
Neil Shepherd 2003
Easy and pleasant climbing. There is a belay 10m back and left.

② Say Hello but Wave Goodbye   10m   6b+ ***
Neil Shepherd 2003
Nice climbing on good holds where it matters.

③ Brain Wave   10m   6b ***
Jeff Ross 2003
Not as easy as it looks from below.

④ On a Different Wavelength   9m   6c
Neil Shepherd 2003
The angle really starts to kick in now. Red bolts.

Non-Tidal Wave

⑤ Closed Project
Initial hangers missing.

⑥ Shockwave   9m   7a+
Neil Shepherd 2003
Best not to hang about on this route.

⑦ Wave Power   10m   7b+ ***
Neil Shepherd 2003
The steepest line on the wall requires powerful moves leading to a horror stretch for the lower-off.

⑧ 7th Wave   11m   7a ***
Jeff Ross 2003
Power will not help on this one, which can succumb to stylish mantel-shelfing or more usually to a belly flop.

Arbroath Sea Cliffs

The Promontory

(NO 6644 4129 - top)   North-West & South-East facing
Map p191

As the name suggests this wall is a small promontory with climbing on both sides. It lies 40m right of Non-Tidal Wave and directly opposite the slab with the exposed step, almost within touching distance. Some of these routes are of high quality.

As the routes are arranged around the small promontory they can all be viewed from various places before committing to the abseil. The seaward facing ones can be viewed in great detail from a large dipping platform of rock lying opposite. The landward facing ones can be viewed from the first path leading down to the Needles E'e (a landmark arch – see next section) from the cliff-top path.

APPROACH

Staple belays will be found on a slab above the wall's hugely undercut south-east face. To the right of these, the top of an open corner will be seen with two further staples just above. An abseil from these down the corner, which is the line of Buoys of Summer, will gain a small ledge below the south-east facing routes. This is equipped with staple belays. For the routes on the north-west side of the promontory it is best to abseil down either Pilgrim's Progress or Barging into the Presence of God. The steep gully, as described for Non-Tidal Wave, can also be descended for the landward facing routes but only in totally dry conditions and taking great care with the loose rock; not recommended.

The first routes face south-east and get a lot of sun, so they are often in good condition. Described from left to right facing the rock and as they are seen from the viewing platform opposite. The first three start from the ledge which is usually non-tidal.

1 Stitch in Time   9m   6b *
Neil Shepherd 1995
A good line up the centre of the wall to the left of the corner. Very enjoyable climbing on some lovely water worn features.

Arbroath Sea Cliffs

**2 Buoys of Summer   9m   6b **
Neil Shepherd 1994
The wide open corner above the belay ledge. Excellent climbing, harder for the short

3 The E'evil Dead   13m   6c *
Neil Shepherd 1994
Climb the previous route until the obvious juggy traverse beckons rightwards. Head out to the wild arete and finish by an exposed sequence. One of the best routes on the coast.

Neil Shepherd on the exposed E'evil Dead (6c), The Promontory (photo Iain Macdonald)

4 Flesh E'eter   18m   7a+ **
Neil Shepherd 2003
The continuation of E'evil Dead round the arete and rightwards to gain the thin hanging groove. Finish up this. Superb climbing in a very exposed position. The continuation of the traverse rightwards is a closed project.

The next route is best reached by a short traverse round from the landward side or by an abseil directly down the arete. Belay staples are in place at the base of the arete.

5 The Abbey Habit   10m   6a
Neil Shepherd 1995
The arete separating the two faces is climbed from a small ledge at the toe of the buttress. Interesting rock structure and a good position make this worthwhile.

The next routes all face the land and can only be seen from the landward side. They have their own starting ledges. This face of the promontory suffers much more from greasiness than the other side and the routes can quite often feel damp when other areas are in condition.

The routes are again described from right to left when facing the rock.

**6 Pilgrim's Progress   10m   7a *
George Ridge 1994
A difficult and sustained route taking the wall to the left of the arete of The Abbey Habit. Once again gives good climbing on some unusual and tenuous holds, the best of which is nicknamed 'the potato'.

The next two routes are not of the same calibre as the others and have not received much traffic.

7 Barging into the Presence of God   10m   6b+
Neil Shepherd 1997
The slightly steeper wall just to the left. Uninspiring climbing and often damp, the rock deserves respect.

Angus

Arbroath Sea Cliffs

8 **The Red Lichtie** 10m 6a+
Neil Morrison 1997
A companion line, but easier and possibly more likely to be dry.

THE NEEDLES E'E

(NO 665 413)   Map p191

This small arch is an obvious landmark on the coast and very popular with the general public. It is clearly visible from the cliff-top path 20m past Post 7, which actually lies just after the approach. There is a variety of easily accessed routes here including a concentration of very good routes which receive a lot of sun and suffer less from greasiness than many other areas. This area is well worth a visit.

Sector Cartoon

South-East facing   Map p191   Diagram p201

This is the first of three sectors which lie on the seaward side of the ridge which holds the Needles E'e. A unique addition to Scottish sport climbing, this area of very short routes was developed as a 'Secteur d'Initiation'. This has been done primarily with younger children in mind but the routes are also quite suitable for older novice climbers. The rock has a profusion of holds with pockets and pebbles predominating. The bolts have been closely spaced. These routes have not been awarded stars but offer enjoyable climbing with easy access. Many of them have been bouldered on in the past but the landings are not appealing and it is not totally unknown for a pebble to 'pop' unexpectedly! In the interests of rock conservation when top roping, climbers are requested to run the active rope through a krab in a loop hung over the edge. This will help to minimize rock scarring.

APPROACH

From immediately before Post 7, take an eroded path down towards the E'e arch. Before reaching the flat gravel filled depression in front of the arch, turn right and cross an exposed step to gain the dipping rock platform. A short wall of rock will be seen on the left. Follow this towards the sea and it gets a little higher. At its right end the first short routes will be seen grouped around a prominent nose of rock.

SOUTH FACE

Above the dipping rock platform these routes are described from left to right.

1 **Loony Tunes** 6m 5+
Unknown 2001
The short arete climbed mainly on its right side packs a lot in!

2 **Fred Flintstone** 6m 3+
Unknown 2001
The left-hand groove with the massive cobble at half-height gives an enjoyable little climb.

3 **Disney Look Too Bad** 6m 6a
Unknown 2001
But feels a lot worse! The right-hand groove leads up to the left of the massive nose.

EAST FACE

(NO 6646 4128 - base)

Traversing round the corner after passing under the huge nose leads to this wall which lies at an amenable angle. It is slightly higher than the south face and gives enjoyable climbing; if only it was three times as high. The routes are described as they are encountered from left to right. Beyond the second crack-line, the ground drops away towards a formidable cave and this marks the start of Sector Parental Guidance.

4 **Cow and Chicken** 7m 3+
Unknown 2001
The first line on the east face climbs the diagonal crack.

5 **Top Cat** 7m 4
Unknown 2001
The wall to the right with some lovely holds, a little rounded to finish.

Arbroath Sea Cliffs

6 **A Grand Day Out** 7m 4+
Unknown 2001
A similar route to the last but a little harder.

7 **The Wrong Trousers** 6m 4
Unknown 2001
The slightly shorter wall just to the right.

8 **Pinky and the Brain** 6m 4
Unknown 2001
The short wall to the left of the crack. Lovely finishing hold!

9 **62 West Wallaby Street** 5m 3+
Unknown 2001
The short crack-line looks easy but can be awkward for the short.

10 **The Pearls of Penelope Pitstop** 5m 6a+
Unknown 2001
The slightly steeper wall to the right of the crack is easy until the final moves!

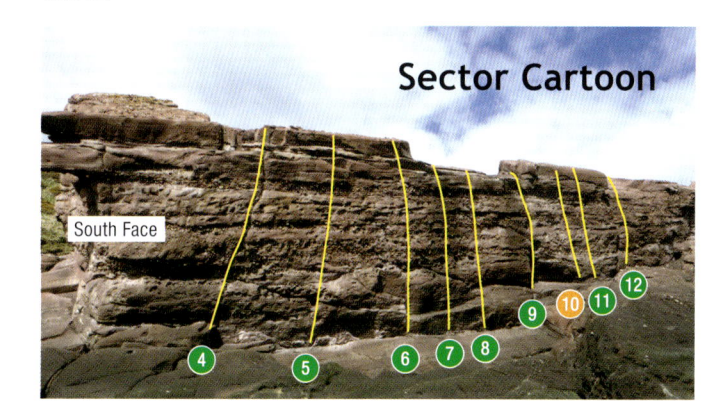

11 **Rugrats' Revenge** 5m 5
Unknown 2001
The wall right again. A bit easier but still tricky for the little un's!

12 **Fantastic Four** 6m 3
Unknown 2001
Alas not a four and barely even a three! The second crack-line is started by stepping out above the drop.

Beyond this route the ground drops in a series of large steps and the wall becomes known as Sector Parental Guidance.

Sector Parental Guidance

(NO 6648 4129)   East facing   Map p191

The grown up version of Sector Cartoon. The routes in the centre which start by the sea cave are unfortunately prone to greasiness and due to the sloping ground above the routes they may be found to be sandy. A quick brush with a SOFT brush will be adequate to clean this off.

The routes on this sector are split into left and right sides when facing the wall due to the different approach required to each.

LEFT SIDE APPROACH

As for Sector Cartoon. From the last route on that sector, drop down the 2m step to the right with care to reach the first of the routes.

1 **Silver Surfer** 8m 4
George Ridge 2001
An easy introduction to the wall on some very positive holds.

2 **Be Calmed** 9m 4+
George Ridge 2001
The slightly more sustained line right and which starts down the next step. Awkward top-out.

Sector Cartoon — South Face

Arbroath Sea Cliffs

Sector Parental Guidance

❻ Pushin' the Limpets   13m   7b ★★
Neil Shepherd 2001
Starts in the same place but traverse airily out along the bar of rock which spans the cave. Pull over the lip in the middle with difficulty. The tall will find the initial reach easier but the short and the flexible have an advantage when it comes to the rock over. The thin wall above presents further difficulty before an easier finish up the short flake.

RIGHT SIDE APPROACH

Interesting and airy, go through the arch of the Needles E'e itself and turn to the right when facing the sea for the first two routes to find belay staples on a thin ledge. This requires care as it can be greasy. The routes are described from right to left facing the rock.

❼ Not for Children's E'en   9m   6c ★
Neil Shepherd 2001
From the belay climb up directly. At the 1st bolt climb out and left in a superb position to eventually gain good holds on the blunt arete.

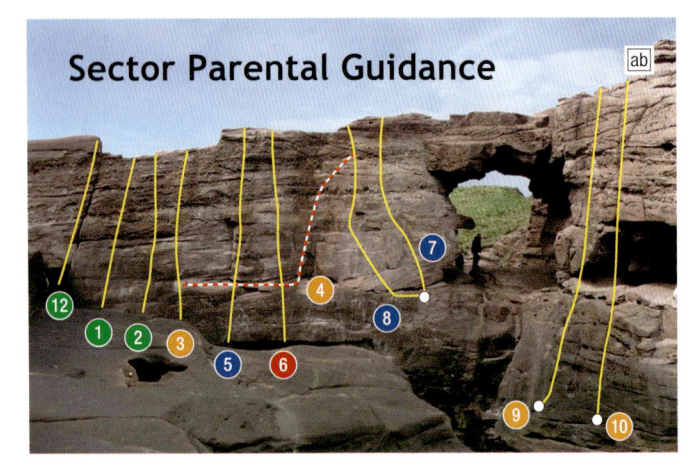

❸ Parental Guidance   10m   6b
Neil Shepherd 2001
A lack of positive holds gives the first taste of the harder climbing on this sector. Pebbles and cobbles are welcome towards the top but dad says don't pull too hard, it might fall off!

❹ Layin' down the Law   15m   6b+ ★★
Neil Shepherd 2001
A well positioned route. Start up the previous route to gain a standing position on the sloping ledge. Traverse delicately right to the groove of 'O' Zone Slayer and then cross Pushin' the Limpets rightwards to gain the hanging corner system. Go up this (crux) with a small run out to finish up the final section of Grounded.

❺ 'O' Zone Slayer   11m   6c ★
Jeff Ross 2001
Start down at the left side of the cave. Hard moves out of the cave lead to the respite of the groove. Finish by further sustained climbing.

Neil Shepherd Pushin' the Limpets (7b), Sector Parental Guidance (photo Iain Macdonald)

Arbroath Sea Cliffs

8 Grounded 11m 7a+ *
Neil Shepherd 2001
Aptly named, as leaving the deck is the crux! From the belay, traverse 2m left along the ledge to gain the obvious sloping shelf directly with some difficulty. Above this another horribly sloping shelf must be overcome before easier ground leads to the top.

The next two routes climb the wall which runs at 90 degrees to the rest of the sector and is on the north side of the E'e. They are reached by abseil to semihanging stances with belay bolts in place. At the top there are belay bolts in place in the unusual rock lump directly above the E'e itself. These are also used for the abseil approach.

9 Do as I Say not as I Do 15m 6a+
Neil Shepherd 2004
The left-hand line, hard at the start if the bolts are followed directly. Great pebble pulling on the upper wall.

10 Loose Lips Sink Ships 15m 6a+
Neil Shepherd 2004
Well this pair must have been on the Titanic! The easy lower wall past the feature which gives the route its name leads to a harder headwall.

The Steppes

East facing   Map p191

These walls are a continuation of Sector Parental Guidance. They provide short, but enjoyable and intense climbing on good rock. They are essentially non-tidal but in high seas might be better avoided. The Left Steppe is vertical to slabby and the smaller Right Steppe is very steep. The rock dries quickly and gets plenty of sun. Many of the holds are pebbles, or bigger still, cobbles and the climbing tends to be harder than would at first appear. If the rock is damp these walls may best be avoided as the pebbles can be loosened in wet conditions. It is possible to do a large number of these climbs in one visit and a good workout is guaranteed! Once again no stars have been awarded to any of these routes as they are so short, but all of them provide good climbing and shouldn't be dismissed.

APPROACH

From the cliff-top path go 30m past Post 7 and take an eroded path down towards the left side of the E'e. Head straight towards the sea onto a sloping area of rock where a group of belay staples will be found. Either make a short abseil from these to large sloping ledges under the Right Steppe or go left for 10m whilst facing out to sea and down a small step to descend an easy and obvious groove leading to the same point.

RIGHT STEPPE

Would have made an excellent bouldering wall if only the landings had been better! Very steep and intense. The routes are described from right to left as reached from the descent. Belay bolts are available in the sloping rock platform above the wall. The grading reflects the shortness of the routes.

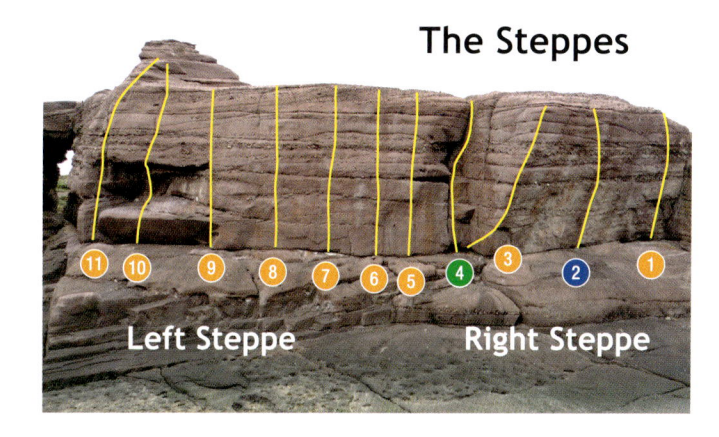

Arbroath Sea Cliffs

1 Welcome to the Steeeppes! 6m 6b+
Neil Shepherd 2001
The first line of bolts as reached from the descent. Very closely spaced but the ground is never far away! Bridging onto the wall by the descent reduces the grade to around 5+ but renders the ascent meaningless!

2 Wicked Steppe Mother 6m 6c+
Neil Shepherd 2001
Packs it in for such a short route and gets harder as each bolt is passed. A go for it attitude helps.

3 Steppe in the Right Direction 7m 6b
Neil Shepherd 2001
The slabby right arete of the central corner. Start in the corner and quickly move out onto the arete; teeter up here on tenuous holds. It is probably best to leave out the go for it of the last route!

4 Steppeladder 7m 4
Neil Shepherd 2001
The deep corner which separates the Left and Right Steppes.

LEFT STEPPE

A more amenable wall but the routes tend to look easier than they are. Again described from right to left starting from the first line left of the corner. Belays at the top for the furthest left routes are a pair of staples in the huge wart of rock above the wall, or for the right-hand lines, three staples on the landward edge of the sloping rock platform.

5 Steppes back in Amazement 7m 6b
Neil Shepherd 2001
The first line left of the corner has a hard start directly below the bolt.

6 Kazakhstani Castaway 8m 6b+
Neil Shepherd 2001
The wall starts to lean back a little but the routes get harder! Surprisingly powerful for a slab.

7 One Steppe Forward 8m 6b
Neil Shepherd 2001
A little easier but still thin in places.

8 Two Steppes Back 8m 6a+
Neil Shepherd 2001
Some big cobbles make this the easiest of this trio and a good introduction to the style of the climbing on this wall.

The next routes start at the huge undercut shelf at the left end of the wall.

9 Put out to Grass 9m 6a
Neil Shepherd 2001
The wall at the right end of the huge sloping shelf and overhang. Recognisable as it has ring bolts instead of staples.

10 High Stepper 9m 6b
Neil Shepherd 2001
Mantel onto the shelf by the belay bolts and cross the roof at the crack by hard moves. Easy once standing above the lip.

11 Steppin' Out 9m 6a
Neil Shepherd 2001
An enjoyable and easy route up the cracked left arete of the wall.

MERMAID'S KIRK

(NO 665 413)   Tidal   West & South facing   Map p191

This is the almost completely enclosed pebbly cove just north of the Needles E'e. Alas it is not completely cut off from the sea and the tide enters through a long rocky tunnel making the routes inaccessible at high tides. The back of the Kirk forms an awesome cave which is prone to prolonged seepage and the occasional nesting house martin, but has some outrageous potential. The barrier wall between the Kirk and the sea is known as Warship Wall and has a couple of below average routes and some bouldering.

Arbroath Sea Cliffs

APPROACH
Take the rutted path 30m past Post 7 as for The Steppes but branch off leftwards as it flattens out. An often slippery path leads down onto the boulder strewn floor of the Kirk. It is usually easy enough to jump down the small step to gain the shingle bank.

Project Wall
(NO 6650 4137 - top)   South facing   Map p191
The vast overhanging wall above the pebbly beach. Ranges from merely frighteningly steep at the left side to ludicrous further right. Unfortunately this wall suffers from seepage a lot of the time and often when it's not seeping, it's greasy! This makes it almost impossible to get the wall in condition long enough to do anything! The rock here is a bit poorer than other areas but does seem to clean up with perseverance.

Diagon Alley   18m   6a+ *
Jeff Ross 2004
An intimidating route, the first to breach this wall, avoids the really steep stuff. Lowering off when the tide is in can prove challenging.

Ossian   16m   8a **
Tomek Kazimierski 2005
At the junction between the frightening and the ludicrous lies a groove line through huge roofs. Very hard to find in completely dry conditions. A totally stunning climb and at present the hardest on the Arbroath coast.

Warship Wall
(NO 6651 4135 - top)   West facing   Map p191
This wall gets the sun late in the day. It has more of a problem with sandiness than other areas which is perhaps due to its sheltered nature; the rock is not as reliable as elsewhere. Only accessible at lowish tide. The height of the pebbles which form the beach can make the starts of these routes harder or easier. There is also some good gymnastic bouldering to be had at the base of the wall with the full traverse of the undercut section fairly trying. There are belay staples in place in the slab above.

Dread Knot   12m   6b
Neil Shepherd 1996
The left-hand line. Quite strenuous at the start and delicate to finish.

Broad Side   12m   6b+
Neil Shepherd 1996
A harder start, especially when the pebbles are low, and a little harder to finish.

Sector Mini
(NO 6655 4136 - base)   South facing   Map p191
This is the small wall which lies on the rock platform above Warship Wall. It has six short routes on lovely featured rock with a 'sector d'initiation' feel. Much like the nearby Sector Cartoon but better. Belay bolts are available on the top. From left to right the routes are.

1 Minitial   5m   4
Unknown 2006
The nicely featured wall.

2 Minitiation   5m   4
Unknown 2006
Start in the little corner and climb the featured wall above.

3 Minimal   6m   4+
Unknown 2006
The arete and tricky featured wall above. Slightly harder than the previous routes.

4 Minimical   6m   6a+
Unknown 2006
Nothing initiation like about this thug.

Angus

Arbroath Sea Cliffs

Sector Mini

5 **Miniquity** 6m 4+
Unknown 2006
The little groove which skirts the roof to its right side. Nice climbing.

6 **Minitiative** 6m 4+
Unknown 2006
Round the seaward end of the wall. Another nice route but avoid in big seas or at high tide!

CONNING TOWER INLET

(NO 666 414)   Map p207

The next area is located in the inlet near Post 10. Known locally as The Cruisie due to the shape of the obvious through cave which is apparently similar to the old oil lamps. This is a complicated area but most of the routes can be viewed from the cliff-top at one point or another before committing to an abseil.

GENERAL APPROACH

Follow the cliff-top path past a large loose looking bay known locally as The Mariners Grave until a narrow peninsula leads out to another tower. This is shortly before Post 10 is reached. Post 10 is at NO 6663 4152, just in case it disappears; it is above the feature in the inlet named as The Conning Tower. The narrow peninsula holds the following wall which forms the south bounding side of the Conning Tower Inlet.

South Wall - Lost Wall

(NO 6662 4147 - top)   North-East facing   Map p207

The first wall with climbing in this area forms the southern side of Conning Tower Inlet. With the wall facing north-east, fairly good conditions are required. The routes at the left end are more exposed and more often dry. It must be said though that in a big swell none of these routes are advisable.

APPROACH

Leave the main path and reach the peninsula at NO 6660 4150. Follow the peninsula out with great care past a very narrow grass section to a large flat area of rock; staple and bolt belays will be found here. An abseil from these leads to starting ledges. Alternatively and probably easier is to carry on to the neck where the tower joins the peninsula and scramble carefully down leftwards to reach wide ledges under the wall.

The routes are described from left to right and can be viewed from the top of the North Wall. There are no belay bolts in place below these routes. However, a large natural thread is present below Lost in Line.

1 **Lost in Line** 12m 5+
Neil Shepherd 1996
The extreme left-hand route. Climb easily to a tricky finish through the slot in the overhangs.

Arbroath Sea Cliffs

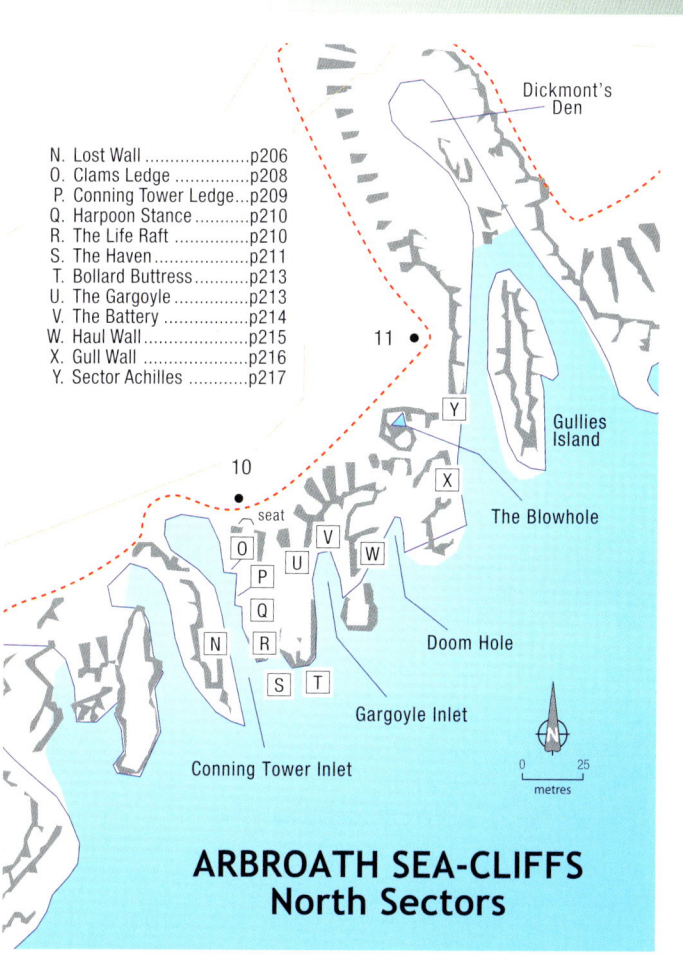

N. Lost Wall p206
O. Clams Ledge p208
P. Conning Tower Ledge...p209
Q. Harpoon Stance p210
R. The Life Raft p210
S. The Haven p211
T. Bollard Buttress...........p213
U. The Gargoyle p213
V. The Battery p214
W. Haul Wall p215
X. Gull Wall p216
Y. Sector Achilles p217

**ARBROATH SEA-CLIFFS
North Sectors**

② Lost but not Least   12m   6c *
Neil Shepherd 1996
Good climbing up the delicate slab to a thuggy finish past the projecting block in the overhang. Usually found to be harder than it looks!

③ Lost the Plot   12m   7a+
Neil Shepherd 2003
The slab just left again is easier than the last route but the capping roof is much harder. A boulder problem in the air.

④ Hanau's Quint   14m   6b *
Neil Shepherd 1996
Another deceptive route which is more awkward than it appears. Steeper than the previous lines, it thankfully has more positive holds, except for that one move....

Things get a bit harder now as the angle steepens.

⑤ Lost at Sea   15m   7a **
Neil Shepherd 1995
This starts at the narrowing of the ledge and climbs a stiff initial wall to reach the scoops. Move past these with some difficulty to reach a sloping ledge and easier ground. It might be a good idea to remind the belayer to keep a firm grip on the belay device as the sea here has developed a taste for Gri Gri's!

⑥ Rust in Peace   16m   7b *
Neil Shepherd 1995
Still a candidate for the hardest vertical route in the area, this climbs the wall directly above the narrowest part of the traverse ledge. A hard start leads to a slight easing and then a dream finish on rounded slopers.

⑦ Pringles Wave   16m   6a
Jeff Ross 1995
Just round the corner from the previous routes and facing back into the inlet this climb is very often greasy and has poorer rock than the others here.

Arbroath Sea Cliffs

Conning Tower Inlet, Clams Ledge

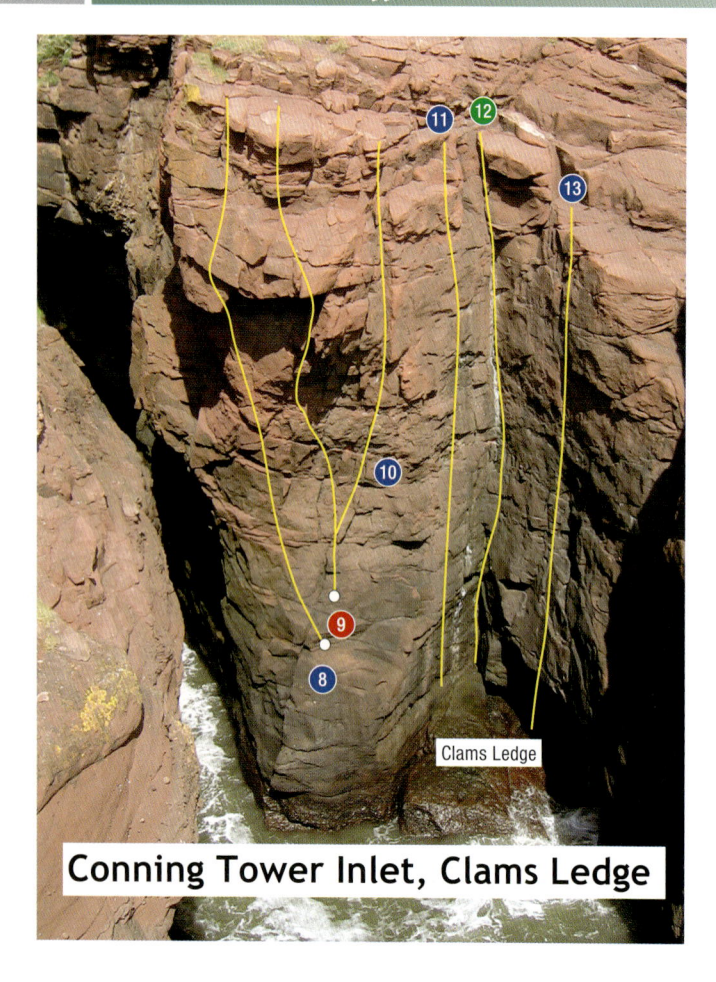

North Wall

Unlike the opposite face, this wall gets a lot of sun and has a friendlier feel although the essential abseil access gives a feeling of commitment. It can be scoped out nicely from the peninsula which tops the South Wall. All of the routes are reached by abseil to four distinct starting ledges at the base of the walls.

GENERAL APPROACH

Reach a seat beside Post 10. The Conning Tower is directly below and seen after two steps forward, although the conning tower shape isn't obvious from here. Head down a little path to reach a flat grassy area above the routes.

The routes and detailed approach for each ledge are described from left to right when facing the cliff.

CLAMS LEDGE

Non-tidal   South-East facing   Map p207

This is the ledge furthest from the open sea and is located below an obvious large corner-groove at the extreme left end of the wall. There are staple and bolt belays above the corner and its right wall, there are also further staples directly above Vast Mango. This corner can be greasy but the ledge is generally non-tidal with the higher ledge below Vast Mango especially so. However as with all of the routes here, none are recommended in a very big sea. A belay bolt is in-situ on the ledge.

8 The Codfather   12m   7a
Neil Shepherd 2003
The wall leading out left from the upper ledge following a line of Eco anchor type bolts. Not the best rock on this buttress but an exposed and difficult section to surmount the overhang.

9 Pretty Clitty Gang Bang   12m   7b **
Neil Shepherd 2003
An outrageously positioned climb taking the enormous nose directly.

… Steep and strenuous at the start becomes steeper and more strenuous higher up to a rounded finish. Intimidating!

10 Vast Mango in Tardis   14m   6c+ ★★
Jeff Ross 1996
A route of high quality and pretty strenuous; big arms are an advantage.

11 Mutton Dressed as Clam   14m   7a+
Neil Shepherd 2002
The wall right of Vast Mango. Feels a trifle eliminate but proves hard and fingery if the temptation of the easy corner is avoided.

12 Silence of the Clams   14m   5 ★★★
Neil Shepherd 1995
One of the best easy routes at Arbroath. Climb the huge corner directly.

13 Galley Slave   12m   6c ★
Neil Shepherd 1995
The wall right of the corner gives another deceptive route. Surprisingly it can be out of condition when the previous routes are all okay. A crimpy crux just above half-height.

CONNING TOWER LEDGE
(NO 6663 4149 - Conning Tower itself)   Non-tidal   South-East facing   Map p207
This spacious ledge is also non-tidal and lies at the foot of the obvious conning tower on its seaward side. Access is by abseil down the gully behind the tower from staple and bolt belays. There are belay bolts in place on the ledge. Six routes start here although Whale of a Time can also be started from the Harpoon Stance. They are described from left to right when facing the rock.

14 Pulling Muscles from a Shell   15m   6c ★
George Ridge 1996
Traverse out left from the ledge to make difficult and delicate moves up the slabby front face of the tower.

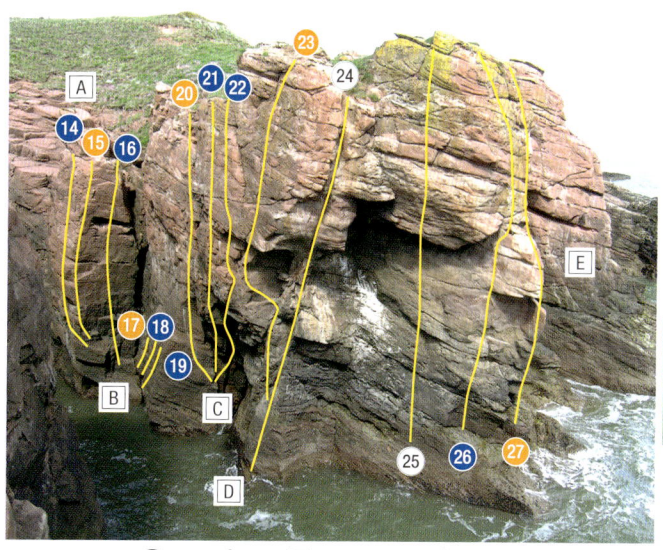

Conning Tower Inlet

A. Conning Tower   C. Harpoon Stance   E. The Haven
B. Conning Tower Ledge   D. The Life Raft

15 Swindlers List   12m   6a+ ★★★
Neil Shepherd 1995
A tremendous climb up the obvious arete of the conning tower.

16 Concentration Cramp   12m   6c ★
Neil Shepherd 1995
Climb the very steep wall above the ledge to the right of the arete; fairly sustained.

Arbroath Sea Cliffs

17 Short Arms, Deep Pockets   14m   6b
George Ridge 1996
The first route on the wall proper. Good climbing on nice features.

18 Peem Machine   15m   6c+   ★★
Jeff Ross 1995
An Arbroath classic. Steep wall climbing with some nice pockets leads to a very rounded crux. This can make an on-sight ascent challenging!

19 Whale of a Time   15m   7a   ★
Neil Shepherd 1995
Another good and well rounded route! Slightly harder than the last one.

HARPOON STANCE
Non-tidal   South-East facing   Map p207
A much smaller ledge than the previous two but not quite a hanging stance! Reached by abseil from either of two pairs of belay staples. One pair is set well back in a large wart of rock; the other is in a short wall of rock near the cliff edge directly above the stance and is probably the best approach. The tide is not a problem here and there are a couple of staples to semihang on. Two routes start here although as previously mentioned, Whale of a Time can be climbed from this stance and in high water, The Mistic can also be started from here.

20 Curse of the Faeroes   12m   6b+   ★
Neil Shepherd 1995
Another high quality route on this section of the wall. Directly above the stance lies a thin open groove with some delicate water worn features. Climb this, a long reach is helpful, to gain easier ground.

21 Neptune's Kiss   12m   7a   ★★
Jeff Ross 2004
Takes the black streak out of the left side of The Mistic's niche. Not often in condition.

THE LIFE RAFT
Tidal   South-East facing   Map p207
This is a small triangular low-tide ledge at the right end of the main wall. It can be seen clearly from the cliff-top path at the head of the inlet; if it can't be seen then the tide is in! It sports a belay bolt and two routes start here. At higher tides a stance can also be taken on the arete at the first bolt of the route, although it is not as comfortable and is only really useful for Haarbinger. Abseil to this ledge from either of the staple belays described as for the Harpoon Stance but ensure the rope runs further right.

22 The Mistic   16m   6c+   ★★
Neil Shepherd 1996
Unfortunately often greasy but a superb climb when dry. From The Life Raft, climb up and rightwards into a recess. Break out of this by the tempting hanging crack to gain the small ledge on Haarbinger. Finish directly up the wall trending a little left. At anything other than low tide, start from Harpoon Stance.

23 Haarbinger   17m   6b+   ★★
Neil Shepherd 1995
Another good route which is dry most of the time. Climb the arete and a crack to gain a sloping shelf. Traverse leftwards round the corner with difficulty to gain a small ledge below the headwall, junction with The Mistic. Pull over the bulge above at its right side and follow the slab above in a fine position. This final slab can be viewed in profile from a position on the main path by an old number 5 post at the head of the inlet (just before post 10).

24 Closed Project 'Jumbobum'   15m
Neil Shepherd 2010
The evil overhanging crease!

25 Closed Project 'Feeding Frenzy'   15m
Neil Shepherd 2010
The hard wall and roof to the right, just left of Killer Wail.

The Haven

(NO 6666 4147 - top)   Non-tidal   Various Aspects   Map p207

The next shallow inlet lies out at the seaward end of the peninsula which forms Conning Tower North Wall and just round the nose northwards from its previous routes; it is not seen from the path. The climbs are situated on all three walls and are some of the most enjoyable and varied at Arbroath. All the routes are worth doing. There is rarely greasiness here except in the most humid weather and at most tides there are spacious ledges below the routes; at low tide the whole inlet is dry. A belay staple is in place below Clean Shaven. A further belay bolt is in place below the roof and this is the usual starting point for the routes from Haven Can't Wait rightwards.

APPROACH

Head down from Post 10 as for the Conning Tower North Wall but continue to the seaward end of the peninsula. To gain the ledge below the routes it is best to abseil down David's Route on the north wall of The Haven from a pair of big staples in a huge rock bollard. Above the roof routes are further staples but these are generally more convenient for belaying, though pre-brushing of the roof to get rid of pigeon droppings might mean abseiling from these.

The routes are described from left to right facing into The Haven from the sea. The first route is actually in Conning Tower Inlet but is best approached from The Haven, so is described here.

26   Killer Wail   16m   6c+   *
George Ridge 1996
Round the left arete as seen facing into The Haven from the sea. Start below a small corner, belay bolt in place. Access only at mid to low tide. Climb the corner and the wall to pull out rightwards onto the slab above with difficulty. Finish up the left side of the prow of the buttress in a good position. One of the first pebble moves in the area.

Sadie Renwick on the top slab of Haarbinger (6b+), The Life Raft (photo Cubby Images)

Arbroath Sea Cliffs

27 Eight Year Itch   14m   6b+ *
Neil Shepherd 2004
Climbs the nose of the left bounding buttress in its entirety. Good rock and lovely moves.

28 Haven Fun   14m   6b *
Neil Morrison 1996
The first line in the Haven itself, climbing featured rock quite easily before the fun begins on the headwall.

29 A Close Shave   14m   6c
Neil Shepherd 1996
Takes a line roughly straight up from the belay bolt, with a very fingery crux low down on small pockets and an easier finish.

30 Shaven Haven   14m   5 *
Neil Shepherd 1996
The steep wall just right looks much more inviting and has a pleasant supply of good holds.

31 Haven Escape Route   14m   3 *
Neil Shepherd 1983
A pleasant easy route on great rock.

32 Haven Can't Wait   14m   6a+
Neil Shepherd 1996
A deceptive route up the steep rock just right of the abseil. Not as easy as it looks and pumpy too. The final holds are strength sappers and need treated with caution!

33 Don't Bridget Neilson   14m   6b *
George Ridge 1996
A harder companion route which saps just that bit more. Make sure you do as the name commands!

Knockin' on Haven's Door (7b), The Haven. Climber Neil Morrison

Arbroath Sea Cliffs

34 Dark Sar-Chasm   15m   5+ *
Neil Shepherd 1996
A truly entertaining climb. Traverse into the depths of the cave before chimneying upwards towards the daylight.

35 Vulgar Display of Power   15m   7b+ **
Neil Shepherd 1996
One of the harder routes in the area. Take the huge roof just left of centre by a strenuous sequence. Easier climbing remains up the delicate and rounded upper left-hand arete.

36 Knockin' on Haven's Door   15m   7b **
Neil Shepherd 2001
The companion line through the right side of the roof and the tenuous slab above.

37 David's Route   13m   5 *
David Pert 1996
The last route in The Haven takes the right wall directly on excellent holds.

GARGOYLE INLET

Map p207

This is the next main inlet north of the Conning Tower Inlet and the seaward end of its south wall joins with The Haven.

Bollard Buttress

East and North-East facing   Map p207

The next two routes are on the buttress below the huge rock bollard on the cliff-top (as used for The Haven access). Slabbier in nature, there are several nice natural lines here.

APPROACH

Either traverse across the narrow chasm from The Haven ledges or abseil directly down from the bolts in the bollard itself.

1 The Grade Escape   12m   5+ *
George Ridge 1996
The first bolted groove out on the east face of the buttress. Good, delicate climbing.

2 Sun Seeker   12m   6a+ *
Janet Horrocks 1996
The second obvious groove to the right is an altogether more deceptively difficult affair. Very delicate climbing.

The Gargoyle

(NO 6666 4150)   Non-tidal   North-East facing   Map p207 Diagram p214

This is the next wall inland from Bollard Buttress and has an unfriendly sloping character to its holds which can sometimes also feel sandy. Consequently the routes feel hard! Easily reached without the need to abseil, it can be viewed nicely from above The Battery. There are two belay points below the wall, both have staples and there are three staples to belay on at the top. The routes are described from left to right as reached from the descent.

APPROACH

Leave the cliff-top path as for The Haven and head down to the grassy area. On the north edge of this a wide and gently sloping gully leads down to the sea. Go down here and turn left at the bottom, facing the water. The Gargoyle looms directly above.

3 Grotesque   12m   7b
Tomek Kazimierski 2005
The left side of the wall is devoid of obvious holds but they are there somewhere!

Arbroath Sea Cliffs

The Battery

**(NO 6667 4151 - top)   South-East and North-East facing
Map p207**

The obvious slabby buttress facing The Gargoyle. The innocuous look of its slabby south-east face belies an imposing north facing aspect in the narrow chasm. There are obvious belay/abseil staples well back on a rock shelf. At present there are two routes here on the slabby south-east face and two lines on the gloomy north face.

APPROACH

Leave the cliff-top path 20m beyond the rough path down to The Haven. A gentle grass slope leads down to a short chasm. The southern wall of this is The Battery. All of the routes here are best approached by abseil. Those on the south-east face by abseil down the slab to a stance at the foot of Artillery Arete. Those on the gloomy north-east face by abseiling down either of the routes to reach a semihanging stance at a small ledge on the Ever Ready Arete. Both stances are equipped with belay staples.

It is also possible to reach the stance below the south-east face by a traverse round at sea-level from The Gargoyle. This removes the need to abseil and is interesting but a little tricky.

The first routes described are on the slabby south-east face and will often be found in condition.

4 Gruesome   13m   6c+ *
Neil Shepherd 1996
A hard climb which is aptly named! A difficult top section and few positive holds make this a pumpy outing.

5 Medusa   12m   6c *
Janet Horrocks 1996
Another deceptively hard route. The crux is gaining the 'antler' but there are few easy moves!

6 Gorgon   12m   6a+
Neil Shepherd 1996
The easiest route on the wall and whilst not as good as the others, it is still worthwhile. Climb the wall by the obvious line up into the thin groove before pulling through onto easier ground.

7 Artillery Arete   14m   5+ * *
Neil Shepherd 2001
The superb slabby arete climbed direct with a very tenuous start. Once over the bulge easier but still interesting climbing leads to the top.

8 Bringing out the Big Guns   14m   6b * *
Neil Shepherd 2001
From the belay, traverse right round the toe of the buttress and across the wall of immaculate sandstone to a hidden bolt and a short groove. Go up this and step right to climb the gritstone like layback crack

Arbroath Sea Cliffs

directly. Pull onto the slab, crux, and then follow the steep corner above to join the previous route where the angle eases. A varied and highly enjoyable route.

The next line is on the arete between the faces and both of the following start from a semihanging stance in the narrow chasm.

⑨ Ever Ready Arete   12m   7a *
Neil Shepherd 2001
The sensational arete behind the pinnacle. You can almost reach out and touch the crux holds from the pinnacle! This makes a true on-sight problematic. Easy for the first 8m then it all goes wrong and hard moves are required to be made to gain the top.

⑩ Fully Charged   12m   6c
Neil Shepherd 2001
The smooth black wall right of the arete. Climb up and rightwards away from the stance until the second bolt is reached. Make a hard reach up left to a good hold and a sloper before heading right again into the centre of the wall. Climb directly to hard finishing moves on the steeper headwall. Good climbing when dry but not often in condition.

DOOM HOLE

(NO 6670 4153 - top of arch)   Varying Aspects   Map p207
This next inlet north is easily recognised by a large archway and collapsed cave roof. This is known locally as the Blow-hole, as in rough seas the spray fountains through the hole in the cave roof. Haul Wall forms the main part of the south bounding wall of this inlet. The walls inside the cave are often greasy but when dry have the potential to provide some awesome routes.

GENERAL APPROACH
As for The Battery but keep to the left of the narrow chasm to reach a large rock platform.

Haul Wall

(NO 6669 4151- seaward end)   East to South facing (Arch)   Map p207
Across the narrow chasm beyond The Battery's north wall lies a large rock apron. The northern boundary of this is Haul Wall, which itself forms the south bounding wall of the Doom Hole and can be well seen from above the opposite wall. A fine wall with some superb sandstone features which although non-tidal, can be greasy in humid or wet conditions. Facing the wall the routes are described from left to right.

There are four belay staples well spread out on the rock apron above the wall for belaying.

APPROACH
Either abseil from the belay bolts on the rock platform or descend at the seaward end of the wall and traverse in to staple belays below the routes.

● In too Deep   10m   6a+ **
George Ridge 1996
A quality route on excellent sandstone features. Good holds where they are needed should ensure its popularity.

● The Jug of Jug Haul   10m   6c *
Neil Shepherd 1996
Another high quality route on lovely sandstone. Similar to the last route except steeper with a hard last couple of moves.

● Haul Anchor   10m   7a+ *
Neil Shepherd 2001
The hardest route on the wall. Climbs the steepest section just before the right-hand arete. The crux is passing the 2nd bolt and a long reach is helpful.

Angus

Arbroath Sea Cliffs

🟢 **Heave Ho! 10m 5+ ***
Neil Shepherd 1996
The obvious rounded arete at the right end of the wall. Good climbing with the crux at the top.

At present there is only one route on the slabby north wall of the inlet, and three on the huge arch at its head. Facing Haul Wall, it is quite easy angled and is best approached by abseil from staple belays. Two staples are in place to belay on at the foot of the slab. All of the following routes start here.

🟢 **Kiss of Doom 13m 4**
Neil Shepherd 1996
One of the easiest routes on these crags, this line takes the big sandy slab directly above the belay.

🟢 **Black and Decker? 17m 5**
Jeff Ross 2002
Climb the easy ramp-line left from the belay then up the big left-bounding corner where the arch meets the slab.

🔵 **The Siren 20m 6c ****
Jeff Ross 2002
From the belay, again climb the ramp left then out over the huge arch in a stunning position following the staple bolts up the prow. A top quality route which requires definite conservation of energy for the finish.

🔵 **Air Raid 24m 7a ***
Neil Shepherd 2002
An aptly named route as big air is possible. Climb Siren to the jug on the arete then continue the hand-traverse left following sandstone coloured bolts to make hard moves up the wildly exposed groove. From the jug on the arete, it is best to unclip the last staple clipped on Siren as rope drag can be significant.

DICKMONT'S DEN

(NO 667 415)   Map p207

The longest inlet in the area is 30m further on from Doom Hole. The only sport climbing at present is on two sectors on the south side of the inlet. The short wall to the left of the descent (when facing the rock) is known as Gull Wall and the higher wall to the right is Sector Achilles.

Gull Wall

North-East facing   Map p207

Named because it faces a local point of interest, Gullies Island, but not because it harbours any of our feathered friends. Nice climbing on good rock but the wall is prone to greasiness and is best regarded as tidal.

APPROACH

As for Doom Hole. Gull Wall and Sector Achilles are the northern boundary of the same promontory of rock. A difficult little step takes you down to ledges below the wall. There is a staple bolt to allow a rope handrail to be positioned for the step down. This would be wise as the descent acts as a seepage line and can be greasy. There are belay bolts in place at the top of the routes.

The routes are described right to left, as they are encountered from the descent.

🟢 **Engullfed 9m 4+**
Neil Shepherd 2004

🟢 **Gulliver's Travels 9m 5+**
Jeff Ross 2004

🟡 **Gullable 9m 6a**
Neil Shepherd 2004

🟡 **Seegull 8m 6a+**
Jeff Ross 2004

Arbroath Sea Cliffs

Sector Achilles

North-East facing   Map p207
The wall to the right of the descent. At present there are only two routes here but there is considerable scope for more on steep rock. Slight greasiness due to the aspect can be found but not nearly as bad as Gull Wall. There are large non-tidal ledges beneath the wall.

APPROACH
The descent is the same as for Gull Wall but once on the ledges go rightwards (facing the rock) with care until more commodious ledges below the routes are reached. There are lower-offs in place for both routes.

● **Beware Geeks Bearing Gifts   12m   7a ***
Neil Shepherd 2005
The left-hand line looks easy enough but is a lot harder than appearances would suggest. A hard pebble pull on the slabby looking bit proves to be the key unless you are lucky enough to have very long arms!

● **Trojan Gift Horse   12m   7b ****
Neil Shepherd 2007
The line through the bulges is as hard as it looks and doesn't give up without a fight.

GRANNIES GARRETT & DEIL'S HEID

(NO 671 418)   Varying aspects   Map p189
This area has some outstanding routes in a tranquil setting. The Deil's Heid is one of the most obvious features on the coast though it may owe more to quarrying than to natural erosion for its shape!

GENERAL APPROACH
Follow the cliff-top path round the long inlet of Dickmont's Den, then carry on up the coast leaving Dickmont's Den behind for about 250m. The stack of the Deil's Heid soon comes into view.

Grannies Garrett

North-East facing

APPROACH
Once the Deil's Heid can be seen clearly from the cliff-top path, cut down rightwards on a gentle path to an area of bare rock. Facing the sea the Garrett is the headland to the south and to the north the Deil's Heid is prominent. To gain the Garrett a bad step needs to be negotiated but the area under the crag is generous and mainly non-tidal.

The routes are described from right to left facing the rock and all have lower-offs.

● **Mushroom Treatment   10m   6b ****
Neil Shepherd 2005
The easiest route has a steep but quite easy lower half before the angle lessens and the route gets harder. Quite high in the grade.

● **Satan's Serenade   10m   6b+ *****
Neil Shepherd 2006
An outrageous line up the huge overhung scoop. Once committed to the angle, speed is of the essence. The rock runs to big flanges and massive jugs. There is a degree of friability but the bolts are closely spaced!

● **Sweet Dreams are made of This   11m   7a+ *****
Tomek Kazimierski 2006
This is one of the most impressive lines at the Arbroath sea-cliffs. Powerful and hard for the grade. Superlatives do not do it justice!

Deil's Heid

All aspects
A prominent local landmark with considerable scope for further routes. It is felt that any development here on the North, South or West faces should have lower-offs and bolts sprayed in a sandstone colour to render them less visually obtrusive.

Red Head

Tilman 'Warg' Schubert climbs Satan's Serenade (6b+), Grannies Garrett (photo Phlip Ebert)

APPROACH
Follow the gentle path as for the Garrett but not as far as the rock area. Contour round a feature known as the Devil's Punch Bowl heading for the Heid itself. There is a very friendly rock and grass area below the Heid, but beware in big seas.

🟢 **Original Route   14m   5+   ***
Unknown 1970s
Climbs a line on the slabby east face above the sea. Start from a belay at the south-east corner where belay bolts can be found. Follow the bolts across the face to an airy perch below a steepening which is the crux. A slightly run out section leads to the final bolt and then the summit. The rock deteriorates and gets quite loose at the top.

There are abseil rings in place on long bolts on the summit but the rope drag pulling it down afterwards is quite severe due to the high friction rock. Walking back up the rock platform towards the cliff-top helps relieve this.

Red Head - Inverkeilor

(NO 703 474) E382 L54   Non-Tidal   East facing   Map p149
This is the highest point on the Angus coast and visible from many miles away. The head rises 90m vertically from the beach on its north-east aspect and provides an intimidating and serious setting. The rock is a thrust of red basalt up into the loins of the surrounding sandstone. The rock is reasonably sound in its upper half where all of the climbing is located to date.

AMENITIES
As for Elephant Rock.

RECOMMENDED TASTY BITES
As for Elephant Rock.

TOP TIPS
Best avoided if you do not have a strong head for heights.

DIRECTIONS

From both the north and the south it is best to locate the pub named The Chance Inn in the small village of Inverkeilor, just off the A92 between Arbroath and Montrose. Opposite the Inn, which is next to Gordon's Restaurant, turn into and follow Station Road. Continue into the country, pass Aniston Farm and after a sharp left bend, turn right signposted Ethie 1 (also Auchmithie and Arbroath). This is about 1 mile (1.6km) from Inverkeilor. Turn immediately left for Ethie. Turn left after 0.4 miles (700m) at Inchock where there is a small sign for Ethie Mains. After 0.4 miles (700m), ignore a left turn for Ethie Mains and go straight on to Ethie Barns. Where the tarmac road turns right at Ethie Barns farm, continue straight on a dirt track. Turn left after 0.25 miles (400m) and follow the track to a small cliff-top car park above Cuthile Harbour (NO 7011 4716). OS map L54 shows all the turns and is useful.

APPROACH

Time: 5mins
Walk north from the car park on an indistinct path to the obvious headland. Go out to the tip of the headland past several old stakes to find a bolt and two staples (3m north of the bolt) at NO 70162 47377.

The only sport route at present climbs the obvious huge arete. An abseil approach is required to a sloping ledge stance located in the main groove. Chain and bolt belays here. The abseil is best from the bolts on the plateau backed up by a stake and possible Friend 3 in a deep crack 15m back from the cliff edge (separate 25m of rope necessary). Escape from the face once committed is difficult, requiring either ascending the abseil rope or an abseil to the beach which is cut off at anything but low tide. There are two traditional routes on the Red Head, **The Engine Driver** (E3) and **Full Steam Ahead** (E2). For details see SMC *North-East-Outcrops* guide 2002.

● **Cock o' the North   25m   6c **
Neil Shepherd, Jeff Ross 2002
From the belay, traverse out left for 5m to gain the exposed hanging arete. Climb this initially with some difficulty and much excitement. Keep to the left of the bolts to reach a semi-rest under a bulge. Pull over this in a wild position, then climb the big wall to the top. There is no sport route in Scotland more out there than this! In 2002 the big wall was climbed up a wide clean swathe but after several years this may need brushing again.

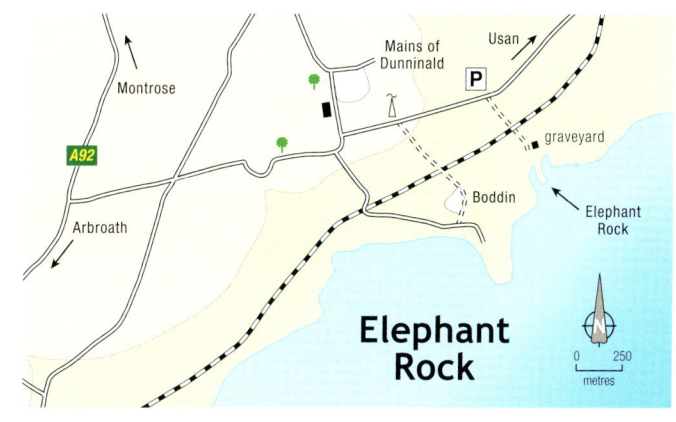

Elephant Rock - Montrose

(NO 7156 5386) L54 E382   Partially Tidal   East facing
Maps p149, p219   Diagrams p222, p224
This venue is situated on the coast mid-way between Lunan Bay and Scurdie Ness, just south of Montrose. Hidden away on a section of coast long overlooked by climbers, it provides a quality venue with routes just that little bit longer than the average Scottish sport climbing crag. Viewed from certain angles and with a degree of imagination the resemblance of the crag to an elephant is clear, especially when seen from the headland just to the north. The crag is formed by a long volcanic dyke projecting from the mainland almost 150m in length but in places less than 10m wide. At these narrow spots the sea has carved two obvious

Elephant Rock

caves through the dyke. These provide the spaces between the beasts trunk and forelegs and its fore and hind legs. They also provide some entertaining sport climbing.

There is not a lot of seepage due to the lack of ground above the crag but the normal sea-cliff problems of humidity and greasiness can be present. In this respect though the crag is less affected than some other areas in the north-east. Nesting seabirds are thankfully uncommon, although those that do nest on the crag are largely fulmars and they are confined to the large central depression above It's a Route Jim and Scratchy and Co. This is the reason for the truncated nature of these routes. House martins are common and it is in the best interests of climbers, and of course the birds, if their nests are not disturbed. They are fairly sociable creatures and will not be put off by climbers right outside their nest. However any damage to a nest will usually result in the loss of the occupants, so take care!

All the climbing takes place on the east face, which makes an early start desirable for those seeking the sun with the crag being shaded from around 1pm onwards. Although a lot of the cliff is tidal, it is possible to gain access to many of the routes for much of the time. By the time you have ticked all the routes above the high water line it will surely have gone out enough to enable the rest of the climbs to be reached!

The rock is a mixed volcanic intrusion which is mainly very sound, especially where it is sea-washed. In some areas the rock can be a bit fragile however and on some routes care needs to be taken especially near the top. The appearance of the rock in certain areas can be very off-putting, such as on Right Wing Extremist. In reality however many of these strange and contorted looking sections are very solid! This venue provides exciting and at times intimidating climbing. All routes finish at twin bolt lower-offs. The rock above these is loose and there are no reliable belays at the top, so please do not attempt to set up top-ropes or abseils as this will only endanger anyone below.

Relations with the locals are friendly at present and visiting climbers should do their utmost to ensure this remains the case. Sensible crag etiquette should apply. This is a local beauty spot and is visited by many local families so please take away your litter and watch your language at all times.

AMENITIES

The usual are to be found in Arbroath with limited climbing supplies found at Basecamp in the West Port.

RECOMMENDED TASTY BITES

Roos Leap in Montrose takes some beating when a proper apres crag feed is required. For the very hungry the Monster Bob Burger is recommended.

Russ Birkett grappling with the Bodysnatcher (7b), Elephant Rock (photo Neil Morrison)

TOP TIPS

Come early to get the sun. Good approach shoes help for the descent down the hill.

DIRECTIONS

The OS map L54 marks Todd's Hole in roughly the correct place for The Elephant. Follow the A92 coastal road north from Arbroath or south from Montrose until a junction signposted Usan 2.5 miles (4km) is reached. This is roughly 3 miles (4.8km) south of Montrose itself. Turn off the A92 at this junction onto a small country road and follow it to a crossroads after 0.3 miles (500m). Continue straight ahead until a series of very tight and blind corners are reached.

Once past these a road sign posted to Boddin Farm will be seen on the right. Go past this to the next road on the right, signed to Usan, 1.25 miles (2km) and turn down here. Continue for about half a mile (800m) until the road bends to the left and a white gate will be seen on the right at the top of a farm track.

Parking is available on the narrow grass verge on the left (NO 7130 5420). Do not take your cars down the track at any time, even if the gate is open. Certain local fishermen have permission from the farmer to park at the bottom of the track but this is not an option for anyone without permission and it is entirely possible that the gate will be locked when you come to leave. Needless to say this would be a tad inconvenient!

APPROACH
Time: 6-8mins

Walk down the track under a railway bridge to reach a small graveyard which has some very old and interesting headstones. Skirt this on the right and a path immediately leads steeply down a grass slope to the beach on the south side of the crag. This can be treacherous when muddy. Go through the first cave on the left to reach the climbs. If the tide is very high and it is impossible to go through the cave then cross over a fence about 20m before the graveyard into a field and follow its edge northwards for about 200m until a stile leads back over the fence. Follow a path down and right to the north-east side of Elephant Rock (where the routes are). This will enable the routes above the high-water mark to be reached. Don't be tempted down the gully just behind the graveyard as it is often wet and unpleasant.

The routes are described from left to right when facing the crag which also means that they are described starting with the most tidal.

1 Can't see the F in Elephant Anywhere   14m   7a
Neil Shepherd 1999
Strenuous to start but with little technical difficulty until the roof. Hard moves out of the bulging crack-line form the crux on mediocre rock. Try to avoid the crack-line once round the bulge as it rapidly loosens, whereas the wall directly below the lower-off is much more solid. Good climbing but spoiled slightly by being a little loose in places.

2 Pas de Charge   16m   6b   **
Neil Shepherd 1998
Bold climbing directly to the niche, strenuous up the wall above and the finish rightwards past the huge block to the lower-off is harder than it looks. The lower-off is shared with the next route.

3 Seeing is Not Believing   15m   6c *
Neil Shepherd 1998
The last route into the niche, but this time pulling directly out over the bulge above with a greater degree of difficulty. A fine upper wall leads to the lower-off.

4 Tale of the Tape   15m   6a+   ****
Neil Shepherd 1998
The narrow pillar of excellent rock gives wonderful climbing in a superb position. Care must be taken not to fall into the huge jug on the final crux wall! One of the best routes at this grade and for those climbing at this standard, a good enough reason to visit the crag in itself.

Elephant Rock

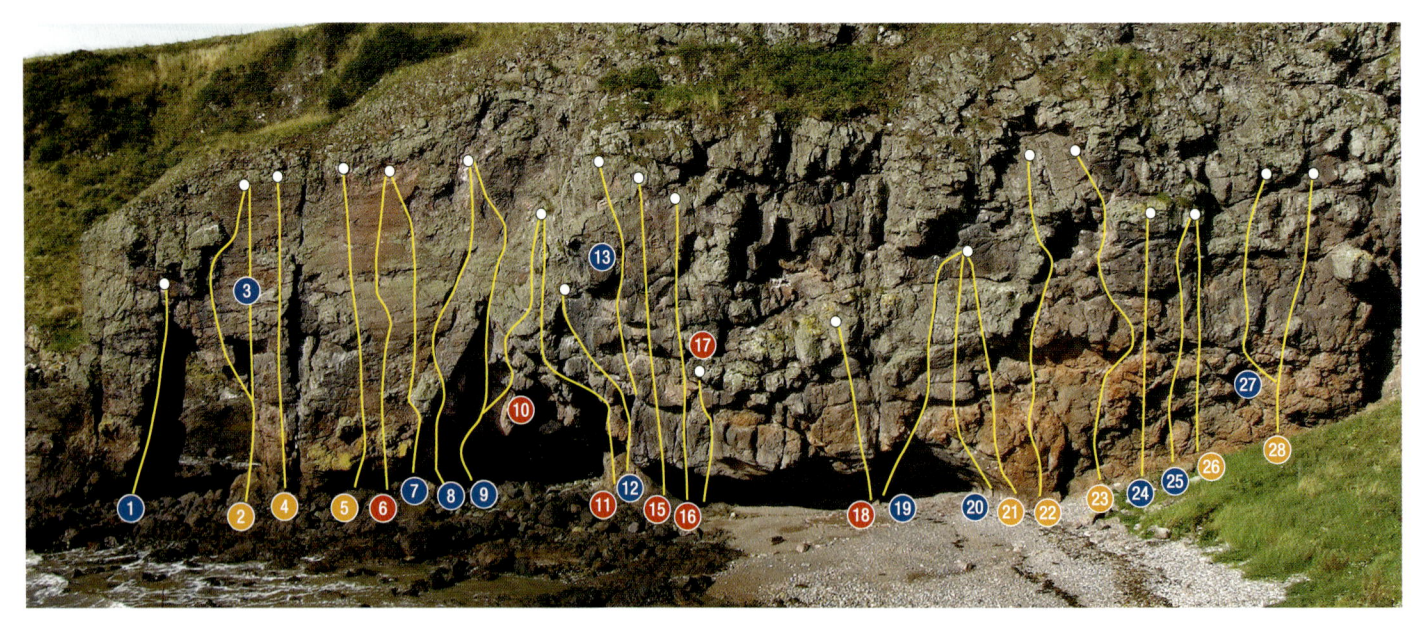

⑤ Big Lug 16m 6b+
Neil Shepherd 1998
The furthest left line on the huge central slab. It gets progressively harder as height is gained. Some big lugs are required to pass the mid-height bulge using a huge ear of rock but the crux is surely reserved for the thin slab above.

⑥ Doigt Attack 16m 7b *
Neil Shepherd 1999
A difficult route up the blankness of the central slab. Only marred by the ease of potential escape onto lesser neighbours. Easy initially over the bulge then some hard cranking is required to reach the sanctuary of the mid-height shelf. On leaving the shelf the second crux involves some further finger straining. If the upper section is climbed directly then it is perhaps a bit sterner than the lower moves.

⑦ Viagra Falls 18m 6c+ **
Neil Shepherd 1998
As expected this one is fairly stiff. The short thuggy initial groove leads to interesting and slightly reachy wall climbing. The crux is low down so persevere as things get a bit softer later on. A shared lower-off with the previous route.

The nature of the crag now changes from the pleasant open walls of the previous routes to a much more intimidating and overhanging arena. This is known as the Outer Limits cave. Thankfully the grades are nowhere near the outer limits, which means it is possible to negotiate some very unlikely looking ground on good holds.

8 The X-philes   20m   6c *
Neil Shepherd 1998
The first route on this section starts in the cave before skirting off left to reach some of the previous pleasant open wall climbing! A varied and technical route with two contrasting sections and excellent positions overlooking the cave proper. Finish high on the left.

9 Hanger 18   21m   7a **
Neil Shepherd 1998
Steep and strenuous, this route contains more contorted positions than any top shelf magazine! The upper slab is easier following the crack to a junction with the previous route before trending up and left to the lower-off shared with that route.

10 Bodysnatcher   18m   7b *
Neil Shepherd 1998
Breaks right from 4th bolt of Hanger 18 to climb the bulges directly. Strenuous to start, then increasingly powerful moves which give the route its name, to a crux surmounting the final large bulge on the right. Go easily up the slab directly to the lower-off.

11 Alien Breed   22m   7b+ **
Neil Shepherd 2001
The steepest and most sustained route in the cave. Follows a contorted line out the huge cleft starting on the right off a small plinth of rock. The initial wall is friable and best climbed just left of the 1st bolt to a good rest before the fun begins. Wide bridging kicks things off before more conventional roof climbing leads out and left in a tremendous position to a junction with Bodysnatcher over the lip of the final roof. Lower off as for Bodysnatcher. The start of this route is very sheltered and is particularly prone to greasiness.

12 Shapeshifter   14m   7a **
Neil Shepherd 1998
The first route on the crag. A good bit shorter than the previous routes but your arms won't be complaining, or maybe they will......! Climb the corner easily for a couple of moves before gaining a hanging arete. Crossing the large capping roof on good holds to reach the upper corner is the crux. Follow this pleasantly to reach the lower-off.

13 The Ex-Pert Route   22m   6c
Neil Shepherd 2000
An intimidating route which is easy in its lower half but really kicks in higher up. Start as for Shapeshifter but continue up the corner before moving right to the top of the arete. The upper section initially follows the broken crack on friable rock before moving slightly left to climb the headwall in an exposed position. The rock on the upper section of the route requires care but the wild position makes up for this. A grade of E4 5c was suggested by the second ascentionist as being more appropriate for this meeting of sport climbing with adventure!

Another change in the crag's character now occurs. The routes are still overhanging but the horizontal component is almost all contained in a huge bulge at the crags base. This has been carved smoothly from the rock by wave action to give a series of formidable starts. The chipping of agate hunters can be seen and sometimes provide useful footholds in the unrelenting smoothness. Some of the starts can require the use of a cheating block to enable the short to reach the starting handholds.
    This is one sector of the crag where a hard winter's gym training will really pay off, as all that extra muscle will allow the use of some gigantic cheating blocks! The routes in the middle of this area are short to avoid the big basin in the upper half of the crag which is home to a colony of fulmars for much of the season.

14 Pert's Buttock   20m   7a *
Neil Morrison 1998
Really a harder and very steep start to The Ex-Pert Route. It gives quality climbing along the lower edge of the hanging slab to join the previous

Elephant Rock

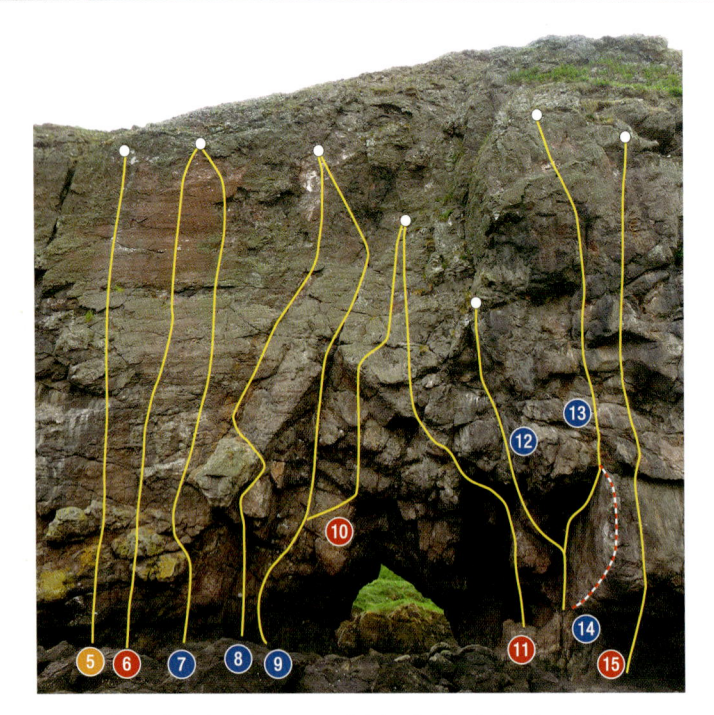

route where it gains the arete. Originally it climbed only the lower arete but now you can go all the way to the lower-off! In wet weather this lower section stays fairly dry and traversing off left after the slab is reached still makes good sense.

15 Smells like Team Spirit   22m   7b **
John Wilson/Neil Shepherd 1998/1999
The start of this climb was originally climbed as a stand alone route before it was extended to the top of the crag. The new upper section does not add any significant extra difficulty although it makes the whole thing more sustained. Some fingery pulls and crafty footwork will gain the easier wall but difficulty returns at the double overhang where further powerful climbing is required. Finish up the headwall in an exposed position.

16 Hannibal   22m   7b
Neil Shepherd 1999
Named more for its liking for human flesh than any elephant associations, this is one route that makes itself felt! A low in-situ cheat stone is in place to start, then the skilful will use a variety of elegant techniques to cross the roof. The less skilled will need to resort to brutal thuggery! The easy corner above crosses another couple of bulges on monster holds to gain the vague crack which trends rightwards to eventually reach a lower-off. In true sea-cliff tradition, a pigeon nests on the final holds of the crux initial overhang. If empty, the nest may need to be removed before an ascent is made.

17 It's a Route Jim!   8m   7b
Neil Morrison 1998
But not as we know it! A much more typical Scottish sport route, very bouldery and short! A convenient block can be rolled in to enable those less than six feet tall to reach the start holds. Once the initial crux of leaving the deck has been overcome it's simply a couple of very powerful pulls to gain the easy corner and a lower-off just under the capping roof. Alternatively, finish up Hannibal.

18 Butt Ugly Martians   11m   7b **
Neil Morrison 1998
Fingery climbing up steep ground makes this a hard undertaking. The height of the shingle bank beneath the route will affect the difficulty of the first moves.

19 Big Girls Blouse   14m   7a+ **
Neil Shepherd 1999
Intimidating! Initially an exercise in overhanging bridging. Once you

run out of leg length or hip flexion, then the remaining section of roof has to be climbed in a more conventional manner. Above the lip another awkward section must be passed before the easier upper crack is reached. Step right at the ledge to the lower-off shared with the next routes.

20 Mahoots Mon   13m   6c+
Neil Shepherd 2000
Very squeezed in! An arching line avoiding the challenge of the huge roof by entering from the right. Follow the staple bolts. Actually gives some fine climbing if one adopts a slightly blinkered attitude.

21 Beware of the Wellyfish   13m   6b ★★
Neil Shepherd 1999
At last the huge undercut relents and things turn more pleasant! A nice warm-up with a steep start and an arm pumping crux bulge at just over half-height.

22 Don't Blame Me!   20m   6a+
Neil Shepherd 1999
A poor route up the slab and groove just right. The obvious short overhanging groove in the middle gives some lovely moves before the rock deteriorates nearer the top.

23 It's not my Fault!   20m   6a
Neil Shepherd 2000
Generally follows the obvious large fault-line above the highpoint of the shingle. Pulling out right and over the small bulge provides the crux. Easier above to reach the right-hand lower-off. Some dubious rock again spoils what would otherwise be an enjoyable and easy climb.

The remaining climbs lie well above the high water mark and a large fallen slab clearly marks the start of this sector. The rock is definitely worth a 9 on the 'weirdshitometer', although it seems sound enough. Occasional crumbly bits may be encountered, most often on the rightmost pair of routes, but in the main the rock is far better than it would appear.

These routes do give some worthwhile climbing.

24 Right Wing Extremist   14m   6c ★
Neil Shepherd 1998
Takes a fairly direct line up from the huge fallen slab. This is a pumpy outing, a lot steeper than it appears. Unfortunately the crux is near the top which adds to the difficulty.

25 Pig on the Rig   14m   6c+
Neil Shepherd 1998
Definitely not a route for porkers! Another pumpy number starting just right and following the ring bolts. The crux is powerful, passing the 2nd bolt going rightwards. The upper section is sustained and strenuous if the bolts are followed directly.

26 The Beggars are Coming to Town   14m   6b ★
Neil Shepherd 1998
Nice climbing which deserves popularity. A little strenuous to be useful as a warm-up, unless the tide is fully in. Finish at the same lower-off as Pig on the Rig.

27 Hornblower   14m   6c
Neil Shepherd 1998
Another route in the Right Wing Extremist mould. 'Interesting' rock and 'pleasant' climbing but not to be underestimated. After the first easy moves, head up and out leftwards with hard climbing to pass a bulge. Continue in a forceful way until easier ground is reached.

28 Whistleblower   14m   6b
Neil Shepherd 1998
A similar line starting as for Hornblower. After the first shared moves, head out rightwards and up to eventually reach some real rock and pleasant climbing to finish at a separate lower-off.

Aberdeenshire

Sport climbing in the North-East of Scotland is not extensive and while it is mainly of local interest, it does provide another enjoyable dimension to the area. The sport climbs fall into three areas with a cluster of crags on the sea-cliffs south of Aberdeen, the Red Wall Quarry north of Aberdeen and Cambus o' May Quarry on Deeside near Ballater.

The sport climbs on the southern sea-cliffs are generally on schist and tend to be short and powerful. The furthest south, Boltsheugh/Newtonhill and The Keel, provide short steep routes with juggy holds in a sheltered setting which are often in condition, while the routes at Clashfarquhar Bay are longer with more awkward access. Sportlethen is another small wall, cruel on the fingers and above the extensive bouldering at Portlethen. Just to the north and standing head and shoulders above the other sport crags, is the Orchestra Cave. This wildly overhanging granite and schist crag has only a handful of routes but they cut through wild ground and are up to 30m long; if 8a is your thing, this is your crag. The granite sport routes in the Red Wall Quarry make the best of a previously unused and dismissed piece of cliff. Although some of them have been sculpted, the sustained and fingery climbing is demanding and rewarding.

Cambus o' May is an altogether different proposition from the sea-cliffs with fingery climbing on quarried granite walls. Although many of the routes have been created through chipping, this is partially compensated by the beautiful setting.

History by Neil Morrison

Sport climbing in the Aberdeen area was slow to start primarily because of the strong ethic of traditional climbing, but was also linked to a lack of both obvious venues and a knowledge of how to go about equipping sport routes. This changed due to the influence of the nearby Angus quarries and the knowledge gained from that area's main developer, Neil Shepherd. In the early '80s many of Aberdeen's climbers logged up impressive mileages down to Angus and particularly to Legaston and Balmashanner. This, coupled with their sport climbing holidays abroad, left some of them wanting sport of their own. The coast was initially regarded as too chancy and the feeling was that there would be a backlash that would lead to bolts being chopped, so investigating all the apparent possibilities Neil Morrison and John Wilson set about developing the disused granite quarries at Cambus o' May in 1993.

The quarries had a few trad routes, with the centrepiece route Idiot Savant having been extensively sculpted. The initial development retro-bolted some of these original routes in addition to adding new lines. Realising the extent of the task, Shepherd and George Ridge were invited and busy spells ensued in both 1993 and 1994. Initial bolting was not without its controversy and some chopping occurred, but after discussion with the original trad developer, Alastair Ross, agreement was reached and development really began. Where routes had previously been led on trad, the guide has acknowledged that ascentionist and date.

The highlights of the development were Ross's retro-bolted Idiot Savant (7c), Morrison's Sun City (7a+), Ridge's …Working Weak (7a), Wilson's Technical Merit (6c+) and Shepherd's Heinous De Milo (7b). Danny Laing and friends

History

Aberdeenshire

1. Aberdeen Sea–Cliffs p230
2. Red Wall Quarry p247
3. Cambus o' May Quarry ...p251

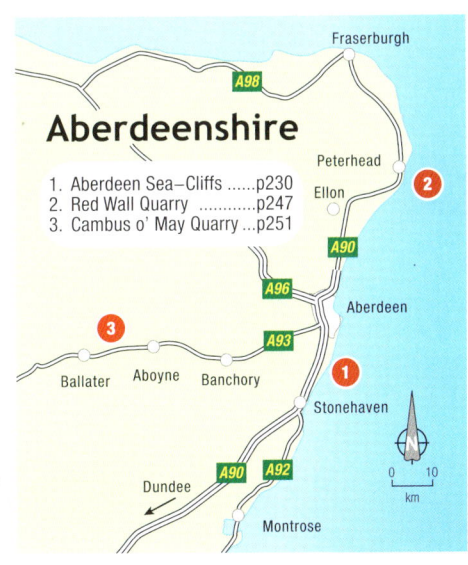

added some easier routes on the back wall although these have been taken over by vegetation. After the initial burst of development most of the obvious lines had been climbed but Shepherd returned in 1996 to add arguably the hardest route with Dinnet Do It (7c). East of the main Idiots Quarry (the original name), another open quarry bay was also developed, but this area was seen as too sensitive due to the presence of nesting raptors and the landowner came under pressure to stop climbing in all the quarries. Fortunately one of the developers knew one of the birdmen and after a bit of negotiation a compromise was reached and the eastern quarry was stripped of bolts while access has been allowed to continue in the main quarry.

After developing Cambus and receiving favourable feedback from many, Morrison and Wilson felt bold enough to develop an area on the coast and after extensive searching they settled on the small but well formed Boltsheugh. Here the best of the first wave of routes were Dark Side (6c+), Down Under (6c) and the difficult Deadheads (7b) which was climbed the morning after Morrison's daughter's head wetting! Controversy however was never far away and as a result of the bolting of coastal rock a meeting was convened in Aberdeen to discuss and draw up guidelines for future development. This resulted in lively but sensible debate and an expression of local democracy led to a distinctly different set of guidelines being drawn up from those proposed by the MCofS. What emerged was that climbers enjoyed the diversity of trad, sport and bouldering on the coast but not at the expense of the overwhelmingly traditional climbing in the area. Boltsheugh became instantly popular both for the sport climbing and bouldering, but it took another 10 years to reach maturity when Tim Rankin set about further development with a clutch of routes at Boltsheugh South from 2004 to 2006. These routes have proven popular and can give sunny sport throughout the winter.

In 2002 Rankin had taken up the mantle of sport climbing development that Morrison and Wilson had slipped away from. Rankin initially used Morrison's tired old Hilti drill to develop the aptly named Sportlethen above the boulders at Portlethen. With his home in Portlethen being so close, he was able to overcome the knackered drill which would only give one or two holes per charge. He practically worked out the whole wall culminating in his ascent of The Portlethen Terrier which, at 8a, gave the areas then hardest sport route. This attracted a swift second ascent by an

Tim Rankin enjoying the Spice of Life (7b+) at Clashfarquhar (photo Neil Morrison)

History

Wilson Moir on the seamy Underbelly (7b) at Newtonhill (photo Neil Morrison)

in form Dave MacLeod. MacLeod promptly stoked east-west rivalry by proclaiming the route was only 7c+ but, suffice to say, it still makes a stiff little outing whatever grade you settle on and you will find easier 8as.

In 2003 Ranken added Fascination Streak (7c/7c+) to the sea-cliffs when he climbed an old project at Findon Ness. This super steep line had originally been equipped by Colin MacLean nearly 10 years previously but the difficulty of finding it dry led to it being abandoned. MacLean's old bolts helped in the re-equipping of the wildly overhanging line. After this route and his further development of Boltsheugh, Rankin cast about for more potential and in 2004 he developed a clutch of routes at Clashfarquhar Bay with Back from the Brink at 7a+ the best of them. In 2005 he visited The Keel, which George Ridge had previously considered developing but had abandoned a partly bolted line in the mid '90s. The rock took a bit of getting used to, but eventually produced eight steep and powerful routes including Ridge's unclimbed prow, The Keel (7b).

A return to Clashfarquhar in 2007 produced the great Spice of Life (7b+), probably the best sport route up to that date on the coast. However it was in 2008 that development of two of the coast's finest sport crags began. The two could hardly be more contrasting with the steep crimpy granite of Longhaven's Red Wall Quarry and the wildly overhanging and atmospheric granite of the Orchestra Cave. Rankin set the ball rolling with four routes at Longhaven with the finest being The King at 7c+. The Orchestra Cave had often been talked about and held a trad route away out on its right wing, but its incredible angles and the difficulty of access both from the bottom and on a rope through steep ground and slatey bands, had put off everyone. Rankin even went to the effort of fixing bolts on the top in 2006 but after swinging about for an hour unable to touch rock only 5m over the lip abandoned the idea! However with his experience in rope access, Ali Coull fitted the bill and duly set about bolting the line which he then led in quick time to give Dangleberries (8a+), surely one of Scotland's finest and most atmospheric sport routes.

In 2009 both the Orchestra Cave and Red Wall Quarry received further development. At the Orchestra Cave, Ali Coull bolted and sent Blobstrop at 8a and arguably the North-East's finest sport route to date. Both Blobstrop and Dangleberries were quickly repeated by Gordon Lennox and Tim Rankin respectively. Gordy's wife, Cheryl and Ali's wife Lynn both need special mention for braving the free abseil and jumar back out to belay them on separate occasions – not something even hardened climbers are keen on. Later in the year and after the birds, Rankin returned to the O-cave to add Bassoon at a highly exciting 7a+. He then extended it to the top of the crag to provide the mighty Double Bassoon at 7c. Beside Dangleberries he added the very improbable Air on a G-String (7c+). This has shut down some powerful lads and hints that it's no pushover at that grade.

At Red Wall Quarry the big news was Rankin's Lucifer, a possible 8b, where crimps from hell lead to a desperate reachy crux and sustained upper wall. Conditions are crucial and it helps to have a low humidity day. Just to the left, Gordon Lennox set about the obvious and even harder alternative start to Lucifer to give the excruciating Dracula (8b); the holds make your fingers bleed just thinking about them and it's definitely a tall man's route. Rankin also added the more amenable Sultan at 7c and both this and The King (7c+) have become popular test pieces at their grades. Ali Coull repeated Lucifer and in the course of his visits linked the start of Messiah to the top of The King to give another 8a, much to the frustration of Rankin who had injured himself trying the line.

In 2010 the sport routes at the O-cave saw some traffic but there was something of a lull. 2011 however, saw Rankin bounce back into action firstly with the development of Newtonhill Cave where Underbelly (7b) is outstanding. He then turned his attention back to the O-cave where he added the short and powerful Crescendo (8a+) and then began development of the viciously overhanging granite wall at the right side of the cave.

Sport climbing in the North-East has a short history and has involved a few developers but the number of repeats of routes at all grades shows their popularity and there is undoubtedly scope for further development of easier routes at Clashfarquhar and one or two desperate routes in the Orchestra Cave. Sport climbing in the North-East is unlikely to ever rival the area's trad climbing, but it definitely adds another dimension to the local scene.

Dave Cowan sorts out The League of Whingers (6b+) at Boltsheugh (photo Neil Morrison)

Aberdeen Sea-Cliffs

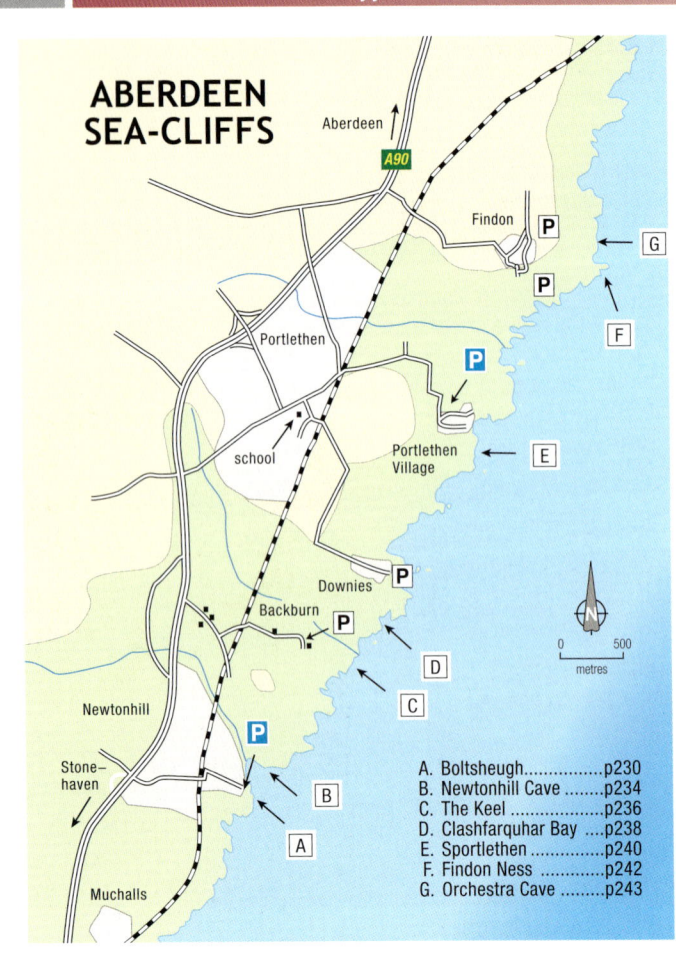

ABERDEEN SEA-CLIFFS

A. Boltsheugh................p230
B. Newtonhill Cave p234
C. The Keel p236
D. Clashfarquhar Bay p238
E. Sportlethen p240
F. Findon Ness p242
G. Orchestra Cave p243

Boltsheugh - Newtonhill

L38 or L45; E406   Map p230

These cliffs lie 200m south of Newtonhill and provide short, steep, often juggy climbing, mostly set well back from the sea. The bolted routes range from 5+ to 7b and are very short. If it wasn't for the poor landings, many of them would be boulder problems. The routes are fine if you are in the area but are not worth a long journey. The main area of Boltsheugh Upper is set well above the sea and is often climbable in rough conditions, particularly when southerly winds rule out most other areas. In addition to the sport routes, it offers some good bouldering with some excellent vertical problems and a couple of fine low-level traverses, although the landings are rocky and a mat is useful. It gets sun until the middle of the day and can provide a sheltered suntrap on mid-winter mornings. Condensation can be a problem as elsewhere on the sea-cliffs, but it is usually possible to get something done.

AMENITIES

Newtonhill has a General Grocery Shop and a couple of pubs. Of an evening the Newtonhill Chippy Van can be found parked at the railway bridge. A pint can be had at the Newton Arms or the more upmarket (very relatively) Quoiters Lounge. All of the above are clustered around the top of Skateraw Road. More extensive amenities are available in nearby Portlethen, or if the bright lights beckon, Aberdeen.

RECOMMENDED TASTY BITES

Newtonhill provides a varied range of options although none stand out particularly. Daily provisions can be had at the ubiquitous Morning, Noon and Night. The impecunious can drive the couple of miles up the road to Asda at Portlethen.

TOP TIPS

Think small and you won't be disappointed. A good bet when the rest of the coast is damp.

Aberdeen Sea-Cliffs

> **DIRECTIONS**

Turn off the A90 dual carriageway into Newtonhill. Follow the road down over a railway bridge and go left after crossing this, then turn right on to Skateraw Road. Go down past the shop(s) to a car park at the foot of the road and overlooking the bay, beside a waterworks vent (NO 9135 9341).

> **APPROACH**

Time: 5mins
From the car park, head 200m south on a footpath, crossing a boggy patch with stepping stones. Shortly after this, descend to the crags easily, either to the north or by easy rock between the two faces. This will take you to the upper platform of Boltsheugh. All areas are easily accessed from here.

BOLTSHEUGH UPPER

(NO 9145 9321)   Non-tidal   East to South-East facing
The upper platform of Boltsheugh and the cliff itself is split into two clear sections, right and left. As well as the routes described, the right-hand section also has some fine bouldering with numerous short problems. In addition the traverse of this section, at low level, gives a superb workout done in either direction. Routes are described from right to left.

Right

1 Deadheads   6m   7b *
Neil Morrison 1994
The first route climbs the steep overhanging wall right of an undercut arete, starting up a flake-crack on the right and traversing left onto the wall. A boulder problem really and has been soloed. The boulder problem from a sitting start at the jug of the next route direct to the upper wall is Font 7b+ ** and a modern classic (probably worth 7c also).

2 Aches in Provence   6m   6c *
John Wilson, Dave Gillan 1994
The steep overhanging arete, which is much more fun if you include a sitting start. Only 6b+ without.

3 Crossroads   6m   6a+
Neil Morrison 1994
The short wall, starting up a flake, leads to the same lower-off as Little Creatures.

4 Little Creatures   6m   6c
Neil Morrison 1994
Gain a good hold on the wall right of a deep crack **The Enemy Within** (HVS 5b) and climb the wall above to the same lower-off as Crossroads. Short with one hard move.

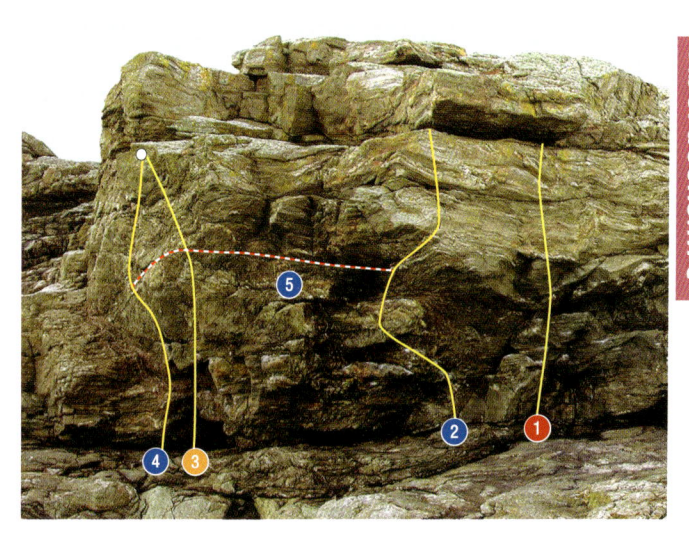

Aberdeen Sea-Cliffs

5 Traverse of the Cods   12m   7a
John Wilson 1994
This is an entertaining, if contrived, traverse taking in most of the routes on this wall. Start up Little Creatures and finish up Aches in Provence, avoiding the temptation to step down or pull over the top of the crag.

The wall to the left of the wide crack gives a Severe route on slightly worrying rock. Strangely there is a bolt lower-off at the top although it is not a bolted route.

Left

(NO 9143 9318)   Non-tidal   North-East facing

6 The Dregs   8m   6a
Neil Morrison 1994
A steep line on poor rock up the vague corner at the right of the steep buttress.

7 Automatic   8m   6c+
Neil Morrison 1994
A steep lower wall leads to awkward moves up and left round a bulge. Avoid the temptation to pull out right towards the top.

8 The Dark Side   7m   6c+ *
Neil Morrison 1994
Powerful moves over the bottom bulge lead to more awkward moves on the second bulge.

9 Mo   6m   6a
Neil Morrison 1994
Steep moves over the bottom bulge at a small corner lead to a shallow ramp feature above.

10 Eany   6m   5+
Neil Morrison 1994
The wall left of the previous route.

11 Meany   6m   5+
Neil Morrison 1994
A juggy lower wall leads to a finish at the short diagonal crack.

Left of the above is a wet cave and left again is a low wall with an overlap which provides some excellent boulder problems including a particularly fine traverse.

BOLTSHEUGH LOWER SOUTH

(NO 9143 9315)   Non-tidal (just)   South-East facing
This section of cliffs lies above extensive partially tidal platforms and while there is a long line of cliffs, much of it is of poor rock. There are now a

Aberdeen Sea-Cliffs

number of sport routes and collectively they provide fine climbing in a very sunny setting.

APPROACH
From Boltsheugh Upper, descend eastwards from the left-hand (southern) end of the cliff. Head to sea-level, then go south onto the platforms which are just washed at high tide, 1min.

The first obvious feature is a large cave.

12 Trouble Monkey   15m   7a+   *
Tim Rankin 2004
The bolt line through the 5m roof of the cave. Climb a fine boulder problem past the 1st bolt onto the ramp. From here it is advisable to clip the next 3 bolts in the roof to prevent a possible knee capping on the ramp (long reach or cunning required). Climb the roof left of the bolts on good but spaced holds to the break at the lip. Finish up right then left to the lower-off carefully using a jammed block below the final roof. A fine roof problem on surprisingly solid rock, although footholds are still friable at present. An inferior variation climbs the roof right of the bolts (6b+) and has proved popular despite avoiding the main challenge.

13 Cheeky Madam   15m   6b+   *
Tim Rankin 2006
The bolt line out the left side of the cave. Climb the fine wall to the roof and move left to the arete, then trend up right to join and finish up Trouble Monkey.

South of this and set back is a large roof some 7m up the cliff, smallest at its right-hand side and to the left of a large corner feature. Five sport climbs cross this roof. All start with easy ground leading to a ledge below the main roof.

14 Laurel   18m   6a   *
John Wilson 1994
Pull over the roof at its smallest point, follow a thin crack a couple of metres left of the corner to ledges and finish with a stiff pull on the headwall.

15 Hardy   18m   6a+   *
John Wilson 1994
Cross the roof just left of Laurel and then head slightly right to a common lower-off with that route.

16 The League of Whingers   18m   6b+   *
Tim Rankin 2006
Great moves through the widest part of the roof. Trend slightly right above the roof to climb the crack left of Hardy to gain its lower-off. Distinctly easier for the tall.

Aberdeen Sea-Cliffs

17 Rankin's Rain Games   18m   6b **
Tim Rankin 2006
The best route here, it gives a wild trip for the grade. Easy ground on the left of the buttress leads to a ledge below the double roofs. Pull along the lip of the first roof until moves up and right lead onto the arete. Pull over the right side of the second roof, then trend left to the lower-off.

18 Morrison's Missed Adventure   18m   7a **
Tim Rankin 2005
An impressively steep route tackling the widest part of the double roofs. Climb easily to the left end of the ledge, then follow the bolts direct through the two roofs to finish up the easy wall above.

John Cooke on The Dark Side (6c+), Boltsheugh Upper Left Side (photo Stuart Stronach)

BOLTSHEUGH LOWER FAR SOUTH

(NO 9138 9313)   Tidal (just)   South-East facing

The final bolted routes hereabouts lie 50m further south, past a small buttress of fine rock topped by broken ground, then a gulch with a small alcove beyond it. All the routes are on a steep wall above a rock pool. This area is affected by high tide.

19 Out Back   12m   6b
Tim Rankin 2005
The right-hand line. Climb to a ledge, cross the roof above going leftwards, then step left into the corner. Pass the flake overhang on the left wall and continue direct to the lower-off avoiding the temptation to walk off right above the flake. A hybrid linking some good features.

20 Down Under   10m   6c **
Neil Morrison 1994
One of the best routes here, taking the central line. Climb the wall and corner clipping the chain from the cliff-top for the full grade.

21 Go West   10m   6b+ *
Wilson Moir 2005
The left-hand line. Hard moves lead to good holds below the 2nd bolt, followed by easier but steeper climbing trending right to the lower-off. More technical but less sustained than Down Under.

Newtonhill Cave - Newtonhill

(NO 915 935)   Non-tidal   South-East facing   Map p230   Diagram p235

A fine, convenient venue developed in 2011. Although not extensive, a visit here can easily be combined with the nearby Boltsheugh routes. The crag is clearly visible from the Boltsheugh parking area and from the right profile is seen as the stunning overhanging left arete of the cave. It is non-tidal and only the biggest of swells would jeopardise access. The cliff runs with water from the field above in the winter but seems to dry out by April or May most years. Once dry the routes will need brushed

Aberdeen Sea-Cliffs

but stay dry even through prolonged periods of rain. The climbing is generally steep and positive on good holds and the routes feel surprisingly long. The rock is a compact schist varying from immaculate to extremely soft and unreliable. Generally the rock is better higher up and the start of all the routes should be handled with care.

AMENITIES
As for Boltsheugh

RECOMMENDED TASTY BITES
As for Boltsheugh

TOP TIPS
Take a clip stick as the starts are on snappy rock and you really do want the first bolt clipped.

DIRECTIONS
As for Boltsheugh and park at the same place.

APPROACH
From the parking area, go north down a well marked path to the beach. Cross the burn by a wooden bridge and either at low tide, scramble round the shore line north to the cliff or at high tide, take a steep path up the hillside opposite the first house which leads up into the field above. Follow the edge of the field east for about 50m until a steep grass ridge leads down to the cave.

The first two routes were bolted and first climbed as dry tooling routes and subsequently climbed as rock routes. Dry tooling is welcome on these lines but not the routes to the right. Crampons should not be worn and trainers or rocks shoes are the accepted footwear. This is to protect soft and potentially loose rock, leaving the climb available for the future.

① Drookit 12m D4 *
Sandy Simpson, Brian Duthie 2008
The furthest left line, starting from the rotten raised ledge. Sustained hooking on flat holds to a perplexing finish for the top ledge. Pumpy climbing.

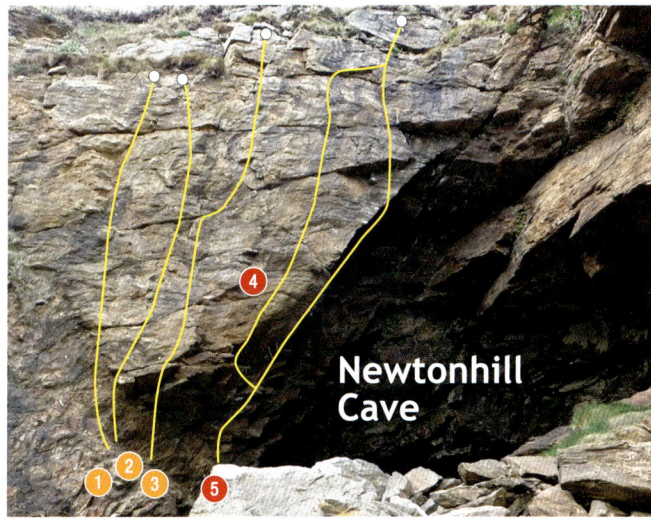

① Drookit 12m 6a
As a sport climb; beware of the rock.

② Credit Crunch 14m D5 **
Brian Duthie, Sandy Simpson 2008
The next route right up a steep crack. Start below the obvious overhang and start pulling hard to a more positive but sustained headwall with some long reaches for the top. A hard start but a good rest can be had before launching up the headwall.

② Credit Crunch 14m 6a+
As a sport climb; beware of the rock.

Aberdeen Sea-Cliffs

③ Tool Bags   15m   6b+ *
Tim Rankin 2011
A good route and the standard warm-up, taking the lower roof direct. Stick-clip the 1st bolt on the lip of the roof.

④ Dog Town   16m   7b+ *
Tim Rankin 2011
Right again is the stunning arete of Underbelly. Start up this to the 2nd bolt, then out left and up the arete to a break. Further hard moves lead to the next break and a final desperate move up the wall left of the last bolt leads to the top break. Move right on this and up to the Underbelly lower-off.

⑤ Underbelly   16m   7b ***
Tim Rankin 2011
The compelling overhanging arete gives arguably the best route of its grade in the area. Climb steep jugs and flakes, then a hard move up the very edge. Use the big side-pull above to gain further jugs in a little hanging corner, then move left and up to the ledge. Finish easily straight up to the lower-off.

The Keel - East Cammachmore

(NO 923 944) L38 or L45; E406   Partially tidal (only high tide)   North-East & South-East facing   Map p230

This is the name given to a short steep area of rock at the back of a partially tidal inlet on the coast roughly mid-way between Newtonhill and Portlethen. The rock is a flakey schist similar to the other coastal sport crags. However it is not always as reliable as it looks but should improve with traffic, especially the footholds. The crag is really only a spring to autumn venue and needs a decent spell of weather to dry it out. It can then remain dry through most summers. Climbing is possible in the rain due to the angle of most of the climbing but it can turn greasy. The left wall faces north-east and is very sheltered, only getting the sun in the early morning, meaning lingering dampness is a problem. The back wall is slightly better being south-east facing. However for both walls the best time to visit is on a sunny morning or when a good northerly has been blowing.

The bolted routes range from 6c to 7c and are very short.

AMENITIES

Head for Newtonhill or the growing metropolis of Portlethen.

RECOMMENDED TASTY BITES

Both Portlethen and Newtonhill are within easy striking distance for a rowie or two if the urge should strike. A rowie is a bread roll special to the North-East.

TOP TIPS

Can look grim but persevere and you might even enjoy it. It might be short but make sure you are feeling strong.

DIRECTIONS

Leave the A90 dual carriageway at a single track road, with a small sign for East Cammachmore. This turn off is easily missed but if approaching from the north, it is some 1.25 miles (2km) south of Portlethen and is preceded by a sign for Cammachmore. From the south it is the first turning on the right after Newtonhill. Follow the single track road for a few hundred metres, passing some cottages until a farm track leads left (small faded sign for Backburn Farm). If you reach a railway bridge you have gone too far. Take the farm track, crossing the railway, forking right then passing between a cottage and outbuildings (which is actually Backburn Farm) to its end at a another farm. Park in the open area before the farm, making sure not to block access, NO 9188 9443.

APPROACH

Time: 10mins
From the farm, head straight down to the coast, arriving just south of a stream. This involves crossing a field on the north side of the farm but it is usually grass (hay) so the farmer doesn't mind. If it is not grass, take the path heading north until it turns east and where it turns back north, continue straight to the coast down the edge of the field. On reaching

Aberdeen Sea-Cliffs 237

③ The Keel   10m   7b ⁎⁎
Tim Rankin 2005
The blunt arete feature marked with both hangers and staples used to be an abandoned project but is now the best hard route here. Very steep and bouldery.

④ The Closer   8m   7c
Tim Rankin 2006
Powerful crimpy moves up the 50 degree overhanging wall right of the staple bolt line of The Keel. The trick is keeping your feet on. Clipping the bolts is probably the crux.

⑤ Span-utan   8m   7a
Tim Rankin 2005
A short route up the right side of the wall, very conditions dependent.

The following three routes are all on the back wall of the inlet. They receive more sun than the other routes so are more often in condition, especially later in the day. Seepage can be a problem in the winter and spring but once the ground above is dry they remain dry even in heavy rain. They all have excellent lower-offs making them ideal training routes.

⑥ The Smile Child   12m   6c ⁎⁎
Tim Rankin 2005
The left-hand line is sustained and steeper than it looks. An excellent training route.

⑦ Lewbee Doobee   12m   7a+ ⁎
Tim Rankin 2005
The central line is a bit of a hybrid but gives good strenuous climbing. Cross the first roof to a reasonable rest below the second. Use a small undercut in the roof to reach right to holds on the lip and traverse the lip hard right to the base of the hanging crack. Go up the crack then the wall above slightly right to the lower-off.

the coast, descend the grass ridge overlooking the stream until it is possible to cut back south down a rocky ramp near the sea, then returning to the back of the inlet.

① Makosi   12m   6c
Tim Rankin 2005
The line furthest left and starting by a detached block. Big jugs with the occasional dirty interlude! Tends to be a bit sandy but worth a star when clean.

Five metres to the right is:

② Titanic   12m   6c+ ⁎⁎
Tim Rankin 2005
Starting from the obvious handrail, forge up and right until a choice of hard moves brings on that sinking feeling! If still afloat, sail on up The Keel clipping its last bolt. Outrageously steep for the grade.

Aberdeenshire

Aberdeen Sea-Cliffs

8 Superlew 10m 7a **
Tim Rankin 2005
The thinner crack-line to the right climbed direct gives an excellent sustained route.

Tim Rankin making short work of Superlew (7a), The Keel (photo Neil Morrison)

Clashfarquhar Bay - Downies

(NO 9251 9462) L38 or L45; E406   Partially tidal   East facing   Map p230

The sport routes at Clashfarquhar are found on a long wall on the west side of the bay. The rock on the wall improves towards the south with the southernmost end holding three or four trad routes. There is also limited but good, if hard, bouldering to be had on the boulders at the base of the cliff. Access is only a problem around high tide. The routes themselves are long for the North-East although ledges do break them up. The rock is a bit flakey but is cleaning up with traffic. Fingery starts and steep upper sections typify the routes.

AMENITIES
Portlethen has Asda, Matalan, Home Base, Snappy Tomato Pizza and pubs. What more could you need?

RECOMMENDED TASTY BITES
Asda cafe awaits your pleasure.

TOP TIPS
Abbing off the routes will spare your nerves and rope so carry a belay plate.

DIRECTIONS
If coming from the south on the main A90(T) dual carriageway, take the first turn into Portlethen (Downies is also on the sign). This takes you on to Bruntland Road and follow it to Portlethen Academy. Turn right just after the Academy; there is a small sign for Downies. Turn left soon after at another small sign for Downies. Follow this minor road to and through the village to a small turning point at the road end. Careful parking is possible for one car (NO 9262 9506), otherwise backtrack into the village and find a parking spot here.

If approaching from the north, head into Portlethen centre and follow signs either for Downies or Portlethen Academy.

Aberdeen Sea-Cliffs

APPROACH
Time: 10-15mins

From the road end, head diagonally south through the fields to cross a low wall and a fence onto Berrymuir Head. Clashfarquhar Bay is the first big bay south of Berrymuir Head. Strike south staying high until atop a steep grass ridge from where the boulders can be seen in the bay to the south.

Descend the steep grass ridge and head south into the rocky bay. In the base of the bay are extensive wave cut platforms sporting one big boulder and many smaller ones. The routes lie south of the obvious large boulder.

There are currently six routes but scope for more. They are located 20m to the south of the largest boulder at the base of the cliff. All have good double bolt abseil points with rings but no lower-off krab. Abseiling may be preferable to lowering off as there are numerous sharp edges near the cliff-top.

The rock is generally better than it looks, but all the routes cross sections of more friable rock which should be handled with care and will hopefully improve with traffic. Due to their position the routes are very sheltered and can stay dry in light rain given a favourable breeze over the cliff-top. However it's worth noting that both the harder lines finish up a slab. This sheltered position can also lead to lingering dampness but the routes are usually climbable even in damp conditions, if a little pumpier.

Seepage isn't too bad so the routes are climbable all year round after a reasonable dry spell. There are a few nests during the nesting season but the routes should still be possible, if a little less pleasant.

① Toll Route   15m   6b+ *
Tim Rankin 2004
The left-hand line of bolts. Use the jug on the next route to get started, then go up and left via a hard move to gain the ledge. Cross the roof direct and climb the fine upper wall to the abseil point/lower-off. Arguably better if started up the next route missing out the hard lower wall (6a+ **).

② Pay and Display   17m   6a *
Tim Rankin 2004
Start up the middle line of bolts to give a fine easier route up the crack and groove line.

③ Sweet Charity   20m   6c+ **
Tim Rankin 2004
Follow the middle bolt line to the ledge, then move right to climb the

steep wall and arete above in a fine position into a hanging groove. Climb the right edge of this and swing right to the abseil point/lower-off.

④ Back from the Brink   20m   7a+ ★★
Tim Rankin 2004
An impressively steep route up the right-hand line. Climb to the ledge, then take the wall above direct on hidden holds. Trend left on the very steep upper wall to a hard pull over onto the slab and the abseil point/lower-off of the previous route.

⑤ Spice of Life   28m   7b+ ★★★
Tim Rankin 2007
Climb Back from the Brink to its 7th bolt in the hanging groove, then break right to climb the obvious line up the left side of the overhanging face passed a demanding final sequence to the lower-off. It needs to be stripped on top-rope. An excellent long, steep and pumpy pitch which is low in the grade but not easy to onsight! Requires 14 clippers.

⑥ Born of Frustration   32m   7c ★
Tim Rankin 2007
Climb a roof crack into the groove of Back from the Brink. Follow this to break out right as for Spice of Life, then step right again to climb the right-hand line of bolts up the middle of the upper overhanging face. Not much new climbing but another excellent workout. By climbing direct up the upper wall and avoiding holds on Spice of Life to the left, it is much harder (7c+) and how it was first climbed.

Sportlethen - Old Portlethen

(NO 9333 9599) L38 or L45; E406   Alt 15m   East to South-East facing   Maps p230, p240
The following routes climb the full height of the Sport Wall, the first wall reached on the approach and also home to a number of boulder problems. With the exception of The Portlethen Terrier, Stray Dogs and Dogs of War, the sport routes are fairly unremarkable but do provide enough entertainment to while away a few hours. The harder routes can feel crimpy. The location is very sheltered and as long as there is no seepage from the fields above, the routes can be climbed at any time of year.

AMENITIES
Old Portlethen has no shops but does have a pub at the top of the village which is fine for a post climbing pint. Portlethen itself has all the shops associated with a settlement of its size including Asda and Homebase (handy for picking up DIY items on the way home). Cash machines and petrol are available at Asda. There are other smaller shops in the village and a couple of pubs. Accommodation is hard to come by although nearby lower Deeside has campsites. Guest houses and B&Bs are available by the shed load in Aberdeen.

RECOMMENDED TASTY BITES
Asda Cafe!? Good cheap breakfast but will provide too much ballast for the routes.

TOP TIPS
Size isn't everything. Strong fingers help on the harder routes.

Aberdeen Sea-Cliffs

DIRECTIONS
Access is from the road linking Portlethen to Portlethen Village (Old Portlethen). From Aberdeen on the A90(T), take the first turning sign-posted to Portlethen (also Marywell and Findon). This goes through some new houses west of the A90 before returning under it to the centre of Portlethen. Go straight ahead at a first mini roundabout in Portlethen, left at a second (across the railway bridge) and continue past a new health centre out of Portlethen and on to Portlethen Village (named as Old Portlethen when you arrive). Park just after entering the village, in a small car park opposite The Neuk (inn), NO 9307 9624. From the south, take the first turning into Portlethen and follow the road (Bruntland Road) to the roundabout at the railway bridge. The route from the north is now joined and followed.

APPROACH
Time: 10mins
From the car park, walk for 150m down the right-hand road (Craigmarn Road) to the last cul-de-sac on the right before the bottom. At the end of this, squeezed between someone's drive and a cottage, a little alleyway at NO 9319 9613 leads as a continuation to the cul-de-sac and turns left after 10m into a pathway between the village and the fields to the south. Walk down to the coast, cross a small fence with a stile and head southwards for 50m until a path descends below the steep little crag. The extensive bouldering lies on the foreshore below.

Routes are described from right to left.

● **Collie Corner 7m 5+**
Tim Rankin 2002
The obvious corner to a break and lower-off. Surprisingly challenging.

● **Long Dogs 7m 6a**
Tim Rankin 2002
A good little eliminate. Climb the wall direct passing to the left of the second bolt. Take the wall above direct on hidden holds to the break. Step right to lower off.

The Portlethen Terrier (7c+) gives Russ Birkett a shake (photo Stuart Stronach)

Aberdeen Sea-Cliffs

● **The Lurcher** 9m 7a *
Tim Rankin 2002
Another fine wee route but don't stray right off the arete. Climb the arete to a good hold at its top. Trend right on good holds to the break and lower-off.

● **Dogs of War** 15m 7c **
Tim Rankin 2002
A strength sapping hybrid making maximum use of the crag. Climb The Lurcher to the good hold, then hand-traverse left (no resting on the ledge) to join The Portlethen Terrier at its 4th bolt. Finish up this.

● **Gone to the Dogs** 10m 7b+ *
Tim Rankin 2004
This climbs the small hanging corner right of The Terrier. Start as The Terrier, then move up right to climb the corner (not the arete of Dogs…) to gain the hand-traverse of Dogs of War. Pull out right to finish up The Lurcher.

● **Stray Dogs** 15m 8a *
Tim Rankin 2004
Follow Gone to the Dogs to join Dogs of War and finish up this. Another excellent hybrid, pumpier than The Terrier.

● **The Portlethen Terrier** 10m 7c+ ***
Tim Rankin 2002
The commanding central line with a tough boulder problem start to gain jugs. The first ascent climbed the groove left of the bolts (8a) but it is now usual to use the big side-pull up right from the jugs. If this wasn't powerful enough for you try the **Power Hound Variation** (8a+*), put up by Tim Rankin in 2006. This is a super direct variation to The Portlethen Terrier missing out all the big holds! Eliminate but superb sustained climbing. Climb the boulder problem start to the Terrier then use only holds on the hanging ramp to the left to gain a break. Take the wall above direct on small crimps to join The Terrier at its 5th bolt and finish up this.

● **Stigmata** 8m 7b *
Tim Rankin 2002
A short vicious route up the line of a thin crack to the left. Climb to the ledge then attack the crack to join and finish up The Portlethen Terrier. Harder for the tall, which makes a change.

● **Dogs Abuse** 9m 7a+
Tim Rankin 2004
A counter diagonal to Dogs of War with a surprising amount of new climbing. Climb Stigmata to the ledge, then go right out the break to gain the hand-traverse of Dogs, reversing this to finish up The Lurcher.

● **Hilti** 6m 6c+
Tim Rankin 2002
Another short stiff route up the next thin crack. The top is slightly easier. The 1st bolt has no hanger (but that may change), and can be climbed by stick-clipping the 2nd bolt.

● **Bosch** 8m 7a
Tim Rankin 2002
A right rising traverse. Pre-clip the first bolt as for Hilti, then traverse right along the break to clip the 2nd bolt. Pull up and clip the 3rd bolt as for Hilti, then continue right, clipping one more bolt to finish at the lower-off of The Portlethen Terrier.

The last route lies on a small buttress to the left of the Sport Wall.

● **The Incredible Sulk** 6m 7b
Tim Rankin 2003
A vicious little number over a bulge. Clipping the 2nd bolt on the lead is a feat in itself.

Findon Ness - Findon

(NO 9438 9739) L38 or L45; E406   Non-tidal   East facing
Maps p230, p243

Aberdeen Sea-Cliffs

The crag at Findon Ness has only one route at present, but what a route, hauling its way through the roof of a huge cave. The crag faces east and the angle of the cave means that the sun does not get into it in the summer months, leading to a serious problem of lingering condensation which can combine with seepage. This makes it difficult to catch the route dry, although it can be climbed when damp and, in fact, was very damp when first climbed. Go on a sunny early morning in spring or autumn before the sun gets too high in the sky to get in under the roofs and after a reasonably dry spell of weather. Take strong arms and abs.

AMENITIES
Findon village has no amenities so Portlethen, with all the delights of Asda, is your best bet. See Sportlethen for more details.

RECOMMENDED TASTY BITES
As for Sportlethen.

TOP TIPS
Incredible patience and luck will be needed to find the only route dry.

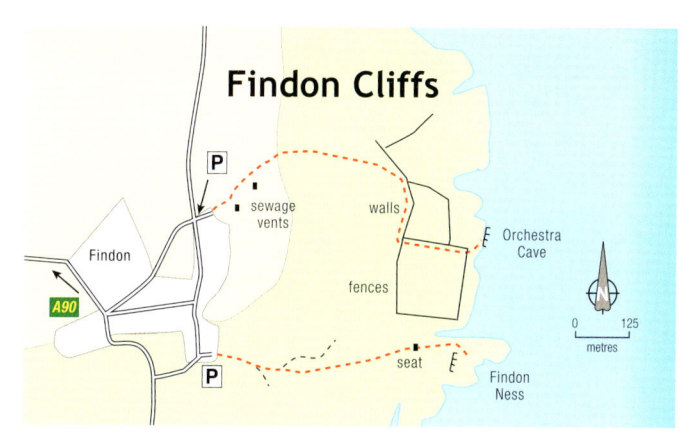

DIRECTIONS
From the main dual carriageway (A90T) from the north or south and just north of Portlethen, take a turn-off signposted for Portlethen, Marywell and Findon. Follow signs for Findon and drive through several turns in the village to its very end where Old Inn Road is a sharp turn on the right. At the bottom of this road where it takes a sharp right and the tarmac ends, there is a cul-de-sac leading left to the start of a path (signposted Findon Moor, footpath to viewing point 600m). Park here without obstructing access (NO 9432 9742).

APPROACH
Time: 10mins
Follow the path and after 100m, take a right branch towards the sea. Once through some gorse, ignore a small left branch and continue straight on, then bending left to reach a bench on a concrete plinth, situated looking out to sea. If all else fails, head to the coast and the bench is very prominent. The big inlet to the north is Kay Hole. Follow a small path (which peters out) down the broad ridge formed by the south wall of the inlet, then cut down and right towards the cave which lies at the back of a big dry bay.

● **Fascination Streak   15m   7c/7c+ **
Tim Rankin 2003
An awesome struggle through the roof of a cave. Possibly easier when in good condition.

Orchestra Cave - Findon

(NO 94433 97655 - top) L38 or L45; E406   Partially Tidal   East facing   Maps p230, p243   Diagrams p244, p246
The Queen of the north-east coast's sport cliffs. It waited some time before its well known potential could be realised and even then it took the seasoned skills of a rope access worker. Luckily there was a new man in town who not only could bolt such a grossly overhanging piece of rock he could climb it too! Once tipped off about its potential, Ali Coull

Aberdeen Sea-Cliffs

wasted no time and often drilled into the dark to equip the first two lines. The cliff is essentially a shallow cave with the roof of the cave set at about 50 degrees. However unlike so many other steep cliffs of micro schist along the coast it is generally excellent quality and uniquely laced with a fine red granite for extra interest. In some places the red granite pushes through the schist in tufa like formations which provides the finest routes (Blobstrop and Air on a G String). On the right side of the cave is an impressive wall of red granite overhanging at about 50 to 60 degrees, the outrageous trad route of **Unchained Melody** (E5 6a) takes the corner where the red rock joins the grey rock. On the left edge of the red wall there is a partly bolted closed project (Ali Coull).

AMENITIES & RECOMMENDED TASTY BITES
Findon village has no amenities so Portlethen, with all the delights of Asda, is your best bet. See Sportlethen for more details.

TOP TIPS
A visit is not recommended in the nesting season due to the volume and stench of the summer residents although Air on a G String is bird free and the nests on the other routes could be avoided. For optimum conditions it is best to visit on sunny mornings in spring and autumn when the sun is lower in the sky and can penetrate its rays deep in to the cave. However a good workout can be had on breezy days but beware of the swell. Although the routes aren't affected by the tide access to them is!

DIRECTIONS
From the A90T just north of Portlethen, follow signs to Portlethen and Findon. Head to Findon and drive through the village to park at the start of Old Inn Road, the last road on the right (see Findon Ness for more details) – park at NO 9381 9769.

APPROACH
Time: 10mins
Take a road north of the furthest north house and follow it towards the sea for 60m where it turns behind the house. Skirt a gate and take a continuation track slightly left; follow it past some sewage vents. When the track turns hard right (south-east), follow this down to cross or skirt a boggy area, then follow the narrowing path beside a wall leading southwards until level with the second of two dykes which lead at a right angle seaward through the fields. Follow this second wall down to the sea on its south side and reach the corner of a field with a fence. Immediately east of this is a V.Diff chimney – descend this and traverse back north to the crag. For an abseil descent, head north-east to the cliff-top and find a block with rope threads (NO 94433 97655). Even at high tide, abseil from the block to reach the routes as long as there is no swell. An alternative set of two bolts 10m further on is above Bassoon. At low to middle tide, you can abseil in directly above Dangleberries from another two bolts 10m further on (the most northerly set). A separate abseil rope is recommended.

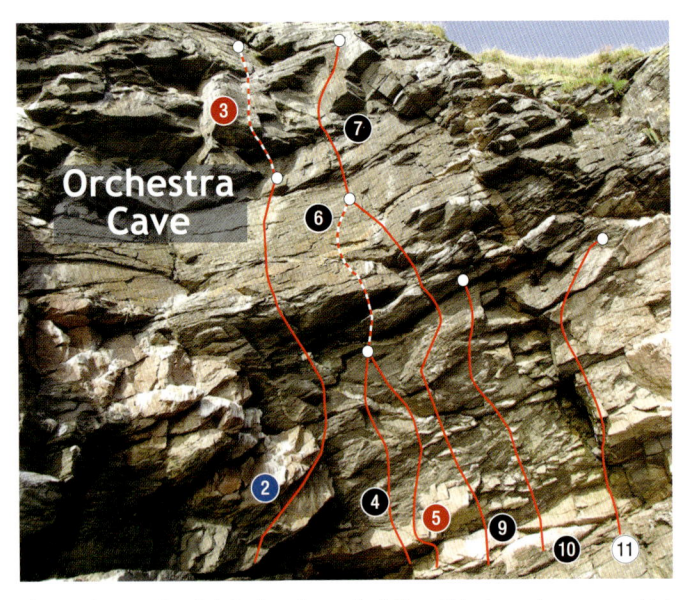

On the far left looking in to the cave is a short but worthwhile warm-up.

1 Mad Cows 10m 6a+ *
Tim Rankin 2009
On the very left edge of the cave is a short route up a pleasant groove and technical upper red wall. It can often look wet when it is in fact perfectly dry!

2 Bassoon 25m 7a+ *
Tim Rankin 2009
On the left side of the cave proper is an obvious hanging red granite groove. Gain this with difficulty and climb it to a hidden rest on the left. Step back right and climb to the bird perch below the roof. Traverse left in a wild position through the roof to a tricky move gaining the lip. Pull over victoriously and continue up the interesting wall to a lower-off above the break.

3 Double Bassoon 35m 7c **
Tim Rankin 2009
As the name suggests this is the extension to Bassoon. Continue above the first lower-off and through the difficult roof above. The top wall is straightforward to a lower-off at the top of the cliff.

On the back wall two routes start close together.

4 Crescendo 12m 8a+ *
Tim Rankin 2011
Stunning sustained climbing up the left-hand line of bolts. Climb through the initial roof to a good hold on the lip, where a hard move up left leads into the line proper. Follow it direct to join Air on a G String at the final hard move to a lower-off in the roof.

5 Air on a G String 12m 7c+ *
Tim Rankin 2009
A short but quality route starting just right of Crescendo. Climb the first roof trending left to gain a large flat hold with difficulty. Pull up right

Wilson Moir pulling victoriously over the lip on Bassoon (7a+), Orchestra Cave (photo Neil Morrison)

Aberdeen Sea-Cliffs

Aberdeenshire

Aberdeen Sea-Cliffs

to jugs then make a dynamic move (crux) past the 4th bolt and up to a rest common with Dangleberries at the quartz break. Return left and up to a break before a final hard move leads to the lower-off in the roof above.

6 O.M.D   20m   8a   *
Tim Rankin 2011
Orchestral Manoeuvres in the Dark is an extension to Air on a G String and provides yet another top quality and outrageously wild trip. From the first lower-off, launch out through the roof. At the lip make a hard rockover to gain a break, and a thin finish up and right to the first lower-off on Dangleberries. Rope drag is an issue at the roof. It is best to reverse aid to the first lower-off to strip.

Unchained Melody E5 6b

7 Bang Tidy   32m   8b/8b+   **
Ali Coull 2012
A stunning voyage of determination and tricky rope work linking all the hardest climbing in one super pitch! Climb Crescendo with two ropes clipping only one. Continue out O.M.D. clipping in the second rope at the lip of the roof. At the Dangleberries 1st lower-off, pause briefly to untie the first rope before launching up this to the top of the crag. A futuristic link up which fell ahead of its time!

8 Air Berries   32m   8b   **
Gordon Lennox 2012
A logical link of O.M.D. into the top pitch of Dangleberries direct up the centre of the crag. Use two ropes as per Bang Tidy. Perhaps low in the grade?

9 Dangleberries   30m   8a+   *
Ali Coull 2009
The original route climbing the full height of the cave. After a tricky first roof tackle the 45 degree wall above to a break and good rest. Climb a steeper bulge and make hard moves up to below the huge roof and a no hands rest. Pull over this roof via an unlikely sequence to another no hands rest (double kneebar). Follow the vague groove above and pull through the final roof rightwards to the lower-off. Brilliant pumpy climbing leading to a boulder crux. To the first lower-off at 20m gives a fantastic 7c+ ***.

10 Blobstrop   20m   8a   **
Ali Coull 2009
The super steep line to the right characterised by the granite blobs. Big moves on good holds leads to the first big blob, wrestle with this (kneebar?) until a high crimp for the right hand can be reached. Swing left to a break and continue straight up until more hard moves lead to below the big roof. Launch through this to get established on the ledge above and lower off. The best sport route in Scotland? Just possibly but certainly a contender.

Aberdeen Sea-Cliffs

The following routes are on a wall which forms the right side of the Cave, and go to the same lower-off.

(11) Closed Project
Ali Coull 2010
A rib right of a huge overhanging chimney-groove line.

(12) Underland 12m 7c ★★★★
Tim Rankin 2011
A superb route taking the obvious challenge of the overhanging groove on the left side of the wall. "More funky moves than a Diversity concert!" The initial roof is hard and there is a knack to taking a hand off to clip the second bolt. It also features a lying down rest on the midway ledge. High in the grade.

(13) Bitter Sweet Symphony 12m 7b+ ★★
Tim Rankin 2011
The central line of weakness trending left across the fine granite wall. Steep juggy climbing except for a tricky move in the middle and a boulder problem gaining the top break. From here traverse hard left, then straight up to the lower-off. It is impossible to strip, so strip on top rope or on reverse. Both options are exciting!

Two more routes are planned to the right. At the right edge of the wall is a trad route **Unchained Melody** (E5 6b).

Red Wall Quarry – Longhaven

(NK 1154 3884) L30 E427 Alt 25m East facing Maps p230, p247 Diagram p249

This large open quarry is probably the most easily accessible of all the major Longhaven Quarries. It is better known as a convenient access point to the Red Wall itself, one of the most impressive traditional climbing areas on the coast north of Aberdeen.

So far two different walls have been bolted, these being the obvious overhanging back wall of the quarry below the descent and the not so obvious steep slab on the south side of the quarry. The rock is generally excellent granite if still a little crumbly underfoot in places but this should improve with traffic. Being granite and never that steep, the climbing tends to be technical and sustained with the overall quality of the climbing being quite remarkable for quarried rock. Both walls face east and catch only the morning sun which can be an advantage in summer. The back wall does suffer from a persistent seep but only the start of The King is affected and this can usually be diverted to allow the holds to dry. The most favourable conditions are on fresh breezy mornings but a good work out can be had even in the worst haar as the climbing tends to be on positive holds. It is also possible to climb on the back wall in light rain or showers.

AMENITIES
Travelling north from Aberdeen, a Tesco at Ellon is conveniently accessed

Aberdeen Sea-Cliffs

Gordon Lennox uses his long reach on the Dracula True Finish (8c), Red Wall Quarry, Longhaven (photo Neil Morrison)

just off the A90 by turning left at the second roundabout. This also provides the cheapest fuel around but it's still not as cheap as Aberdeen. Longhaven village itself has a shop, but what an experience and not to be missed in its own right. Dubbed the porn and pie shop, it provides a much needed rest stop for the tired trucker or a good place to pick up your climbing snacks! Peterhead, 5 miles (8km) to the north, is a sizeable town with all the amenities you would expect including a McDonald's. There are two pubs and a small well stocked shop in Cruden Bay.

DIRECTIONS

From Aberdeen take the A90 towards Peterhead and reach Longhaven village 5 miles (8km) before Peterhead. About 500m after Longhaven, turn right off the A90 onto a wide track signposted Longhaven Quarry. Follow the track to a Scottish Wildlife Trust car park at NK 1146 3941 and beside an old ruined cottage.

APPROACH

Time: 10mins

Follow a path east past the cottage (away from the quarry road) to a signpost. Turn right (signposted Cruden Bay) and follow the footpath round the rim of the huge (occasionally) working quarry until it descends to an old track. The track goes left (east) into Longhaven Quarry (many trad climbs), but go right to a fence. Don't go through a gap into the working quarry but stay outside the fence and follow the waymarked path which soon leaves the quarry fence and heads towards a ruined wartime lookout seen on the crest ahead. Continue past the lookout on the waymarked path, which soon descends slightly to cross an old track. Continue for 50m to where the path goes to within 5m of the cliff edge. The edge is actually the rim of an old quarry (Red Wall Quarry) facing out to sea. In 2010 there was a fixed rope on stakes leading diagonally down a ramp into the quarry (but not difficult even without the rope). The Back Wall is on the left of the descent. For the Bridal Slab approach from the Back Wall, go down a boulder field staying close to the south wall of the quarry.

Aberdeen Sea-Cliffs

BACK WALL

The most impressive wall in the quarry looks blank on first appearance and overhangs by about 10 degrees. It gains in height from left to right with the first route starting off a raised platform.

1 Joker 12m 6b+ *
Tim Rankin 2012
The leftmost line on the wall. Climb a short crack to a flake, move right on this, then stand up using a good undercut flake (common with Harley Quinn). Move up left to the big undercut flake, then climb the thin crack above to the lower-off.

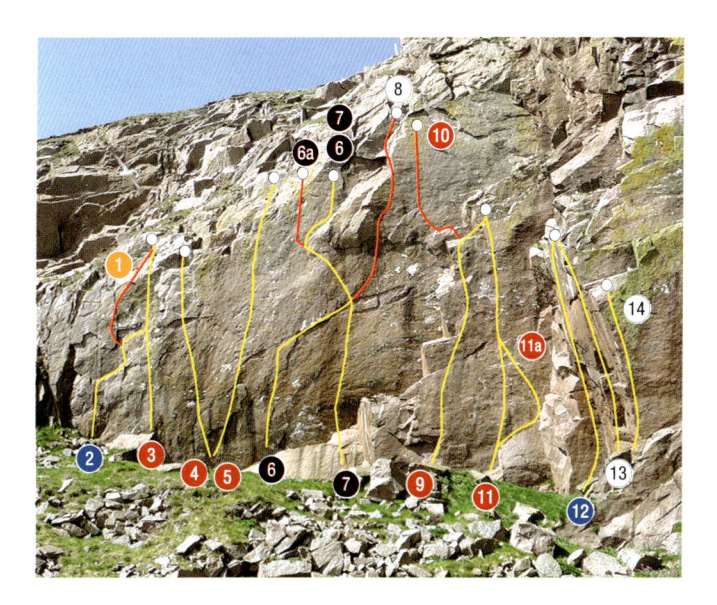

2 Harley Quinn 12m 6c *
Tim Rankin 2012
A logical link to give a reasonable warm up. Start as for Joker. Climb a short crack to a flake, move right on this, then stand up using a good undercut flake. Leave Joker and make a hard move right to join Jester at the foot of the upper crack. Finish up Jester. It is best to stick-clip the first bolt and ignore the tempting undercut flake out left of the 2nd bolt – this is Joker.

3 Jester 10m 7b
Tim Rankin 2008
The left-hand line climbing cracks and flakes. Passing the first two bolts is an initial crux. It can provide its own warm-up by pulling past the initial two bolts but care must be taken clipping its 3rd bolt.

4 Messiah 12m 7c+ **
Tim Rankin 2008
The thin crack on the left side of the wall gives an excellent sustained struggle. Start as The King and swing left into the crack. It usually seeps from the bottom of the crack but this doesn't affect the holds. High in the grade.

5 The King 18m 7c+ **
Tim Rankin 2008
The compelling central line weaving its way up flakes and edges. The start up the flake is often wet but a rag in the top of the flake stems the flow and it quickly becomes dry to climb. Easy to do the moves but frustrating to redpoint. In the opinion of some it is low in the grade.

6 Dracula 22m 8b **
Gordon Lennox 2009
The desperate thin flake leads to an even more desperate move to gain a good thin flake. A wander up this leads to a finish up the sustained wall and groove of Lucifer.

The independent **Dracula True Finish** (8c **, route 6a) starts at the base of the right-slanting ramp. Step left and make desperate moves directly up the wall to a lower-off

7 Lucifer 20m 8b ✶✶
Tim Rankin 2009
The skilfully enhanced blank wall leads to a semi-rest at the undercut break, then continues up the fine sustained upper wall and groove. The crux is a very height dependant move above the rest and the route may be only 8a+ for those of average stature.

8 Closed Project
Tim Rankin 2012
The wall right of Lucifer after starting up that route to the point where it joins Dracula.

9 Solomon 14m 7b ✶
Tim Rankin 2012
A worthwhile eliminate taking in the most challenging line up the wall left of Sultan. Step onto the wall and immediately overcome a hard sequence to gain the sloping ramp direct (no holds in groove on left) move up again and step right to use an undercut to gain holds level with the big ledge. Either make an ugly mantle onto the ledge or nicer, use a side pull on the right. From the ledge climb the arete then swing right and up the next arête to jugs. Step right then up to lower off as Sultan. Hard climbing all the way but not sustained.

10 Road to Perdition 22m 7c ✶
Tim Rankin 2012
The fine traditional style finger-crack in the upper wall climbed in its entirety from the flake at its base. Climb Solomon to before its step right where it joins Sultan, then step up to the ledge. Span hard left to gain the flake below the crack. Desperate moves gain a good pod. Further sustained climbing leads to the lower-off.

11 Sultan 12m 7c ✶✶
Tim Rankin 2009

The blank looking wall just left of the right-bounding corner **Rough Diamond** (E1 5b) gives excellent sustained face climbing.

A 7b+ right-hand **Variation Start** to Sultan (route 11a) is popular. Climb the starting flake right into the right-bounding corner, have a picnic, then return back out left up an easy flake-line to join the original at the 3rd bolt.

12 Diamond in the Rough 6c ✶✶
Neil Shepherd 2012
A groove right of Rough Diamond.

Right again are two closed projects.

13 Closed Project
Neil Shepherd 2012

14 Closed Project
Neil Shepherd 2012

BRIDAL SLAB

(NK 1154 3880)   Alt 20m   East-South-East facing
The huge inverted triangular slab in the south-east corner of the quarry, facing away and therefore not seen from the Back Wall.

15 Kingdom of Granite 22m 7a+ ✶
Tim Rankin 2008
This climbs the centre of the inverted triangular slab set at a lower level and to the south of the back wall routes. Start up an easy groove then bridge to gain jugs on the left arete. Clip the 2nd bolt with care then relax and pull onto the wall proper. Follow flakes then a shallow scoop to below the obvious overlap; cross this with difficulty and continue to a ledge. The final wall provides a tricky finish. An absorbing and sustained route avoiding a loose easy crack to the left of the overlap.

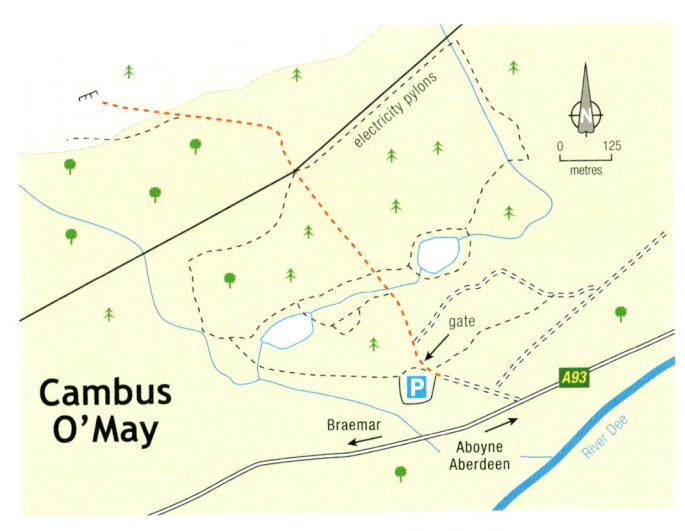

Cambus o' May Quarry - Ballater

(NO 3971 9866) L37 or L44; E395 or E405   Alt 270m
East, South & West facing   Maps p230, p251   Diagrams p252, p253, p255

Cambus o' May on Deeside is an altogether different proposition from the sea-cliffs with fingery, edgy climbing on vertical or slightly overhanging granite walls. Many of the routes have been created through enhancement of features or wholesale chipping. The setting is beautiful and goes some way to offsetting the created nature of the routes. The quarry containing all the climbing is part of an area of disused granite workings set amidst open birch and pine woodland forest north of Cambus o' May on Royal Deeside. They lie on part of The Dinnet National Nature Reserve and this should be kept in mind when climbing there. The approach walk provides fine views up Deeside to the more traditional fare of Lochnagar.

The routes offer interesting and generally sustained climbing on good rock at a variety of grades, although the emphasis is on difficulty. The routes tend to be vertical and crimpy with a good stiff pair of shoes helping considerably – don't wear your slippers. Many, if not all, routes rely on man made holds. A number of the older routes have been retro-bolted with the agreement of the first ascentionists.

The main quarry is box shaped, faces south and despite some persistent damp patches, tends to offer warm dry climbing, even early in the year, when the more exposed traditional crag at the Pass of Ballater is too cold for comfort. The rock is very compact and marble like in nature so can be sweaty in hot weather and the sheltered nature of the crag can make for midge and mosquito hell so choose a cool day with a breeze for optimum conditions.

Development also occurred in the other quarries to the east. However, concern over nesting birds (in consultation with the Forestry Commission) led to these other venues being de-bolted. Please stay away from them in the future or access to the whole area will be jeopardised.

AMENITIES

Ballater, almost 3 miles (5km) west of Cambus, offers all the visiting climber needs with pubs, cafes, cash machines and an outdoors shop selling climbing gear. The Old Station Cafe is particularly fine. Accommodation is well catered for with a campsite and a host of B&Bs. The well heeled climber may wish to stay at The Stakis Craigendarroch Hotel and Leisure Club.

RECOMMENDED TASTY BITES

At Cambus o' May itself the Crannoch Guest House and Cafe serves excellent food including superb scones.

TOP TIPS

Don't climb here with dodgy fingers. Do climb here with edging shoes.

DIRECTIONS

Heading west from Aboyne on the A93 towards Ballater, turn right at a signpost for Cambus o' May Forest Trails (NO 405 980). This is about

Cambus o' May Quarry

8 miles (13km) after Aboyne, 1.5 miles (2.4km) after a road on the right to Strathdon (B9119) and 1.1 (1.7km) miles after the Cambus o' May Hotel. It is just before the Crannoch Guest House and Cafe at Cambus o' May (if you see a trout fishery on your right you have gone too far). Go up the rough track for 200m into a car park at NO 404 981. If approaching from Ballater the signs and car park are on the left, immediately after Crannoch Guest House and Cafe (nearly 3 miles; 5km). This is fairly soon after a long straight which is just after where the Pass of Ballater road joins the A93. The hillside with the quarries and other broken rocks is visible from the A93 at NO 400 979.

APPROACH
Time: 15mins

From your parking spot, return to the entry track and go along it past a "danger electricity overhead" sign to a locked gate. Go round this and on for 20m to where the main track bends right. Leave it and go straight on along a wide footpath (actually wide enough for vehicles) for 5mins (440m) to pass under electricity lines (ignore the waymarked paths). Five minutes (400m) after this, the track forks at NO 3983 9863. Follow the right fork (actually straight on), going diagonally uphill until the western quarry is reached after 140m. This is where all the climbing activity is concentrated.

WEST WALL

1 Scuffer   12m   4+
Ian Davidson 1988
The steep wall on the left of the quarry is bounded on the left by a slab. Climb the middle of the slab to a big ledge, then continue up the edge of the slab above. Retro-bolted.

The next five routes are on the overhanging west wall.

2 Boulder Problem   7m   7b
Colin Stewart 1988
The right-slanting thin crack to the big ledge, starting just right of the crack. Short and desperate. Retro-bolted.

3 Dinnet Do It   12m   7c *
Neil Shepherd 1996
Climb out directly from Idiot Savant, then into the small triangular niche high on the wall, finishing direct.

4 Edgelands   12m   7b *
Neil Morrison 1993
Climb Idiot Savant past its 2nd bolt. Quit the crack and climb the wall

to the left to rejoin Idiot Savant near the top. Well nigh impossible for climbers under 5ft 10in.

5 Idiot Savant   15m   7c *
Alastair Ross 1988
A work of art and a bit different from your normal sport route. Follow the continuously interesting crack to underneath the obvious pot-hole, then move left to finish up the thin crack. Can be dirty at the crux due to a drainage line but brushes up easily. Retro-bolted.

6 Sticks 'n' Stones   10m   7a+ *
Neil Morrison 1994
The line of holds up the wall right of Idiot Savant. Dodgy single bolt lower-off.

BACK WALL

The following routes were revealed after heavy excavation, though nature has since reclaimed the terrain. The lines are on very blocky rock and will not appeal to everyone's tastes. There appear to be more routes recorded than lines bolted but no one has had the desire to resolve this mystery.

All of the routes on the Back Wall were equipped and climbed by Kev Smith, Danny Laing and John Mackie, but all would need re-cleaned before an ascent.

7 Slip of Death   15m   5
Kev Smith, Danny Laing, John Mackie 1994
Start at the foot of the slab between twin cracks and climb to a lower-off point.

8 Deathwish 2   15m   5+
Kev Smith, Danny Laing, John Mackie 1994
Start at a block and climb up to a roof. Finish directly up the headwall above.

9 Suicide Bat   15m   6a
Kev Smith, Danny Laing, John Mackie 1994
Start as Deathwish 2. Climb directly to an overhanging arete. Surmount this and trend right to finish.

10 Pinball Wizard   15m   6b+
Kev Smith, Danny Laing, John Mackie 1994
Start at an obvious stepped block. Climb up and left to an overhanging wall. Surmount this leftwards and finish as for Suicide Bat.

Cambus o' May Quarry

Amanda Lyons in Sun City (7a+), Cambus o' May East Wall (photo Mel Hayes)

11 Magic Bus   15m   5+
Kev Smith, Danny Laing, John Mackie 1994
Start as for Pinball Wizard. Climb to the 1st bolt and move left to below the overhanging arete. Follow the corner to a roof before traversing left to finish up the headwall.

12 Anyway, Anyhow, Anywhere   15m   5+
Kev Smith, Danny Laing, John Mackie 1994
Start at the stepped block and move up rightwards to the 1st bolt. Step right and climb blocks to finish.

EAST WALL

13 Heinous De Milo   20m   7b ★★
Neil Shepherd 1994
The left-hand line on the big wall gives sustained and sequential climbing. It can have a little damp streak and, at the time of writing, needs re-cleaned.

14 Sun City   20m   7a+ ★★★
Neil Morrison 1994
A classic sustained and sequential trip up the central line on the main east wall, left of the hanging groove. Along with Idiot Savant the reason for climbing at Cambus.

15 Tornado of Souls   20m   7b+ ★
Neil Shepherd 1994
The hanging groove line starting directly up the wall past the twin monos. A very technical lower wall. The groove can be dusty.

16 Welcome to the Working Weak   15m   7a
George Ridge 1993
The thin seam and flakes, right of the hanging groove; 4 bolts to lower-off. At the time of writing it was seriously overgrown and often wet.

Cambus o' May Quarry   255

17 Indian Summer   15m   6c+
John Wilson 1993
A short way along the east wall is a superb flake-crack. Climb the left-hand side of the flake to a ledge. Climb the wall above starting with a reachy move (often a full blooded flying leap).

18 Sharp Practice   15m   6a ★★
Ian Davidson 1988
Climb the right-hand side of the flake to a ledge. Move right and up (crux) to finish. Retro-bolted.

19 Technical Merit   15m   6c+
John Wilson 1993
The escapable arete right of Sharp Practice, climbed on its left-hand side and gained from below by a long reach.

The following routes are very short and finish at a big ledge but can be extended by climbing either of the lines on the bolted wall above at no change in grade. Both extensions are 5+ (routes 20 and 21).

22 Bonsai Pipeline   6m   6a
George Ridge 1993
Right of Technical Merit is a ledge with a Scots Pine. Climb the very short wall, past one bolt, under the tree.

23 Wimpey Construction   6m   6a+
John Wilson 1993
The next line right, like the inside of a Wimpey House – small.

24 Wind in the Willows   6m   6b
John Wilson 1993
Right again. Short and fingery.

25 Quality Street   10m   6a
Colin Stewart 1988
The left-hand line on the taller wall to the right. It trends up left. Retro-bolted.

26 Roses   8m   5
Unknown 1980s
At the right end of the east wall there is a series of horizontal breaks. Climb these to finish on small holds. Retro-bolted.

Aberdeenshire

Highlands East

This is a more recently developed area where seven of the ten sport crags are conglomerate. The climbing is surprisingly similar to some of Spain's world famous conglomerate cliffs, for example Mallos de Riglos, but much smaller of course. Enthusiasm is growing quickly for this style of climbing, which is surprisingly fingery rather than strong arms despite the very steep overall angle. The proliferation of positive holds produces many climbs in the lower grades and guarantees the popularity. The climbs are hard to read from below as one pebble looks much like another, but some give excellent holds. A first visit to conglomerate feels very tentative, but as confidence grows that the pebbles will stay in place, the grades feel easier as your climbing style relaxes and you stop gripping quite so hard. Having said that, the lines are initially very loose and heavy cleaning is required to create a route. So early ascents can be quite spooky as holds can still come off, but the routes soon become enjoyably solid, if never quite the same as traditional rock types.

Conglomerate also has few cracks so there has been little or no criticism of the bolting from hardline trad climbers. The climbs dry very quickly as there is often little drainage from above. New routes will continue to appear and some are planned, but not all conglomerate crags can clean up sufficiently to be good venues. The first two crags have more conventional rock but have particularly steep impressive walls which offer fine climbing in the higher grades.

History by Andy Wilby, Neil Shepherd, Ian Taylor, Andy Nisbet, Rab Anderson & Simon Nadin

Dunlichity Crag

This crag had been lying untouched and overgrown since the early 1980s until its impressive main wall was picked out in 2005 by Andy Wilby as a potential sport venue near Inverness, at the time rather short on sport crags. He bolted all the lines except Kids with Guns and his group of friends paid various visits to the crag taking turns at trying routes.

Brin Rock

Andy Wilby noticed that this clean sunny crag received few visits from trad climbers and its overhanging nature attracted him and his drill. Initially he kept it secret and unfortunately drilled through a new trad line which was also being kept secret. Moving of some bolts and changing the line has meant an uneasy truce, and it seems likely that the sport climbing will be much more popular than the serious trad routes. Later in 2011, several more routes were drilled; some have been climbed but the remaining ascents are not far away.

The Camel

Neil Shepherd first visited in 1981, an ultimately fruitless traditional day was had, and further tentative sport climbing visits in 1985 and 1992 ended because the available bolting technology could not cope with the particular demands of the crag. On a visit with Shepherd, Rab Anderson bolted what was to eventually become Sand in my Pants, the line having been adopted, with permission, by George Ridge.

By 1997 however drills and bolts had improved to a level where the first route could be equipped and climbed. Two Humps are Better than One (6b) showed the crag's potential but still required a retreat to base in Inverness for a battery

History

recharge. The following year the increased drilling firepower of George Ridge and Shepherd and a passing mention in that year's Highland Outcrops guide brought the crag to the attention of others.

While 1999 saw a lot of equipping, only Shepherd actually got anything climbed. A cold day in October with a gale force wind blowing down the gully saw the Shepherd family out with three year old daughter firmly attached to a bolt so she didn't blow away! Stone of Destiny received its first ascent; numb fingers prompted an initial grade of 7a+ but this quickly settled to 6c+ with traffic the following year.

Inverarnie Schwarzenegger (7a) and The Final Straw (7a) were climbed the following year but access problems were not far away. Firstly rare lichen and an SSSI designation meant protracted negotiations for the MCofS, the result of which limited development to the gully sidewall. The next blow arrived when the local raptor study group, ignoring advice from its parent body the RSPB, insisted on a total crag ban for the bird nesting season despite the nest site being distant and out of sight of the climbing. In recent years the birds have not nested and access has been open.

By 2004 the access issues had been resolved. However, Ridge had lost interest in his equipped lines and Shepherd climbed the left-hand one to give Paralysis by Analysis (7a+) whilst the same day Ali Robb climbed the other to give There's Sand in my Pants (7a). The standard of difficulty rose slightly in 2005 with Giza Break (7b) but went to a far higher plane in 2007. Late that year Dave Redpath, who was always on the lookout for new hard lines to climb, climbed the overhanging wall left of Two Humps to create Ubuntu (8a). This was matched in 2009 by strong local climber Andy Wilby who added Death is a Gift (8a) to its left. The same year it was left to Dave MacLeod to round off development to date by linking the hardest climbing of both the previous routes to give the eliminate Gift Link (8a+).

Moy Rock

Although Moy Rock had been climbed on in the 1970s by bold traditionalists, it wasn't until 2007 that the first sport routes appeared. Andy Wilby put in a mammoth effort by cleaning and drilling five routes on the Big Flat Wall, ranging from Little Teaser (6b+) to The Seer (7b). Intent on keeping a low profile, some of the bolting even occurred under cover of darkness, accounting for some of the route names. These routes became instantly popular as the sunny sheltered location allowed climbing right through the winter.

The following year the right side of the crag was developed. Easy Slab (4+), The Fly (6a+) and the lengthy Clansman (7a+) were done by Andy, while Will Wilkinson added Pebble Party (6a). Over the course of a few visits Richie Betts earned the title The Old Man of Moy by managing to flash the entire crag. No small achievement given the high chance of ripping a hold.

Ian Taylor, whilst recovering from a finger injury, bolted a couple more routes with The Herring (6c+) and Constant Flux (7a). Later in 2010 Andy bolted up The Silver Fox (7a), named in memory of Will Wilkinson who was tragically killed by an avalanche on Ben Nevis.

The cliff was deep in the forest until autumn

Highlands East

1. Dunlichity..........p260
2. Brin Rock..........p262
3. Creag Dhearg....p264
4. The Camel p265
5. Moy Rock..........p268
6. Princess Cairn...p276
7. Little Torboll p277
8. Creag Bheag p279
9. Silver Rock........p283

Tess Fryer was Fighting off the Vultures (6a+) to get this first ascent at Moy Rock (photo Ian Taylor)

2010 when the ground below was clear felled. This left an open sunny face with the potential for all year round climbing. In 2011 Andy Nisbet was determined that this fine crag should have enough lower grade routes for a worthwhile day, so five more routes were drilled with the help of Ian Taylor and Andy Wilby, making Nisbet the first SMC president to place a bolt.

The rush of development continued in 2011 with first Ray Wilby maintaining the family's drilling tradition with three more routes, then Neil Shepherd with two more and finally Gary Kinsey adding three easier routes to make the crag an excellent venue for lower grades. Development continued rapidly with two more routes in October 2011, two more in November and several attractive lines still remain.

Princess Cairn

Lichenous rock and difficult access had discouraged anyone until the unusual hot weather of March 2012, when local climbers Seb Rider, Topher Dagg and Greg C found solid rock and accessed their lower-offs by climbing a difficult trad line. The routes were drilled in a weekend using a generator, and a second generator when the first broke down. Despite secrecy, the bolts were spotted very quickly by another local climber Dave Allan out for a walk. Andy Nisbet and friends then did substantial cleaning and improved the lower-offs to provide another good conglomerate venue in this small area between Dornoch and Golspie.

Little Torboll

This roadside crag had been used for top-roping

along with Keith Geddes, he climbed The Turbinator, then in 2012 three more lines were added with Andy Cunningham and Chris Anderson.

Creag Bheag

Between spells of work on a nearby wind farm Rab Anderson visited this crag, which he had spotted from the road. Signs of chalk showed that someone had been using it for bouldering and top roping, however not being one to hang about Anderson set about its development. In 2008 ten routes were added with assistance from Fraser Fotheringham, Dave Cuthberston, Chris Anderson and Andy Cunningham. In June 2008 a further six routes were added by Anderson and Cunningham and in 2009 Chris and Rab Anderson added another. Working here again in 2012 Anderson along with assistance from Brian Dickson, Dave Cuthbertson and Chris Anderson completed development of the right side of the crag with a further six routes and also plugged a gap further left.

Silver Rock

After moving up to the area, Simon Nadin was looking for rock to climb locally. Following a brief look at Creag Bheag, the more prominent Silver Rock was chosen. Ag Rippa, the first route in 2007, and Fleet of Foot were climbed with wife Louise, then the easier Extreme Lichen and High School Blues with daughter Bethan, before moving on to the more impressive roofed area. Highland Wildcat Trails, a local mountain bike centre, contributed to the cost of bolts. There is still scope and route developers are welcome.

Beth Nadin doing Extreme Lichen (3) on Silver Rock (photo Simon Nadin)

by locals and Scout groups but its sport climbing potential was realised by Rab Anderson when in the area working on wind turbines. In 2011,

Dave Redpath on the move on Ubuntu (8a), The Camel (photo Michael Tweedley)

SOUTH OF INVERNESS

There are four sport crags in an area between Loch Ness and Strathnairn, between 7 and 11 miles directly south of Inverness.

Dunlichity Crag - Dunlichity

(NH 6577 3329) L26 E416   Alt 250m   South-East facing
Maps p257, p260

This sport crag lies on Creag a' Chlachain above the hamlet of Dunlichity. It is easily seen when approaching Dunlichity from the east or south. The rock is gneiss, but a younger type than the Lewisian gneiss to the west.

AMENITIES
The crag is fairly remote so it is best to stock up with petrol and supplies at either Inverness to the north or Aviemore to the south. There is a small but friendly village shop in Inverarnie, passed en route from the A9.

RECOMMENDED TASTY BITES
Nothing close by.

TOP TIPS
Due to the poor rock quality in the lower section, all these routes have been done with the first bolt high and pre-clipped. Take a clip-stick.

DIRECTIONS
From the A9 south of Inverness, turn off just south of Daviot onto the B851 Fort Augustus road. Follow this for 2.6 miles (4.2km) to Inverarnie (named Tombreck on the OS maps), then turn right onto the B861, signed to Inverness and the Dunlichty Trout Fishery. Take the first left after 0.5 miles to Dunlichity, passing the fishery and Dunlichity House. Turn right at Dunlichity village, signposted Bunachton. The crag is visible from the turning. Parking is best at the top of the hill, at a wide track entrance about 400m past the crag (NH 6584 3367). There is a more direct route on smaller roads from Inverness town centre.

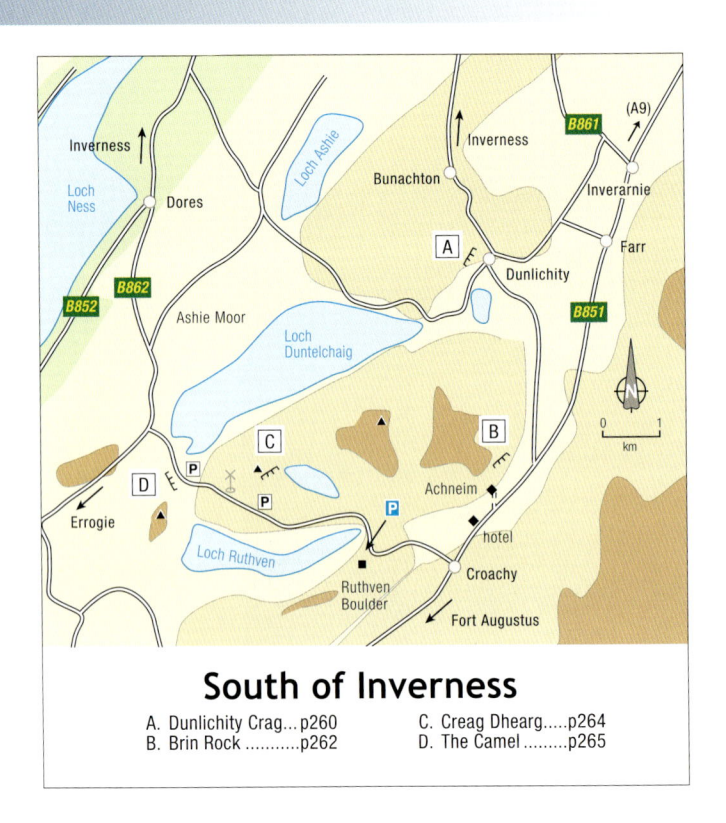

South of Inverness

A. Dunlichity Crag... p260
B. Brin Rock p262
C. Creag Dhearg p264
D. The Camel p265

APPROACH
Time: 6mins
A power line crosses the road immediately north of the parking spot. Cross a fence and follow the power line until it is obvious where to traverse to the crag. Summer bracken can increase the approach time.

Dunlichity Crag 261

① Kids with Guns 20m 7c *
Murdoch Jamieson 2006
The furthest left line on the main wall. Start with a boulder problem (V4) and climb up into a good rest. Pull round onto the wall, and then break off left onto a good hand ledge. Get stood on this, then go up a flaky arete.

② Psycho 20m 7b+ **
Richie Betts 2005
The same bolder problem start as Kids with Guns but continue straight up the wall, good sustained technical climbing.

Andy Wilby dealing with Kids with Guns (7c) (photo Richie Betts)

③ Closed Project 20m
Andy Wilby

④ Shame it's no Name 20m 7b **
Andy Wilby 2005
Make hard moves to gain the big undercuts. Pull over the overlap onto better rock and up to jugs at half-height. Easy to the top.

⑤ Gods Gift 20m 7c ***
Ben Lister 2005
Start as for Shame it's no Name. Move right along the overlap, up the wall to a jug, then slightly left to the chain.

Highlands East

Brin Rock - Strathnairn

(NH 6602 2921)   Alt 350m   South-East facing
Maps p257, p260

A schist crag which dominates the valley below and with the strata offering overhanging rock on positive holds. It was only bolted in 2011 so the routes have seen few ascents.

AMENITIES
As for Dunlichity Crag.

RECOMMENDED TASTY BITES
Brin Herb Nursery (see Directions) offers good hot drinks and excellent home baking. You must try out their freshly picked herbal teas! But only open Thursday to Monday, April to September, 11am to 5.30pm. The Grouse and Trout Hotel (also called The Steadings) has a lounge bar open after 6pm.

TOP TIPS
Don't miss the path, as the going can be extremely rough. A breeze can help to keep temperatures down in the summer (!). Overhanging crimpy is the style.

DIRECTIONS
From the A9 south of Inverness, turn off just south of Daviot onto the B851 Fort Augustus road. Follow this past Inverarnie and continuing to where the overhanging cliff of Brin Rock dominates the view high on the right, after 6.8 miles. The overhanging buttress is The Needle and the sport climbing is on the buttress just beyond and on the skyline. 0.3 miles further on is the Brin Herb Nursery and after another 0.5 miles is a right turn with a sign for Achneim House B&B. Park on the verge 100m beyond the turning where the verge is wider, just short of the Grouse and Trout Hotel, 7.7 miles in total from the A9, NH 6559 2816.

APPROACH
Time: 30mins
The crag is in view throughout. Follow the tarmac road across a bridge and immediately turn right on a track towards a field. Pass a shed and enter the field. Take a left fork round the edge of the field. Leave the field on the left and follow a zigzag track across heathery ground until a quad bike track heads leftwards uphill, slightly away from the crag. This uphill section can be seen from the main road. When a fence is reached, follow a path cut in the bracken and immediately below the fence; it may overgrow again. Keep on this line higher than you might think and reach the second last fence post (the last is 5m further on and lies against rock). Five metres below this post is a cairn and the start of a cut path down a ramp through broom (whin) to reach the left end of the crag base. The wall above has two short routes.

For the other routes, keep traversing along a line of lopped and sawn broom, very rough if you miss the line, until a fixed rope leads up a bulge to the start of the remaining routes.

❶ The Path   8m   6c
Andy Wilby 2011
Difficult moves up the vertical wall, not as easy as it looks.

❷ Gillette   8m   6b *
Andy Wilby 2011
A better quality route, straight into the crux, then nicely sustained to the top. A shame it's a bit short.

❸ Snow on the Ben   12m   7a
Andy Wilby 2012
A right-slanting line on the wall left of an overhanging corner. Start up the arete of the wall to the 2nd bolt, then makes hard moves back into the middle, then back out to the arete to finish at the same lower-off as the following route.

❹ Despicable Me   12m   7a+ **
Andy Wilby 2012
Start on the sloping ledge just left of the corner. A strenuous start leads to a good hold and rest, then a reachy move to gain better holds and a

puzzling finish to the same lower-off as Snow on the Ben.

5 The Pink Wall   15m   7b *
Andy Wilby 2011
Start up an overhanging corner to a good hold at the base of the pink wall. Crimps lead slightly left then right to a jug underneath the last few strenuous moves. Awesomely steep but surprisingly good holds.

6 Dodged a Bullet   15m   7c+ *
Nick Duboust 2012; bolted by Andy Wilby 2011
Start as for Pink Wall clipping the first 2 bolts and gaining the jug. Make a long clip out right, then hard moves gain the arete. Go up this to turn it about halfway on to the front face and a welcome jug before the crux. More difficulties lie in wait trying to clip the chain.

7 Brin it On   15m   7c **
Andy Wilby 2011
Strenuous from the start and does not let up. Start directly below the roof. Climb the corner to a shallow slot, make a long move left to an undercut, then run your feet round on nothing. Don't even breathe as you pull the slack out to clip.

**8 Whinging Consultants   15m   7b+ **
Murdoch Jamieson 2011
Very bouldery once the wall is gained. Hard moves on sidepulls lead to a rest, then good crimps and jugs to the top.

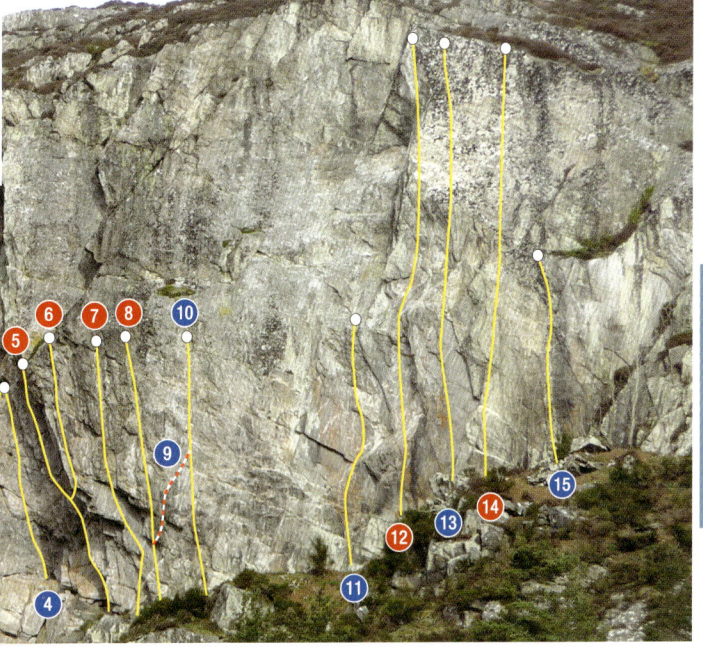

Creag Dhearg

9 Snake in the Grass 16m 7a+ **
Andy Wilby 2011
A slightly harder start to the following route. Start as for Whinging Consultants to the first bolt, then follow a fingery handrail right clipping 2 independent bolts to join The One and Only at its 4th bolt.

10 The One and Only 15m 7a ****
Dave Douglas 2011
A white overhanging wall on surprisingly incut crimps or jugs; amazingly sustained.

11 Captains of Crush 12m 6c *
Pete Clarkson 2012
About 10m right and 3m left of the longer route, The Power of Three, is this good, sustained technical climb with a stiff pull at the finish

12 The Power of Three 25m 7b+ **
Andy Wilby 2011
Three scoops with hard exits and clipping the chain is perplexing. Hard to on-sight, with thin climbing followed by blind moves out of the scoops, but with hands-off rests in each. A different challenge to the rest.

13 Overdose 27m 7a+
Dave Douglas 2012
A line to the right of The Power of Three.

14 Christmas 1937 25m 7b+ **
Andy Wilby 2011
A line on the wall right of The Power of Three.

15 The Secret Garden 10m 7a *
Andy Wilby 2012
Sustained moves until a good hold is reached at half way then it gets a bit technical with an interesting finish.

Creag Dhearg – Loch Duntelchaig

(NH 620 293) L26 or L35; E417   Alt 350m   South-East facing
Maps p257, p260

Set high above Loch Duntelchaig in a beautiful location, this large conglomerate crag can be seen when driving north past Loch Ruthven. Unfortunately, the rock is an inferior conglomerate to that of the nearby Camel, and would have great potential but for that poor rock quality. As a result Andy Wilby has abandoned his development of the crag. There are some boulders below the crag and at nearby Brin Rock, as well as the excellent Ruthven Boulder.

AMENITIES
As for Dunlichity Crag.

RECOMMENDED TASTY BITES
As for Brin Rock.

TOP TIPS
Wear a helmet when belaying.

DIRECTIONS
From the A9 south of Inverness, turn off just south of Daviot onto the B851 Fort Augustus road. Follow this to pass the obvious Brin Rock on the right of the road and reach the village of Croachy after 8 miles (12.8km).

Immediately after the first house (as in 2011), turn right on a small road, signed RSPB Loch Ruthven Nature Reserve. Follow this for 1 mile (1.6km) to pass a car park at the tail end of Loch Ruthven, above which sits the visible Ruthven Boulder. Continue past a house on the right before gently rising up a long hill to its highest point next to some fields. Park on the verge next to the fields, 2.6 miles (4.2km) from Croachy, NH 6172 2828. You've gone too far if you start to descend towards The Camel and pass a lone wind turbine.

From Inverness it is best to follow the B862 South Loch Ness road to

Dores. Here follow the same road uphill heading towards Errogie. Once the road levels out onto Ashie Moor and the south-western tip of Loch Duntelchaig is reached, a small road leads down steeply to the left again signed to RSPB Loch Ruthven Nature Reserve. Follow this for 2 miles (3km), with a lone wind turbine after 1.5 miles (2.4km), to park on the verge next to a field near the highest point on the road.

APPROACH
Time: 30mins
From the parking spot, walk across the field towards the summit of Creag Dhearg (407m), the hill to the north. From below its rocky final cap, the left end of the crag can be seen on the right. Cross a fence and head right above the top of a forest to reach the left end of the crag. Traverse rightwards along its base, sometimes rough, to reach the routes near the right end of the crag.

Battle of the Bulge   20m   6b
Andy Wilby 2002
Near the right end of the crag is a pale wall above the last flat terrace below the cliff. The wall has a bulge at mid-height which decreases rightwards. The route is in the centre of the wall where the bulge becomes quite small. Climb an easy angled wall to start, then up overhanging terrain above.

A Game of Two Halves   20m   Open Project
Climb the middle of an easy slab about 20m right of Battle of the Bulge to the roof (3 bolts missing). The continuation is a hard project.

Suicide Wall   20m   6b+
Andy Wilby 2002
At the very right end of the crag is a buttress with a big roof on its crest. This route climbs the smooth left face of the buttress. Bridge up the corner for the first few moves, then go straight up the wall.

The Camel - Loch Duntelchaig
(NH 6004 2892) L26 or L35; E417   North facing   Alt 280m
Maps p257, p260   Diagram p266

Lying on Creag nan Clag at the south-west end of Loch Duntelchaig, the essence of this outstanding crag lies in its height and in the rock type which is a hard conglomerate. It has very few cracks and little scope for natural protection. Seepage is only occasional but run off from the top overhangs can sometimes be a problem. The crag does not get much sun and the gully can sometimes be a wind funnel but at least that helps keep the midges at bay! All the routes have been equipped to a high standard.

ACCESS RESPONSIBILITIES
The Camel has SSSI status for two species of rare lichen and as such future development should be limited to the area of rock between Inverarnie Schwarzenegger and the top of the gully.

A Schedule 1 species of bird often nests on the left-hand side of the crag. It is an offence in law to disturb such birds and as such the local Raptor Study Group, the RSPB and the landowner have asked climbers not to climb on the crag between February and July. This situation may change at any time and current details can be found on the MCofS website <www.mcofs.org.uk>.

AMENITIES
As for Dunlichity Crag.

RECOMMENDED TASTY BITES
As for Brin Rock.

TOP TIPS
Bring a 60m rope. Best avoided on a still day.

DIRECTIONS
From the A9 south of Inverness, turn off just south of Daviot onto the B851 Fort Augustus road. Follow this to pass the obvious Brin Rock on

The Camel

the right of the road and reach the village of Croachy after 8 miles (12.8km). Immediately after the first house (as in 2011), turn right on a small road, signed RSPB Loch Ruthven Nature Reserve. Follow this for 1 mile (1.6km) to pass a car park at the tail end of Loch Ruthven, above which sits the visible Ruthven Boulder. Continue past a house on the right before gently rising up a long hill to its highest point next to some fields, the parking for Creag Dhearg. With the crag visible ahead, descend past a lone wind turbine and park on the grassy verge directly below it (NH 6023 2898), overlooking the end of Loch Duntelchaig. This is 4 miles (6.4km) from Croachy but the crag would be hard to miss!

From Inverness it is best to follow the B862 South Loch Ness road to Dores. Here follow the same road uphill heading towards Errogie. Once the road levels out onto Ashie Moor and the south-western tip of Loch Duntelchaig is reached, a small road leads down steeply to the left again signed to RSPB Loch Ruthven Nature Reserve. Follow this for 0.8 miles (1.3km) to reach the parking below the crag.

APPROACH
Time: 7mins
Go straight up the hill to reach the foot of a big gully towards the right side of the cliff. The climbing is on its left-bounding wall.

The left-bounding wall of the gully is the only wall where climbing is permitted on the crag. Thankfully it is also the best area of steep rock here. The routes are described from left to right as reached from below.

**1 Inverarnie Schwarzenegger   25m   7a **
Neil Shepherd 2000
The first line up the left side of the huge vertical wall is easily identified because of its resin ring bolts. Sustained climbing to a crux at 20m then easier to the lower-off.

2 Stone of Destiny   26m   6c+   **
Neil Shepherd 1999
The sustained line up the centre of the almost always dry wall is arguably the best route at the grade in the country. Gaining and leaving the biggest pebble on the crag will constitute the crux for most.

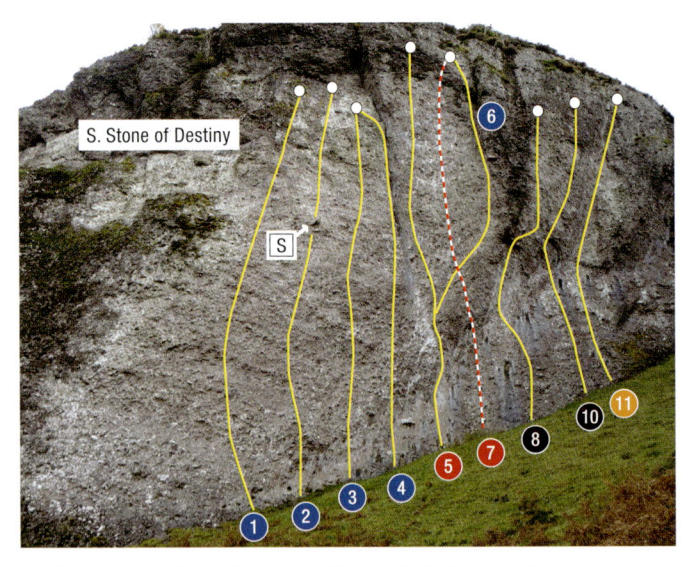

The line of bolts through the capping roof above is an open project, but often damp and the rock is less good.

3 Paralysis by Analysis   25m   7a+   ***
Neil Shepherd 2004
Continuously overhanging, this line is a challenge to route reading and forearm stamina and makes an excellent training route. Starting just right of Stone of Destiny, it keeps right of that line up the impending wall. Lower off two large staple bolts.

4 There's Sand in my Pants   25m   7a **
Ali Robb 2004
This one heads for the huge fissure which starts 10m up. Gain it by

easyish wall climbing where some harder moves up the fissure lead to easier climbing, a ledge and the lower-off on Paralysis by Analysis.

5 Eye Balls Out   30m   7b+   ***
Murdoch Jamieson, bolted by Andy Wilby 2011
Starts at the same place as The Final Straw, clipping the first 5 bolts to the base of the ramp, then heading straight up the wall staying right of the fissure. Take 15 quick draws and some extra stamina.

6 The Final Straw   30m   7a   ***
Neil Shepherd 2000
Outstanding climbing up the hanging right-trending ramp. Hard moves up the initial wall are rewarded by exposed and easier climbing up the ramp. The final groove provides a further test before the lower-off is gained over the capping overhang.

7 Giza Break   28m   7b   **
Neil Shepherd, Ali Robb 2005
This line crosses the ramp of The Final Straw and continues up the wall to share the same lower-off.

8 Death is a Gift   25m   8a   ***
Andy Wilby 2009
Climb a slab to the left of Ubuntu to an obvious hole. Climb through a bulge above (keeping right of the loose arete) and make a long move rightwards to the block on Ubuntu. Climb directly up the steep wall above. Excellent sustained climbing.

9 The Gift Link   25m   8a+   **
Dave MacLeod 2009
This links the start of Death is a Gift with the finish of Ubuntu.

10 Ubuntu   25m   8a   ***
Dave Redpath 2007
After an easy start up the slab at its highest point, this line breaches the centre of the sweeping bulge. Tenuous moves on undercuts lead right to

Tom Lee confronts the Stone of Destiny (6c+), The Camel (photo Cubby Images)

Death is a Gift (8a), The Camel. Climber Andy Wilby (photo Tim Rankin)

a powerful crux on small edges to reach a handrail. Then follow the line of cobbles above.

11 Two Humps are Better than One   23m   6b
Neil Shepherd 1997
The highest ramp-line near the top of the gully. Dirtier than the previous routes. The crux is just below the lower-off.

NORTH OF INVERNESS

There are five conglomerate sport crags north of Inverness. Moy Rock is about 20mins drive towards the North-West whereas Princess Cairn, Little Torboll, Creag Bheag and Silver Rock are in Sutherland, about an hour's drive up the A9 north of Inverness. Finally, in the far north at Wick, is the small crag of The Powe.

Moy Rock - Contin

(NH 4952 5494) L26 E431   Alt 120m   South facing
Map p257   Diagrams p269, p273

Moy Rock is a conglomerate crag which is located immediately above the main A835 to Ullapool and the North-West Highlands, some 15 miles (24km) to the north of Inverness and a short distance to the east of Contin. Following tree felling, much of the crag is now open and sunny. The climbing is steep on positive holds and surprisingly fingery, but its real attraction is that it is accessible, dries very quickly and has all grades except the hardest. One wall even stays dry in the rain, as long as wind doesn't blow the rain on to the crag. It can sometimes be too hot in the summer as the pebbles, originally river polished, can be quite slippery and sweaty hands can make this worse. The crag is popular with nesting birds, visitors from March to June inclusive should watch out and minimise disturbance if necessary. The MCofS website will provide information and detail any restrictions which happen in the future.

AMENITIES
The nearest big town with all facilities is Dingwall, 8km (5 miles) away. The nearby former Victorian spa town of Strathpeffer has several tearooms and cafes, including The Station Cafe, by the old station.

Moy Rock

RECOMMENDED TASTY BITES
There is an excellent restaurant in the Pavilion, The Red Poppy, with brilliant burgers!

TOP TIPS
Belayers are advised to wear a helmet as pebbles can pop occasionally. A 60m rope is convenient for lowering from the longest routes but 50m is fine for all the easier ones.

DIRECTIONS
After leaving the A9 at Tore, follow the A835 to the Maryburgh roundabout, then continue west on this road towards Contin. When the road reaches its highpoint there is a straight with a left turn for Brahan. Then there is a long right bend followed by another straight which is definitely downhill. Almost immediately after the bend is a lay-by on the left (south). After another 200m there is a wide tarmac entrance on the right to a gated forestry track; this is just over 3 miles (5km) from the roundabout and nearly the same distance from Contin. Park here (NH 4957 5481) on the grass verge, or back at the lay-by if full. The landowner has no objection to climbing here but has specifically asked that the entrance be kept clear. After the 2010 felling, the crag is highly visible.

APPROACH
Time: 5mins
Go 30m rightwards up the track, then head up left on a track made by felling machinery. At its end, take a zig-zag track through the brashings to the crag, arriving at The Chimney Zone. Big Flat Wall is the big wall left of the arrival point. At its left end is a big tree. Thirty metres further on and beyond a gully is the start of Ravens' Wall.

LEFT - THE BAY

This is the furthest left wall with climbs to date and about 110m left of the arrival point. Heading left from the arrival point, one passes along the flat base close under Ravens' Wall. Beyond this is a gully 15m wide and then a steep wall with a huge flake at its base and a large holly growing out of the wall behind the flake.

**1 Holly Tree Groove   18m   6a **
Sandy Allan, Andy Nisbet 2011
This climbs a shallow groove in the wall just right of the holly. Start by scrambling up the chimney behind the flake to belay off the holly and a bolt. Sustained and sometimes technical, but occasional bridging takes the sting out of the steepness. The lower-off is just below the arete of the following route.

2 Conglomarete   25m   4 *
Sandy Allan, Andy Nisbet 2011
Climbs the right arete of this wall, but usually on the slabby wall just to

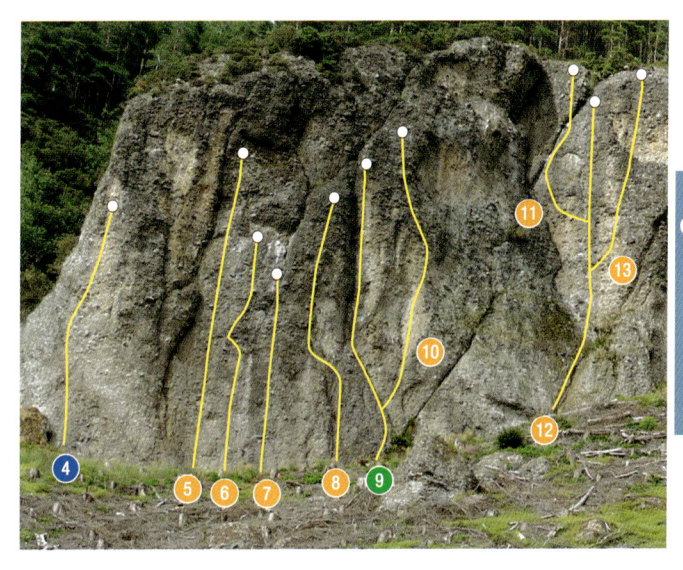

Moy Rock

Rory Mackenzie on The Herring (6c+), Moy Rock (photo Andy Nisbet)

its right. Graded for starting just right of the base, but climbing direct from a tree stump at the base is better (4+).

RAVENS' WALL

This wall lies about 60m left of the arrival point and is the next main wall left and slightly down from Big Flat Wall. Because of overhanging ground above, the section from Fighting off the Vultures to Pebbledash stays dry even in heavy rain unless there is wind blowing rain onto the cliff.

3 Moy Racer   14m   6a *
Andy Nisbet 2012
A line at the very left end of the wall, starting from a raised vegetated platform left of the main cliff base. One move on the first bulge is much harder than the rest.

4 The Herring   15m   6c+ *
Ian Taylor, Andy Wilby 2008
This lies at the left end of the wall. Good climbing, with a tricky bulge.

5 Fighting off the Vultures   22m   6a+ *
Andy Wilby 2011
The main wall has two corner systems and a level bare earth terrace below. The left corner is loose and this route is on the wall just to its right. Sustained steep climbing on good holds; enjoy the reinforced ones! Ignore the bolts of the following route and its lower-off just to the right, although the lower quick-draws can be placed from it (it is slightly easier).

6 The Old Man of Moy   17m   6a+ *
Andy Nisbet 2011
A line up the centre of the wall between the corners. The first bolt is quite high but easily reached. Gain and climb near a shallow grey groove, then go diagonally left through a bulge (crux). Go more easily up rightwards and go up to the lower-off. An extension can be made by finishing up the previous route.

7 Moy Bueno 14m 6b *
Andy Wilby 2011
The right line on the wall. More sustained, especially in the upper section, than the previous route. Low in the grade.

8 Pebbledash 20m 6b **
Andy Nisbet 2011
A shallow left-slanting groove in the rib at the right end of the wall gives a sustained climb. The ring bolts are an older, thicker type. Go straight up a shallow groove towards Corvus, then move left low down into the slanting groove. Keep just left of pale rock (which holds the bolts), then over a bulging section which is probably the crux. There is some poorer rock low down but the route is generously bolted.

9 Corvus 22m 5+ **
Andy Nisbet 2011
The right corner system. Start just left of a vegetated patch at its base. Climb the wall before moving right into the corner (more of a ramp low down) above the vegetation. Follow the ramp and gently overhanging corner to its top. Ignore the lower-off on the left, as that is Pebbledash.

10 Scoopy Doo 22m 6b *
Ray Wilby 2011
A pale overhanging groove in the wall right of Corvus. Start up Corvus to reach its ramp, then move out right to the overhanging groove. Climb it with distinctly technical moves out right at its top on to the right arete. The grade is lower if you are tall or flexible. Continue up and slightly left (not straight up) on poorer rock until the angle eases. A popular option which reduces the grade to 6a is by stepping down from the bolt high in the groove and traversing to the right arete, then climbing it, but the best climbing is missed and a fall here would mean a swing back into the groove. A harder line leading out left from the overhanging groove is planned.

The following three routes are on a wall some 10m to the right of Corvus and set above a low-angled groove. This is the last wall facing the

Deziree Wilson Chadwick pulls pebbles on Moy Bueno (6b), Moy Rock (photo Andy Nisbet)

Moy Rock

road before reaching the gully and ramp between this area and Big Flat Wall. The routes should not be climbed between mid February and the end of May as long as there is an active ravens' nest.

11 Ravens' Nest   26m   6a+ *
Ray Wilby 2011
This route branches off left from Black Steak. It has the same start, clipping the first 7 bolts. Move up, clip a bolt on the left, then traverse left with hands at the top of a smooth pale section before going up. Go diagonally left to a big crack, then follow the crack rightwards until the bolts go straight up. Climbing more directly and gaining the big crack higher up is 6b. The same bolts are clipped from either version. If using a 50m rope, thread the lower-off with the end of the rope (not a bight) to ensure enough rope to reach the ground.

12 Black Streak   25m   6a+ **
Ray Wilby 2011
A dark streak in the centre of the wall. Climb the mucky groove to reach the wall and climb the centre of this on good holds to a separate chain.

13 Pyramid   25m   6a+ *
Ray Wilby 2011
This route branches off right from Black Steak and is the hardest of the three. Clip the first 5 bolts of Black Streak, then move out right to clip a bolt. Step back down and climb to the right of this and the next two bolts with deviations left to clip. Continue to a ledge rest, then finish up the steep upper wall.

A popular variation, after clipping the bolt out right, is to climb the rib left of the bolt but rather too close to Raven's Nest, before moving out right to join the previous version. Good direct climbing but less independent.

BIG FLAT WALL

This is the big, slightly concave wall on the left of the arrival point, left of a right-slanting ramp, and is the showcase wall of Moy Rock. A knotted rope on the left provides access.

14 Match if you are Weak   20m   6c+ *
Andy Wilby 2008
Sustained climbing, starting up above the knotted access rope.

15 The Dark Side   20m   6c **
Andy Wilby 2007
Follow the line of the orange streak, with a sting in the tail.

16 Little Teaser   20m   6b+ ***
Andy Wilby 2007
This excellent route is 6a to the second last bolt, 6a+ to the last and leaves its crux to the end. A wild grab for the lower-off has been known.

17 Pulling on Pebbles   20m   7a+ **
Andy Wilby 200
Climb the wall to the bulge, then make sequency moves to the two large stones above.

18 The Ticks Ate all the Midges   25m   7a ***
Andy Wilby 2007
Good sustained climbing in the upper half.

19 Cloak and Dagger   25m   6c+ **
Andy Wilby 2007
Start a few metres up the slab. Pull over a roof near the top.

CHIMNEY ZONE

The next area lies right of the right-slanting ramp and is a recessed wall with a huge right-slanting chimney separating walls of smoother rock.

20 One Man went to Moy   15m   7a *
Neil Shepherd 2011
A shallow pale scoop just right of the ramp. Thin and fingery, finishing up the right edge of the scoop.

Moy Rock 273

23 Constant Flux   15m   6c+   *
Ian Taylor 2009
The precarious slab on the right of the chimney followed by cranking through two bulges.

OAK TREE AREA

Some 20m right of the previous zone and still in the trees in 2011 (though it seems likely the trees will be felled), is a rambling oak tree below a cirque with eight easier routes and two harder ones. The first is on a slabby pillar immediately right of the right arete of the previous recessed area.

24 Easy Slab   20m   4+   *
Andy Wilby 2008
The left side of the cirque, left of a deep gully, holds two slabs separated by a chimney. The left side of the left slab gives this route, hardest at the start, and also a little mossy low down.

25 Ankle Biter   20m   4+
Gary Kinsey, James Edwards 2011
Start 1m right of Easy Slab. Follow the right edge of the slab ending at the same lower-off as Easy Slab. The least clean of the routes but likely to improve.

26 Ephemeral Artery   24m   4+   *
Gary Kinsey, Christine Paterson 2011
The left side of the right slab. Start at the base of the gully and slant up left over an overhang at the base.

27 Venus Return   24m   4+   **
Gary Kinsey, James Edwards 2011
The right side of the right slab. Start at the base of the gully as for Ephemeral Artery. Clip the same first bolt but branch right and continue up the right side of the slab to the same lower-off. Grade 5 if you don't bridge on to the wall on the right to start.

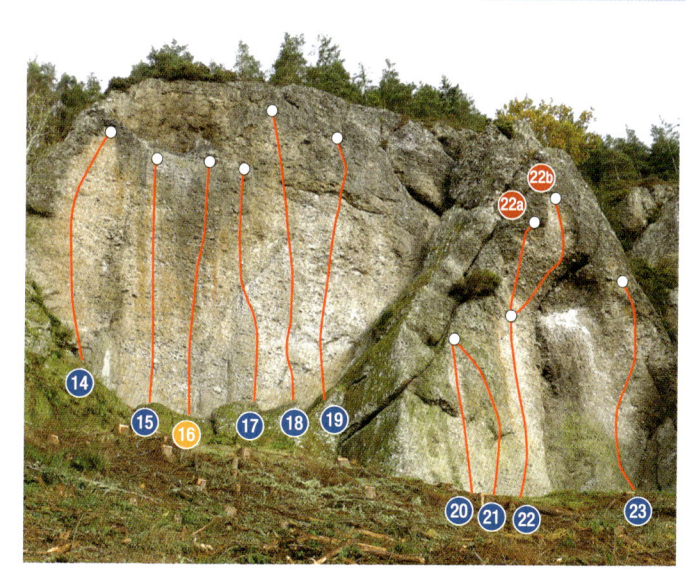

21 Burning Barrels   15m   6c   *
Neil Shepherd 2011
On the grey rock between the pale scoop of One Man and pale rock of The Seer to the right. It shares a lower-off with One Man went to Moy.

22 The Seer   12m   7a+   **
Andy Wilby 2007
The steep slab on the left of the chimney gives a short and technical climb with just enough holds. It has a hard crux followed by sustained moves to the chain.

There are two extensions which are included in a single overall pitch. Continuing above (22a) makes the overall grade 7b, while continuing diagonally right above the chimney (22b) provides a combination worth 7b+ (**The Fear** Alan Cassidy 2012, bolted Andy Wilby 2010).

Highlands East

Moy Rock

Paula Betts on Little Teaser (6b+), Moy Rock (photo Ian Taylor)

28 Moy Soldiers   15m   5+   *
Ian Taylor, John Mackenzie 2011
The first of three routes on a smaller pillar right of the biggest vegetated gully. This takes its left rib to its top followed by a steep finish.

29 Pebble Party   15m   6a   *
Will Wilkinson 2008
The centre of the pillar is more sustained followed by the same steep finish.

30 L-Plate   15m   5   *
Andy Nisbet 2011
Start up a corner formed by the right edge of the pillar, then follow its flake edge left. A final crack brings a reach left for the lower-off (same final bolt as the previous two routes).

31 The Fly   15m   6a+   **
Andy Wilby 2008
On the wall right of the pillar, starting at the highest left of three ramps leading up right. A vertical route, sustained and fingery after the first 4m.

32 Round the Bend   28m   6a   **
Andy Nisbet 2012
This route starts up the lowest right and largest ramp, thereby crossing the following two routes. The crux section above the ramp has close bolts. From the top of the ramp, start up the right arete of the cirque, but after about 3m, move out right on its slabby right side going first up, then left parallel to the arete. To reduce potential rope drag, clip the first bolt of The Silver Fox above the ramp using a 2m sling. The next bolt is at the top of a small overlap on the ramp. 13 quick-draws required.

33 The Silver Fox   25m   7a   **
Tess Fryer 2010
Start up the wall below the central of the three ramps. Gain the ramp past one bolt. Take a line of bolts leading up left across the right wall of the cirque.

34 The Clansman 30m 7a+ **
Andy Wilby 2008
The line of bolts up the left side of the right arete of the cirque, finishing up the steep headwall. Start up the lower wall right of The Silver Fox (3 bolts) to reach the ramp. Continue up keeping left of the arete.

35 Hidden World 30m 6a+ *
Gary Kinsey 2012
Start below and right of the base of the right arete, some 6m right of The Clansman, at the foot of a slightly white streak coming down from a gap in the small overhang above. Climb on poorer rock to the gap in the overhang, then pull through to the wall above. Continue up on much better rock, then right into a left-facing corner. Climb this and continue up the wall above. The route is a full 30m; thread the lower-off with the end of the rope (not a bight) to ensure enough rope to reach the ground. With a 50m rope, it is necessary to abseil to the 5th bolt, which is a double set with maillons, and to descend from there. There is an easier start up a flake line 4m to the right. This reduces the overall grade to 6a but the rock is still not good.

36 Forbidden Forest 12m 7a *
Andy Wilby 2012
A line on the overhanging wall some 10m right of the right arete. Steady wall climbing leads to a good hold below the bulge. There are some strenuous moves through the bulge, then steady to the top. The rock has still to settle down.

37 It's Rock Jim, but not as we know it 12m 6c+
Sue Wood 2012; bolted Andy Wilby
A central line up the wall and bulge. Start to the right of Forbidden Forest. Steady climbing leads up the wall to the bulge. Strenuous moves up and rightwards gain a good hold. A long move back left gains a good hole in the middle of wall, then sustained climbing to the top.

38 Collywobbles 12m 7a
Sue Wood 2012; bolted Andy Wilby
The green streak a few metres right of It's Rock Jim. Climb the vertical green wall to the 4th bolt, then traverse left under the bulge to join It's Rock Jim at its 4th bolt. Finish up this.

FOREST WALL

A separate wall hidden in the forest to the right of the main area. The wall is very sheltered and can feel quite cold on a chilly day, but might be ideal when windy. The shelter can be an advantage on a hot day, but humidity can also bring dampness. All this may change if and when the forest is cleared. The routes are long, sustained and slightly intimidating but not as hard as they look. This is typical Moy but those who prefer a short sharp crux may find the grades in this sector hard. The routes have hangers typical of expansion bolts, but they are glue-ins. More routes are planned further right.

APPROACH
From the right end of the main area (Collywobbles), follow a slightly rising traverse path for 60m to the start of the wall and the following two routes.

39 Robert the Bruce's Spider 17m 6a *
Gary Kinsey 2012
Start at the left hand edge of the wall near the top of a soil cone. Climb the middle of the wall passing a small pocket (hidden surprise) and head for an obvious flake. Use the flake, pull through the horizontal break and continue to a double ring lower-off.

40 Don't Look Down in Anger 20m 6a+ **
Gary Kinsey 2012
Start at, or just below an old tree stump halfway up the soil cone. Climb the blunt arete above using holds on both sides. Climb through the horizontal break to a double ring lower-off which is on the right of the arete.

Princess Cairn

㊶ Curse of the Strong   20m   6a+ ★★
Gary Kinsey 2012
This has a harder section than the routes on either side, but has better rests. Originally graded 6b. Start 3m to the right of Don't Look Down in Anger, just to the right of a granite coloured Fixe hanger at foot level (for light belayers with heavy leaders). All the hangers on this route are granite coloured. Climb straight up skirting the left side of a shallow broken ledge. Continue on to a diagonal crack and move right up this to a semi-rest. Above this, the crux leads to a horizontal break. Continue up just left of the two remaining bolts to reach the lower-off of Don't Look Down.

㊷ Summer Solstice   24m   6a+ ★★
Gary Kinsey 2012
Start 3m to the right of Curse of the Strong, just right of a grey coloured Fixe hanger at foot level. All the hangers on this route are pale grey coloured. Climb straight up skirting the right side of a shallow broken ledge. Continue on up the wall above to the end of the difficulties at about 18m. Easier ground leads to the two hanger with rings belay, just below the overhanging crest of the wall.

㊸ 'Ave it!   10m   7b ★★
Andy Wilby 2012
The smooth wall in the middle of the buttress. A slightly right-trending line through the smooth wall just to the right of the holly gives technical, tricky climbing.

Princess Cairn - Golspie

(NH 7598 9752)   L21 E441   Alt 170m   South-East facing   Map p257
This crag is clearly seen from the A9 on the east side of Creag an Amalaidh, or Princess Cairn, the distinctive hill opposite Mound Rock overlooking Loch Fleet. It is a hillside conglomerate crag, sunny and scenic but exposed to the wind, with seven routes from 5 to 6c+. The rock is good quality for conglomerate but slightly lichenous in the upper sections, although this should improve as the routes get more ascents.

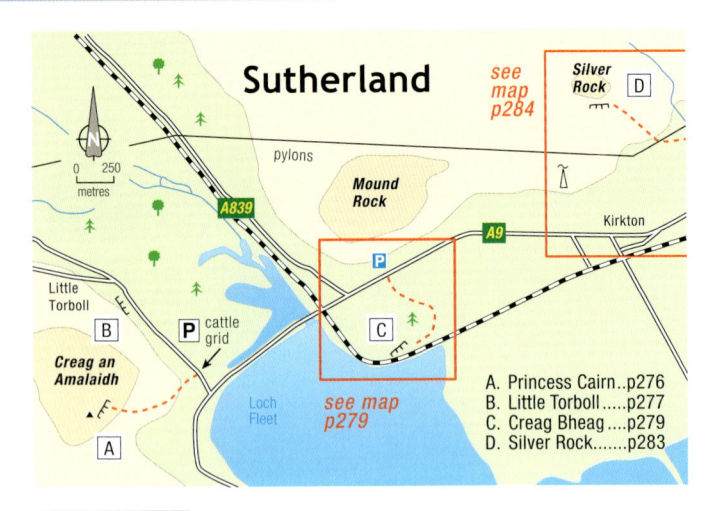

AMENITIES
As for Creag Bheag.

RECOMMENDED TASTY BITES
As for Creag Bheag.

TOP TIPS
Hidden pockets make some routes easier than they look.

DIRECTIONS
Head north up the A9 from Inverness for 45 miles (72km) measured from the roundabout just south of the Kessock Bridge to The Mound causeway across Loch Fleet. On the south side of The Mound causeway, turn off at a cottage and take the unclassified single track road with a small sign to Lochbuie, initially heading north-west. After 170m is a cattle grid; park immediately after it on the left (NH 7675 9780).

Little Torboll

APPROACH
Time: 20 to 25mins
Walk uphill through the woodland past the boulders (bouldering to be had here) picking the easiest line. Trend increasingly left as the angle eases and the trees thin. Contour left, taking a line close to or just above a fence. Follow this until an estate track comes up from below. Follow the track until the crag is seen above. Head steeply up to a clean plaque of rock with a double overhang on its left side (not a larger single overhang further right). There is a small level platform at the crag base.

1 Moonlighting Meercat 10m 6c *
Start just to the left of the lower roof. Climb past its left end, then go through the upper roof to a lower-off shared with the following route.

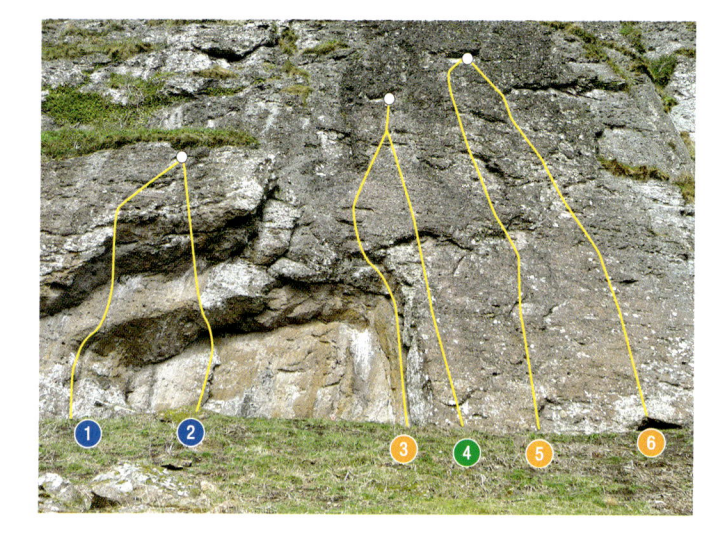

2 Badass Honey Badger 10m 6c+ *
Start at a flake-crack in the lower roof. Move left through the lower roof, then leftwards through the upper roof to share a lower-off with Moonlighting Meercat.

The flake-crack is a trad route, a steep E1 5b.

3 The Great Rock 'n' Route Swindle 15m 6b *
Formed between the lower roof and the clean plaque is a big left-facing corner. Climb the corner, through the roof and up the wall above to a lower-off shared with the following route.

4 One in the Eye for the Duke 15m 5+ *
Start 1m right of the right arete of the big corner. Climb the smooth slabby wall, then trend slightly left through bulges to the shared lower-off.

5 Creative Commoners 18m 6a *
Start 3m right of the right arete. Climb the smooth slabby wall to rippling bulges.

6 Sleekit 18m 6a *
Start 6m right of the right arete. Climb the smooth slabby wall to trend left through bulges to the shared lower-off.

7 Jenny 22m 5 *
The final route lies on a thinner section of wall 25m to the right.

Little Torboll - Golspie

(NH 7622 9837) L21 E441 Alt 10m North facing
Maps p257, p276
This useful little crag lies on the north side of Creag an Amalaidh, or Princess Cairn, the distinctive hill opposite Mound Rock overlooking Loch Fleet. The crag lies within The Mound Alderwoods, a SSSI that is one of the UK's largest and best examples of alder woodland on

Little Torboll

estuarine floodplains, and an important habitat for breeding wetland birds. It is quickly and easily accessed from the minor road which runs north-west from the south side of The Mound causeway across Loch Fleet, about 1km to the south of the Creag Bheag layby. The left fork of this road passes a few houses at Little Torboll, after which the crag has been named. It provides pleasant climbing on pocketed, waterworn rock and is sure to become popular given its proximity to Princess Cairn and Creag Bheag and the fact that it is right next to the road.

Although north facing, the crag is surprisingly dry and has the added benefit of having the car near to hand. The climbs are squeezed-in close to each other to get as much as possible out of this venue.

AMENITIES
As for Creag Bheag.

RECOMMENDED TASTY BITES
As for Creag Bheag.

TOP TIPS
Cragging from the back of a car, no need for rucksac or walking boots!

DIRECTIONS
On the south side of The Mound causeway, turn off at a cottage as for Princess Cairn crag, and take the unclassified single track road signposted to Lochbuie, initially heading north-west. Follow this for 1km to park on the left beneath the crag where the road forks left to Little Torboll. Just beyond the cottage at the start of the road there is some bouldering in the trees beside the road, accessed by parking at the cattle grid (where the Princess Cairn crag approach starts).

APPROACH
There isn't one! This is the closest sport crag to a road in Scotland.

1 KG Max   15m   6a
Rab Anderson 2012
The wall right of the central cracked groove.

2 The Turbinator   15m   6a *
Rab Anderson, Keith Geddes 2011
Climbs the centre of the crag at its highest point, between the black streaks and to the right of the cracked groove which curves into an overlap. Taking the top bulge directly makes it harder.

3 Veggiemight   15m   6b+
Rab Anderson 2012
Take the right side of the black streak immediately to the right of The Turbinator. The top bulge provides the crux.

4 Mr Angry   12m   6a+ *
Rab Anderson 2012
Start on the right and climb the right side of a clean streak to the upper ledge. Step right to a lower-off, or a step left and finish up the crux of Veggiemight.

Further lines might be added in 2013.

Creag Bheag - Golspie

(NH 7830 9794) L21 E441 Alt Sea-level South-East facing
Maps p257, p276, p279 Diagram p282

This pleasant crag with its sunny disposition lies just south of Golspie in Sutherland, on the north side of the tidal estuary of Loch Fleet, from which it is separated by the main, though in no way busy, Inverness to Wick railway line. The base is flat grass and the climbing on positive holds, even jugs in places, so many routes can be done in the day and ticking the whole crag is an obvious challenge. It is not a sea-cliff but there is a tidal pond at the foot of the cliff and during spring tides, water does touch the cliff base.

The routes have been equipped with 10mm stainless steel expansion bolts and twin bolt, single ring stainless steel lower-offs, which have to be threaded. The rock is a solid conglomerate and where it is steeper and discoloured it is generally sound, offering pocketed climbing. The top-outs on these steeper routes are onto pebbles and boulders in the matrix, which on occasion could be prone to breaking, something which belayers and those on the grass below should be aware of. After heavy rain parts of the crag suffer from seepage from the forest above but it is still possible to climb here throughout the winter, given a few days dry weather and some sunshine.

Trees in the forest above the crag are 40m above its base and the top can be reached by a rough path starting from right of any steep ground. There is a long low-level traverse along the base of the entire crag.

It is worth noting that this area can be dry when it's raining on the west coast and it takes about an hour to get here via Lairg from Laxford Bridge, or Ledmore Junction. With a westerly wind, showers often pass over, barely wetting the rock.

Little Torboll is a useful roadside crag about 1km along the minor road to Lochbuie on the south side of The Mound causeway. Princess Cairn is also accessed from the start of this road, which has some bouldering in the trees about 200m along, and Silver Rock lies above the road 2 miles closer to Golspie.

AMENITIES

Golspie is 3 miles north along the A9 with cafes, shops and toilets. Also for anyone with energy left to burn, there are the Highland Wildcat mountain bike trails <www.highlandwildcat.com>. Situated on the slopes around the Ben Bhraggie monument, they offer 16 miles of the finest trails in the country and cater for all standards. With fabulous beaches, great wildlife, fine golf courses and three splendid distillers nearby (Glenmorangie & Balblair either side of the bridge over the Dornoch Firth and Clynelish at Brora) there is much to see and do here.

RECOMMENDED TASTY BITES

Located by the car park in the centre of Golspie, the Coffee Bothy does a good selection of cakes, sandwiches and as the name suggests, drinks. Dornoch has a choice of four cafes, Luigi's, Butter Fingers, Harry Gow's and The Dornoch Patisserie, with the cakes at the latter perhaps being the best sampled to date.

TOP TIPS

A great place for lower sport grades.

Creag Bheag

DIRECTIONS
Head north up the A9 from Inverness for 45 miles (72km) measured from the roundabout just south of the Kessock Bridge to The Mound causeway across Loch Fleet. Just north of the causeway is a left turn to Lairg and Rogart (A839). Continue on the A9 for 200m to a lay-by on the left side of the road (NH 7801 9844).

APPROACH
Time: 10mins
Opposite the lay-by is a gated forestry track. Carefully cross the road (fast traffic!) and follow the track for 60m, then turn left on a less-used track beyond the gorse and follow it across a felled area, bending left into forestry plantation (120m). Continue through the trees until the track turns sharply right (250m), then head off left and diagonally down through the trees to a wall and fence which bound fields (100m). Follow the wall, then the side of a drainage ditch beside the fence until there is a cross fence on the other side (100m). Cross the joining point to the outside and walk on grass bending right to the crag (180m).

The climbs are described from right to left, as met from the approach.

① The Bheagining 10m 6a+ *
Rab Anderson 2012
Climb the steep wall just left of the chimney at the right end of the crag (2 bolts) and finish up The Pebble Parlour.

② The Pebble Parlour 10m 6a **
Rab Anderson 2012
The bulging wall just right of the crack is climbed via an undercut; nice but short.

③ Edge of Reason 15m 6a *
Rab Anderson 2012
This takes the edge just left of the crack; a bit friable in places.

Brian Dickson enjoying Glug (5+), Creag Bheag (photo Rab Anderson)

Creag Bheag

4 Life's a Beach 15m 6a+ **
Rab Anderson 2012
The smooth, scooped wall just right of a lug of rock is graded for being taken directly between the bolts via a pocket, though this section can be bypassed at an easier grade to the right.

5 Vincent's Lug 15m 6a *
Rab Anderson 2012
Climbs up to and onto the ear shaped rock then continues to the top. From the last bolt choose the lower-off up right, or up left.

6 Pablo's Pebble 15m 6a *
Rab Anderson 2012
Passing to the left of the lug of rock, this steps left at the top overlap to avoid turf, then finishes up right.

7 Glug 12m 5+ *
Andy Cunningham 2008
This climbs a white streak and has a tricky bulge low down as the crux.

8 Twintrack 12m 6a *
Rab Anderson 2008
Climbs through two tricky bulges leading to an easier upper section.

9 Pickpocket 12m 5+ **
Rab Anderson 2008
Passing the left end of the overlaps, this contains a bucket sized pocket.

The next set of routes lie on steeper and smoother rock capped by a wave overhang with a prominent white streak below its right side. There are three routes right of the white streak which go to a common lower-off.

10 Above the Line 15m 6a **
Rab Anderson 2008
The first passes right of the wave overhang. Sustained climbing without any bulges.

John Lyall on Pickpocket (5+), Creag Bheag (photo Andy Nisbet)

Creag Bheag

11 Crazy Horse 15m 6a+ ★★
Rab Anderson 2008
This passes through the right end of the wave overhang to reach a lower-off shared with Above the Line. A fingery crux below the overhang, but leave something in reserve.

12 Jib Test 15m 6b ★
Rab Anderson 2008
This is immediately right of the white streak. The roof is a distinct crux. The lower-off is shared with the previous two routes.

To the left of the white streak there are 5 routes which climb above a ledge that rises up left to end in a big flake shaped like a lizard's head. The 1st bolts on some of these climbs are above the ledge and although easily gained, care should be taken in damp conditions.

13 Blade Runner 12m 6a+ ★
Rab Anderson 2008
The first climb is immediately left of the white streak. The roof isn't the crux!

Silver Rock

**14 Jailbird 12m 6b **
Rab Anderson 2008
This lies 2m to the left and passes through the wave overhang where it begins to decrease in size. Sustained climbing, with the crux low down on smaller holds.

15 Fleet Street 12m 6b **
Rab Anderson 2008
The classic of the crag, this lies right of a less obvious pale streak. It is best finished at the lower-off of The Mound but can be finished at Jailbird. It is quite sequency on pockets, so can seem easy if you get it right.

16 The Mound 12m 6b+ **
Rab Anderson 2008
Left of the less obvious pale streak, passing a small rock scar. The holds improve higher up, but it gets steeper and you get more tired!

17 Turbine Charged 15m 6a+ **
Rab Anderson 2008
Passes through the big lizard's-head shaped flake at 3m height. Fine sustained climbing to share a high lower-off with the next two climbs.

18 Tain Spotting 15m 6a **
Rab Anderson 2008
Passes just where the lizard's tongue would capture you! Steep on good pockets through the overhang leading to a lower-off shared with Turbine Charged.

19 Off the Rails 18m 5+ *
Rab Anderson 2008
The red bolts are hard to see but a high 1st bolt is easily gained above a large pocket. Go up through the roof to the left of Tain Spotting on a good undercling. Again steep and on excellent holds, leading to a lower-off shared with Turbine Charged.

20 Tied Up 20m 5 *
Rab Anderson 2012
Just to the left of Off the Rails, climb to a turf ledge (5 bolts) then step left to finish as for Gift Wrapped through the gap in the turf ledges.

21 Gift Wrapped 20m 5 **
Chris Anderson 2009
Some 5m left of the lizard's head feature, this climbs the crag at its highest point where it is less steep, through a gap between turf ledges. Another high 1st bolt is easily gained above a good pocket.

22 Splat 10m 5+ *
Andy Cunningham 2009
The first of three shorter climbs towards the left end of the crag. Start 3m right of red rock formed by a shallow flake-corner. Climb green rock, then trend left through a bulge right of a capping roof above the red rock. The lower-off is shared with the following route.

23 Squelch 10m 5 **
Andy Cunningham 2009
Climb the red corner to a capping roof, step left and go up through the bulge on good holds to a lower-off shared with Splat. Moving slightly right through the bulge is 5+ but joins Splat. The quickest route to dry on the crag.

24 Manitou 8m 5
Rab Anderson 2008
The furthest left route starts easily but steepens.

Silver Rock - Golspie

(NH 795 995) L21 E441 Alt 180m South facing
Maps p257, p276, p284 Diagram p285

This crag of predominantly very sound conglomerate lies just outside Golspie on the north side of Loch Fleet, over which there are fantastic views. Creag Bheag lies about 2 miles (3km) to the south. There are

Silver Rock

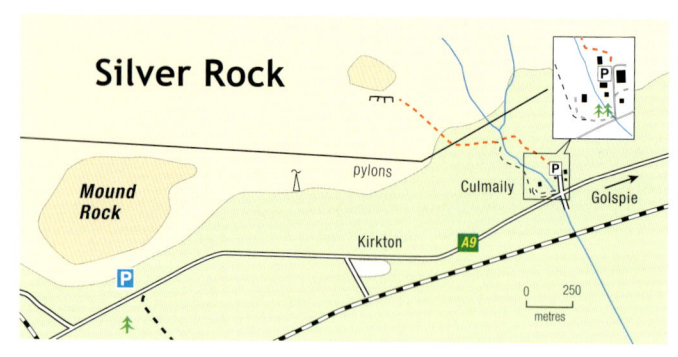

climbs from grade 3 to 7a+, with plenty of scope for new lines. The steeper section of the crag stays dry in the heaviest of rain but unfortunately the lower-offs are on the slabby wall above this. The crag can remain wet for a few days after prolonged heavy rain due to run off.

AMENITIES
As for Creag Bheag.

RECOMMENDED TASTY BITES
As for Creag Bheag.

TOP TIPS
You need faith to succeed; however the pebbles don't come with a guarantee. Belayers and picnickers beware! Some of the grades may be stiffer than on other conglomerate crags.

DIRECTIONS
Head north on the A9 from Inverness for 45 miles measured from the roundabout just south of the Kessock Bridge to The Mound causeway across Loch Fleet. Just north of the causeway is a left turn to Lairg and Rogart (A839). Continue on the A9 for 2.0 miles, and then turn left into Culmaily Farm (small sign). Before reaching the turn-off, the grand Culmaily House is seen up on the left. The farmer Angus McCall has kindly allowed access and parking at Culmaily Farm behind the two white holiday cottages (NH 8069 9921), or just beyond if this is full with farm machinery.

Please avoid parking inconsiderately and avoid blocking any gateways or machinery etc. It takes about an hour to get here via Lairg from Laxford Bridge, or Ledmore Junction on the west coast.

APPROACH
Time: 25mins

From behind the last farm building, the crag is visible up on the left. Head up a tractor track in that direction into a field and out through a gate in a wall at its top end. After 10m, take a line left (some gorse has been cleared here) across a burn and out the far side of more gorse. Join another tractor track and follow it and the field beyond to cross its top boundary deer fence by a metal gate. Go up to the crag across open ground. If the burn is likely to be in spate or bulls are in the field, avoid them by heading back towards the main road, before going part way along the track to Culmaily House to go through the first gate into the field and follow the west side of the burn. The first route on the crag is the furthest left at NH 7956 9957.

① Extreme Lichen 8m   3
Bethan & Simon Nadin 2008
At the left end of the crag base is an old fence. This route climbs a scoop 10m right of the fence. A good introduction to climbing.

② High School Blues 10m   4
Bethan & Simon Nadin 2008
Some 20m right, just right of a section where the base is undercut. Pleasant climbing on good rock.

③ Czech Connections 12m   HVS 4c *
Simon & Louise Nadin 2008
In 2012 there was only a bolt lower-off but the route is included in this guide as the intention is to bolt it throughout. The crack is climbed directly to the lower-off. Originally climbed with knotted slings!

Silver Rock

4 Fleet of Foot 13m 5+ **
Simon & Louise Nadin 2008
Nice climbing up the pink streak starting above a level spot at the cliff base. Awkward passing the last bolt.

A low-level traverse from here to the next route is 20m 5c.

5 Ag Rippa 23m 6b+ *
Simon & Louise Nadin 2007
Start some 20m right and just left of where the cliff base becomes a rock slab. An easy wall leads to a bulge. Steep moves on good holds lead to groping pulls around the bulge (crux) before a rest in the alcove above. The bulges above are tackled on good holds in a fine position.

6 Sans Peur 20m 6c **
Simon Nadin 2009
This climbs red rock near the left end of the rock slab. Start in an obvious shallow corner with technical climbing leading past the first two bolts. Easier but airy climbing follows until the final headwall is reached. A committing sequence of moves hopefully leads to the lower-off above.

7 Silver Darlings 14m 7a+ ***
Simon Nadin 2009
Near the right end of the rock slab, a series of pockets is followed dynamically to a large pebble. Technical and fingery moves pass under and just left of an obvious patch of bird poo. Finish more easily through the bulge on the right.

8 Champ at the Bit 11m 7a+ **
Simon Nadin 2008
At the very right end of the rock slab and 1m right of Silver Darlings. Another dynamic start (crux) leads to sustained climbing passing just right of the bird poo to surmount the final overhang.

9 Ground Clearance 12m 6c **
Simon Nadin 2008
Start from a smaller rock platform close on the right of the main slab. Excellent climbing based on the line of the shallow runnel. Tricky moves lead over the bulge directly above (crux).

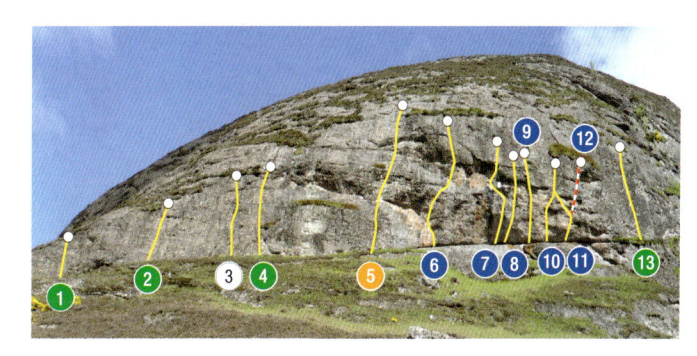

10 Dashed Pebbles 10m 7a *
Simon Nadin 2009
From the smaller platform 2m right of Ground Clearance, the obvious large pockets are followed to an abrupt end. A fierce pull on a painful two finger pocket may gain easier ground above.

11 T.B.C. 13m 6c+ **
Simon Nadin 2010
Start as for Trust in Me, from a rock flake at the right end of the smaller platform. From the 2nd bolt, stretch out left to a small pocket before continuing to a larger pocket left again. Move up and left to reach Dashed Pebbles. Finish up this.

12 Trust in Me 11m 6c *
Simon Nadin 2009
Start from a rock flake at the right end of the smaller platform. Stretch up for pockets (hard for the short) and climb slightly rightwards before attacking the bulge and wall above. From the last bolt to the lower-off is easier.

Highlands East

Silver Rock

Simon Nadin – Champ at the Bit (7a+) on Silver Rock (photo Bethan Nadin)

The next route starts from a green ledge 10m above and to the right of Trust in Me.

13. To Infinity and Beyond 15m 5+ **
Simon & Louise Nadin 2010
Make a tricky scramble up to the ledge from below to belay in a shallow alcove. Climb out of the right-hand side of the alcove past a large pocket. Continue directly up a water cleaned streak. It is possible to lower off back to the ground, below the scramble, but take care with a 50m rope.

The Powe - Wick

(ND 373 492) L12 E450 Non-Tidal South-East facing

This small sea-cliff comprised of angular leaning walls, sits above large flat sea platforms in a picturesque setting with a pleasant ambience. The climbs are fairly short (8-12m) and the rock is an unusual hard slatey sandstone, horizontally banded, and slightly friable in nature. The climbing is generally steep on small edges. There are three sport routes at present, three projects, traditional lines and ample opportunities for bouldering. The Powe is best visited between late spring and early autumn when long days and prevailing westerly winds provide ideal conditions with minimal midges.

AMENITIES
Wick is a well appointed town with several petrol stations (a little pricey though), no shortage of banks and a couple of supermarkets. There's a caravan/campsite on the A882 Thurso road and if you're feeling a bit flush there are many hotels. The brave, feeling hot and bothered at the end of the day, can go for a dip in the nearby Trinkie outdoor swimming pool!

RECOMMENDED TASTY BITES
Wetherspoons in Wick is a good retreat for food, coffee or a well earned pint, or head down to the Harbour Cafe for a snack.

TOP TIPS
Keep an eye out and you may be lucky enough to catch a glimpse of killer, pilot or minke whales. The platforms make a lovely picnic spot on a summer's day.

DIRECTIONS
Head to Wick, either by the A9 and A99 if coming from the south, 100 miles (160km) north of Inverness, or on the A882 if coming from Thurso, 20 miles (32km). Once in the town of Wick, follow signs for the Castle of Old Wick/Trinkie (outdoor swimming pool). This road takes you through a residential area and on out towards the headland via a single track road, passing an old white tower on the right, to a car park at the road end, approximately 1.25 miles (2km) from the town (ND 373 492).

APPROACH
Time: 2-4mins

From the car park, locate a small path at the left end of a low stone wall. Follow this down to a large sloping platform (slippery when wet) and the crag.

BARNY'S WALLS

🟢 **Mystery Machine 12m 3+**
Shauna Malcolm 2005
On the left end of the crag, just left of the large orange graffiti BARNY, is a corner and arete. Start 1m left of this corner. Climb to a lower-off above a small roof.

🟢 **At Ma Wick's End 11m 5b**
Raymond Wallace 2005
Climb the left side of the arete (without using the wall on its left) to a break, move right and over the bulge. Lower-off on a large ledge above.

🟠 **Da Ma Wick 11m 6a**
Allan Wallace 2006
Climb the steep right side of the same arete to finish as for that route.

There are three other bolted lines with lower-off chains which were too hard for John Malcolm and Raymond Wallace who bolted them.

⚪ **Open Project 6b?**
The flake 1m right of Da Ma Wick.

⚪ **Open Project 6c?**
Climb an arete 15m right of Route 4, past another orange BARNY, then up the line of slopers rising leftwards to a corner.

⚪ **Open Project 6b+?**
Some 25m right again and past three corners is a blank wall with an overlap in the middle. Climb directly through the middle of the overlap past a very thin ramp on the left, then climb the right side of a hanging arete.

Creag Dhubh, Loch Loyal

(NC 609 498)   Alt 240m   North Facing
This crag lies on the eastern flank on Beinn Heil, and is the obvious clean slab seen up on the right when driving south along Loch Loyal. The rock is a very fine-grained granite with good friction, although it takes a while to dry out. The one route done so far is very good, and whilst not enough to justify a visit on its own, could be combined with a visit to the high crags on Ben Loyal, or the North Coast sea-cliffs.

AMENITIES
Tongue, 5 miles to the north, and Lairg, some 30 miles to the south, are small but have many facilities.

RECOMMENDED TASTY BITES
The Crask Inn, some 17 miles to the south, is situated on the roadside at a uniquely remote moorland spot and has good bar meals.

TOP TIPS
Look out for new route descriptions, as more routes are planned.

DIRECTIONS
Head north from Lairg on the A836, passing Altnaharra. A sufficiently robust attitude to your car's suspension should allow you to drive up a short track to park at some concrete ruins at NC 612 497.

APPROACH
Time: 10mins
Walk up the hill to the crag.

🔵 **Friend or Foe 30m 6c ***
Simon Nadin, Neil Wilson 2012
To the right of the toe of the slab is a broken overlap. Step left through the left end of this overlap to gain the 1st bolt, then continue straight up, linking together occasional pockets and flakes.

Highlands West

This section covers the cliffs principally in Wester Ross, in the area enclosed by the triangle created between the arms of the A835 Ullapool road, the A832 & A890 to Kyle of Lochalsh road and the rugged Atlantic coastline.

The majority of the crags lie in the Gairloch and Gruinard area and have been developed since 2004 and are therefore well bolted with modern equipment. There is a wide range of grades and the crags are accessible, so there really is something for everyone. The crags vary from Clown Slab with Grade 4s to Goat Crag which is big and steep and with some of the best hard routes around. The rock is Lewisian gneiss, so mostly of high quality, and many of the sport walls are judged too poorly protected to give any pleasure for trad climbing. Some of the crags do have existing trad routes but never ones that have seen many ascents. The setting is true North-West with beautiful scenery and quiet, but beware in the summer when tourists and midges arrive. However, most of the crags are in open country where a breeze can be a saviour. Further south and on schist, there is the fierce Duncraig, containing the two original routes in the area, but with current development by the locals. Another recent development, Leacanashie Woods Crag is mainly for dry tooling but with some sport routes also. Finally the first Torridonian sandstone crag has been developed, Creag nan Òrd near Dundonnell.

History by Paul Tattersall

The first bolted lines in Wester Ross were established in autumn 2001 by Paul Tattersall (Tat) and Colin Meek. After years of bouldering at Am Fasgadh, they finally started the process of creating some sport climbing by bolting Toiseach (7b), and The Brown Streak (7b+). In the beginning drilling resources were very limited. Tat had acquired a Bosch in Germany and Mick Holmes was recruited to help out as he had Bosch batteries stashed in the side pockets of his backpack. Lewisian gneiss is a lot harder than German sandstone. Three batteries and a blunt drill bit would sometimes result in no more than two holes from a bolting session but there was always bouldering to fall back on. In this relaxed West Coast way, Bog Talla (7c) and The Crack (7b+) were added. Tat had climbed the latter as Tatapult at E6, but his and everyone else's feeling was that as the heart of Wester Ross sport climbing, Am Fasgadh should be a bolted venue and so it was. There was always plenty of chat among the few local climbers about bolting the other lines but not much happened due to the lack of drilling power and a reluctance to give up precious climbing time when at the crag.

The situation changed when George Ridge loaned his mothballed petrol drill to the cause with a note to say "get on with it". Bolts and resin were bought, ear defenders dug out and The Beast was duly put to action. Tat opened up Creag nan Luch Lower Tier producing Old Snapper (6b+), Astar (6a+), Ni Dubh (6b), Walkaway (7a) and the classics of the crag Toss (6c) and Superblue (7b+). At Am Fasgadh he added The Warm Up (7b) and The Pillar (8a).

That was early Spring 2004 and it was at this time that Lawrence Hughes suddenly got enthusiastic about forging on at Am Fasgadh. He stepped up, chose his line, bought the bolts, got some rope access tips and created a classic with Black Sox (7c+). It was a big effort fraught with many, now amusing, setbacks. The funniest prob-

Highlands West

1. Duncraig.............................p292
2. Leacanashie Woods Crag.....p293
3. Creag na Cadhag.................p296
4. Grass Crag..........................p300
5. Creag nan Luch p302
6. Kuhjo Crag p310
7. Goat Crag & Am Fasgadh......p312
8. Creag nan Òrd p320

ably being the occasion he had the holes drilled for the lower-off and came back to resin the anchors in. A 45 minute drive down from Ullapool after work, walk in with all the gear, get kitted up, jug up his ropes to check the holes. Back to the ground then get set with the resin whilst following the instructions and grinning with excitement. It was a gorgeous day and elsewhere everyone else was sending routes on lovely, dry warm rock. Back up to the anchor, put the nozzle in the hole, pump the trigger… nothing. Tat swears he heard the scream in Melvaig, 30 miles away! Lawrence had primed the resin on the deck and with all the faffing about, on a hot day it had set in the nozzle. The final error was only having one nozzle. He came back the next day, sorted it out then gave the drill back to Tat and retired from the bolting scene.

Tat was left to soldier on alone, but relief was at hand. Paul Thorburn, aka Storky, appeared in the Spring of 2005. For the next few seasons he would arrive with the swallows, unannounced, climb a bit, spend days on end in all weather hanging and drilling on the steepest bits of Wester Ross, creating the hardest sport routes in the area and then disappear. Lawrence's epic pales into insignificance when you know what Storky went through trying to tame The Beast. Days and days of sheer hard graft, and the results? Creag nan Luch - the lines of Stalks (8a+) and Hola. Am Fasgadh – Storkies (8a+). Goat Crag – the brilliant Leaning Wall (8a) and The Prow Right-Hand (7c+). Creag nan Cadhag – the lines of Ronald Raygun (7b+) and Nuclear Nightmare. He made no fuss, left no names, and often didn't even climb much. Throughout the long days of May and June he tidied up messes of half-done things that Tat had on the go by fixing or finishing off anchors, gluing holds, adding extra bolts or the few last bolts to incomplete lines. True to life, everything moved on and the migrating Stork became a thing of the past. Once again Tat was left to nurse The Beast alone.

By the end of 2005 Creag nan Luch Upper Tier was becoming a good summer venue with big

The Deaf Violinist (7a), Creag nan Cadhag (photo Murdoch Jamieson)

Andy Wilby on The Shield (7b+), Am Fasgadh (photo Ian Taylor)

things for the locals to do and cash in on their strength acquired from wintering on Am Fasgadh. The big trio of Whip and Ride (7c), Stalks (8a+) and the project Remember to Rock 'n' Roll will keep most people occupied for a while.

Late January 2006 was cold. Tat had had enough and bought himself a Hilti for Christmas, so The Beast was laid to rest, sort of. The bogs of Wester Ross were frozen solid down to sea-level for a week or more and whilst the sun shone brilliantly out of blue skies and the hard core locals were revelling in the stickiest conditions ever at Am Fasgadh, Tat bolted Grass Crag. The routes might be short but they pack the climbing in. With lots of sixes and easier grades it has proved popular with the masses.

Around this time a major force appeared on the bolting scene and the crags haven't had a chance since. Andy Wilby, the North's strongest man, bought himself a Hilti and came over to test the system at Grass Crag. He was also involved at Kuhjo Crag with Tat and Claire Hayden. Like Grass Crag, Tat had done a few trad routes here in the past which no one had ever shown any interest in for fear of mortal injury. Since being bolted, people have been queuing night and day. Wicked and Weird (7a+) is a mini classic.

The big action in 2007 was at everyone's secret crag. You know the one just above the road that looks really awesome, the one you can see from everywhere, even when you are on the Ullapool ferry – Goat Crag. Colin, Murdoch Jamieson and Tat headed up there and got things moving in March. Murdoch, being youthful and just doing what he was told to do, got on with Teepee (6a+), TP being Tom Paine or Tom Patey. Colin added Mac Talla (7b) which has the best route in Wester Ross award and Tat made a bee-line for The Prow LH (7c). It was a big joint effort. Through April and May, Andy and Storky got involved and when the dust eventually settled the premiere sport venue of Wester Ross was up and running. Tom Paine's Bones (6b+), Too Old To Be Famous (7b), The Mighty Atom (7b+) and The Prow RH (7c+) having been fully equipped.

It was around this time that there was a breach of security with the arrival of Dave Redpath from the Central Belt. He was spotted on the Upper Tier of Creag nan Luch and whilst displaying a friendly manner and a basic level of climbing strength he was allowed to unlock the sequence on Whip and Ride that had been confusing the local hard core. To everyone's delight he invested time and energy in hold maintenance and stood back to let the queue of waiting ascentionists strut their stuff. Having been given the time of day he obviously felt part of the inner circle and went round to Goat Crag and bolted Broken Silence (7c) before heading south to Yorkshire.

In late 2007 Ian Taylor entered the fray. He adopted Am Fasgadh and Goat Crag and started plugging away at filling in the remaining lines that were crying out to be bolted. With the thumb pressing hard, the first thing he did was make the real warm up route at Am Fasgadh, The Groove (6c+) then add The Shield (7b), climbed with Tat. In 2008 at Goat Crag, he bolted Between the Monsoons (6c+) and Hydrotherapy (6c+), two great climbs that are almost always guaranteed to be dry and went on to add the fine Primo (7c) to Am Fasgadh with Lawrence Hughes, returning to the fray again. Not being one to miss out on the action, Andy Wilby added Batman and Robin (7b) and the Joker (7b) to Goat Crag.

Tat was keeping his fuel bills to a minimum and developing the coastal venues of Melvaig, close to his house, as well as enjoying seeing the fruits of the keener elements of the extended Wester Ross climbing family get on with some hard work and the emptying of their bank accounts! It was 2007 when Martin Moran got in touch with Tat wanting to find out what all this bolting shenanigans was about. He had a few places down his way around Lochcarron that he was keen to turn into dry tooling venues. Tat agreed to meet up and introduce Martin to The Beast. A neutral venue was chosen, Creag na Cadhag, where Tat, Murdoch and Storky had already bolted some lines but more action was needed. Martin got on quite well with his new friend and Axe Grinder (7a+) was the result. This completed the trio of excellent sevens on that section of crag, the others being The Deaf Violinist (7a) and Drip Drip Drip (7a). Martin cleaned the line to the right, Tat put the bolts in and Ball Park Incident (6c+) was the result. Martin was soon suffering under The Beast's tyranny and when it finally packed in altogether he went online and got himself a Hilti. The Beast is back in its box in Tat's shed.

In 2008 Colin Meek found time to start developing Creag nan Òrd near Dundonnell. This 30m sandstone crag has four routes to date and when Colin sees a window of opportunity, he has a mass of bolts hanging in the byre awaiting a good home.

Continuing his work at Goat Crag, between 2009 and 2012, Ian Taylor added a further ten routes and although he climbed harder, Caberfeidh (6b), Fidgey Muckers (7a) and Snow Flake (7a+) stand out. At Am Fasgadh in 2011 he added two more routes to the right end of the crag and Murdoch Jamieson climbed Black Sox Direct Finish at (8a+).

In 2009 Tat started developing Creag an Oisean where The Otter Final (7a+) is the best and the following year at Creag nan Cadhag he added Bovnahackit (6a+), one of the finest 6a+s in the area. Also here, in 2011, Andy Wilby, as well as adding 3 easier routes, climbed Game Over (7b) and in 2012 went on to complete one of Storky's open projects, Ronald Raygun (7b+). Andy has obviously set himself the task of having a project he can play on no matter which venue he ends up at! At the time of writing his closed projects are Poison Ivy on Goat Crag, The Counter Diagonal at Am Fasgadh, Pesto Macho on the Lower Tier, and Remember to Rock 'n' Roll on the Upper Tier. They are all going to be hard. In 2012 with the areas reputation growing, Ali Coull added the Fun Prow (7c+) hybrid link to Goat Crag and another of Storky's drilled projects was finally climbed by Alan Cassidy, Stalks (8a+) at Creag nan Luch. And to the future? There is somewhere called Super Crag but Tat is too old and knackered and thinks youngsters these days just want it all on a plate!

Amy Tattersall on The Snatcher (4), Clown Slab of Kuhjo Crag (photo Angela Tattersall)

PLOCKTON & LOCHCARRON
There are two cliffs in this area; one at Duncraig near Plockton and the other, a mainly dry tooling venue, at Leacanashie Woods Crag near Lochcarron.

Duncraig - Plockton

**(NG 8404 3380) L24 E428   Alt 50m   North facing
Map p289**

The small crag of Duncraig sits just above the road near to the scenic seaside village of Plockton. The rock is excellent quality schist and the crag has had some recent attention to make for a good sport climbing venue. Bouldering at the base of the cliff comes recommended.

AMENITIES
A castle, palm trees, sea views, pubs, grocery store, hotel and B&Bs – Plockton has it all and set the scene for the BBC series Hamish MacBeth!

RECOMMENDED TASTY BITES
The wee chippy in Plockton does a good fish supper.

TOP TIPS
Avoid this crag during the summer months as it's a midge haven!

DIRECTIONS
Heading south on the A890 (which links the Lochcarron area with the A87 to Kyle of Lochalsh), follow signs for Achmore, passing through the village to a junction just to its south. Coming north on the A890, turn left signposted Braeintra. Go through Braeintra to the same junction. From the junction, head west signposted Plockton. After 1.1 miles the crag is on the left, almost overhanging the road but only visible above the trees (look up through the sunroof!). Park discreetly somewhere nearby.

APPROACH
Time: 15 seconds!
From the road, up the bank to the crag.

Routes are described from left to right (east to west). All routes have been bolted using 12mm X 85mm Hilti Rawl bolts (not stainless steel) with Petzl hangers.

○ **Hang Over   16m   Project**
Neil Smith, Roger Lupton 1989
This was first climbed with scarce natural protection and has still to be bolted. It climbs the wall just left of the corner where Long Reach starts. Keep to the right and step right through the overhang near the top.

● **Long Reach   25m   6b**
Neil Smith, Roger Lupton 1989
Originally climbed in 1989 with virtually no protection; 2 bolts were added in 1993 and a further 5 in 2010. The route starts at the base of a large corner with a large overhang at mid-height. Climb the corner until possible to traverse right onto the slab. Use small holds to climb diagonally up to the right side of the roof. Climb through the overhang and continue up trending left to below a bulging wall; traverse left and up a small slab to finish.

● **Hare   25m   6b**
Neil Smith, Roger Lupton 1993
Originally climbed using scarce natural protection; it now has 7 bolts. Start 4m to the right of Long Reach at a large boulder. Climb the small corner to a cracked block and pass this on the left. Climb the slab trending rightwards to the base of a corner at the far right end of the roof. Climb the corner, step left and then traverse right under a bulging wall to finish right of the tree.

● **Gordon's Route   24m   6c**
Gordon Bisset, Neil Smith 1988
Originally climbed with scarce natural protection; 2 bolts were installed in 1993, but it now has 7. Start 4m to the right of Hare at the base of a smooth wall below an overhang at one-third height. Climb the wall (crux) up to the overhang, move left, then pull through the overhang and

climb easier ground to a recess. Climb a crack on the left side of the recess to join Hare.

🔴 **Pine Martin   23m   7b**
Neil Smith, Gordon Bisset 1989
This is the left-hand bolt line up the west end of the crag. At the lip of the first overhang is a large nose. Gain this using a flake, then continue up the wall above on good holds and side-pulls (7a, strenuous). Climb slightly right up to a small overhang at the horizontal break (good rest). Climb direct through the overhang by means of an Egyptian (crux) to vertical cracks; follow the cracks to the top.

🔴 **Wild at Heart   24m   7b**
Neil Smith, Roger Lupton 1989
This is the right-hand bolt line just right of Pine Martin. Climb through the double roof (7a, strenuous), then continue up and right into to a large recess. Climb directly over the overhang using a large hold. Climb the steep wall (crux) up to the horizontal crack, then traverse left to a rest; climb directly to the top.

⚪ **Levitation   70m   Project**
Neil Smith, Alan Forrest 1986
Originally climbed using sparse natural protection. A long rising east to west traverse with an exposed finish. Still to be bolted. The grade is expected to be 6b.

Leacanashie Woods Crag - Lochcarron

(NG 855 356) L24 E428   Alt 75m   South facing
Maps p289, p293

This overhanging crag has an attractive southerly aspect in oak woods on the north side of Loch Carron (Leacanasigh on recent maps). The crag is up to 16m high and is composed of crushed and banded gneiss, with some friable rock and few cracks. The cliff is a great gymnasium for dry-tooling, technically absorbing rather than brutally athletic, and also offers a few sport rock climbs, ideal for an autumn or winter day, when it captures every available hour of sunlight. The venue offers a sanctuary for winter climbers driven off the mountains by bad conditions or weather. Stainless steel bolts and lower-offs were placed by Martin Moran, and the climbs were completed by Moran, Nick Carter, Murdoch Jamieson, Pete Macpherson, Alex Moran and Martin Welch. Rock shoes were worn on most ascents, avoiding unsightly scratching of the rock, and the climbs may be half a grade harder wearing crampons. Any pre-drilled holds are mentioned in the descriptions. The only established dry-tool rule here is that use of hands is strictly forbidden! The bolt spacings are adequate but most routes give a real sense of commitment due to the fierce angle and friable rock and a few cams are advised on some routes. Helmets are essential. There is no topo because the crag is in trees.

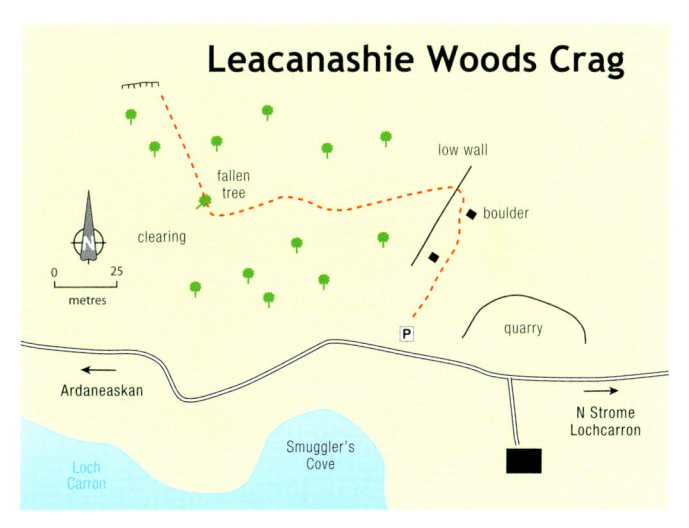

🟥 AMENITIES

Lochcarron village has a bank, garages and shops.

Leacanashie Woods Crag

RECOMMENDED TASTY BITES
Cafe/tearooms at Lochcarron Weavers (1 mile from crag) and in Lochcarron village; bar meals in Lochcarron Hotel.

DIRECTIONS
From Lochcarron village take the minor road signposted Ardaneaskan – North Strome. Follow this for 3.8 miles (6km), ignoring a left turning to Strome Castle after 3.3 miles. The road dips steeply down past the shingle bay of Smugglers Cove. Park on the right of the road above the cove, just after an old gravel cutting and just before the woods (NG 8559 3545).

APPROACH
Time: 8-10mins
The key to the approach is following a small path, so take care at the start. Finding it is much harder (but still possible) in the summer when the bracken is high. Walk up a grass hollow to a boulder at 35m and a bigger one at 65m. Five metres past the bigger boulder, turn left over a low wall at 5m and go diagonally back left (not straight up into jungle) for 70m into the oak woods to a shoulder, from where the car is just visible directly below. Continue along the path, 30m gently up then level, then 50m descending and level to the start of a clearing. Just before the clearing, leave the path and go diagonally left uphill under a part fallen tree after 10m from where the crag can be seen in the same direction.

An overhanging prow forms the centrepiece of the crag. To its left is a right-angled corner recess with another bulging wall on its left side. To the left of this is a smooth 6m wall, which forms the left wing of the cliff.

LEFT WING
This offers several short introductory routes with two lower-off points. At the left end of the crack-lines on either side of two bolts give:

Warm-Up 6m D4

Warm-Down 6m D4

Smuggler 8m D6 *
The thin seam in the centre of the wing. A hard start leads to thin wall climbing (3 bolts).

Plunderer 9m D6 *
Climb cracks at the right end of the wing to a roof (3 bolts), then move left (large cam for protection) to a delicate finishing move.

Buccaneer 14m D7 **
The bulging wall left of the easy corner gives an arm sapping route. Start just left of the corner on a sloping shelf, pull up past friable breaks and cut loose rightwards over the main bulge. Pull back left then move right to a finishing crack and lower-off (6 bolts).

Free Trader 12m D3 *
The 'easy' corner would be about Scottish technical 5, and is a good beginners' lead route.

MAIN WALL
This has some terrific strenuous dry tool challenges.

Freebooter 14m D5
Climb enjoyably up the crack-line in the left arete of the wall (2 bolts) to a ledge under the roof. Move left and delicately up to a bolt and holds and finish just right of Free Trader.

The Gibbet 18m D8 **
The horizontal roof crack looks unremittingly strenuous but proves surprisingly technical. Start up Freebooter, then move delicately right into a little groove under the roof. Gain the roof crack and try not to swing off a crucial placement, before going hell for leather to gain lodgement on the balcony above. Go up the wall on the right to the lower-off (7 bolts).

Leacanashie Woods Crag

○ **Gutbuster** 15m D8 **
Start 2m right of The Gibbet and climb the bulging lower wall to a ledge. Go up a thin layback seam, swing left to cross The Gibbet under the roof. Pass a worrying projecting block and make a strenuous and tenuous move direct over the roof to a tree.

○ **Credit Crunch** 16m D9 ***
This line takes the blank roof 2m right of The Gibbet and has three drilled or improved placements. Start delicately up the lower wall to gain the ledge at 6m. A thin pull gains the first drilled hold in the base of the roof. Three big reaches gain a bomber horizontal crack just over the lip (hidden bolt!). Pull over and finish up the wall to the lower-off (7 bolts).

○ **Ribcracker** 16m D8 ***
The classic of the crag climbs the prow to gain a bottomless finishing groove. Consider the route's name before attempting any figure fours! Start up a flake-crack, then make wobbly moves on to the 6m ledge. Climb the wall above to gain the roof where drilled placements lead left. A big reach gains the finishing groove and lower-off (7 bolts).

○ **The Shield** 16m D9/10 ***
This route tackles the smooth headwall above Ribcracker. Climb that route to the roof then swing up right over the prow to the smooth headwall, which is extremely thin and in 2012 had not been led cleanly. A slightly easier option is to move left on the lip of the prow and finish up the arete just right of the groove of Ribcracker.

○ **Predestination** 16m D8 **
The central wall and groove offers technical and forceful climbing. Swing up right to a ledge, then climb a steep wall and pull over the first roof to an awkward rest under the second roof. Break out leftward using a crucial side flake to gain the finishing groove and lower-off (6 bolts). The dry tool version breaks out left at the lip of the first roof.

Leacanashie Woods Crag – Predestination (D8) takes on Pete Macpherson (photo Murdoch Jamieson)

Highlands West

Creag nan Cadhag

● **Predestination   16m   6c **
As a sport climb.

○ **Consternation   16m   D9 ***
The triple roof system just right of Predestination provides reachy moves and exciting clips on the lips (5 bolts). Go easily on to a ledge (cam runners under roof), then swing up left to a crack-line in the wall (2 bolts and small cam recommended). At the 2nd roof make fascinating moves (bolt) to gain a precarious rest squeezed under the 3rd roof. Pull over with a long reach up right to easier finishing moves.

● **Consternation   16m   6c+ ***
As a sport climb.

○ **Macpherson's Mountain Sports   16m   D9 ****
This eliminate climbs Predestination to a bum-rest under the final roof, then moves right to finish up Consternation.

○ **No Questions Asked   17m   D8**
The bulging wall right of Consternation is climbed using hidden natural holes to gain an easier but bold upper corner finishing with rightward moves to the chain.

● **No Questions Asked   17m   7a ***
The bulging wall has a strenuous crux moving left to gain good crimps on hidden breaks.

○ **Murdoch's Reach   17m   D8 ***
A blind crack seam on the right side of the wall, 2m right of No Questions Asked, has hard reaches to gain a ledge at 10m (stick-clipping advised for 2nd bolt). Trend up left rather boldly on the upper wall to the lower-off. With a point of aid at the crux, the route would be a better and more consistent 6b.

● **Murdoch's Reach   17m   7a+ ***
As a sport climb. With a point of aid at the crux, the route would be more consistent 6b.

NEARBY BOULDERING

A clean shoreline bouldering wall is found 120m west of Smuggler's Cove (NG 853 354) and offers protectable mini-routes or extended boulder problems from V1 to V5 up to 8m in height with a shingle landing from most. The venue is tidal. Approach along the shore.

GAIRLOCH & POOLEWE TO DUNDONNELL

There are six crags in the vicinity of Gairloch. These are Creag nan Cadhag above Loch Maree to the south of Gairloch, Grass Crag just outside Gairloch to the north-east and to the south of Poolewe at the north-western end of Loch Maree, Creag nan Luch, Creag an Oisean and Kuhjo Crag. Some 13 miles (21km) further north and east on the A832 around the coast is the fabulous Goat Crag at Gruinard and its near neighbour Am Fasgadh. The area ends with Creag nan Òrd overlooking Dundonnell at the end of Little Loch Broom.

Creag nan Cadhag - Loch Maree

(NG 864 723) L19; E433 or E434   Alt 160m   North-West facing   Maps p289, p297   Diagram p298
Also known as Stone Valley Sport Crag, the crag is clearly visible on the south side of the A832, Gairloch to Kinlochewe road, at the top of the Slattadale pass. Despite its green appearance, the rock is compact Lewisian gneiss which gives superb steep climbing with edges, slopers, cracks and even the odd pocket. The parking spot is also used to access the Stone Valley trad crags (see SMC *Northern Highlands Central*).

AMENITIES

Gairloch has two supermarkets; the Strath Stores is very good whilst the Wildcat (the one at the T-junction) stays open until 9pm in summer. The Chemistore at the harbour is a general store and open on Sundays. There is a bank (ATM), petrol station (closed Sunday), cafes and pubs, fish and chips (the best being at Strath Square), restaurants, B&Bs and hotels, two campsites (the one at Big Sand is particularly good) and a SYHA hostel. Many places are closed out of season but the Harbour Lights

Creag nan Cadhag

Gairloch to Poolewe

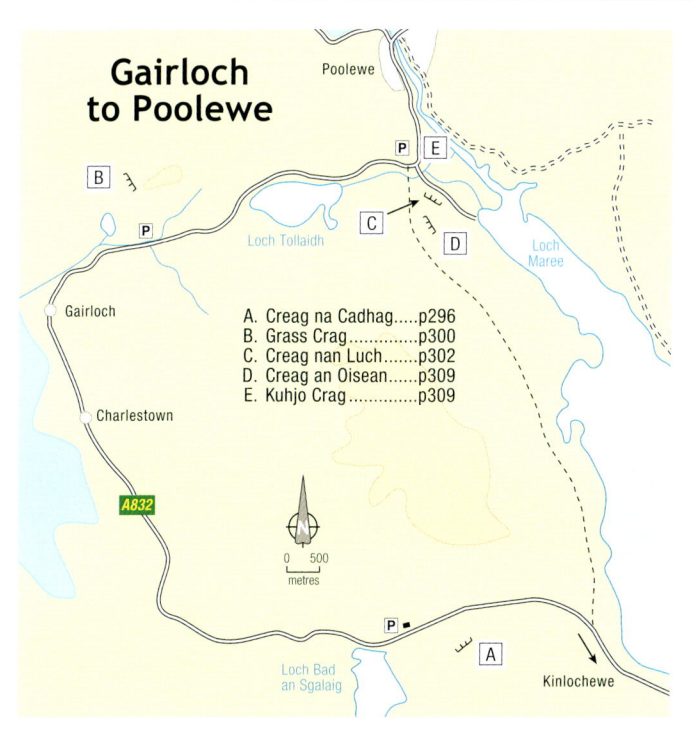

A. Creag na Cadhag.....p296
B. Grass Crag.............p300
C. Creag nan Luch.......p302
D. Creag an Oisean......p309
E. Kuhjo Crag.............p309

Cafe and the Na Mara Restaurant stay open all year. The petrol station in Kinlochewe opens on Sundays. Inverness or Dingwall are the nearest places with full town facilities. There is a new climbing wall in the Leisure Centre in Gairloch (01445 712345).

RECOMMENDED TASTY BITES

The Badachro Inn is very good. In Gairloch, the Na Mara Restaurant for cappuchino, cakes and food or The Shieling for meals or a coffee whilst lounging in the leather sofas. The Old Inn has lots of real ales, serves good food and has live music at the weekends.

TOP TIPS

The sun doesn't come round until about 4pm so it is a good option in hot weather. Being exposed there is often a breeze making it worth trying on a midgy day. The steep part of the crag is sheltered in showery weather and doesn't suffer from seepage.

DIRECTIONS

From the south, take the A832 towards Gairloch. After Kinlochewe the road follows the shore of Loch Maree for about 10 miles (16km), then it leaves the loch up a long straight. At the top of this is a cattle grid from where the crag first becomes visible on the left. Continue beyond the crag to where the road becomes single track. After a further 400m there is a green hut on the right and a parking area on its far side, NG 8566 7207. Do not park in the passing places directly below the crag.

From the north (Gairloch), reach this point, which is just past the end of Loch Bad an Sgalaig, via the A832; 5.5 miles (9km).

APPROACH

Time: 15mins
Walk back up the road to where it became single track and climb over the deer fence at a strainer post, then head diagonally up the tussocky hillside.

1 Old Man's Beard   18m   6a *
Andy Wilby 2011
The first of two routes which are left and lower down than the rest of the routes. A deceptive start leads to an easier section and a good ledge. Big jugs over a bulge to a more technical finish.

2 Bovnahackit   20m   6a+   *
Paul Tattersall 2010
Start in a depression. Go up a crack to start, then a smooth pale wall above which has lots of hidden holds.

Highlands West

Creag nan Cadhag

③ Battle Axe   12m   6c ★★
Murdoch Jamieson, Paul Tattersall 2007
The line on the left wall of the big central corner. The corner is VS 4b but overgrown.

④ Ronald Raygun   20m   7b+ ★★
Andy Wilby 2012; bolted by Paul Thorburn 2007
Up a slight scoop in the green overhanging wall 6m right of the big corner. Bridge up the wall to the 2nd bolt, then make a long move right to a good hold. More big moves to good holds lead to the crux, then easier to the top.

⑤ Nuclear Nightmare   20m   Open Project (8a?)
Bolted by Paul Thorburn 2007
The steepest section of wall. Go up a groove passing a roof on the right and up the headwall.

Creag nan Cadhag

6 Game Over   20m   7b
Andy Wilby 2011
A third line on the steepest section of wall. The grade is to a lower-off below the top. A one-bolt extension to the top is a much harder open project.

7 The Deaf Violinist   15m   7a **
Paul Tattersall 2007
Start up a big right-slanting ramp, leaving it to finish up a left-facing corner. Interestingly steep and crimpy in the middle, then a juggy finish.

8 Drip Drip Drip   15m   7a **
Paul Tattersall 2007
A crimpy lower wall gains the ramp. Head up from its top to finish leftwards up a diagonal crack to the same lower-off as Ronald Raygun. Suffers seepage unfortunately.

9 Axe Grinder   15m   7a+ **
Martin Moran 2007
The centre of the wall right of the ramp. The crux is making the moves into the finishing crack.

10 Ball Park Incident   15m   6c+
Paul Tattersall 2008
The flake-line come corner. Hard climbing past the first two bolts.

11 Volturi   10m   6b+ *
Andy Wilby 2011
This one might bite you! A short pillar with a crack on its left has some strenuous moves.

12 Flying Scotsman   10m   5+
Andy Wilby 2011
The centre of the slabby wall at the right end of the crag has a short crux section in the middle.

Andy Wilby on Battle Axe (6c), Creag nan Cadhag (photo Andy Nisbet)

Grass Crag

13 Born to Run 10m 5 *
Andy Wilby 2011
Sustained on positive holds.

Grass Crag - Gairloch

**(NG 817 789) L19 E434   Maps p289, p297
Diagrams p300, p302**

This crag lies on the north side of the road between Gairloch and Poolewe. It is a small secluded venue with an open sunny aspect. With a good spread of easier climbs it has a family picnic atmosphere and is a good place to let children run around. The rock is Lewisian gneiss of varying quality and the right-hand crag particularly has a snappy feel. Most routes dry quickly but there is some seepage down the middle of the right-hand wall after prolonged rain.

AMENITIES
As for Creag nan Cadhag.

RECOMMENDED TASTY BITES
As for Creag nan Cadhag.

TOP TIPS
Wellies recommended for the approach in anything but a dry spell of weather. The crag makes a good all year round venue, having a sunny aspect and being quick drying. For those who climb 6a and below, a combination with climbing on nearby trad crag, Aztec Tower, which has several good VS and HVS routes, makes a full day (see the SMC guide Northern Highlands Central). It lies at NG 815 784 but park at the same place for both crags.

DIRECTIONS
Driving north from Gairloch, seen from the crest of the first hill is a knoll with a prominent red slab. This is Aztec Tower, but behind and left of it is Grass Crag. Drive past Aztec Tower to where the road bends right and leads on to a long uphill straight. This is about 200m before a trad crag on the left (Creag Bhadan an Aisc). Park on the outside (north) of the bend, NG 8226 7809.

APPROACH
Time: 15-20mins
Head uphill (west of north), immediately crossing a couple of small burns and keeping left of a fenced enclosure, towards a wall on the skyline. Cross this and continue to a crest from where the crag is seen in profile. Keep right of the lochan to a flat area which should be passed on the right unless conditions are dry (or you are wearing wellies). Wet bogs can increase the approach time.

LEFT-HAND CRAG

(NG 8172 7891)   Alt 160m   South-West facing

1 Like it Hot? 12m 6c *
Paul Tattersall 2006

A central pillar.

2 Waiting for the Man   12m   6a+ **
Paul Tattersall 2006
A shallow corner at the right side of the pillar to the same lower-off as Like it Hot. Fine sustained climbing.

3 Side Flake   8m   5+
Paul Tattersall 2007
A flake and upper wall towards the right side has a sting-in-the-tail.

4 Sign of the Jug   8m   5+
Paul Tattersall 2007
The wall to the right also has a sting unless you're very tall. No escaping the sting to the right.

RIGHT-HAND CRAG

(NG 8175 7888)   Alt 150m   South-West facing

5 Joint Account   8m   6a *
Paul Tattersall 2006
A blind crux moving right.

6 Invest Wisely   8m   6a
Paul Tattersall 2006
Sustained climbing to a shared lower-off with Joint Account.

7 The Thinker   8m   6a+ *
Paul Tattersall 2006
Not as helpful as it looks, especially the last move.

8 Constipated Miser   8m   6b *
Paul Tattersall 2006
A bulging left-slanting crack is sustained to a shared lower-off with Joint Account. It's best to reach the cliff top, then step left to the lower-off.

Invest Wisely (6a), Grass Crag. Climber Sonia Rae (photo Andy Nisbet)

Creag nan Luch

Creag nan Luch - Creag Mhòr Thollaidh
L19 E434   Maps p289, p297

This crag has an accessible and popular lower tier with mostly easier grades and an impressive upper tier with two sections and some wild routes which have seen few ascents. The adjacent Red Mouse Slab has one easy route so far. The crag is just south of Poolewe, at the base of Creag Mhòr Thollaidh, which is a well known trad venue.

AMENITIES
The village of Poolewe has a grocery shop and Post Office. The Poolewe hotel is open to non-residents. Also in Poolewe is the Bridge Cottage Coffee Shop. There is a daytime restaurant at the world famous Inverewe Gardens run by The National Trust for Scotland (one mile north of Poolewe on the A832). There is a small outdoor shop on the premises of the Slioch outdoor clothing factory in Poolewe and nearby is the local swimming pool. The nearest petrol station is in Gairloch but this is closed on Sundays. Inverness or Dingwall are the nearest places with town facilities. There is a new climbing wall in the Leisure Centre in Gairloch (01445 712345) which may save an otherwise wasted weekend.

RECOMMENDED TASTY BITES
The Bridge Cottage Coffee Shop, with a friendly welcome and great food, is the only place to be if you are not at the crag cranking.

DIRECTIONS
Heading north from Gairloch on the A832, pass Loch Tollaidh and start descending into Poolewe with lovely views into Fisherfield. Just after a sharp left bend, go down a small tarmac road on the right. From Poolewe, the turning is about 1.5 miles south. The road leads down past Tollie Farm to the shores of Loch Maree at Tollie Bay. Park on the right at a shapely rowan tree just past the farm gate, from where the crag is clearly visible, NG 8643 7854. Do not park in the passing place a little further down the road as this causes an obstruction.

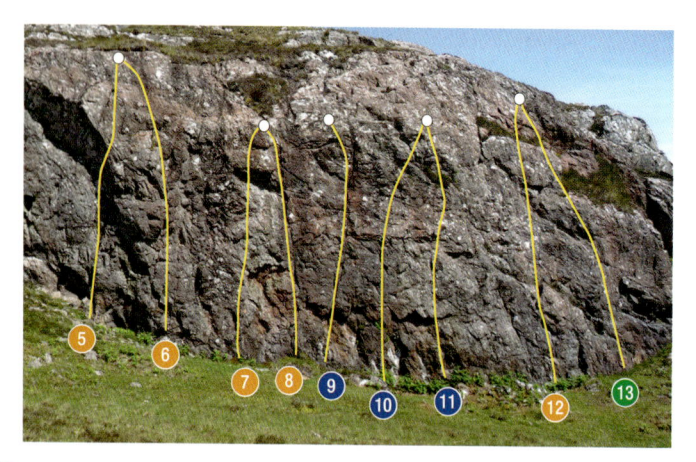

**9 The Dump   8m   6c **
Paul Tattersall 2006
A diverging crack to the right.

10 Pants on Fire   8m   7a
Paul Tattersall 2006
The wall 2m to the right.

11 All the Arts   8m   6c
Paul Tattersall 2006
Start over an undercut flake to a shared lower-off with Pants on Fire.

**12 Kick Ass Yoga   8m   6a+ *
Paul Tattersall 2006
A deceptively tricky initial flake gives a boulder problem start, then easier.

**13 Third and Final   10m   5 *
Paul Tattersall 2006
A shared lower-off with Kick Ass Yoga.

Creag nan Luch 303

LOWER TIER

(NG 8641 7824)   Alt 70m   North-East facing
Diagram p304

A very accessible and popular venue with a good range of climbs mostly in the 6s. It is sheltered and dries quickly. It loses the sun around 11am in the summer but gets no sun at all in the winter. The rock is rough crystalline Lewisian gneiss of excellent quality.
There is some reasonable bouldering on the blocks close to the foot of the crag.

TOP TIPS

It is sheltered from typically wet south-west or westerly weather and as long as it is only showery conditions, rather than prolonged rain, it is a good venue to escape to when more exposed crags are getting soaked. Midges can be a problem in the summer!

APPROACH

Time: 5mins
Walk down the road for 130m and cross the deer fence at a stile. A small worn path leads up to the crag.

1 Pumpernickle   25m   6a+
Paul Tattersall 2008
High up the slope at the very left end of the crag. A hard start leads to a long easy slab.

2 Old Snapper   15m   6b+ *
Paul Tattersall 2004
Start rightwards up a small hanging slab, leading to intricate groove climbing with a thuggish finish.

3 Hairdubh   18m   6c+ *
Paul Tattersall 2004
A thin bouldery start, then head rightwards up a steep smooth wall.

Andy Wilby on Superblue (7b+), Creag nan Luch (photo Richie Betts)

Highlands West

304 Creag nan Luch

Creag nan Luch

(4) Pesto Macho   18m   Closed Project
Andy Wilby 2010
A direct line up the smooth wall.

(5) Superblue   18m   7b+   ★★★
Paul Tattersall 2004
Absolutely superb climbing up a big curving flake, shame there is a no-hands rest before the upper headwall.

(6) Shottabeena   18m   7b+   ★★
Paul Tattersall 2005
Great moves on the steep lower wall.

(7) Astar   20m   6b   ★★★
Paul Tattersall 2004
The left-trending line in the centre of the crag. The 1st bolt is high but only the start is hard; a lower bolt would have been more generous but a clip stick solves it. Curve left up the flake to start, then finish much more steeply. Low in the grade, particularly if you are feeling strong.

(8) Ni Dubh   20m   6b   ★★
Paul Tattersall 2004
Start as for Astar but soon go direct. The crux is at the top getting into the short hanging groove.

(9) Toss   20m   6c   ★★★★
Paul Tattersall 2004
Superb wall climbing. The best route on the crag.

(10) Walkaway   20m   7a
Paul Tattersall 2004
About 3m left of a big fault with a tree. A thin frustrating crux at half-height.

(11) Alice in Wonderland   25m   6a
Paul Tattersall 2009
The fault. Pull on the tree if you need to!

Astar (6b), Creag nan Luch. Climber Blair Fyffe (photo Allen Fyffe)

Highlands West

Creag nan Luch

Colin Meek on Remember to Roll (7a), Creag nan Luch Upper Tier (photo Paul Tattersall)

**12 Psychopomp   20m   6a+ ** **
Paul Tattersall 2005
About 2m right of the fault is this fingery route. Two cruxes, one low down and the other at the top. Originally graded 6b.

13 So Phia so Good   20m   6c *
Paul Tattersall 2008
Clean reddish rock 4m right of the fault. Surprisingly tricky.

14 Unfinished Business   15m   7a+ *
Murdoch Jamieson 2005
Reachy moves to a hard finish.

15 Mister Smooth   15m   6c *
Murdoch Jamieson 2005
The last route on the crag to dry out.

UPPER TIER

An amazing place that is interestingly steep and has the grades to match, most routes being 7b and upwards. The two walls are about 75m apart, separated by an area of damp and lushly vegetated vertical terrain. The outcrop is Lewisian gneiss with pink/pale feldspar rich rock that is smooth and blocky and a black hornblende rich rock which is flakier and softer. It only gets the sun on long summer evenings and is a good place to be in hot weather. Some of the climbs can be slow to dry out in the spring and even through the summer there can be seepage but it often doesn't restrict the climbing. Once the autumn has really set in then forget it, the place is way too cold and uninviting!

TOP TIPS
The central section of the left-hand crag is virtually perma-dry and sheltering from the rain is possible as long as it is not too windy.

APPROACH
Time: 10mins
Walk down the road for 130m and cross the deer fence at the stile and

gate. Branch off right from the path leading to the Lower Tier just after crossing the small burn and follow another worn trail up to the crag.

Left-Hand Crag

(NG 8636 7823)   Alt 120m   North facing

There is an in-situ handrail rope for access to the first three routes which start up a gully at the left end of the crag.

1 Little Leaf   12m   6c *
Paul Tattersall 2006
The short pumpy climb at the top of the grotty gully/ramp.

2 This is Jazz   15m   7b *
Paul Tattersall 2005
Directly up the steep dark wall.

3 King of the Swingers   25m   7a *
Paul Tattersall 2005
Start at the same place as for This is Jazz but head diagonally up rightwards to the lower-off on the skyline. Back clean the runners, then do The Swing.

4 Big Knives   25m   6c *
Paul Tattersall 2005
Start at the bottom of the grotty gully/ramp and climb directly up through King of the Swingers.

5 Whip and Ride   25m   7c *
Paul Tattersall 2005
Fantastic.

6 Stalks   25m   8a+ *
Alan Cassidy 2012, bolted by Paul Thorburn 2005
Climb directly up the wall below the hanging groove to a semi rest at 8m. Turn up the power and make a hard and powerful series of moves to get established in the groove. Follow this with very sustained interest to the top.

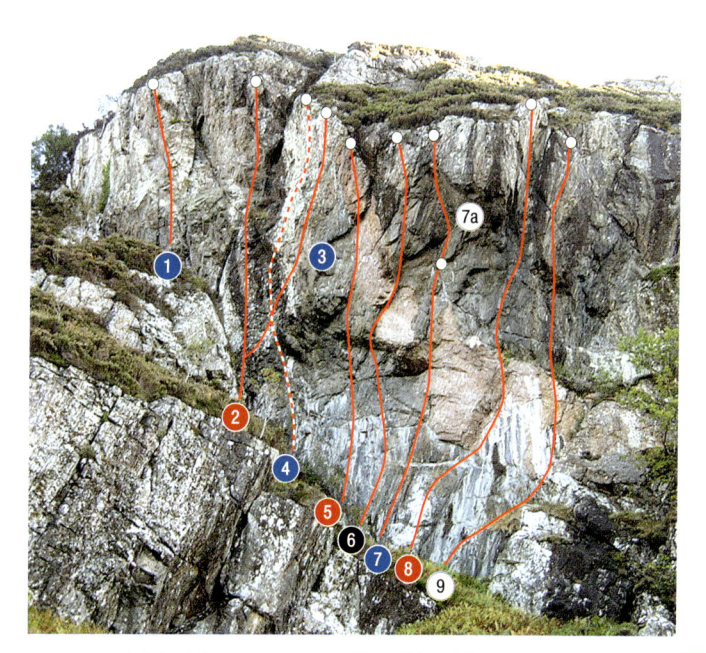

7 Remember to Roll   15m   7a *
Paul Tattersall 2005
Up to a mid-height lower-off. The extension **Remember to Rock 'n' Roll** is a closed project.

8 I'm a Tit, I Love Flying   25m   7b+ *
Paul Tattersall 2005
The right-leaning groove/flake through the pink rock and hanging groove

Creag nan Luch

(crux) in the black rock above. The finish suffers seepage after heavy rain but the crux stays dry.

9 Hola   25m   Open Project   ***
Bolted by Paul Thorburn 2006

Right-Hand Crag
(NG 8632 7822)   Alt 110m   North-West facing

10 Behaving Badly   25m   7a   **
Paul Thorburn 2006
Harder than it looks. Surprisingly varied and sustained up pink rock at the very left edge of the crag.

11 Fighting on all Fronts   25m   7a   **
Paul Thorburn 2006
Start as for Behaving Badly but go direct to the tenuous crux around a sentry box.

12 Happily Married   25m   7a   **
Paul Tattersall, Paul Thorburn 2006
From 3m up left from the flat crag base at its right end, scramble up rightwards to reach the 1st bolt. Excellent slopey fun. Graded for grabbing the anchor chain.

13 The Power of Tears   25m   7a+   **
Paul Tattersall 2005
Start as for Happily Married but scramble further right. Two cruxes, one to get started, one to snag the finishing jug which is just past the chain.

14 Swingers   25m   7b   **
Paul Tattersall 2005
Start up a chimney-groove at the very left end of the flat area. Superbly slopey, spoilt only by a no hands sit rest at half-height.

15 Swallows   25m   6b+
Paul Thorburn 2008
Start from the centre of the flat area. A steep start then sustained slabby climbing. Often wet.

RED MOUSE SLAB
(NG 8637 7843)   Alt 70m   North-West facing
A fine slab above the parking spot. Originally lichenous but cleans to good rough rock and will provide more than the one easy route done to date.

Kuhjo Crag

APPROACH
Time: 5mins
Start as for Creag nan Luch but once over the stile, head up right to the crag. The crag can be seen all the time.

🟢 **Red Mouse   12m   5**
Paul Tattersall 2010
Climb a central shallow scoop left of a heathery fault.

Creag an Oisean - Creag Mhor Thollaidh
(NG 861 778) L19 E434   Alt 180m   South-West facing
Map p297
A good afternoon venue as the sun comes round from about mid-afternoon. The rock is good quality Lewisian Gneiss. At the time of writing the crag was being developed and most lines will be 5s and 6s.

AMENITIES
As for Creag nan Luch p302.

RECOMMENDED TASTY BITES
As for Creag nan Luch p302.

TOP TIPS
Climb on Creag nan Luch Lower Tier in the morning, then walk up past the Upper Tier to follow the sun round on to Creag an Oisean.

DIRECTIONS
On the A832 between Gairloch and Poolewe, about 1.5 miles south of Poolewe, is a rough pull-out on the inside of a bend in the road (NG 859 790). There are panoramic views over Tollie Bay up Loch Maree and of the Fisherfield hills from here.

APPROACH
Time: 25mins
Cross the road from the car park and follow the Tollie Path which is heading over to Loch Maree at Slattadale. After about 20mins the constructed path rises sharply then levels off again. From here the crag is up on the left, a few minutes above the path.

🟢 **Stormy Monday   12m   5**
Paul Tattersall 2010
A line up the left arete starting up an open groove.

🟡 **A Game of Towels   12m   6b ****
Paul Tattersall 2009
Directly up the middle of the wall left of the corner.

🟡 **Oshan Toshan   18m   6a ****
Paul Tattersall 2009
The corner.

🔵 **The Otter Final   12m   7a+ *****
Paul Tattersall 2010
The central line up the plumb vertical wall.

Kuhjo Crag - Poolewe
(NG 863 791) L19 E434   Maps p289, p297
Two crags on a small hill named Tòrr a' Mhuillir on E434. These are unusual crags for Wester Ross, being sheltered by trees. The climbs are short but pack in as much climbing as possible. There is a whole range of grades and even a bit of bouldering. The crags do suffer from seepage, but being sheltered and getting any afternoon sunshine, means they can be considered as all year round venues. The usual Wester Ross midge warning applies.

AMENITIES
As for Creag nan Luch.

RECOMMENDED TASTY BITES
As for Creag nan Luch.

Highlands West

Kuhjo Crag

> **TOP TIPS**
> Clann (pronounced clown) is Gaelic for children.

> **DIRECTIONS**
> About 1.5 miles south of Poolewe on the A832 is a pull out next to a small white building which is a water pumping station (North of Scotland Water authority sign). Park here (NG 8610 7902). The top of both crags can just be seen above the trees to the left when taking in the spectacular view down Loch Maree (not the smaller more obvious crag towards Loch Maree).

KUHJO CRAG
(NG 8631 7913)   Alt 55m   North-West to West facing

> **APPROACH**
> *Time: 6mins*
> Step over the rickety fence right of the pumping station and initially head in the direction of Loch Maree. After almost 100m keep left and drop down through the birch trees to cross the boggy ground leftwards over to the crags which are now hidden in trees. There is a vague path in the heather.

The first four routes are on a sidewall at the left end of the crag.

1 Whittled Into Kindling   8m   6c
Paul Tattersall 2007
Short but steep.

Kuhjo Crag

2 Slave Trade 8m 6c
Paul Tattersall 2007
Short and steep.

3 Cowskull 10m 7a *
Paul Tattersall 2006
A tricky, thin crux finish.

4 Spiderman 8m 6c **
Andy Wilby 2006
Just left of the arete. Perfectly pumpy.

The next route is 10m right of the arete.

5 The River Gods 10m 6a+ *
Paul Tattersall 2006
A wet streak appears at the start after heavy rain.

6 Eco 12m 6c **
Paul Tattersall 2007
A tricky lower wall.

7 Polluted Planet 12m 6c **
Paul Tattersall 2006
A very deceptive slab followed by a long reach on the crux which may be impossible unless you are a tall orang-utan.

8 Permanent Rage 12m 7c+ **
Paul Tattersall, Andy Wilby 2006
The desperate thin crack-line and fingery wall above.

9 Wicked and Weird 12m 7a+ ***
Paul Tattersall 2006
The hanging groove and pumpy finish. Brilliant fun.

10 Don't Kick the Bolt 10m 6a *
Claire Hayden 2006
A slab forming the left wall of a deep groove.

11 Cocohead Arete 10m 6b **
Paul Tattersall 2007
The right arete of the groove. The bolts on the right are an unfinished open project.

Andy Nisbet at home on Cocohead Arete (6b), Kuhjo Crag (photo Sandy Allan)

CLOWN SLAB

(NG 8633 7907)   Alt 65m   South-West facing
All routes are slabby and covered in holds, just perfect for the job.

APPROACH

As for Kuhjo Crag. To get to Clown Slab from Kuhjo Crag (assuming you don't find Clown Slab first), head right (facing up) from its right end. Follow the base of a slightly lower continuation crag and from its end Clown Slab would be visible 30m away except it faces slightly away (50m in total).

1 Futures Bright   10m   4 *
Paul Tattersall 2007
An open slab on the left.

2 The Snatcher   10m   4 **
Paul Tattersall 2007
A more broken slab left of a central crack.

3 Wonders of the Woods   10m   4 *
Paul Tattersall 2007
The central crack.

4 Path to Power   10m   5 **
Paul Tattersall 2007
A slab at the right end, just left of a large perched block.

Goat Crag - Gruinard

(NG 9644 9114) L19 E435   Alt 90m   South-West facing
Map p289   Diagram p314

Without doubt the premiere venue of Wester Ross sport climbing. One of the most obvious crags in the Gruinard area, it stands proud above the Gruinard River behind the estate house at Inchina. The rock is grey Lewisian gneiss which is wonderfully compact and clean. It gets afternoon sunshine and there is often a breeze which can keep the midges at bay, well it's worth a try anyway!

Seepage lines are a hassle after prolonged rain and even during dry spells of weather some routes can suffer bits of overnight seepage that needs the afternoon sun to dry it off, nothing that really gets in the way though. There are still a few lines to bolt up.

AMENITIES

The crag is equidistant between the thriving, small port of Ullapool and the much quieter port of Gairloch. Both places have plenty of shops, accommodation and places to eat and drink. Gairloch virtually closes down on a Sunday whereas Ullapool keeps going, in the summer anyway. North West Outdoors in Ullapool is the only climbing shop in the whole area.

Goat Crag

RECOMMENDED TASTY BITES
The Dundonnell Hotel serves food and the local ale (brewed in Dundonnell) all day. Out at Mellon Charles, The Perfume Studio is worth the trek and stays open till 6pm; it is closed on a Monday. Over in Poolewe the Bridge Cottage Coffee Shop is highly recommended for the good cakes. Otherwise it is up to Ullapool where there is plenty of choice; The Ceilidh Place serves good tea, coffee and food.

TOP TIPS
An all year round venue.

DIRECTIONS
Park just south of the bridge over the Gruinard River which is 1.0 miles north of Gruinard beach car park on the A832; the crag is dramatically obvious from here – NG 9612 9114. Coming from the north, it is one mile south of the prominent crag (Gruinard Jetty Buttress) which almost overlooks the road when it reaches the coast again. Avoid obstructing private parking for people fishing on the river and do not park by the track to Inchina House.

APPROACH
Time: 10mins
Walk over the bridge and turn down a track on the right. Halfway between an initial gate and a dilapidated garage, step over a fence at a place with a log step on each side. There is a vague path from here leading up with a zigzag to the crag.

The second route goes just left of a big patch of ivy.

1 Flowsnake 15m 7b+
Ian Taylor 2012
The steep corner at the left end of the bolt wall. Start up the project Poison Ivy until a hard move leads into the corner. Continue very steeply until able to move right to the Poison Ivy lower off.

Tess Fryer on her way up Mac Talla (7a+/7b), Goat Crag, Gruinard – the best route in Wester Ross (photo Ian Taylor)

Goat Crag

Goat Crag

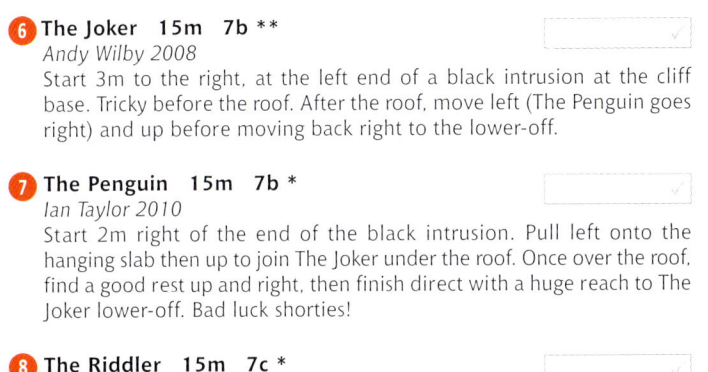

② Poison Ivy   Closed Project
Andy Wilby 2010

③ The Noose   15m   7b+
Ian Taylor 2012
Climb Snow Flake until it moves right to the flake. Move left and make funky moves into a niche. Finish with a strenuous clip.

④ Snow Flake   15m   7a+   ***
Ian Taylor 2010
This is just right of the big patch of ivy. Climbed in a snow storm. Plenty big holds. Lots of fun.

⑤ Batman and Robin   15m   7b   **
Andy Wilby 2008
Start as for Snow Flake but go straight up at the 2nd bolt. Break out right under the small roof. There is a closed project (5a) heading left through the roof and up to the same anchor (no grade yet but hard).

⑥ The Joker   15m   7b   **
Andy Wilby 2008
Start 3m to the right, at the left end of a black intrusion at the cliff base. Tricky before the roof. After the roof, move left (The Penguin goes right) and up before moving back right to the lower-off.

⑦ The Penguin   15m   7b   *
Ian Taylor 2010
Start 2m right of the end of the black intrusion. Pull left onto the hanging slab then up to join The Joker under the roof. Once over the roof, find a good rest up and right, then finish direct with a huge reach to The Joker lower-off. Bad luck shorties!

⑧ The Riddler   15m   7c   *
Ian Taylor 2009
The name says it all. Start 2m to the right of The Penguin.

⑨ Bamboozle   15m   6c   *
Ian Taylor 2010
Clip the first four resin bolts of The Riddler, then break right and follow four stainless expansion bolts back to The Riddler anchor.

⑩ Broken Silence   12m   7c   *
Dave Redpath 2007
A crack-line in a much more overhanging section. Short and burly, and a hassle clipping bolt 3.

⑪ Tom Paine's Bones   15m   6b+   **
Paul Tattersall 2007
Climbs near the arete at the right end of this overhanging section. A steep bouldery start with easier climbing above. A popular variation is starting to the right and bypassing the hard start; 6a+ overall.

⑫ Teepee   20m   6a+   **
Murdoch Jamieson, Colin Meek, Paul Tattersall 2007
The big corner-line.

⑬ Young Man's Link   6c+   *
Breaking right at the 5th bolt to join Too Old to be Famous above its crux gives a good climb.

⑭ Too Old to be Famous   20m   7b   *
Murdoch Jamieson, Colin Meek, Paul Tattersall, Paul Thorburn 2007
The white wall right of the corner has a distinct crux through the mid-height bulge. Young Man's Link allows the upper section to be climbed at 6c+.

⑮ The Mighty Atom   20m   7b+   **
Murdoch Jamieson, Colin Meek, Paul Tattersall, Andy Wilby 2007
A thin right-slanting crack-line leads to an easing before a steep grey shield which provides the crux.

Goat Crag

16 Pensioners' Link   7a+ *
If you feel too old, hand-traverse left below the shield to finish up Too Old to be Famous. Also known as The Combo.

17 Mac Talla   20m   7a+/7b ***
Murdoch Jamieson, Colin Meek, Paul Tattersall 2007
Direct up the wall right of centre provides the best route in Wester Ross!

18 The Prow – Left-Hand Finish   20m   7c ***
Murdoch Jamieson, Colin Meek, Paul Tattersall 2007
Another best route in Wester Ross!! The right edge of the wall.

19 The Prow – Direct Finish   20m   Open Project
Bolted by Paul Tattersall 2007

20 The Prow – Right-Hand Finish   20m   7c+ **
Paul Thorburn 2007
Another superb route. Clipping the last bolt is a heart fluttering quandary.

21 The Leaning Wall   20m   7c+/8a **
Paul Thorburn 2007
Superb. Always dry.

22 The Fun Prow   20m   7c+ *
Ali Coull 2012
A hybrid route linking the bottom half of The Leaning Wall into the top half of The Prow via two bolts.

23 Hydrotherapy   20m   6c+ **
Ian Taylor 2008
Start at the right end of the whitest section. Excellent fun, don't miss out on the tufa pocket at the start!

Tess Fryer getting Hydrotherapy (6c+) at Goat Crag (photo Ian Taylor)

Am Fasgadh

**24 Between the Monsoons   20m   6c+ ** **
Ian Taylor 2008
Sustained and pumpy, starting 1m right but diverging. Nearly always dry. A good warm-up for the crag.

Right again is a full height crack-line which is **Liquidator** (E3 5c).

25 Cloudburst   15m   7a *
Ian Taylor 2011
A line just right of Liquidator going over bulges and slabs to finish with a boulder problem in the sky. Harder for the short. Finishing rightwards as for Caberfeidh gives a more balanced 6b+.

**26 Caberfeidh   15m   6b ** **
Ian Taylor 2011
A line starting just right of Cloudburst and curving left to the same lower-off. Steep and juggy, after a tricky start.

27 War Cry   20m   7b *
Ian Taylor 2012
Climb Caberfeidh to the 4th bolt, then trend up and right to the left-leaning crack in the headwall. Good climbing up the crack leads to a vicious final move.

**28 Fidgey Muckers   25m   7a ** **
Ian Taylor 2012
A line right of Caberfeidh. Two steep sections with a more leisurely middle.

Am Fasgadh - Gruinard

(NG 966 909)   L19 E435   Alt 60m   South-West facing
Map p289   Diagram p318

The original sport crag of the area. Through the winter it is the outdoor climbing wall to the locals. It is a total sun trap and nearly always dry, due geologically to a quartz intrusion that runs diagonally across the crag and sheds the rain off most of the routes. The routes are fairly short but relentless requiring a determined approach. You always leave with that Am Fasgadh Feeling!

AMENITIES
As for Goat Crag.

RECOMMENDED TASTY BITES
As for Goat Crag.

TOP TIPS
Not the best venue in warm weather as the rock quickly gets a greasy feel. Virtually perma-dry. Good bouldering.

DIRECTIONS
As for Goat Crag. Park just south of the bridge over the Gruinard River (NG 9612 9114).

APPROACH
Time: 10mins
Walk over the bridge and turn down a track on the right. Go through the gate at Inchina, the white estate house, and follow the track on the north bank of the Gruinard River. Pass a green tin bothy and where the track bends leftward and back right (before a white estate house) follow a worn path up the bracken covered slope directly to the foot of the crag. Only the top of the crag is just visible from the river side because it sits in a hollow at the cliff base. Alternatively, traverse the cliff base from Goat Crag. 5mins.

1 Toiseach   12m   7b *
Colin Meek, Paul Tattersall 2001
The original route in black rock near the left end. Often wet in the winter.

**2 The Brown Streak   12m   7b+ ** **
Paul Tattersall 2002
Stick-clip the first bolt.

318 Am Fasgadh

Am Fasgadh

3 Warm-Up 10m 7b ★★
Paul Tattersall 2004
The one bolt extension makes it 7b+ if you make the move over the roof.

4 The Pillar 10m 8a ★★
Paul Tattersall 2004
Funky climbing, something different, up the small pillar.

5 Black Sox 12m 7c+ ★★★
Lawrence Hughes 2004
About 2m metres right of the pillar. Hard past the first bolt, then a race to the final dyno before the pump sets in.

6 Black Sox with Direct Finish 10m 8a+ ★★★
Murdoch Jamieson 2011
Start as for Black Sox up to half-height, clipping the first 3 bolts to a bolt on the left. Make a hard long move up and left to a good edge that allows a span left into a crack. More sustained hard moves lead to the chain.

7 Storkie's 15m 8a+ ★★
Paul Thorburn 2005
Hard and bouldery!

8 Bog Talla 12m 7c ★★★
Paul Tattersall 2002
Just right of a stone drying kiln. Step off the structure to start. Hard at half-height, then a thin finish.

9 Primo 25m 7c ★★★
Ian Taylor, Lawrence Hughes 2008
A small white streak right of a bigger one; 7b+ to an intermediate lower-off.

10 The Counter Diagonal 12m Closed Project
Andy Wilby 2009

Richie Betts climbing Black Sox (7c+), Am Fasgadh (photo Ian Taylor)

11 The Crack 25m 7b+ ★
Paul Tattersall 2002
A desperate boulder problem start that can be avoided by stick-clipping the 1st bolt and pulling past it, then it's 6c to the top. There is an intermediate lower-off so that this route, also routes 8 and 11 can finish at the quartz band if the upper section of the crag is wet.

12 B Movie 10m 7a
Paul Tattersall 2007
An easier start to The Crack is 2m to its right.

13 The Shield 15m 7b ★★★
Paul Tattersall, Ian Taylor 2007
A great route. Start up a crack to a diagonal easing, then a headwall.

Highlands West

⑭ Scorchio 15m 7a **
Ian Taylor 2011
Takes a line up the wall right of The Shield, finishing direct if dry enough or more usually, pulling left to The Shield anchor at a slightly harder grade.

⑮ Teasel 15m 6c+ *
Ian Taylor 2011
A route squeezed in between Scorchio and The Groove, with surprisingly good climbing.

⑯ The Groove 15m 6c+ **
Ian Taylor 2007
The real warm-up is some 8m further right, towards the right end of the crag.

Creag nan Òrd - Dundonnell

(NH 1007 8661) L19 E435 Alt 170m North-West facing
Map p289

The crag is clearly visible on the south side of the A832 from Braemore Junction to Dundonnell. The outcrop is very clean Torridonian sandstone offering varied climbing with strenuous sections on the lowest part of crag giving way to vertical rock and steep slabs. At the time of writing there are only four lines, but they offer a substantial amount of quality climbing as all are close to 30m long. There is potential for other shorter routes on both sides of this longer central section.

AMENITIES
The Dundonnell Hotel has a petrol station, but there are no big shops nearby. The nearest independent hostels are Sail Mhor Croft at Camusnagaul and Badrallach Bothy at Badrallach.

RECOMMENDED TASTY BITES
The Dundonnell Hotel has a bar which offers snacks, meals, teas and coffee. Maggie's tearoom at Camusnagaul is another good stop for snacks in a sun room overlooking the loch. It also has a raised decking area with tables outside. There is a small shop further along the road at Durnamuck.

TOP TIPS
The crag dries quickly, catches a lot of breeze and doesn't suffer from any significant seepage so is a good choice when other lower lying crags may be too wet, humid or midgy. A 60m rope is essential. The top of the crag offers a sunny place to admire the view over the loch. The crag catches the evening sun during the summer.

DIRECTIONS
Follow the A832 from Braemore Junction towards Dundonnell. The road takes a sharp left bend 0.8 miles (1.3km) after the turn-off to Badrallach. 0.1 miles after this is a layby on the left, a possible parking place. After a further 0.3 miles is a gravel turn-off on the north side of the road at NG 1040 8716. One car can park here without blocking the entrance and the crag is clearly visible up left on the hillside above.

APPROACH
Time: 20mins
Cross a fence opposite the turn-off and follow the left side of the burn on nearly level ground at first (can be boggy). At a sharp bend in the burn walk directly south-west to the crag.

The routes are on the right and cleaner wall of the crag, the first being just right of the base.

① Guga Direct 28m Closed Project
Colin Meek 2010
Clip the 1st bolt from an obvious ledge and continue strenuously up the steep undercut face. Surmount the bulge to reach the small roof. After difficult moves to get established on the near vertical wall (crux), continue to an independent lower-off. Maybe 7c.

Creag nan Òrd

② Guga 30m 6c+ **
Colin Meek 2008
A long adventure over the best features of the crag offering excellent, strenuous and varied climbing. Start up Guga Direct but move right to an obvious large niche. Make hard moves out of the niche and continue up on more delicate but easier ground.

③ Siostan 26m 6c *
Colin Meek, Alf Chammings 2008
A few metres to the right of Guga Direct is a slab leading up to a large roof below the large niche. Climb delicately to the roof and pull strenuously onto a shelf. Climb to the top of the large niche and then follow Guga to the top.

④ An Sinnoch Mòr 25m 6b+ ***
Colin Meek, Alf Chammings 2008
The next line to the right follows an obvious corner which although short, is sustained and technical but well bolted. Follow the corner and make hard moves over a bulge onto the easier face. Continue up the broken crack-lines and trend carefully left to the lower-off shared with the previous two routes.

⑤ Carnyx 24m 6a **
Colin Meek 2011
The face left of a higher corner offers delicate climbing up immaculate rippled rock. At the time of writing there is a long runout between the 4th and 5th bolts, but there are plans to add an additional bolt. If this hasn't happened yet, then you need to place a 2m sling on the 5th bolt. The crux above the 4th bolt is climbed by moving right and traversing back left, however more direct is better, although harder at 6a+. A lower-off is also expected to be placed soon, however it is easy to top out to place a sling on a spike.

Highlands West

Islands

There are some small sport climbing venues on the Islands; at Castle of Yesnaby on Orkney, at Raasmi on Shetland and four crags on Mull. All are recent, with the participants particularly concerned about upsetting trad climbers in the small climbing communities. A further crag has been bolted in Shetland but its as yet controversial nature has meant that it has not been included in the guide. Access to the Islands by ferry or plane adds another dimension and while it is unlikely that anyone will visit just for sport climbing, the crags can add a different day to a trad climbing trip.

On Mull local enthusiast Colin Moody was spotting potential sport crags while watching controversy on the mainland. After an initial route at Creag Ghillean in the south-west of the island survived through 2009, he recruited friends for drilling at Stac Liath, near the ferry terminal at Craignure in the east of the island, and The Staple in the south.

History by Orkney Climbing Club & Colin Moody

Mull

Colin Moody bought some bolts in 1996 for a couple of routes on the limestone at Balmeanach. After deciding where the bolts would go, he led one route with traditional gear. Julian Fisher was going to help with the bolting of a harder line but also led it on trad gear, although he was keen for it to be retro-bolted.

In 2009 outdoor instructor Andy Spink bolted a route at Creag Ghillean near Tavool, opening the floodgates. The next year Colin and Steve Jones started work on Stac Liath.

Stac Liath (Mull)

Colin Moody checked out the crag around 1982, but there were no obvious natural lines. Years later Michael Tweedley and Danny Brooks both thought it should be bolted. After getting permission from the landowner, the chief of Clan MacLean, Colin and Steve Jones started this in 2010 following Andy Spink's sport route at Creag Ghillean. An earlier MacLean chief tied his wife up and left her to drown on the tidal rock that can be seen from the crag. There is now a lighthouse on the subsequently named Lady's Rock.

The Staple (Mull)

These crags have mostly been used for top roping since the mid-'80s. But in 2011, Colin Moody bolted two lines.

Balmeanach (Mull)

A handful of routes were bolted on the quick drying pillar in 2012. The original two bolt projects have not yet been equipped because they are slow to dry.

Josef Goeth came from Sweden to climb Smoked Out (5+), at Balmeanach, Mull (photo Colin Moody)

History | 323

Mull
1. Stac Liath.....p324
2. Balmeanach .p325
3. Creag Ghillean .p326
4. The Staple.......p326

Orkney
1. Castle of Yesnaby Quarry....p327

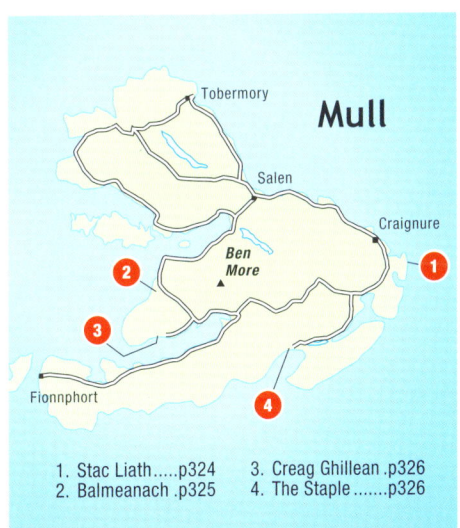

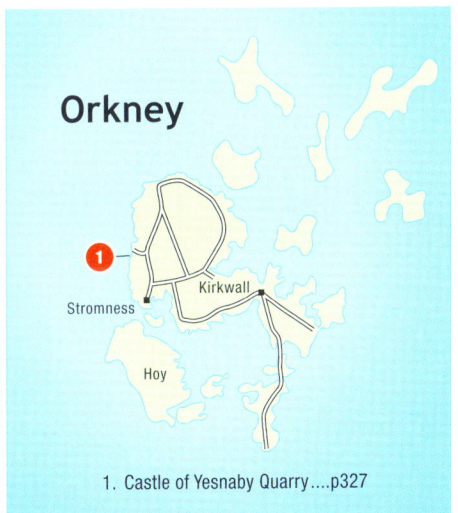

Shetland
1. Raasmi.....p330

The Future (Mull)
There are a few steep fingery lines to go at Stac Liath. More routes are likely at Loch Buie. These will be recorded in the SMC Journal and at <www.colinmoody.com/Site/Topos>

Orkney Mainland - Castle of Yesnaby Quarry
The quarry has been used as a venue for outdoor groups for several years and various bolts had been placed on the top for rigging. The first sports routes appeared in 2003 when Iain Miller and Steve Herd added two routes. With funding from the Orkney Climbing Club, Chris Jex and Tim Deakin then added a further 12 routes in 2007 making this a popular venue with the local climbing fraternity.

Raasmi (Shetland)
The first climbing was in 2003 but only two trad routes were feasible due to the difficulty of gear placements on the main wall and the slightly snappy rock. In 2007 the rest of the crag was cleaned and bolted, mostly by brothers Al and Paul Whitworth, and mainly as a training venue for the climbers living nearby. The original routes were left as trad, but they may be bolted in the future.

Al Whitworth on Revolution (5) at Raasmi, Shetland (photo Paul Whitworth)

Islands

MULL

The island of Mull has four sport crags, recently developed and more routes are likely to follow.

DIRECTIONS

There are two main ferries to Mull, one from Oban to Craignure and a cheaper but longer to drive to (for most) crossing from Lochaline to Fishnish, which is 5 miles (8km) from Craignure <www.calmac.co.uk>.

Stac Liath, South of Craignure - SE Mull

(NM 752 345) L49 E359 Alt 10m East-North-East, South-South-East & West-South-West facing Map p323

Stac Liath is a basalt dyke about 6m wide and which overlooks Duart Point (Black's Memorial) Lighthouse. A fair amount of shipping can be seen and there is also a fine outlook to Ben Nevis, Ben Cruachan and other hills. The midges don't seem to be as bad as the crags on the west of Mull and the area get less rain than expected.

Stac Liath consists of a fast drying west face, a short south facing end that also dries quickly and a longer east face that takes some seepage. There is a ravens' nest on the east face which is occupied some years, so climbing may not be possible in the spring.

DIRECTIONS

The ferry from Oban to Craignure is very convenient for this crag.
By car; drive 1.3 miles south from Craignure and turn left (east) for Kilpatrick (in summer there is a large sign for Duart Castle). Continue for 1.5 miles and park on the left after a slight uphill at the last corner before the castle (NM 749 345).
By bus; In summer buses run three times a day from Craignure to Duart.
By bike; Craignure Tourist Office hires out bikes during the summer and are considering doing so in the winter (01680 812377).

APPROACH
Time: 7mins
Go through a gate and walk diagonally across the field (south-east) then down towards the lighthouse.

WEST FACE

🟠 **Man the Lifeboats** 12m 6a
Colin Moody, Cynthia Grindley 2011
Climb the line at the right-hand side of the face, starting 4m left of the edge.

🟠 **Women and Children First** 12m 6a+ **
Colin Moody, Andy Hyslop, Cynthia Grindley 2011
Climb the wall 2m left of Man the Lifeboats, passing right of a recess about 5m up.

🟠 **Breeches Buoy** 12m 6b **
Colin Moody, Cynthia Grindley 2011
The third route from the edge. Climb up easy rock to a high bolt in the recess. Go over a bulge with difficulty then continue up.

SOUTH FACE

There are two ribs facing the lighthouse.

🟢 **The Saving Light** 12m 5
Colin Moody 2010
Start up the left-hand rib, step right and bridge up the rift between the ribs.

🟢 **Let There be Light** 12m 5 *
Colin Moody 2010
Climb the right-hand rib to finish slightly left. At a ledge move left to the top of The Saving Light.

EAST FACE

The right end of the face is the highest; left of this the rock is easier angled with some grass ledges. Left again is a clean scoop taken by Shipwrecked.

Closed Project
Colin Moody 2012
Start left of Shipwrecked and climb a left-facing scooped corner up leftwards to the top. Traverse right and finish up the easy top section of Shipwrecked.

Shipwrecked   16m   6a+   **
Colin Moody, Steve Jones 2010
Climb the scoop and continue between the heather breaks to the rib above.

Closed Project
Colin Moody 2012
A line just right of Shipwrecked, moving left to finish up the easy top section of Shipwrecked.

Balmeanach, Ardmeanach, SW Mull

(NM 442 322)   L48 or L49 E373   Alt 50m   West facing   Map p323

This is an unusual cliff, possibly unique, composed of quartz conglomerate topped by limestone, so the holds are angular rather than round. The main central face is slow to dry but the left and right sections are quick to dry. Some easy routes have been soloed on the boulders below the cliff. The sport routes are on the left-hand pillar. There are a couple of creaking flakes that should be treated gently.

DIRECTIONS
From Salen head west, then follow the road (B8037) along the south side of Loch na Keal past the Gribun cliffs. When the road starts to gain height, take a minor road on the right past a house to a car park (NM 448 334).

APPROACH
Time: 20mins
Follow the footpath to Mackinnon's Cave (going round left of the farm buildings), boggy in places. After dropping down towards the shore the crag comes into sight on the left. As an alternative dropping down towards the shore, walk left along the cliff-top and abseil in.

LEFT-HAND PILLAR

Underexposed   12m 6a *
Colin Moody 2012
The second line left of the flake-line. Move left at the top to the anchor of the next route.

Flashing Images   12m 5+ *
Colin Moody 2012
Climb up just left of the flake-line.

Are You a Man?   12m   5 *
Colin Moody 2012
There is a step on the ground around the middle of the pillar. Start left of the step and climb the flake-line to the lower-off of Thirty One.

Thirty One   12m   5+ *
Colin Moody 2012
Start just left of the step.

Smoked Out   12m   5+ *
Colin Moody 2012
Start right of the step.

Incomplete   12m   5+ *
Colin Moody 2012
The next route right.

Ready   12m   5 *
Colin Moody 2012
A line just left of the right edge of the pillar.

Mull

MAIN FACE

🟠 **La Paroi Noire** 16m 6b **
Colin Moody 2012
A line on the left side of the face. Climb up to a right-facing corner, then over the overhang and continue up.

Creag Ghillean - Ardmeanach, SW Mull

(NM 455 272) L48 or L49 E373 Alt 60m South facing Map p323

This dolerite crag can be seen by looking across the bay to the north from the road to Fionnphort and Iona. There are also trad climbs which are on good sound rock, but there is seepage so three days of good dry weather will be needed for some of the routes. It is steep, however, and the odd shower does not affect a lot of the routes. Ravens may nest on the crag, and if so, avoid climbing in the spring.

APPROACH

Park at the National Trust car park just past Tiroran (NM 478 275). Walk or cycle along the continuation track (passing aerials) till the forest ends (2km from the car park). The crag lies below; an old fence runs down to the left (west) end of the crag. About 30mins walk. Walk in from either end or abseil from pine trees.

🟢 **Hendrix** 10m 5
Andy Spink, Ben Starkie 2009
The only sport route on the crag in 2011 is easily seen around the centre of the crag. Move up right to gain bolts on a prow, which gives lovely steep climbing with good holds. Either belay on trees at the top or lower off the top bolt.

The Staple, Loch Buie - South Mull

(NM 602 247) L48 or L49 E375 Alt 20m South facing Map p323

This basalt crag (Druim an Aon Stapuill) was once a sea-cliff so is undercut in places, but it is now on a raised beach. From right to left, the sections of cliff are Fisherman's Slab, The Arch (Staple), Queen Victoria, some overhanging cliffs, then Bat Rock with 2 sport climbs at present.

ACCESS RESPONSIBILITIES

The track in front of the crag is popular with walkers. An attempt has been made to equip the routes when there was nobody around. The buttress forming the profile of Queen Victoria is a well known landmark and is probably best left without bolts.

DIRECTIONS

From Craignure, head south on the A849 towards Bunessan. Turn left after 6 miles (10km) and drive for 8 miles (13km) to Loch Buie. After reaching Loch Buie, bear right past the triangular monument, from where the crag can be seen ahead. Continue for 100m over two small burns and park near the bridge.

APPROACH

Time: 5mins
Walk along the continuation track past Fisherman's Slab, The Arch, Queen Victoria and some overhanging rock to the last buttress, Bat Rock, which is below an oak tree.

BAT ROCK

🟢 **Mass of Knots** 12m 5+ *
Colin Moody 2011
Climb the rib left of a left-slanting vegetated crack. Move right above the bulge and finish below the oak tree.

🟢 **Nobody Listening** 14m 5+ *
Colin Moody 2011
Climb up to the right of the left-slanting vegetated crack, then move left above the bulge to the finish of Mass of Knots.

Orkney

ORKNEY MAINLAND
Castle of Yesnaby Quarry

(HY 219 153) L6 E463   Non-tidal   North facing   Map p323
Diagrams p327, p328

The Orkney Isles off the far north coast of Scotland have a long tradition of adventurous trad climbing, but are definitely not associated with sport climbing!

AMENITIES
The harbour town of Stromness has all amenities; grocery store, cash machine, petrol station, hotels, B&B, shops, cafes and restaurants.

RECOMMENDED TASTY BITES
Try Julia's Bites opposite the ferry terminal in Stromness.

TOP TIPS
Bring a trad rack too!

DIRECTIONS
Orkney is best reached by Northlink ferries from Scrabster (near Thurso) to Stromness, or by Pentland Ferries from Gills Bay (north of Wick) to St Margarets Hope. For full details of travel and accommodation details see <www.visitorkney.com> or contact the tourist information office (01856 872856).

Castle of Yesnaby Quarry lies beside the popular and impressive sea-stack of Castle of Yesnaby, 5 miles (8km) north of Stromness. Unless you have a car, the best means of travel is by taxi (or hire a bike). From Stromness, the quarry is reached by following the A965 to the outskirts of Stromness then turning left on the A967 which is signposted to Skara Brae and Skaill House.

This is followed for 2.5 miles (4km) until at a sharp right-hand bend, turn left onto the B9056 for 400m before making a left turn at the signpost marked Yesnaby. Parking is at the car park by the old military buildings at the end of the road.

APPROACH
Time: 15mins
Walk south to the ancient millstone quarry, which lies just to the north of the stack itself.

RIGHT-HAND WALL
The routes are described right to left.

1 Mr. Tim   10m   5+
Tim Deakin 2007
Start on the raised platform below a small undercut on the right-hand end. A couple of thin moves lead to a vague flake-line which is followed to the top (2 bolts for belay on top).

Orkney

2 **Mr. Chris** 10m 6a *
Chris Jex 2007
About 2m left of the last route, follow the vague crack-line direct to the top (belay as for the last route)

3 **High Tide Alternative** 10m 6a+ *
Iain Miller 2003
Starting 3m left of Mr Chris, this crimpy route follows a very vague crack to a small overhung corner.

4 **Splashing Out** 13m 6c+
Steve Herd 2003
Start 6m to the left is an obvious thin crack. Ascend the crack to a small ledge (rest), followed by a hard sequence to a good pocket and the top.

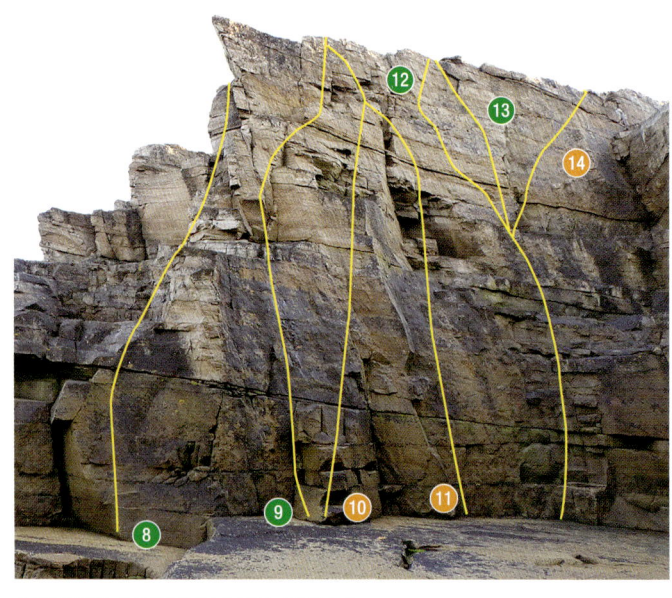

UPPER LEFT-HAND WALL

This wall gives three vague crack-lines with a stake and bolt anchors on top.

5 **The Quarry Man** 7m 5+
Chris Jex 2007
The left-hand line direct to the top.

6 **Up the Middle** 8m 6a *
Tim Deakin 2007
The central thin crack followed direct.

7 The Stretch   8m   6a+   *
Chris Jex 200
The right-hand line has a hard move to reach a small crimp after the 1st bolt.

LOWER LEFT-HAND WALL
Affected by a very high tide and a westerly wind.

8 The Prow   13m   4+
Tim Deakin 2007
On the left a short wall leads to a ledge with a blocky rib on the right which is followed to a small ramp to finish.

9 Wet Feet   13m   5+
Chris Jex 2007
Start 4m right of The Prow. Climb the black slab to a large ledge (possible belay) which is followed by further ledges direct to the top.

10 Rib Wall   13m   6b   *
Tim Deakin 2007
Start in the open corner with a hard move to the 2nd bolt, then climb direct to the big ledge using the rib on the right. Trending right, climb to the next ledge and the top.

11 Daddy Long Legs   13m   6a+
Chris Jex 2007
To the right of Rib Wall is a protruding nose of rock which is climbed awkwardly, then via a slab on the right which leads to a ledge below an undercut. Move up the wall on the left to finish as for Rib Wall.

The next three routes have a common start to reach a big ledge.

12 Sunset Slab Left-Hand   13m   5+   **
Tim Deakin 2007
Climb up the corner in the bay to the large ledge. Trend left up ledges

Ian Rendall climbing Mr Chris (6a), Castle of Yesnaby Quarry, attended by Greg Whitton, Colin Linklater and Baillie the dog (photo Ian Rendall)

until in the centre of the slab, then move up to climb direct to the top in a fine position.

13 Sunset Slab   13m   5+ ★★
Tim Deakin 2007
From the large ledge, climb the slab direct until it is possible to move left to reach the top again in a fine position.

14 Olive Oil   14m   6a+
Chris Jex 2007
From the large ledge, move right to reach a ledge below the top wall (possible nut belay on right). An awkward mantelshelf is followed by a rising rightward traverse to the top (2 bolts for belay on top).

SHETLAND MAINLAND
Raasmi

(HU 228 802)   L3 E469   Partially Tidal   West facing   Map p323

Shetland's first sport crag. It offers varied climbing on good sheltered rock, and is a fine option for a summer's evening as it catches the evening sun. The first three routes are non-tidal, but the others require a low tide and a calm sea. There is also a small bouldering traverse wall on the beach to the west of the crag. The whole traverse is around V6 but easier variants can be done. The landing is mostly sand so mats are not needed.

AMENITIES
The nearest shops are at Hillswick, Ollaberry or Brae, Ollaberry and Brae also having petrol. The nearest pub is the St Magnus Bay Hotel at Hillswick. There are no hostels on Shetland Mainland; the cheapest accommodation is at camping böds, <www.camping-bods.com>.

RECOMMENDED TASTY BITES
The Braewick cafe sources meat and veg from their own adjoining croft.

DIRECTIONS
In 2012 there are daily sailings in both directions from Aberdeen to Lerwick in Shetland, a 12hr crossing; see <www.northlinkferries.co.uk>. There are regular flights from Edinburgh, Glasgow, Aberdeen and Inverness to Sumburgh, 25 miles south of Lerwick; see <www.loganair.co.uk>. For full details of public transport and accommodation on Shetland, see <http://visit.shetland.org>.

Eshaness is a peninsula in the north-west of Shetland Mainland. Here is much of Shetland's trad climbing. From the B9078 which heads out on to the peninsula, take the Leascole road and follow this over a cattle grid and to Ure Croft at the end of the road. Park here (HU 225 801), taking care not to block any gates or the turning area.

APPROACH
Time: 5-10mins
Walk through a gate next to a walled garden, then north over the brow and alongside a fence, eventually crossing a stream on metal planks. The crag is now clearly visible in front of you. The belays are in place at the top of the climbs (not lower-offs). There are also belays situated further

back from the cliff allowing self belaying at the crag or for abseils back down. The crag is sheltered and the first three routes are non-tidal, but the others require a low tide and a calm sea to guarantee access. The two original trad climbs at the crag, climbed in 2003 have been left unbolted and require a small trad rack. Routes are described right to left.

1 Magicman 6m 4
Al & Paul Whitworth 2007
The first route up this short wall.

2 GG Grease 6m 4+
Al & Paul Whitworth 2007
Nice moves through the better rock

3 Turtle Turtle Up 8m 5
Paul Whitworth 2007
Mantel the ledge and thug your way to the top!

4 Ure Kiddin' 8m 6a *
Al Whitworth 2007
A brilliant route. Start right (tricky) and keep right for the full effect!

5 Raasmi 8m 4+ **
Paul Whitworth 2007
The line of least resistance up the pocketed wall.

The corner crack to the left is **Werther's Original** (VD). The obvious crack left again is **Heritage** (HVS 5a) and harder than it looks.

6 Revolution 12m 5
Paul Whitworth 2007
Steeper than it looks.

7 Wavey Longs 15m 5 *
Andy Long 2007
Start up Revolution to mid-height, then traverse left to finish up Resolution.

8 Continuum 12m 5 *
Al Whitworth 2007
Interesting and varied. Reachy in places.

9 Resolution 12m 5+
Paul Whitworth 2007
Climb the wall on pockets up to the huge flake. Tricky start move.

10 Hilti's Big Adventure 18m 6c *
Al Whitworth 2011
Traverse the overhangs and finish up the corner.

Paul Whitworth on Turtle Turtle Up (5) (photo Al Whitworth)

Minor & Historical Venues

Cambusbarron Quarries - Fourth Quarry

(NS 770 921)   Alt 90m   West facing
The large open quarry contains many trad lines but has two sport routes. Follow the quarry track beyond the barrier for 200m, then swing left into the open quarry base (5mins).

● **Scales of Injustice   12m   7b+ ★★**
Mark Somerville (2001)
An unusual but good route on the off-vertical wall which is hidden behind trees near the left edge of the quarry face. Technical moves lead through a crux bulge with slightly easier climbing above. The demise of a large block near the top has made the route slightly harder. 5 bolts to a lower-off.

● **Unnamed   10m   6b+**
This lies well to the right – grade unconfirmed. 5 bolts to a lower-off.

Balgone Heughs

(NT 563 824)
A long north-west facing escarpment in the trees about 1 mile to the south of North Berwick Law. The land lies in the ownership of the nearby Balgone House. The rock is not great but between 10-15 routes of up to 7b+ were developed. Routes were never recorded and for some reason most (if not all) the hangers were removed, although the studs remain. It may be worth approaching the landowner with a view to redeveloping this cliff.

Dalachy Quarry

(NT 209 863)
A remarkable south facing square-cut hole of huge proportions just off the A921 between Aberdour and Burntisland in Fife. Known as the shoe box there were a number of manufactured fingery routes from 6c to 7b+. Although sheltered from the elements the rock can suffer from condensation. The rock is Newbigging sandstone and the climbs are obvious but due to access problems at the time, the hangers were removed although the studs remain. With the current access legislation it is perhaps worth investigating again. The quarry is located about 1 mile to the east of Aberdour. Park just off the main road at a tree stump and take the left-hand track, turning off right, just before a house, onto a path leading to the quarry.

Northfield Quarry

(NO 431 285)   Alt 70m   North facing
A basalt outcrop in a small quarry visible on the hillside above the Fife (south) end of the Tay Bridge. Four short routes were bolted in the mid–'90s but the hangers removed soon after. This was not due to a debate over sport climbing here, but because the locals failed to recompense the bolter as promised. The rock requires care.

St. Douane's Den

(NJ 496 683)
A cave at the north-west (Portknockie) end of the sandy beach in Cullen Bay on the Moray coast was bolted but the short routes may never have been climbed and the bolts are now rusty. This cave and others nearby have become a good bouldering venue – see <www.scottishclimbs.com/wiki/Cullen_Caves>.

Index

100 Ways to be a Good Girl	143	Angels with Dirty Faces	46	Badly Overdrawn Boy	157	Bend it like Beckham	73
21st Century Citizen	146	Ankle Biter	273	Bahama Breeze	29	Bends, The	99
62 West Wallaby Street	201	Another Green World	153	Ball Park Incident	299	Benny and the Banshees	115
7th Wave	197	Anvilfire	50	Balmashanner Bomb Shell, The	168	Benny Goodman – King of Swing	115
99 Flake	168	Anyway, Anyhow Anywhere	254	Balmashanner Buttress	171	Benny Hill	115
		Apollo	42	Bamboozle	315	Benny Lane	116
A		Appliance of Violence	21	Bananas in Pyjamas	41	Benny's Black Streak	115
'Ave it!	276	April's Arete	163	Bang Tidy	246	Benny's Groove	115
Abbey Habit, The	199	Aqua Vitae	25	Barging into the Presence of God	199	Benny's Route Left-Hand	22
Above the Line	281	Arc of a Diver	94	Bark Bacherache	139	Benny's Route Right-Hand	22
Abstract Art	20	Arcadia	64	Barrel of Laughs	165	Bennydorm	115
Aches in Provence	231	Are You a Man?	325	Bassoon	245	Between the Lines	183
Aching Arms and Dragging Heels	35	Ariel Man, The	101	Batman and Robin	315	Between the Monsoons	317
Admission	60	Arm Carnage	56	Battle Axe	298	Beware Geeks Bearing Gifts	217
Aerodynamic	187	Arms Limitation	99	Battle of the Bulge	265	Beware of the Wellyfish	225
After the Flood	94	Armygeddon	181	Batweeman	143	Beyond the Call of Nature	174
Ag Rippa	285	Art Attack	111	Be Calmed	201	Bheagining, The	280
Age of Aquarius	84	Artillery Arete	214	Beach Ball of Kirriemuir, The	155	Bible Babble	46
Age Old Problem Rears its Ugly Head, The	97	Astar	305	Beat the Bulge	158	Big Bad Wolf, The	126
Ain't no Rolling Stone	184	At Ma Wick's End	287	Becalmed	153	Big Girls Blouse	224
Air Berries	246	At the Crossroads of Destiny and Desire	194	Beef Monster	29	Big J, The	185
Air on a G String	245	Atlantic Strikes Back, The	50	Been Caught Stealin'	84	Big Knives	307
Air Raid	216	Atonement	73	Beg Issue, The	116	Big Lug	222
Airhead	29	Autobahn	176	Beg Pardon	117	Bill and Benny the Flower Pot Men	114
Alice in Wonderland	305	Automatic	232	Beg to Differ	116	Bitter Sweet Symphony	247
Alien Artefact	140	Awaken	25	Beg'tastic	116	Black Adder	70
Alien Breed	223	Awe!	161	Beggar, The	116	Black Again	73
All Chalk, No Traction	154	Axe Grinder	299	Beggar's Banquet	110	Black and Decker?	216
All Electric	87	Axiom	60	Beggar's Banquet	116	Black as Bill's Mothers	71
All the Arts	302			Beggars are Coming to Town, The	225	Black Beard	71
Ally's in Wonderland	116	**B**		Beggars Belief	115	Black Beauty	70
Amateur Hacker	49	B Movie	319	Begone	117	Black Death	71
An Dialtaig	89	Back from the Brink	240	Beguile	115	Black Dog	71
An Sinnoch Mòr	321	Bad Attitude	21	Behaving Badly	308	Black Eyed Peas	72
Anarchic Law	34	Bad Religion	102			Black for Good	72
		Badass Honey Badger	277			Black Friday	71

Entry	Page
Black Hawk	72
Black Heart	70
Black Holes of Calcutta	73
Black in the Day	73
Black in Time	73
Black int' Back	155
Black is Back	72
Black Jack	71
Black Magic (Black Rock)	73
Black Magic (Lower Lednock)	121
Black Mamba	71
Black Pig, The	71
Black Power	73
Black Sabbath	70
Black Seal of Approval	70
Black Sox	319
Black Streak	272
Black to Black	71
Black Velvet	73
Black where we Belong	72
Blackberry	72
Blackout	52
Blade Runner	282
Blind Faith	101
Blithe Spirit	96
Blobstrop	246
Blood Diamond	49
Blood Fire	49
Bloody Shocking	88
Blue Velvet	68
Boarding Party	155
Body Blow	49
Bodysnatcher	223
Bodyswerve	49
Bog Talla	319
Boldfinger	91
Bomber	183
Bon the Edge	155
Bonsai Pipeline	255
Bonzai	124
Boomhead	137
Born of Frustration	240
Born to Run	300
Bosch	242
Boulder Problem	252
Bovnahackit	297
Brain Wave	197
Brass Monkeys	144
Breathe the Pressure	26
Breeches Buoy	324
Brian the Snail	183
Brian the Snail Direct	183
Bridging the Gap	86
Brin it On	263
Bringing out the Big Guns	214
Broad Side	205
Broken Silence	315
Brown Streak, The	317
Buccaneer	295
Bulldog Drummond	67
Buoys of Summer	199
Burn Baby, Burn	112
Burn it Up	113
Burning Barrels	279
Burning Desire	174
Burning with Anxiety	191
Burnt Offerings	112
Butt Ugly Martians	224
By Hook or By Crook	159

C

Entry	Page
Cabaret	146
Caberfeidh	317
Caledonia Dreaming	143
Can't see the F in	
Elephant Anywhere	221
Caned and Unable	154
Captains of Crush	264
Car Pit Baggers	180
Carnyx	321
Carry On Up the Corbetts	102
Carsonagenic	95
Casanostra	22
Cast Adrift on the Ocean of Uncertainty	194
Cat Scratch Fever (Rockdust)	146
Cat Scratch Fever (Ley)	162
Caught in the Act	165
Caught Red-Handed	193
Cauldron of Fire	121
Cauldron of Spite	98
Cease Fire	92
Celebration Day	35
Ceuse Jimmy	105
Chain Lightning	93
Champ at the Bit	285
Charred and Damned Desire	185
Chasing Dragons	156
Chasing Shadows	68
Chasing the Bandwagon	104
Cheeky Madam	233
Chemical Generation, The	140
Children of the Revolution	93
Chimera	110
Chip 'n' Pin	67
Chocoholics	106
Chopping Block, The	133
Christmas 1937	264
Circuit Bored	88
Circuit Breaker	87
Clairvoyant	121
Clam Chowder	86
Clansman, The	275
Clash of the Titans	44
Climb and Punishment (Diamond, Glen Ogle)	94
Climb and Punishment (Rob's Reed)	179
Climbers Wear Platforms	194
Cloak and Dagger	272
Close Shave, A	212
Closer, The	237
Cloudburst	317
Clutching at Straws	105
Cock o' the North	219
Cocohead Arete	311
Codfather, The	208
Cold Shoulder	66
Collie Corner	241
Collywobbles	275
Comfort Machine, The	170
Concentration Cramp	209
Confession of Faith	137
Conglomarete	269
Consolidated	22
Constant Flux	273
Consternation	296
Constipated Miser	301
Continuum	331
Cony the Calvinist	101
Corvus	271
Counter Diagonal, The	319
Cow and Chicken	200
Cowal Crusaders	50
Coward of the County	106
Cowskull	311
Crack, The	319
Cracking the Lines	86
Crazy Horse	282
Creative Commoners	277

Credit Crunch (Newtonhill)	235
Credit Crunch (Leacanashie)	295
Crescendo	245
Crocodile Corner	159
Crossed Wire	86
Crossfire	52
Crossroads	231
Crouching Tiger	45
Crowing at the Enemy	139
Crushed by the Wheels of Industry	140
Crystal Myth	156
Curse of the Faeroes	210
Curse of the Strong	276
Curtain Call	160
Cut Loose	95
Czech Connections	284

D

D.I.V.O.R.C.E	175
Da Ma Wick	287
Daddy Long Legs	329
Dam That River	62
Dance into the Groove	127
Dangleberries	246
Dark Sar-Chasm	213
Dark Side, The (Boltsheugh)	232
Dark Side, The (Moy Rock)	272
Dark Skies (Roadside Wall, Glen Ogle)	108
Dark Skies (Wild Swans)	83
Darkmoon Rising	165
Darkness Falling	34
Dashed Pebbles	285
David's Route	213
Dazed and Confused	105
Dead Pull	179
Deadheads	231
Deaf Violinist, The	299
Death is a Gift	267
Death is the Hunter	182
Deathwish 2	253
Debt of Pain	98
Declaration of Intent	196
Deer Hunter	175
Deil, The	121
Delivery Man	169
Demolition Man	185
Dennis Caravan	178
Dennis the Menace	167
Desperate Dan	168
Desperate Measures	184
Despicable Me	262
Devastation Generation	25
Devil's Advocate	67
Diagon Alley	205
Diamond Back	61
Diamond Groove	61
Diamond in the Rough	250
Dig Deep	158
Digital Quartz	92
Digital Sclerosis	169
Dilemma	54
Dinnet Do It	252
Direct Access	186
Direct Start	194
Dirt Digger	98
Dirty Deeds	89
Dirty Dozen, The	106
Dirty Harry	179
Dirty Sanchez	25
Disney Look Too Bad	200
Diss!	187
Distant Cries	44
Do as I Say not as I Do	203
Dodged a Bullet	263
Dog Town	236
Dogmatic	154
Dogs Abuse	242
Dogs of War	242
Doigt Attack	222
Don't Blame Me!	225
Don't Bridget Neilson	212
Don't Do Today what you can do Tomorrow	141
Don't Fight the Feeling	107
Don't Kick the Bolt	311
Don't Knock the Block	143
Don't Look Down In Anger	275
Don't Pass Me By	97
Done and Dusted	160
Double Bassoon	245
Down to the Last Heartbreak	138
Down Under	234
Downshifting	146
Dracula	249
Dracula True Finish	249
Dread Knot	205
Dregs, The	232
Drifting Too Far from Shore	55
Driller Killer	182
Drip Drip Drip	299
Driven round the Benny'd	115
Driven to Distraction	98
Drookit	235
Dropping like Flies	163
Drowning by Numbers	165
Drowning Pool, The	98
DTS Spirit	126
Dubh be Dubh	155
Duchess, The	73
Dum Dum Boys	20
Dump, The	302
Dun Moan'in1	119
Dunira or Die	119

E

E'evil Dead, The	199
Eany	232
Easy Ley	163
Easy Over	92
Easy Slab	273
Eat Y'self Fitter	97
Eco	311
Edge of Darkness	185
Edge of Ecstasy, The	95
Edge of Reason	280
Edge, The	47
Edgelands	252
Egyptiana Jones	147
Eight Year Itch	212
El Boa	160
El Captain	160
El Mundo Fanatico	80
El Ringo	127
Electric Sunday	101
Electrodynamics	86
Elysium	42
Embrace My Weakness	99
End Justifies the Means, The	92
End of Silence, The	136
End of the Line	61
End of the Road	178
Endgame Project	56
Enforcer, The	179
Engullfed	216
Ephemeral Artery	273
Esperanza	67
Essential Balmashanner, The	171

Index

Entry	Page
Event Horizon	41
Ever Ready Arete	215
Every Last Drop	137
Everything Must Go	185
Exodus	188
Ex-Pert Route, The	223
Extreme Lichen	284
Eye Balls Out	267

F

Entry	Page
Face the Heat	112
Faithless	143
Fantastic Four	201
Far Beyond Driven	98
Far From the Malham Crowds	84
Fascination Streak	243
Fast and Furious	126
Fat Boy Slims	159
Fat Chance	103
Fat Eagles Fly Low	102
Fat Groove, The	62
Fat Man Starts to Fall	166
Fat of the Land	158
Fated Mission	59
Fated Path	59
Father Figure	132
Fear and Self Loathing	84
Fear of the Dark	132
Feeding Frenzy	210
Fidgey Muckers	317
Fight Fire with Fire	97
Fight or Flight	103
Fighting the Feeling	64
Fight the Flab	103
Fighting off the Vultures	270
Fighting on all Fronts	308
Filth Infatuated	24
Final Straw, The	267
Fingers of Fudge	107
Fire at Will	184
Fire Down Below	185
Fire in the Hold	174
Fire Power	50
Firestarter	169
First Night Nerves	195
First to Fall	185
Fishing for Compliments	165
Five Magics	163
Flaked Out	191
Flashing Images	325
Fleet of Foot	285
Fleet Street	283
Flesh E'eter	199
Flesh for Fantasy	25
Flight of the Mad Magician	182
Flown back from Boston	35
Flowsnake	313
Fly, The	274
Flyboy	159
Flying Scotsman	299
Fogtown	33
Footfall	164
Forbidden Forest	275
Forbidden Fruit	143
Forfaraway	175
Fort Dundurn Gurner, The	119
Foundering on the Rocks of Obsession	194
Frankenstein	127
Fred Flintstone	200
Free Trader	294
Freebooter	294
Friend or Foe	287
French Connection UK	127
French Onion Soup	147
Fretting over Nothing	176
Friendly Fire	50
Frigging in the Rigging	96
Fully Charged	215
Fun Prow, The	316
Futures Bright	312

G

Entry	Page
Galley Slave	209
Game of Towels, A	309
Game of Two Halves, A	265
Game Over	299
Gatecrashers Galore	176
Gentle Mass Touching	25
George's Bush	119
Get a Grip	97
Get Shorty	177
GG Grease	331
Ghost Trail	105
Gibbet, The	294
Gift Link, The	267
Gift Wrapped	283
Gillette	262
Gimme Shelter	147
Ginger's Jewels	158
Give Me Sunshine	123
Giza Break	267
Glaikit Folly	156
Glass Ceiling, The	140
Glen Bolt'achan Big Gun's	119
Glug	281
Go West	234
Gods Gift	261
Going through on Aggregate	174
Golden Shot, The	184
Gone to the Dogs	242
Good Boy Jo Jo	179
Good Training for Something	125
Goosey Goosey Gander	67
Gordon's Route	292
Gorgon	214
Gotta Sin to Be Saved	97
Grade Escape, The	213
Grand Day Out, A	201
Grand Jorassic	161
Grand Theft Auto	176
Granola Head	133
Grapes of Ratho, The	31
Grasping the Nettle	177
Grassy Knoll	154
Gravity's Rainbow	171
Great Rock 'n' Route Swindle, The	277
Greenhouse Defect, The	107
Grey Edge	70
Groove, The (Am Fasgadh)	320
Groove, The (Ardvorlich)	55
Grooviliscious	124
Gross Indecency	94
Grotesque	213
Ground Clearance	285
Grounded	203
Gruesome	214
Guga	321
Guga Direct	320
Guilt Trip, The	97
Gullable	216
Gulliver's Travels	216
Gurrie Appeal	65
Gurrie, The	64
Gut Feeling	158
Gutbuster	295

H

Entry	Page
Haarbinger	210

Index

Hairdubh	303	Heinous De Milo	254	Hurlyburly	125	Jailbird	283
Half Breed	21	Hell Bent for Lycra	170	Hydrotherapy	316	Jaws of the Law	33
Half Covered	106	Hell's Bells	185	Hyper Hyper	98	Jenny	277
Half the Battle	170	Hendrix	326			Jerusalem	44
Hamish Teddy's Excellent Adventure	131	Heritage	331	**I**		Jester	249
		Herring, The	270	I Can't Believe it's Not Black	71	Jib Test	282
Hammerhead and the Quarryman	127	Hidden World	275	Ice Scream Wall	168	Joining the Debt Set	157
		Hideous Kinky	80	Idiot Savant	253	Joint Account	301
Hammertime	52	High and Dry	106	Idiot Wind	103	Joker (Red Wall Quarry)	249
Hanau's Quint	207	High and Mighty	81	If Six was Nine	25	Joker, The (Goat Crag)	315
Hand of Andromeda	42	High Pitched Scweem	136	Igneous Intruder	34	Jug of Jug Haul, The	215
Hang Free	95	High School Blues	284	I'm a Tit, I Love Flying	307	Jumbobum	210
Hang On!	104	High Stepper	204	Immaculate Conception	67	Jungle Run	68
Hang Over	292	High Tension Lead	86	Imodium Crack	29	Junk Man Blues	183
Hanger 18	223	High Tide Alternative	328	Imodium Wall	29	Jupiter	110
Hanging out on the Smalls	95	High Voltage	174	Impaled on the Horns of Indecision	193	Justice	144
Hannibal	224	Highland Cling	81	In at the Deep End	192		
Happily Married	308	Hill Billies	157	In too Deep	215	**K**	
Happiness in Slavery	24	Hill has Eyes, The	157	In with the In Crowd	194	Kazakhstani Castaway	204
Happy Campus	104	Hilti	242	Incomplete	325	Keel, The	237
Happy Hooker	124	Hilti's Big Adventure	331	Incredible Sulk, The	242	KG Max	278
Hard Labour	154	Hive of Industry	97	Indian Summer	255	Kick Ass Yoga	302
Hardy	233	Hobble	83	Infinite Gravity	97	Kids with Guns	261
Hare	292	Hola	308	Infrarete	112	Killer Wail	211
Harley Quinn	249	Hold the Press	108	Insane in the Membrane	124	Killing Fields, The	181
Harry Snotter	121	Hole, The	73	Inverarnie Schwarzenegger	266	Killing in the Name of	44
Harry Trotter	173	Holly Tree Groove	269	Invest Wisely	301	King of the Swingers	307
Haul Anchor	215	Holy Water	165	Irn Age	62	King, The	249
Haul or Nothing	165	Holyman	46	It Ain't Over till it's Over	106	Kingdom of Granite	250
Haven Can't Wait	212	Hoochie Coochie Man	35	It's a Route Jim!	224	Kinmont Times	105
Haven Escape Route	212	Hornblower	225	It's not my Fault!	225	Kirrie on Regardless	157
Haven Fun	212	Horny Deer	175	It's Rock Jim	275	Kirrie Sutra	160
Havering Skate	98	Horrid	97	Italian Stallion	175	Kiss of Doom	216
Having a Little Flutter	105	Hot Chocolate	107			Kissing the Witch	139
Head of Medusa	43	House of Pain	25	**J**		Kneed 4 Speed	67
Head of the Queue	178	Hunger	50	Jacksonville Hip	55	Knockin' on Haven's Door	213
Heave Ho!	216	Hunt the Ratbag	182			Krab, The	196
Heavy Metal	50	Hunting Swan, The	185				

Index

L
L-Plate 274
La Paroi Noire 326
La Plage 157
Lady of the Loch 81
Lady Willoughby 115
Lake Lomond 55
Lakey Hill 68
Landward 29
Lapdancing 138
Last Gasp 136
Lateral Thinking 67
Laurel 233
Law and Disorder 33
Law of Gravity 33
Law of the Flies 33
Law of the Rings 34
Layaway to Haven 66
Layin' down the Law 202
Le Bon Vacance 170
League of Whingers, The 233
Leaning Wall, The 316
Left on the Shelf 142
Left-Hand Route 33
Lemon Squeezy 184
Leonardo da Pinchy 175
Leopold 64
Les Morts Dansant 188
Let it all Hang Out 103
Let There be Light 324
Let there be Rock 155
Levitation 293
Lewbee Doobee 237
Leyed to Rest 165
Lichen Virgin 105
Life in the Fat Lane 104
Life's a Beach
   (Creag Bheag) 281
Life's a Beach (Ley) 166
Lighten Up 138
Like a Virgin 127
Like it Hot? 300
Link, The 93
Little Bo Peep 180
Little Creatures 231
Little Leaf 307
Little Teaser 272
Live-in Skin 80
Llama Parlour, The 138
Long and Winding Road 68
Long Dogs 241
Long Good Friday, The 137
Long Reach 292
Loony Tunes 200
Loose Cannons 173
Loose Lips Sink Ships 203
Loose Living 105
Lost at Sea 207
Lost but not Least 207
Lost in Line 206
Lost the Plot 207
Lucifer 250
Lurcher, The 242
Lymphomaniac 187

M
Mac Talla 316
Macpherson's Mountain
   Sports 296
Mad Cows 245
Made to Suffer 169
Magic Bus 254
Magic Carpet Ride 54
Magic Pockets 162
Magic Thumb 166
Magicman 331
Mahoots Mon 225
Make my Day 179
Making the Grade 165
Makosi 237
Man the Lifeboats 324
Maniaxe 95
Manifestations 170
Manitou 283
Manpower 137
March of Dimes 184
Markerhorn 161
Marlina 130
Mars 110
Mass of Knots 326
Match if you are Weak 272
Maxwell's Demon 62
Meany 232
Meaty Hefts 196
Medusa 214
Merchant of Menace 171
Messiah 249
Metal Guru 94
Metalcore 49
Midge Patrol 92
Mighty Atom, The 315
Millennium Madness 145
Mind of Metal, A 124
Mini the Minx 168
Minimal 205
Minimical 205
Miniquity 206
Minitial 205
Minitiation 205
Minitiative 206
Missing Link, The 143
Mister Poops 29
Mister Smooth 306
Mistic, The 210
Mo 232
Modern Tart 111
Moments of Enlightenment 42
Mona Sleaza 111
Monkey See, Monkey Do 159
Moonbeams and Honey
   Dreams 41
Moonlight Sonata 83
Moonlighting Meercat 277
Morrison's Missed
   Adventure 234
Motion Sickness 142
Moulin Rouge 146
Mound over Matter 154
Mound, The 283
Moy Bueno 271
Moy Racer 270
Moy Soldiers 274
Mr. Angry 278
Mr. Chris 328
Mr. Tim 327
Munrobagger 101
Murdo's Reach 296
Mushroom Heads 153
Mushroom Treatment 217
Mutton Dressed as Clam 209
My Own Private Scotland 81
Mystery Machine 287

N
Natural Born Drillers 22
Necktie 33
Necrosis 188
Nectar 163
Need for Speed 176
Negative Creep 21
Negotiations with Isaac 29
Neptune's Kiss 210

New Beginning	115	
New Power Generation	86	
Ni Dubh	305	
Niagara	68	
Niche, The	171	
Nirvana	163	
Nitrogen	99	
No Questions Asked	296	
No Remorse	186	
No Respect for your Elders	175	
Nobody Listening	326	
Noose, The	315	
Northern Exposure (Concave Wall, Glen Ogle)	99	
Northern Exposure (Terraces, Glen Ogle)	111	
Not for Children's E'en	202	
Not the Risk Business	164	
Nu Mettle	52	
Nuclear Nightmare	298	
Nymphocyte	187	

O

O.M.D	246
Off the Beaten Track	93
Off the Couch	170
Off the Rails	283
Old Law Breaker	34
Old Man of Moy, The	270
Old Man's Beard	297
Old Snapper	303
Old Wives' Tail	94
Olive Oil	330
Omerta	19
On a Different Wavelength	197
On the Never Never Land	157
On the Up	154
One and Only, The	264
One Can Dan	168
One Foot in the Door	176
One in the Eye for Stickmen	94
One in the Eye for the Duke	277
One Man went to Moy	272
One Pig One	137
One Step Beyond	138
One Steppe Forward	204
Original Route (Deil's Heid, Arbroath)	218
Original Route (The Platform, Arbroath)	194
Oshan Toshan	309
Ossian	205
Otter Final, The	309
Out Back	234
Out of the Red and into the Black	195
Outshined	112
Overdose	264
Over the Top	109
Overkill (Glen Ogle Asteroid)	109
Overkill (Legaston)	184
Overlord	109
'O' Zone Slayer	202

P

Pablo's Pebble	281
Pack Horse, The	97
Pants on Fire	302
Paradise Road	97
Parallel	25
Paralysis by Analysis	266
Parental Guidance	202
Parson's Nose	193
Pas de Charge	221
Path to Power	312
Path, The	262
Paws for Thought	154
Pay and Display	239
Payback Time!	19
Pearls of Penelope Pitstop, The	201
Pebble Parlour, The	280
Pebble Party	274
Pebbledash	271
Peddle Power	160
Peem Machine	210
Pelican Brief	68
Penguin, The	315
Pensioners' Link	316
Permanent Rage	311
Persistence of Vision	19
Pert's Buttock	223
Pesto Macho	305
Phantom	133
Pharmacist's Apprentice	156
Pickpocket	281
Pig on the Rig	225
Pilgrim's Progress	199
Pillar, The	319
Pin Ball Wizard	68
Pinball Wizard	253
Pine Martin	293
Pink Wall, The	263
Pinky and the Brain	201
Pit Bull	162
Pitscandly Chainsaw Massacre	175
Playing with Fire	188
Plums of Ratho, The	31
Plunderer	295
Poison Ivy	315
Polluted Planet	311
Pool of Despair	165
Poop Deck	29
Portlethen Terrier, The	242
Pot Calling the Kettle Black	71
Power Flower	174
Power of Tears, The	308
Power of Three, The	264
Power Shower	92
Power Sink	86
Power Surge	87
Predestination	295
President Shhean Connery	142
Pretty Clitty Gang Bang	208
Primo	319
Pringles Wave	207
Protection Racket, The	138
Prow, The (Castle of Yesnaby)	329
Prow, The (Goat Crag)	316
Psycho	261
Psychopomp	306
Psychosis	41
Pulling Muscles from a Shell	209
Pulling on Pebbles	272
Pulliscious	124
Pullover	109
Pumpernickel	303
Purgatory	84
Pushin' the Limpets	202
Pushover	109
Put out to Grass	204
Putting Shame in your Game	169
Pyramid	272

Q

Quality Street	255

Index

Quarry Man, The	328	Rib Wall	329	**S**		She Conceives Destruction	187
Quiet Revolution	146	Ribcracker	295	Sans Peur	285	Sheep of Things to	
Quidditch	121	Riddler, The	315	Satan's Serenade	217	Come, The	180
		Ride 'em Cowboy	193	Satan's Slaves	95	Shield of Perseus	43
R		Ridge, The	83	Saturation Point	110	Shield, The (Leacanashie)	295
R n D Dubz	173	Right in the Face	142	Saturation Right-Hand	111	Shield, The (Am Fasgadh)	319
Raasmi	331	Right Wing Extremist	225	Savage Amusement	169	Ship Ahoy	95
Race for the Prize	55	Ring Cycle, The	30	Saving Light, The	324	Shipwrecked	325
Rack, The	184	Ring of Steall	64	Say Hello but Wave		Shockwave	197
Railway Children, The	59	River Gods, The	311	Goodbye	197	Shoot to Kill	184
Raksasha	81	Roadkill Recipes	84	Scales of Injustice	332	Shore Beats Working	195
Rankin's Rain Games	234	Road Rage	191	Scaramanga	91	Short Arms, Deep Pockets	210
Raspberry Beret	95	Road to Hell, The	121	Scarred for Life	162	Short Circuit	86
Rat Attack	170	Road to Perdition	250	Scooby Snacks	138	Short Haul	177
Rat Race Face	168	Robert the Bruce's Spider	275	Scoopy Doo	271	Short Sharp Shocked	97
Ratbag	182	Rock is Dead	107	Scorchio (Bennybeg)	115	Shottabeena	305
Ravens' Nest	272	Rocket's Secret Machine	185	Scorchio (Am Fasgadh)	320	Side Flake	301
Raving Lunatics	95	Rocking Stone, The	184	Screamin' Demon	196	Side Issue	56
Reaching for the Pilot	35	Ronald Raygun	298	Screaming Weem, The	136	Sign of the Jug	301
Reaching the Limit	105	Roofiliscious	124	Screwless	156	Silence of the Clams	209
Ready	325	Room with a View	44	Scuffer	252	Silk Purse, The	131
Real Mackay, The	137	Roses	255	Seam, The	29	Silk Teddy	131
Rebel Without Applause	84	Rotweiller	162	Seaside Special	194	Silver Darlings	285
Recreational Chemistry	95	Round the Bend	274	Second Sights	26	Silver Fox, The	274
Rectified	175	Route 10	115	Seconds Out	182	Silver Surfer	201
Red Lichtie, The	200	Route One	114	Secret Garden, The	264	Sinners Paradise	131
Red Mouse	309	Route Two	114	Seegull	216	Siostan	321
Reinforcer, The	179	Roxanne	187	Seeing is Not Believing	221	Siren, The	216
Remain in Light	188	Rubbin' Salt into		Seeing the Light	160	Six Fours-les Plages	131
Remanufacture	140	the Wound	194	Seer, The	273	Skullduggery	180
Remember to Roll	307	Rubrique	146	Selfish Shellfish, The	196	Slaphead	103
Republic of Scotland, The	142	Ruby Slippers	84	Sending the Wrong Signal	146	Slave to the Rhythm	96
Resident Evil	121	Rugrats' Revenge	201	Serious Beef	158	Slave Trade	311
Resolution	331	Rum Ration	96	Shadowlands	50	Sleekit	277
Restless Souls	108	Running Blind	67	Shame it's no Name	261	Slim Pickins	158
Retribution	102	Rush	95	Shapeshifter	223	Slip of Death	253
Revolution	331	Rust in Peace	207	Sharp Practice	255	Slip Sliding Away	68
Rhumba al Sol	80	Ruthosaurus	161	Shaven Haven	212	Smee Day	159

Index

Smells like Team Spirit	224	Spitfire	52	Sufferance	20	That Sinking Feeling	
Smiddy, The (Bennybeg)	116	Splashing Out	328	Suffix	20	(Ardvorlich)	55
Smiddy, The (The Anvil)	50	Splat	283	Suicide Bat	253	That Sinking Feeling	
Smile Child, The	237	Squeal like a Piggy	174	Suicide Wall	265	(Glen Ogle)	98
Smoke on the Water	42	Squelch	283	Sultan	250	There's Sand in my Pants	266
Smoked Out	325	Stag Night	191	Summer Solstice	276	Thinker, The	301
Smokies	193	Stalks	307	Sun City	254	Third and Final	302
Smuggler	295	Starboard	110	Sun Seeker	213	Third Eye, The	60
Snail's Pace	178	Staring at the Sun	137	Sunset Slab	330	Thirty One	325
Snake Eyes	54	Start the Fire	169	Sunset Slab Left-Hand	329	This is Jazz	307
Snake in the Grass	264	Static Discharge	86	Superblue	305	Thorny Issue	154
Snatcher, The	312	Static in the Air	139	Superlew	238	Ticks Ate all the	
Sneaker Freaks	67	Steall Appeal	65	Swallows	308	Midges, The	272
Snipe Shadow	99	Steallworker	62	Swan Lake	65	Tipping Point	62
Snow Flake	315	Stegosaurus	161	Sweet Charity	239	Tied Up	283
Snow on the Ben	262	Step on It	104	Sweet Dreams are made		Tim'rous Beastie	156
So Be It	25	Steppe in the Right		of This	217	Titanic	237
So Phia so Good	306	Direction	204	Sweet Revenge	182	To Infinity and Beyond	286
Sold Short	177	Steppeladder	204	Swimming against the		Toiseach	317
Solitaire	91	Steppes back in Amazement	204	Tide of Tradition	195	Tolerance	21
Solitary Soul	34	Steppin' Out	204	Swindlers List	209	Toll Route	239
Solomon	250	Sticks 'n' Stones	253	Swine Flew	173	Tom Paine's Bones	315
Sombre Reptiles	153	Stiff Little Fingers	161	Swingers	308	Tomorrow Never Comes	141
Sometime Soon	141	Stigmata	242	Sye of Relief	168	Too Fast Too Furious	126
Sonsie Face	156	Sting, The	125	Syes don't Matter	168	Too Old to be Famous	315
Sorry Tess	107	Stitch in Time	198			Tool Bags	236
Soup Dragon	138	Stolen	62	**T**		Top Cat	200
Spandex Ballet	186	Stone Junky	98	T.B.C.	285	Torch Lite, The	126
Spanner, The	115	Stone of Destiny	266	Tain Spotting	283	Tornado of Souls	254
Span-utan	237	Storkie's	319	Take a Hike	101	Toss	305
Spark Thug	87	Stormy Monday	309	Take the Plunge	192	Totally Trashed	177
Speedfreak	98	Strathearn Shangrila	120	Tale of the Tape	221	Touch too Much	158
Spent	157	Stray Dogs	242	Tales of Creation	170	Towed in the Hole	179
Spice of Life	240	Stretch, The	329	Tanning Salon, The	29	Towing the Line	194
Spider Pig	173	Strut yer Stuff	191	Tarrier	20	Traditional Imperfections	165
Spiderman	311	Stuck in a Rut	192	Teasel	320	Tragically Hip	26
Spiral Tribe	93	Submersion	98	Teepee	315	Trailer Trash	178
Spirits Drifting	153	Sudden Alchemy	107	Technical Merit	255	Traverse of the Cods	232

Index

Trench Warfare	53
Trial by Dimension	182
Trial of Brother Number 1, The	138
Tribeswoman	59
Tribute	147
Trick of the Tail	62
Trojan	110
Trojan Gift Horse	217
Trossachs Trundler	94
Trouble Monkey	233
True Path	160
Trust in Me	285
Tullybannocher Tea Room	119
Turbinator, The	278
Turbine Charged	283
Turtle Turtle Up	331
Twenty Shilling Woodworm	118
Twilight Shift	146
Twilight Zone	165
Twintrack	281
Twister	26
Two Humps are Better than One	268
Two Steppes Back	204

U

Ubuntu	267
Ukranian Mermaid	196
Ultima Necat	130
Ultraviolet	112
Uncertain Emotions	59
Under Mind	96
Under the Same Sun	112
Under Where?	95
Underbelly	236
Underexposed	325
Underland	247
Unenforced Layoff	153
Unfinished Business (Black Rock)	71
Unfinished Business (Creag nan Luch)	306
Unforgiven	22
Uninvited, The	176
United Colours of Bennyton	115
Up the Middle	328
Ure Kiddin'	331

V

Va Va Voom	124
Vanishing Point	45
Vast Mango in Tardis	209
Vector Space	59
Veggiemight	278
Venga Boys	80
Venus Return	273
Viagra Falls	222
Vibe Heads	133
Vibes, The	133
Vincent's Lug	281
Virtual Life	146
Volturi	299
Voodoo Magic	24
Voodoo Ray	107
Voyage of the Black Pearl	70
Vulgar Display of Power	213

W

Waiting for a Train	97
Waiting for Godot	56
Waiting for the Man	301
Walkaway	305
Walking the Plank	159
Walking the Straight Line	184
Wall of Hate	195
Wandering Minstrel	147
War Cry	317
Warm-Down	294
Warm-Up (Leacanashie)	294
Warm-Up (Am Fasgadh)	319
Watchtower, The	143
Wave Escape	197
Wave Power	197
Wave, The	47
Waves of Emotion	193
Wavey Longs	331
Way out West (Ranochan Wall)	67
Way out West (The Anvil)	52
Weasel, The	188
Weigh Anchor	96
Weighty Issue	158
Welcome to the Big Pocket	177
Welcome to the Steeeppes!	204
Welcome to the Working Weak	254
Werther's Original	331
Wet Feet	329
Whale of a Time	210
What Every Woman Wants	157
When Annabelle met Tinkerbelle	160
When the Wind Blows	67
Where there's Muck, there's Brass	157
Whinging Consultants	263
Whip and Ride	307
Whiplash	29
Whistleblower	225
Whitehouse, The	118
Whitewash	118
Whittled Into Kindling	310
Whole Lotta Kirrie	155
Wicked and Weird	311
Wicked Steppe Mother	204
Wild at Heart	293
Wild Goats	83
Wild Iris	34
Wild Swans	83
Wimpey Construction	255
Wind in the Willows	255
Wings would Help	159
Witch Hazel	121
Women and Children First	324
Wonders of the Woods	312
Wounded Knee	31
Wristy Business	94
Wrong Trousers, The	201
Wrong Turn	160

X

Xmas Xcess	158
X-philes, The	223
XX	95

Y

Ya Butey	41
Young Man's Link	315

Z

Zombie Nation	121
Zoo, The	159

SCOTTISH MOUNTAINEERING CLUB
SCOTTISH MOUNTAINEERING TRUST

CLIMBERS' GUIDES

Northern Highlands North	£22.00
Northern Highlands Central	£25.00
Northern Highlands South	£25.00
Skye The Cuillin	£25.00
Skye Sea-cliffs & Outcrops	£25.00
The Cairngorms	£25.00
Ben Nevis	£22.00
Glen Coe	£22.00
Highland Outcrops	£16.00
North-East Outcrops	£22.00
Lowland Outcrops	£22.00
Arran, Arrochar and Southern Highlands	£15.00
Scottish Winter Climbs	£25.00
Scottish Rock Climbs	£25.00

SCRAMBLERS' GUIDES

Skye Scrambles	£25.00
Highland Scrambles North	£19.00

HILLWALKERS' GUIDES

The Munros	£23.00
Munros GPS data disk (via SMC website)	£8.00
The Corbetts and Other Scottish Hills	£23.00
North-West Highlands	£22.00
Islands of Scotland Including Skye	£20.00
The Cairngorms	£18.00
Central Highlands	£18.00
Southern Highlands	£17.00

OTHER PUBLICATIONS

Ben Nevis – Britain's Highest Mountain	£27.50
The Cairngorms – 100 Years of Mountaineering	£27.50
Rising to the Challenge – 100 Years of the LSCC	£24.00
Hostile Habitats – Scotland's Mountain Environment	£17.00
Munro's Tables	£16.00
A Chance in a Million? Avalanches in Scotland	£15.00
The Munroist's Companion	£16.00
Scottish Hill Tracks	£18.00
Scottish Hill Names	£16.00

Visit our website for more details and to purchase online: www.smc.org.uk

Distributed by **Cordee Ltd**,
(t) 01455611185 (w) www.cordee.co.uk